SURVEYS IN ECONOMICS

Public sector economics

SURVEYS IN ECONOMICS

Series editors: Robert Millward, Michael T. Sumner and George Zis

Public sector economics

ROBERT MILLWARD
DAVID PARKER
LESLIE ROSENTHAL
MICHAEL T. SUMNER
NEVILLE TOPHAM

Public sector economics

LONGMAN
London and New York

LONGMAN GROUP LIMITED
Longman House, Burnt Mill, Harlow
Essex CM20 2JE, England
Associated companies throughout the world

Published in the United States of America
by Longman Inc., New York

© Longman Group Limited 1983

First published 1983

BRITISH LIBRARY CATALOGUING IN PUBLICATION DATA
Public sector economics. — (Surveys in economics)
  1. Finance, Public — Great Britain
  I. Millward, Robert II. Series
  336.41 HJ1001
  ISBN 0-582-29566-1

LIBRARY OF CONGRESS CATALOGING IN PUBLICATION DATA
Main entry under title:
Public sector economics.
  (Surveys in economics)
  Includes bibliographical references and index.
  1. Industry and state. 2. Taxation. 3. Subsidies.
  4. Local government. 5. Government business enterprises.
  I. Millward, Robert E. II. Series.
  HD3611.P8 1983 338.9 82–4609
  ISBN 0-582-29566-1 (pbk.)

Set in 10 pt Linotron 202 Times
Printed in Singapore by
Selector Printing Co (Pte) Ltd

Contents

Editors' preface

The aim of this series is to survey the primary literature on selected economic topics at a level designed for intermediate and advanced undergraduate students. Few textbooks contain an adequate perspective on the development of their subject, and still fewer portray the focus of current research; but it has become progressively more difficult to supplement textbooks by selecting journal articles which provide a satisfactory comprehensive, coherent and self-contained treatment of a topic, at a length and level of technique within the capacity of a student. The widening gap between the pedagogic and the professional literature stems partly from the increasing volume of the latter, the consequent pressure to abbreviate manuscripts, and the dissemination of research in a growing number of more specialised journals. It also reflects the increasing technical sophistication of the subject in all spheres of application, and particularly the integration of theoretical and empirical analysis which characterises much recent research, in marked contrast to the teaching of economics and econometrics in separate compartments of most undergraduate courses.

The surveys have been written for those who are studying or have completed intermediate courses in economic theory and quantitative methods. They aim to guide the reader through the professional literature, paying particular attention to the introduction of empirical work and to synthesising relevant contributions from different areas of specialisation. The major issues are explained and attention is directed towards the most useful sources for further study. By providing a comprehensive overview of its subject, each survey enables users to pursue particular aspects of the topic in greater depth through the medium of primary sources, within a frame of reference which enables the significance of those individual contributions to be assessed in their broader context.

The subjects of the surveys have been selected for their economic importance and for the extent and inaccessibility of the literature in journals and monographs devoted to them. Each is complete and self-contained, and can be read without reference to the surveys of related topics which appear in the same volume. The volumes themselves are not intended to replace textbooks by providing comprehensive coverage of their area, but to supplement textbooks by conveying the current flavour of the state of the art.

The series as a whole has been designed for second- and third-year undergraduate students at universities and polytechnics, but individual surveys will also appeal to postgraduate students and to practising economists in government, nationalised industries and the private sector who wish to update their knowledge of the subject. Economics has developed rapidly in the last two decades, and even active members of the profession have experienced difficulty in keeping pace with progress outside their own field of specialisation. It is hoped that the series will prove useful to this wider readership of continuing students as well as those beginning their education in economics.

Robert Millward
Michael T. Sumner
George Zis

Acknowledgements

Several economists have read first drafts of this volume and appropriate acknowledgements are given at the start of each chapter. The collation of different pieces of work into one volume with a common index has benefited from the efficiency of Susan Mullins and Shirley Woolley who did all the typing magnificently.

CHAPTER ONE

Introduction

Robert Millward and Michael T. Sumner

A sign of the rapidity with which the study of government expenditure and revenue has recently been changing is the use of new titles for the area. As late as the 1960s many texts still carrried the label 'Public Finance' and were still dominated by the theory and practice of taxation. The nineteenth-century tradition was that since government expenditure was largely devoted to the regrettable necessities of law, order and defence, there was little that could be said of it save that it should be provided efficiently and at least cost. The problem was finance. With the long history of embarrassments to governments from borrowing and currency debasements, the issue was finding a tax structure which did least damage to the workings of the economy and a tax base, whether on land, heads, hearths or work, which kept down collection costs. In 1958 Samuelson was lamenting not only that Pigou's outstanding 1928 treatise on 'A Study of Public Finance'[1] contained hardly anything on government expenditure and production, but that matters had not improved much in the intervening period. That can no longer be said, and modern texts now include sections on cost-benefit analysis of public expenditure, the choice between taxes and prices for the provision of public services, analytical aspects of public goods, and pricing policies of public utilities. In reflection of this wider coverage the new titles are often 'Public Economics' or 'Public Sector Economics', though a well-established American text, recently updated, stubbornly keeps to 'Public Finance in Theory and Practice'[2] despite its quite extensive treatment of issues other than finance. The authors acknowledge that this description is too narrow to be accurate, but argue that public economics, properly defined, embraces topics like monetary and antitrust policies which lie outside the scope of their book. The examples are interesting because of their analytical connections with public finance in its strictest sense. The interrelationship between monetary, fiscal and debt management policies has provided the focus of the recent literature on the macroeconomic implications of the government's budget constraint, and the analogy between the inflation tax on money balances and the partial equilibrium analysis of conventional excise taxes is well established. The choice between regulation through administrative edict and taxation has been extensively debated in the literature on pollution control. While fiscal substitutes for legal constraints on monopolies, mergers and restrictive practices have attracted less attention, the effects of the present corporate tax system on industrial structure, and hence indirectly on the task which confronts the legal guardians of the public interest in such matters, have not escaped notice.[3] Thus the boundaries of public sector economics, as currently defined, which these examples might suggest, are far from rigid or impenetrable; and the only justification for even these amorphous boundaries rests on the division of labour among economists rather than any intrinsic logic. Public policy cannot be divided into watertight compartments.

Whilst the literature has changed in its recognition that both sides of the budget are important and also in its recognition of the increased scale and diversity of government activities, other features of change stem from the development of economics as a subject. Each of the contributors to this volume was invited to write on areas close to his own research which, in his view, were important enough to be part of an undergraduate's education in public sector economics but which had been neglected, wholly or partly, in the literature accessible to students, including that in textbooks. In the traditional area of taxation, perhaps the most significant development from the point of view at least of the policy maker is the increasing stress on quantitative work. The underpinning of prescriptions for changes in corporation tax or income tax is an expectation of their impact on the workings of the economy. Since the rate of corporate investment and the number of hours worked are each functions of a large set of variables, quantitative estimates are vital and Sumner's chapter on the incentive effects of taxation is partly concerned with work in this area. Analogously, assessment of the relative efficiency of public and private enterprise has often been of an impressionistic nature but has recently been put on a much firmer quantitative footing, as the latter part of Millward and Parker's survey indicates. Empirical work on housing and food subsidies is covered in Rosenthal's survey and whilst Topham's survey of the fiscal federalism literature is, for reasons which will be discussed shortly, mainly analytical, there are many indications of the growing empirical work in this field, at least for the United States.

A second important feature of recent advances in public sector economics is the increasing recognition that the structural features of both the public and the private sectors are much more complex than those embodied in simple models. One interpretation of the theory of public goods is that it explains how some goods tend to be produced and sold by the private sector whilst the supply of other goods is financed through taxation with no user prices. National defence has externality properties, in the sense that its technical characteristics are such that provision for one person in the community cannot be arranged without supplying the service to the rest of the community, including those who for philosophical reasons would prefer to reject it. A private market in defence services will therefore not emerge because, even if everyone sets a positive value on the service, each individual member of the community will underreveal his willingness to pay for defence, on the grounds that his consumption of defence will depend as much on the purchases of others as on his own purchases. In practice, however, few goods with externality properties have spillovers of a national dimension; roads, refuse collection, certain health and educational services, flood control schemes, diffuse benefits over a limited geographical region of a country. In so far as the provision of such services is made by local governmental units, an element of choice is open to economic agents who can in principle be viewed as determining the location of their residence or factory partly in response to varying levels of provision in different local governments and associated differences in local tax rates. The implications of this have been developed at length in the literature on fiscal federalism which is surveyed by Topham. Much of this arises from America where state and local governments have more autonomy than UK local governments, but the issues are equally important in the UK. The introduction of publicly provided comprehensive education has had massive implications for family choice of residential location. What does this imply about the level of property taxes (rates) in different regions? What are the implications for house prices? These and similar questions have been neglected by recent generations of British economists, and not merely in their pedagogic writing. The intellectual vacuum has not been filled by the numerous official enquiries into various aspects of the economics of local government. Indeed, Topham suggests that the economic analysis associated with a major inquiry into local government organisation in the UK in the early 1970s, the Redcliffe-Maud Report, was virtually zero. His survey provides a comprehensive introduction to the analytical issues which are now attracting the attention of UK economists, and which will in the future prompt the questions which act as the starting point for empirical work.

In assessing the role of public goods in the economy and the methods of taxation, certain assumptions have to be made about the structural features of the private sector. The implications of profit maximisation and competition are not only well known to economists but also involve clear-cut propositions about output, pricing and investment policy. Much work in public sector economics over the last decade has tried to allow for different assumptions about the private sector. Perhaps the key issue is that ownership and control in the large modern private sector company are divorced, with company activities decided on the balance of strengths of management on the one hand and shareholders on the other. Sumner evaluates the literature which has reassessed the impact of corporate taxation when objectives such as company growth maximisation are deemed to be more relevant than profit maximisation. This follows a discussion of one of the key corporate tax issues, namely that when the tax treatment of capital costs allows more or less than their full deduction from taxable income, the firm's output and investment policy is likely to be significantly affected, whatever its objective. The fact that private sector industries are sometimes dominated by firms where ownership and control are divorced also has implications for the performance of private firms relative to public enterprises. In the past, predictions of the likely relative performance of these two types of organisation have often presumed an environment of profit maximisation enforced by competition in the private sector. A thorough reconsideration of the meaning of 'private' and 'public' enterprise is taking place in the literature, and

Millward and Parker take up the analytical features of this in the earlier part of their survey.

What governments provide, or at least finance, is not restricted in any obvious way to areas where externalities exist. The positive implications of their extensive intervention constitute the fourth general feature of the surveys in this volume. Housing, food, higher education, regional aid have often attracted government interest, even though the precise rationale for this interest is not always clear. Concern over income distribution or what Pigou called the 'defective telescopic faculty' of consumers often seems dominant. Economists have always sought clarification of government objectives in these areas since the appropriate fiscal instrument will vary with objectives. What is the motive behind provision of free school milk – concern that some families do not have enough income for basic nutritional requirements, or that household decision-takers are ill-informed about these requirements? Many such issues crop up in association with subsidies of various kinds to the household sector of the economy, and Rosenthal brings the analytical considerations together in his survey. It is perhaps not too dangerous a generalisation to suggest that public finance specialists have tended, in their policy prescriptions, to favour using different policy instruments for distributional and allocative ends. They have often explicitly recommended the use of the price system for allocating resources, confining intervention through indirect taxes or subsidies to the correction of identifiable distortions, and the direct tax system for redistributing income; tax relief for, or transfer payments to, low income groups is preferred to subsidised provision of housing. There are some signs, however, of a more positive approach to the analysis of government policies, in the form of a growing willingness to take the policy as a datum and look carefully at its economic implications without challenging its rationale directly. Rosenthal exemplifies this tendency in comparing various kinds of specific help to the personal sector with the standard prescription of tax relief or direct income transfers. In a similar vein Sumner considers the impact of particular fiscal instruments on the choices made by households or firms: for example, how particular forms of regional aid influence production methods, and hence employment levels and the geographical distribution of investment. One of Topham's concerns is to predict the influence of different forms of central government grant on the behaviour of local goverments. Another is to appraise the role attributed to the median voter. Indeed an increasingly prominent theme in the general literature of public sector economics is the positive explanation of government behaviour, a task which raises new questions about the role of bureaucracies, the nature of competition among political parties and the sources of political popularity. One area where both analytical and empirical work has concentrated on these positive issues is in the study of the behaviour of public enterprise, especially in US transport and electricity, which is comprehensively covered by Millward and Parker.

Normative analyses have not been neglected in the recent literature. On the contrary, in traditional areas like the study of taxation the adoption of explicit welfare functions which, however tentatively, quantify the trade-offs between efficiency and equity has provided a new and highly contentious focus. One consequence is that prescription has become more overtly conditional, and more restricted in its scope. Few analyses of optimal taxation have examined the choice between alternative tax bases, and fewer still have incorporated government spending. Samuelson's lament has been heeded, to the extent that both sides of the budget are now included in the scope of public economics as a matter of course; but the integration of the two sides has continued to pose serious problems.

The boundaries of public sector economics, like those of the public sector itself, have expanded rapidly during the period covered by these surveys. At the extensive margin new specialisms have developed and connections with other branches of economics have been strengthened. At the intensive margin, established areas of study have been changed by new techniques of theoretical and empirical analysis, and by the introduction of new questions for consideration. The abundance of intellectual problems which remain at every level and their immediate or potential relevance to practical issues indicate the scope for further development.

Notes

1. **P. A. Samuelson**, Aspects of public expenditure theories, *Review of Economics and Statistics*, **40**, 1958:332–8. The year 1928 is actually the date of the third edition of A. C. Pigou's book. Samuelson's complaint was anticipated by Hugh Dalton in his *Public Finance* (5th edn 1929; first published 1922, Routledge: London). He satirised the older writers' restrictive view of state functions, and criticised 'modern economists, especially in this country' for their failure 'to correct vulgar prejudices on this matter and to place the whole question, from the point of view of principles, upon a proper footing' (p. 190). Interestingly enough, in view of his subsequent role as Chancellor of the Exchequer in 1945–47, he drew some comfort from '[o]ne fortunate result of this lack of theoretical discussion... [viz] that the path of economic wisdom in public expenditure is practically unencumbered by doctrines of equity'. He also pointed out that Pigou's *Study* 'only professes to cover selected parts of the field' (p. 292), and cited the same author's *Economics of Welfare* (4th edn, 1932, first published as *Wealth & Welfare,* Macmillan: London 1912), as a source of 'valuable fragments of a theory of public expenditure'.
2. **R. A. Musgrave and P. B. Musgrave**, (3rd edn) McGraw Hill: New York, 1980.
3. See, for example, **J. A. Kay & M. A. King**, *The British Tax System*, OUP: Oxford 1978 ch. 12.

CHAPTER TWO

The incentive effects of taxation

Michael T. Sumner[*]

1. Introduction

The study of taxation, one of the oldest identifiable specialisms of economics, has undergone a fundamental change in character during the last two decades. One reason for this is force of circumstances: the extended range of responsibilities assumed by modern governments has expanded the size of the budget everywhere, raising old taxes to new levels and stimulating an enormous variety of fiscal innovations, thus enlarging the range of questions for study and intensifying their practical significance. In addition, however, developments within economics have played an important role in this transformation. One particularly relevant example is the general theory of second best, crystallised by Lipsey and Lancaster (1956), which demonstrated the very limited usefulness of the traditional public finance practice of showing how particular taxes violated the Pareto conditions for a welfare maximum, and which subsequently generated the now very extensive literature on the optimal method of raising tax revenue. A common characteristic of second-best problems is that the information required for their solution is quantitative rather than qualitative. In this respect, the questions raised by economic theorists have reinforced the more immediate stimulus to quantitative research on taxation imparted by fiscal innovations and by the questions posed by those responsible for tax policy. Consequently, the use of econometric techniques has become one of the distinguishing features of the recent literature on taxation.

Few economic choices can be exercised without some fiscal consequence, and they are therefore subject, in principle at least, to fiscal influence. Indeed, a surprising number of choices which are not primarily economic, such as whether to marry or when to have children, often involve fiscal consequences. To emphasise the potentially pervasive influence of taxation, this survey is sectionalised in terms of the decisions made by firms and households; though to keep the discussion within manageable limits and to avoid the charge of claiming too much, the decisions considered are confined to those which fall within the

* Thanks are due to Roy Houghton, Bob Millward, Neville Topham and George Zis for discussion and comments.

scope of economics narrowly defined.

The distinction between the decisions of firms and households corresponds roughly to a classification in terms of taxes. The major influence on business decisions is exercised through corporation tax; unincorporated businesses, although they are subject to a more progressive structure of tax rates, may be subsumed under the same heading for most purposes because the receipts and payments which constitute the tax base are similarly defined for both types of firm. The personal income tax and sales taxes primarily affect household decisions, but their influence also extends to a subset of business decisions. For instance, firms' choices between distributing dividends and and retaining profits will depend partly on the fiscal implications for their shareholders, and hence on the relative tax treatment of capital gains and 'unearned' income; and sales taxes may influence decisions on product quality and pricing policies.

Analysis of fiscal influences on the behaviour of individual economic agents emphasises the actual or potential effect of taxation on resource allocation. The positive aspect of this relationship provides the focus of this survey. Normative propositions, i.e. policy prescriptions, are treated on a piecemeal basis rather than being derived from some grand vision of the government as a mechanism for maximising welfare through the design of a new fiscal structure. This partial treatment of normative questions is in any case an unavoidable consequence of separating tax and expenditure decisions, but it also corresponds to the practical problem of fiscal policy, which is to reform or replace existing taxes rather than to design a completely new structure.[1] The danger of a partial treatment is that it diverts attention from the interaction among different taxes and leaves unexplored the relationship among different potential reforms. It therefore does not provide an ordered agenda for future political action; but as long as this limitation is clearly understood, no misunderstanding will ensue.

Tax changes will in general affect the distribution of income as well as the allocation of resources, though in many cases their distributional consequences will be so diffused and indirect as to be unpredictable *ex ante* and impossible to isolate *ex post*. In any event, the existence of distributional effects does not veto specific reforms directed towards improved resource allocation, despite frequent suggestions to the contrary. What is significant is the distributional consequences of the fiscal system as a whole; attempts to answer this question, which superficially appears to be well defined in principle if inordinately complex at the practical level, are surveyed in the final substantive section.

The tax system is evaluated not only on the basis of allocative and distributional criteria, but also in terms of its contribution to the achievement of macroeconomic objectives. Standard multiplier analysis of changes in tax rates is most usefully carried out in the context of a large-scale macroeconometric model, and thus clearly lies outside the scope of this survey; some examples, using all the main British models, are reported by Laury, Lewis and Ormerod (1978), Lewis and Ormerod (1979) and Ormerod (1979). In a pioneering study,

Dorrington and Renton (1975) extended the standard analysis of changes in direct taxation to a more finely disaggregated level in an augmented version of one such model; but even in that extended form, only a limited range of changes in tax structure could be accommodated. Two particular changes in the tax structure have been advocated on macroeconomic grounds in recent years; both lie outside the analytical scope of existing macro models but can be conveniently examined in an allocative context. These proposals, for tax-based prices or incomes policies and for explicitly temporary changes in expenditure tax rates, will be evaluated as extensions, respectively, of the argument for commodity taxation to expand the output of a monopolist, and for the replacement or augmentation of income tax by a personal expenditure tax. The macroeconomic implications of other actual or proposed features of the tax structure will be treated as a secondary matter, to be noted only in passing. For instance, the indexation of the personal income tax system would affect its built-in flexibility and hence the economy's automatic response to macroeconomic shocks; but in an assessment of the case for indexing a personal tax these consequences are incidental to the effects on allocation and distribution. Similarly the macroeconomic requirement of built-in flexibility has little influence on the progressivity of the present income tax, but the latter certainly influences the former.

　　Empirical studies are introduced and discussed as an integral part of the modern literature on taxation. British investigations are cited wherever possible, but examples are also drawn from studies of other economies to illustrate important methodological principles and procedures.

2. Taxation and business decisions

INTRODUCTION

A standard proposition of elementary economic theory is that a profits tax will not affect the decisions of a profit-maximising firm, provided the tax rate (t) is less than 100 per cent. If pre-tax profits, π, are maximised at a level of output Y, then the highest attainable level of post-tax profits will be $(1 - t)\pi$, and this will be achieved at the same output level. Yet there is a large body of literature which analyses and attempts to measure the effects of business taxation on the firm's decisions about its output, inputs, location, and sources of finance. The apparent contradiction stems from two primary sources: the difference between the profits tax of the elementary textbooks and the base of the tax on business income defined in tax law; and the pursuit of objectives other than profit maximisation. These two considerations are the focus of this section.

　　The firm's tax base is the difference between the value of its sales revenue and the value of its factor inputs of labour, capital and bought-in materials. There is no difficulty in calculating the value of labour input, which is simply the wage bill; but capital inputs are usually owned by the firm rather than being hired, and their economic life extends over a succession of accounting periods. The problem which faces the tax authorities is therefore to allocate the joint cost of a capital good over these periods in order to determine the firm's taxable 'profits' in each one. Changes in inventories of raw materials (and of finished goods) require similar treatment. This process inevitably involves a large element of arbitrariness, and also provides the authorities with an opportunity to influence investment decisions deliberately, by varying the tax treatment of capital goods, as an element of regional, industrial and macroeconomic policy. Less frequently the authorities have changed the cost of labour to firms operating in particular industries, e.g. by the Selective Employment Tax (1966–73) or particular regions, e.g. by the Regional Employment Premium (1967–77).

The tax on 'profits' affects not only the 'real' decisions of the firm on output and inputs, but also its financial policy. Interest payments are treated as a deductible expense, but dividend payments to shareholders are not. In addition, the form of corporation tax determines the shareholders' liability to personal income tax on dividends. Under the 'classical' corporation tax which was in force in the UK from 1965 to 1973, the shareholder was charged income tax on dividends with no allowance for the corporation tax previously paid by the company. The present imputation system was introduced in 1973 with the avowed intention of eliminating the so-called discriminatory tax on dividends. All profits are now taxed at a uniform rate (currently 52 per cent), and dividend payments are deemed to have borne tax at the basic personal rate. The dividend pay-out decision therefore has no fiscal consequence for basic rate taxpayers, who are no longer liable to make any additional payment; but discrimination between distributed and retained profits inevitably remains for other classes of shareholder, who make additional tax payments on dividend receipts or receive refunds. The other classes of shareholder include the average dividend recipient: King (1977: Appx. A) calculates that, although the modal and median marginal tax rates on dividends have coincided with the standard rate of income tax, the mean marginal rate has been consistently higher. Thus for the 'representative' shareholder, retentions are still cheaper in net of tax terms than distributions.

The additional taxes payable on dividends will influence the firm's pay-out policy but not its real decisions, for the maximisation of post-tax profits precedes choices about their distribution. In what follows, the real and financial decisions of a profit-maximising firm are therefore considered sequentially, and finally the assumption of profit maximisation is discarded.

FACTOR INPUTS

In the elementary textbook world with no profits tax, the firm hires labour up to the point where its marginal revenue product equals its marginal cost. In the real world the revenue derived from hiring an additional unit of labour is taxed, but its cost reduces the firm's tax bill. Consequently, because marginal costs and revenues are reduced in the same proportion, the employment decision is unaffected by the profits tax. In the short run at least, when the firm's capital input is fixed, its real decisions remain the same as in a world without taxes.

Capital input decisions are rather more complex because a time dimension is unavoidable. To minimise inessential difficulties, assume that by incurring an initial outlay of Q and constant annual replacement expenditures of δQ, the firm can make a permanent addition to its capital stock which yields an increase in annual revenue of $P\partial Y/\partial K$, where P is product price and $\partial Y/\partial K$ is the marginal product of capital, both of which are assumed to remain constant over time. In a world without taxes the net present value of the investment will be

$$\sum_{i=1}^{\infty} \frac{P\partial Y/\partial K - \delta Q}{(1+\rho)^i} - Q$$

where annual revenues net of annual replacement expenditures are discounted over the indefinite future at the shareholders' marginal rate of time preference, ρ. Under competitive pressures the net present value of the marginal investment will be driven down to zero. Imposing that condition and solving the infinite geometric progression yields, after rearrangement, the expression

$$\frac{\partial Y}{\partial K} = \frac{Q}{P}(\rho + \delta) \tag{1}$$

as the equilibrium condition for capital inputs. The right-hand side has been variously described as the user cost of capital, the implicit rental price of capital services, or simply the cost of capital.

It is now an easy matter to superimpose business income taxation. Revenues are taxed at rate t, and purchase of a capital good entitles the firm to deduct from its taxable income a stream of depreciation allowances $d_0, d_1 \ldots d_n$ in successive years, for each pound of expenditure. Define the present value of these tax allowances as

$$d_0 + \frac{d_1}{(1+\rho)} + \cdots \frac{d_n}{(1+\rho)^n} = Z$$

Then proceeding as before, the net present value of an investment becomes

$$V = \sum_{i=1}^{\infty} \frac{P\partial Y/\partial K(1-t) - \delta Q(1-tZ)}{(1+\rho)^i} - Q(1-tZ) \tag{2}$$

and the equilibrium condition is

$$\frac{\partial Y}{\partial K} = \frac{Q}{P} \frac{(\rho+\delta)\,(1-tZ)}{(1-t)} \tag{3}$$

It is immediately obvious that equations [1] and [3] will be identical only under special assumptions. In general, therefore, the tax treatment of investment expenditures will not be 'neutral' as in the case of labour hiring decisions. The profit-maximisers's choice of factor inputs, and therefore output, will be altered by changes in the tax rate or in other fiscal parameters, in this instance the tax allowable depreciation rates, d_i.

This framework was introduced and developed by Jorgenson and his collaborators in a series of papers on investment behaviour; a good example is Hall and Jorgenson (1971). The simplified derivation above was first presented by Coen (1968). Its application to the analysis of investment behaviour combines the equilibrium condition [3] with an assumption about the form of the production function. In the Cobb-Douglas case, for example, the marginal product of capital is

$$\frac{\partial Y}{\partial K} = a \frac{Y}{K} \qquad [4]$$

where a, the elasticity of output with respect to capital input, is a constant. Interpreting this as a technological relationship and equating it with [3] enables the optimal capital stock, K^*, to be expressed as

$$K^* = \frac{aYP(1-t)}{Q(\rho + \delta)(1-tZ)} \qquad [5]$$

Net investment, the change in the actual capital stock, follows changes in the optimal capital stock with a distributed lag. Replacement expenditure, as in the preceding argument, is proportional to the existing capital stock. The observable variable, gross investment, is the sum of these two components.

Several aspects of this procedure have been heavily criticised by subsequent writers; Brechling (1975) provides an accessible introduction to this later literature. Nevertheless, Jorgenson's approach offers a useful method of analysing the effects of tax policy on investment, and in various modified forms it has remained the dominant framework for empirical studies. Three of its specific characteristics are worth singling out for comment.

First, apart from the tax rate, there is only one fiscal parameter, Z, which represents a variety of fiscal instruments used at different times in different countries. Annual depreciation allowances have been provided in several different forms.[2] Additional allowances have been granted at the beginning of an asset's life in some periods: in Britain, the 'initial allowance' reduced annual allowances in subsequent years, whereas the 'investment allowance' raised the (undiscounted) value of depreciation deductions above an asset's costs. Tax allowances have been partially replaced by cash grants. All these individual instruments can be reduced to a present value, but only on the basis of an assumed discount rate. If firms cannot borrow at that rate, if they have insufficient taxable income to absorb the allowances available to them, or if they are deceived by the fanfare which has accompanied each successive fiscal innovation, then their perception of the cost of capital will be distorted by the calculation of Z. For instance Sumner (1981) presents evidence that cash grants were regarded in a different light than tax allowances of the same apparent present value at discount rates within the relevant range.

Secondly, the expression for the optimal capital stock contains output and the cost of capital in a multiplicative rather than additive form. This feature arises from the explicit derivation, and contrasts sharply with the *ad hoc* tradition in applied econometrics of entering variables which 'seem' relevant in linear form on the right-hand side of a regression equation. On the other hand, the specification is restrictive in assuming a Cobb-Douglas production function. This means that the influence of the cost of capital on investment is imposed rather than being estimated. For that reason most economists who have used this approach subsequently have replaced Jorgenson's Cobb-Douglas assumption with a more general form of the production function which does not constrain the elasticity of substitution to be unity.[3] One example of this modification applied to British data is a study by Boatwright and Eaton (1972). Significant features of their results include a substitution elasticity well below unity, and a long distributed lag, which severely limits the usefulness of changing fiscal investment incentives for counter-cyclical purposes, in the response of net investment to a change in the optimal capital stock; specifically, it takes more than nine quarters for one-half of the total effect to materialise.

Thirdly, even after modifying the production function, the specification constrains changes in output and in the cost of capital to influence investment with the same distributed lag. A movement to a higher isoquant (in the 'long' run) will often involve the firm in purchasing more equipment of the type already used. In contrast, a movement along an isoquant in response to a change in relative factor prices will often involve a change in the type of capital used; this can be accomplished only when the firm's existing capital is replaced. An alternative approach permits a faster response to output changes than to fiscal or other influences on relative factor prices. The level of the cost of capital, relative to the wage rate, determines the capital-labour ratio selected for gross investment, whether for output expansion or replacement; consequently, the full effect of a change in the (relative) cost of capital is completed only when the entire capital stock which exists at the time of the change has been retired. British examples of this more realistic but more complex representation of 'putty-clay' technology include King (1972), Malcomson and Prior (1979), and Sumner (1981).

In addition to its positive applications, this framework for the analysis of factor input decisions also sheds considerable light on an important normative question. Two further steps are required before that issue can be raised. First, the irrelevance of the additional taxes levied on distributed profits for the firm's input decisions can now be clarified. If the returns on the investment are paid out to shareholders as dividends, these additional taxes will be charged at rate t_p ; but if the cost of the investment, net of tax deductions, is financed from retained earnings, then this opportunity cost to shareholders is also subject to the personal tax adjustment because they would have received only $(1 - t_p)$ per pound invested.[4] Thus the net present value of an investment to shareholders is $(1 - t_p)$ of the value at the level of the firm; and since the latter is driven down to zero, in equilibrium, by competition, the additional taxes on distributed profits do not affect the investment decision. Under the imputation system of corporation tax a basic-rate taxpayer is not liable to additional imposts on dividends, and so the same result holds trivially (because $t_p = 0$) even if the investment is financed by a new share issue; but for other classes of shareholder, and for all taxpaying classes under the 'classical' system, personal tax liabilities cannot be ignored when new shares are issued to finance capital expenditure.

Secondly, investments may be financed not only from equity sources, whether new shares or retained profits, but also by issuing debt, an operation which has direct implications for the firm's tax liability because interest payments are deductible. Suppose a permanent addition to the firm's capital stock is financed by borrowing. From the shareholders' perspective there is no initial outlay, because profits need not be retained to purchase the asset. The investment will be worth undertaking if the annual incremental revenue covers net replacement expenditures and net debt service payments, or if

$$(1 - t)P\,\partial Y/\partial K - \delta Q(1 - tZ) - r(1 - t)Q(1 - tZ) \geqslant 0$$

where r is the pre-tax interest rate. The firm borrows $Q(1 - tZ)$ to purchase the asset, after allowing for depreciation deductions; the annual interest payments on this debt are deducted from its taxable income. At the margin,

$$\frac{\partial Y}{\partial K} = \frac{Q}{P}\,\frac{(r(1 - t) + \delta)(1 - tZ)}{(1 - t)} \tag{6}$$

Comparison of this equilibrium condition for debt-financed investment with the expression [3] derived earlier raises obvious questions about the relationship between debt and equity discount rates, and about the firm's choice between these sources of funds. These are explored in a later section.

The more immediate question is whether a 'neutral' tax system, meaning that investment decisions are not influenced by taxation, can be designed. It is clear from equation [3] that this condition will be fulfilled for an equity-financed project only if $Z = 1$, i.e. if the cost of capital goods can be deducted from taxable income in the year of purchase, rather than being spread across a period of years. Such a provision, often described as expensing or, less precisely, as 'free depreciation', has applied to purchases of equipment in the UK, but not to other types of capital, since 1972.

If marginal investments are financed by borrowing this treatment will be more favourable than is warranted by the neutrality criterion. That condition would be fulfilled if the firm were permitted to deduct, in addition to interest payments, a periodic tax allowance which corresponded to economic depreciation, the decline in the value of the asset.[5] It is not feasible, however, to determine the tax treatment of individual investments by relating them to particular forms of finance. Moreover, even if there were good reasons for believing that debt is the marginal source of funds, determination of the physical depreciation rate for each asset would be wholly impracticable, except in the rare cases where active resale markets exist. The facts that in practice economic depreciation will depend on use as well as age, and that there would in any case be possibilities for substituting more favourably treated maintenance expenditure for replacement, are sufficiently indicative of the difficulties involved.

Two reactions to these difficulties are to be found in the literature. The first is exemplified by Coen's (1975) attempt to determine the pattern of true economic depreciation in individual (2-digit) industries, by comparing econometric estimates based on different assumptions about the life and decay of equipment and structures, in the belief that 'to achieve tax equity and neutrality, the treasury should strive to keep tax depreciation in line with economic depreciation' (p.59). As already indicated, this exercise represents the pursuit of an unattainable goal. The alternative course is to abandon the search for precise measures of true economic income, and to base corporate tax liabilities on cash flow rather than profits. This alternative, which has been advocated by many economists, most recently Meade *et al.* (1978), on grounds of certainty and simplicity, would involve two steps: the extension of expensing to all forms of capital expenditure, including inventory investment (Sumner 1975a); and the abolition of interest deductibility, or equivalently the addition of new borrowing to the tax base.

The neutrality discussion would probably have aroused little interest had it not been for the rise of the inflation rate during the 1970s. In a fiscal context, the rapidly growing literature on inflation accounting presupposes that a tax system free from inflationary distortions can be achieved only by an elaborate system of indexing. Specifically, depreciation for tax purposes would have to be based on replacement cost, and capital gains on existing assets and liabilities taxed as they accrued. The difficulties already inherent in the measurement of true profit would therefore be magnified enormously. In sharp contrast, a cash-flow base would require absolutely no adjustment for inflation: tax relief on capital expenditure would be granted in the same period and, therefore, the same 'pounds', as the purchase itself; and nominal interest payments would not reduce tax liabilities, so their increase when the inflation rate rose would not reduce the real interest rate. Whatever its importance in providing information to shareholders, therefore, inflation accounting would not be necessary for tax purposes. This point was acknowledged in the influential Sandilands Report (1975), but only for a limited range of assets, and without recognition that interest deductibility plus expensing would be more than 'neutral'.

A number of writers, including Nickell (1977) and Sandmo (1979), have stressed that a cash-flow base does not provide neutrality if the tax rate is expected to change. The effect of such anticipations, perhaps contrary to intuition, would be to depress investment when the tax rate is temporarily reduced, and vice versa. The reason is that the returns from the investment will mainly be taxed at the 'normal' rate, while tax relief on investments executed currently will be granted only at the lower rate. There is therefore an incentive to postpone investment until the tax rate has risen back to its normal level[6]; or conversely, to concentrate investment into periods of temporarily high tax rates.

Sandmo (p. 176) asserts incorrectly that 'by increasing the tax rate one reduces the demand for capital goods'; such an effect would be produced by an increase in the *anticipated* tax rate. Nevertheless, some interesting light is cast on his inaccuracy by studies of the response to predictable tax changes. Eisner and Lawler (1975) record that when the tax liabilities of US corporations were temporarily surcharged in 1968, firms responding to a questionnaire reported a decrease in planned capital spending, rather than the acceleration that would be predicted on *a priori* grounds. In the UK, the transition to the imputation system, which involved an increase, predictable two years in advance, in the corporate tax rate, was associated with a level of investment that was much too *high*, relative to an econometric estimate of what would have happened *ignoring* the expected tax change, in the period before the change; the opposite, and equally puzzling, prediction error was registered in the period immediately after the tax change (Sumner 1981). Whatever the explanation of these apparently perverse results, they diminish the attractiveness of the suggestion that 'one might wish to introduce an element of non-neutrality in order to increase the usefulness of the tax as an instrument of stabilisation' (Sandmo 1979: 176) by making announcements of future tax rates, since it would be difficult to predict even the direction of response. Moreover, variations in expected future tax rates, whatever their macroeconomic impact, would diminish the allocative advantages of a neutral tax base by generating uncertainty.

DISCRIMINATORY FACTOR TAXATION

What are the practical consequences of a non-neutral tax system? One immediate answer to that question is that a less favourable tax treatment of capital than of labour inputs will make the capital-output ratio lower than it would otherwise have been; the level of output, for given labour force and technical knowledge, will therefore be reduced. If technical knowledge in endogenous, as for instance in Arrow's (1962) model of learning by doing, where it depends on cumulated gross investment, these effects will be intensified. If the tax treatment of capital is not uniform, but discriminates among the equipment used in different industries, an additional and less obvious effect on output occurs.

In the textbook model the firm chooses its factor input ratio from the technically efficient set represented by the relevant isoquant according to the relative price ratio, $W/Q(\rho + \delta)$, where W is the wage rate. As we saw in the previous section, the existence of taxation influences this ratio, which now becomes $W(1 - t)/Q(\rho + \delta)(1 - tZ_j)$, where the j subscript has been inserted to indicate that firms in different industries face differences in the tax treatment of their capital expenditures. For simplicity labour and capital inputs will be treated as homogeneous; that assumption can be relaxed, provided possibilities of substitution between different types of labour and between the production of different types of machine are admitted, but only at the cost of inessential complexity. To simplify further, assume that the output of the capital-good industry remains fixed because the total demand for equipment is not affected by taxation; and that after allowing for the labour requirements of the equipment industry there remains in the economy a fixed quantity of labour available for the two consumption-good industries, denoted by subscripts $j = 1,2$.

These simplifications enable the effects of discriminatory factor taxation to be treated diagrammatically, in a form popularised by Johnson (1966). Figure 2.1 represents an Edgeworth-Bowley box in which the fixed amounts of labour and capital available to the two consumption good industries are shown on the axes. In the absence of taxation, cost minimisation would ensure that

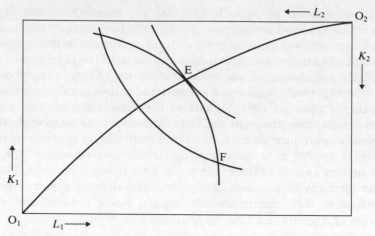

FIG. 2.1 Productive efficiency

production in the consumption-good industries took place at a point such as E, on the efficiency locus which represents tangency of the two sets of isoquants. The economy would then be operating on its production possibility frontier, achieving the maximum attainable output of good 1 for any specified output of good 2 in each time period. When taxation is introduced, however, that result no longer holds if the equipment purchases of the two industries are treated differently. Different values of Z will cause different factor price ratios; cost minimisation will now ensure that the factor allocation deviates from the efficiency locus, and instead occurs at a point such as F where a pair of isoquants intersects. For a given output of good 2 a smaller output of good 1 will result: the transformation surface is pulled below the production possibility frontier, provided both industries remain in existence. This departure from productive efficiency is additional to any departure from neutrality 'on average', which would change the relative size of the equipment industry.

Departures from productive efficiency impose a more tangible, and therefore more obvious, form of loss than many other tax-induced distortions. The most transparent application of the analysis is to the British selective employment tax (SET), introduced in 1966 and abolished in 1973, which discriminated between labour employed in different industries. The mechanism was a uniform increase in the employer's National Insurance contribution which was refunded, initially with a premium, to firms engaged in manufacturing and other specified industries. The effect was to raise labour costs in the service sector and other industries which did not qualify for refund by a maximum of about 8 per cent.[7] In quantitative terms, however, the difference in labour costs induced by SET was dwarfed by a difference in capital costs imposed almost simultaneously. Between 1966 and 1970, investment in equipment by manufacturing and other favoured industries attracted a cash grant of 20 per cent, while equipment purchased by other industries qualified only for an initial allowance of 30 per cent. The effect was to raise comparative net capital costs in the service sector by a minimum of about 18 per cent. The latter difference was less apparent than SET, and was misunderstood by even well-informed commentators. For instance, in his report on SET Reddaway (1970) contrasts the 'clearly valid principle' that the tax would encourage substitution of machines for men with the results of his discussions with those liable to the tax; these revealed only 'very few cases' where the principle 'had become effective'. As the principle was *invalidated* by the accompanying change in capital costs, the results of his discussions are rather less surprising than he believed. This example underlines the importance of basing empirical investigations on a sound theoretical framework.

The SET instance also indicates that it is *relative* factor prices which affect productive efficiency. If industry 2 faced uniformly higher prices for both factors than industry 1, the factor allocation would be changed but would remain on the efficiency locus. The effects would be analogous to those of an excise tax on industry 2's output or sales. Thus productive efficiency would be unaffected by levying a higher tax rate on, say, industry 2's net income; it is much more closely related to the definition of the tax base than to relative tax rates.

Two corollaries follow from this. The first emphasises the practical significance of neutrality. Departures from this principle, by accident or design, are unlikely to be uniform; hence their consequences for the capital intensity of production in aggregate, with its implications for the time-profile of output, will be combined with changes in the inter-industry allocation of factors. Secondly, the best-known analysis of discriminatory factor taxation is inadequately specified and consequently misleading.

The allusion is to Harberger's analysis (e.g. 1966) of the corporation income tax. The essential features of his model can be illustrated by Fig. 2.1 where the relatively capital-intensive industry 1 represents the corporate sector, a form of organisation which predominates in manufacturing, and industry 2 represents the characteristically unincorporated provision of housing and other services and agriculture. In both sectors personal income tax is levied on the income of the owners of capital, but those in the corporate sector pay an additional surcharge in the form of a (classical) corporation tax. An increase in the rate of corporation tax generates a flow of capital to the unincorporated sector until post-tax rates of return are equalised; but this necessary condition for equilibrium is accompanied by unequal pre-tax rates of return, and therefore productive inefficiency, because tax rates differ. His analysis of the efficiency effects of corporation tax is complemented by an examination of its incidence (e.g. Harberger 1962), which demonstrates how the 'burden' will be transmitted to all owners of capital, and considers its effect on relative factor shares.[8]

The merit of his efficiency analysis consists in isolating the determinants of the loss caused by a fiscal distortion. The relevant parameters are shown to be the elasticities of substitution in the two sectors, which characterise the curvature of the isoquants in Fig. 2.1, and the elasticity of substitution in consumption, which measures the response of demand composition to a change in the relative price of the two consumption goods. Parenthetically, to estimate the magnitude of these effects Harberger used calculus techniques, which are

appropriate only when the corporation tax is the sole distortion and is introduced on an infinitesimal scale; nevertheless, the application of more appropriate numerical simulation techniques (Shoven and Whalley 1972) has not
produced radically different estimates.

The defect of the analysis lies in the characterisation of the fiscal
distortion as a surtax on net income from capital in the corporate sector.
Harberger's initial assumption is that to achieve a return of X per cent net of a
50 per cent corporation tax, the gross rate of return (on an equity-financed
investment) must be $2X$ per cent. This would be true only if the tax code
permitted the deduction of economic depreciation. Since more generous deductions are usually granted (e.g. Hall and Jorgenson 1971), the distortion caused
by corporation tax is typically overstated, perhaps even misdirected (Sumner
1973), in his analysis because the tax base is incorrecty specified. In his empirical
work on the US tax system, Harberger uses the average tax rate (total
corporation tax revenue ÷ total income from corporate capital); this will be
positive provided some investments have a strictly positive net present value,
even if the tax rate on a marginal investment is zero, as it would be under a
neutral tax. As we have seen already, a neutral corporation tax would not alter
corporate investment decisions; but Harberger's use of the average rather than
the marginal tax rate obscures that important result.

As a practical matter, corporate tax systems have approached but
seldom achieved neutrality, except for special forms of investment singled out
for particularly favourable treatment, so Harberger's analysis retains some
substance. Moreover, even if decisions are unaffected at the margin, because
'the whole corporate profits tax structure is just like a lump sum tax on
corporations' (Stiglitz 1973:33), the fact remains that positive tax will be
collected as long as net present values are on average positive, and that tax could
be avoided by not incorporating. Why, then, do firms incorporate? Are their
decisions to do so affected by the tax structure? A comprehensive treatment of
these questions is not available in the literature, but when they are raised it is
usually suggested (e.g. Stiglitz 1973; King 1977:ch. 4) that non-tax considerations, such as the risk of bankruptcy and the separation of ownership from
control, carry greater weight. King shows that the possibility of retaining
earnings within the firm on favourable terms may influence the decision to
incorporate in certain circumstances; but he also reports failure to find a
significant (partial) relationship between the relative size of the corporate sector
and the appropriate fiscal variables in either the USA or the UK.

A caveat is necessary before concluding this section, for the desirability of productive efficiency has not been questioned; yet in a second-best world
none of the first-best welfare conditions can be assumed to remain unchanged.
Cases in which productive inefficiency is optimal have been constructed by
Dasgupta and Stiglitz (1972) and by Mirrlees (1972), using both distributional
and allocative arguments. The former seem unconvincing provided 'enough'
fiscal instruments are available; the latter do not apply if returns to scale are
constant, which is not an unreasonable first approximation. The final word is left
to Sandmo (1976:48): 'Perhaps ... one should not worry too much about the

exceptions to the rule that productive efficiency is desirable; the administrative and informational costs of deviating from the rule might easily be too high for it to be an interesting alternative.'

LOCATIONAL DECISIONS AND REGIONAL FACTOR INTENSITIES

The regional pattern of economic activity has been a matter of explicit concern to successive British governments since the interwar years; but it is only in the period since 1963 that fiscal instruments have been directed towards the regional problem. Since then investment in both equipment and buildings has attracted higher tax allowances or cash grants when located in what are now described as assisted areas. Over the shorter period 1967–77 the regional employment premium reduced the wage bill in qualifying industries. In quantitative terms the proportionate reduction in labour costs was considerably smaller than that in capital costs. Both forms of assistance have been confined to the 'industrial' sector, mainly manufacturing, mining and construction.

In the model used in the previous section, regionally differentiated factor-price ratios have no role; indeed, there are no regional problems, or even regions! To assess these instruments, therefore, the model must be expanded and 'the regional problem' must be characterised. The long-running debate as to whether work should be taken to the workers or workers to the work suggests that at least one feature of the problem is regional immobility of labour. This can be incorporated in the two-sector, two-factor model by postulating that each industry is located in a particular geographical area, and that there is a fixed maximum quantity of labour available in each of these regions; this additional constraint is represented by the vertical line AB in Fig. 2.2, in which the subscripts now represent both industries and regions.

This additional constraint means that only one point on the efficiency locus, viz. E, is attainable. If a higher level of industry 1's output is desired, say Y_1^2, it is not possible to operate at point C, where industry 2's output is Y_2^3. To

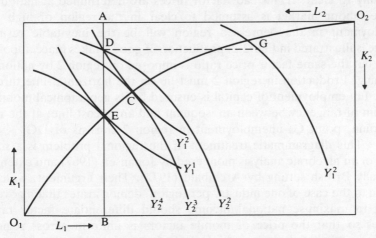

FIG. 2.2 Regional immobility of labour

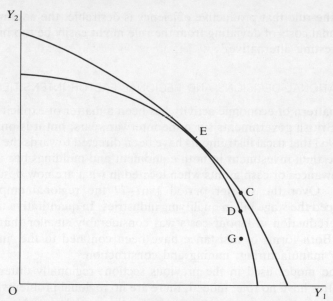

FIG. 2.3 Effect of labour immobility on the production frontier

attain points on the constraint AB other than E, relative factor prices must differ in the two regions if factor allocations are determined by a decentralised decision-making process. The locus of feasible outputs along AB is shown in Fig. 2.3, along with the production possibility frontier that would obtain in the absence of the regional constraint on labour mobility.[9]

To attain points such as D along AB, relative factor prices must differ in the two regions. The appropriate differentials would be created automatically if factor prices adjusted immediately to clear markets; but the most casual form of empiricism reveals that wage rates for a given type of labour in different regions do not differ sufficiently for labour markets segmented by geographical immobility to clear. If, instead, factor prices are determined at national level, and the labour market is assumed to clear in the region of high activity, unemployment in the depressed region will be the inevitable result. This outcome is illustrated in Fig. 2.2: production of good 1 takes place at point D, as before, but the same factor-price ratio is imposed on region 2 by national wage bargaining. Production in region 2 must lie on the horizontal line through D, because full employment of capital is ensured by its geographical mobility, and at a point of tangency between an isoquant and an isocost line; at the resulting equilibrium, point G, unemployment in region 2 consists of DG.

This diagrammatic treatment of the regional problem is a simplified version of an algebraic analysis pioneered by Johansen (1967) and extended in a specifically British setting by Archibald (1972). Their argument, which is not confined to the case of one industry per region, demonstrates that a government wishing to maximise national income should differentiate factor taxes and subsidies so that the price of mobile factors is uniform across regions and industries, and that the price of immobile factors is uniform across industries within a region but, in general, differs among regions.[10] If minimising the regional variance of unemployment *per se* is a government objective, the case for regionally differentiated taxes or subsidies on labour input, and the case against offering investment incentives in depressed areas, would appear even stronger; yet successive governments have not heeded these prescriptions.

This discrepancy between analysis and policy suggests that at least one of them is defective. Three objections to the analysis have been suggested. The most simplistic is that the choice of production techniques is more limited than the smooth convex isoquants of Fig. 2.2 suggest. The information available on this question is conflicting. Moore and Rhodes (1976) 'can find little evidence' of intra-industry substitution of capital for labour in the UK, though the significance of their statement is diminished by their failure to record where and how they searched. On the other hand, using regional differentiated data from the 1968 Census of Production, Buck and Atkins (1976) report elasticities of substitution differing significantly from zero in 33 out of 77 industries; a less disaggregated analysis of the same data by Tooze (1976) yielded 9 or 12 (depending on specification) significantly non-zero cases out of 14. In any case, the possibility of intra-industry substitution is fundamentally irrelevant to the argument in question, as indeed the title of Johansen's paper indicates. Even if the capital intensity of each industry is a technologically determined constant, the capital-labour ratio can be varied across regions by variations in the industry mix. Attracting capital-intensive industries to labour-abundant regions remains an odd policy.

Secondly, Blake (1976) has argued that capital may be regionally immobile, either because of 'external economies and linkages' or because of 'inertia'. The consequence of capital immobility, however caused, is a situation in which 'depressed regions ... obtain less than their proportional share of investment' (p.96). It is difficult to rationalise the implied judgement that this situation is undesirable without treating the regional allocation of investment as an end rather than a means and, as Johansen observed, a regional objective of this kind 'would seem rather odd'. If the original objective of maximising the value of national output is retained, then a distinction needs to be drawn between the two suggested explanations for capital immobility. The invocation of 'external economies and linkages' implies that investment is more productive, *ceteris paribus*, when concentrated in established locations that when it is diverted to green-field sites; differential labour subsidies would then remain the appropriate instrument for maximising national income. If geographical concentration generated discrepancies between social and private valuation, additional measures to deal with externalities might be appropriate; but these would be directed against activity in narrowly defined localities, rather than in favour of investment in whole regions. In contrast, if firms are 'inert' in their response to policy changes, then the assumption of cost-minimisation becomes questionable; but in that event the efficacy of any fiscal instrument becomes dubious.

The third and most convincing objection to the foregoing analysis is that it starts from an incomplete characterisation of the regional problem. An alternative justification for special assistance to particular regions might be couched in terms of high initial costs; provided these set-up costs were indeed transitory, the case for subsidising them would be analogous to the infant-industry justification for tariffs. It would be difficult, however, to justify regional *investment* incentives on the basis of this argument, even if the existence of higher initial costs were adequately documented. Investment expenditures in assisted, or for that matter other, regions are not incurred solely to initiate new production; and infants incur other forms of expenditure. The infant-industry argument is a case for lowering input prices uniformly, or more directly for levying a lower tax rate on sales revenue, for a specified period after establishment. It is certainly not a case for lowering machine prices in greater proportion than new building costs, as current and past policies have done, or for confining regional assistance to particular industrial categories. At most this argument suggests that the case for regionally differentiated labour costs based on regional immobility should be augmented by subsidisation, at a lower rate, of capital expenditures incurred by identifiable infants.

FINANCIAL DECISIONS

The choices at issue in this section concern the sources and uses of funds: what proportion of debt and equity should the firm adopt, and how should it divide its net profit stream between dividends and retentions? The literature bearing on these questions, particularly the former, is enormous. For present purposes, it starts with the question of whether the firm's decisions on financial policy make any difference to its market value. The answer given by Modigliani and Miller (1958), and later generalised by others, was negative, for a world in which the risk of bankruptcy could be ignored, and in which firms and individuals faced a perfect capital market. In those conditions individuals would be able to arrange their personal portfolio of equity and debt (or loans) to exploit, and thereby eliminate, any profitable opportunities, rendering the firm's debt-equity choice irrelevant.

In a world where the tax rate is not uniform, either among individuals or between the household and corporate sectors, the terms of borrowing differ correspondingly. Such differentiation creates new opportunities for profitable arbitrage. In particular, if the corporate tax rate exceeds 'the' personal rate, firms can borrow more cheaply than individuals; it would then be profitable for the firm to borrow in unlimited amounts, not only to finance investment but also to pay dividends in excess of profits.[11] To use a corporation in this way as a conduit for what would in effect be personal borrowing would be illegal, but there is no prohibition on financing the firm's entire expansion plan by issuing debt. Deferring the question of its feasibility or desirability, it is worth digressing to examine the consequences of an all-debt policy.

Neutrality through offsetting errors

We have seen that if investment is financed by borrowing and the firm can deduct economic depreciation from its tax liabilities, corporate taxation will not distort investment decisions. Boadway and Bruce (1979) have shown that this neutrality property can be applied more generally, provided the firm finances its entire net investment by borrowing. Suppose, as before, that economic depreciation occurs at the constant rate δ, but that tax-allowable depreciation is granted at some different rate, μ. These two different depreciation schedules imply two different valuations of the net capital stock at each moment of time: the 'true' economic value,

$$K = I + (1 - \delta)K_{-1}$$

where I is gross investment and K_{-1} is the 'true' capital stock at the end of the previous period; and the 'accounting' stock,

$$\hat{K} = I + (1 - \mu)\hat{K}_{-1}$$

determined by the tax-allowable depreciation rate. Conversely, the gross investment of any period can be divided into its expansion (ΔK, $\Delta \hat{K}$) and replacement components (δK_{-1}, $\mu \hat{K}_{-1}$) in two different ways. Any excess of tax-allowable over economic depreciation ($\mu \hat{K}_{-1} - \delta K_{-1}$) will be exactly matched by an excess of 'true' over the 'accounting' measure of net investment. Therefore, if the firm is legally constrained to borrow only what is necessary to finance its net investment as measured by 'accounting' conventions, the present value of the tax deductions on its interest payments will deviate from those that would be generated by its 'true' net investment; and it will do so by an amount which exactly compensates for the discrepancy between tax-allowable and economic depreciation. Thus, if the constraint on borrowing in excess of net investment is based on the measurement conventions built into the tax code, *any* tax system will be neutral. Paradoxically, if lenders, who impose the constraint, are sufficiently sophisticated to perceive the true economic situation through the veil of tax conventions, neutrality will not be achieved.

The flaw in this ingenious argument is the hidden assumption that the measures used by accountants, who fulfil a major role in providing information to shareholders and creditors, are based on fiscal conventions. The converse proposition, that taxation is based on accounting conventions, is a more accurate generalisation; but a specific exception applies to capital expenditure, at least in the Anglo-Saxon world. Before business accounts can be used to assess tax liabilities, accounting depreciation must be added to income and statutory capital allowances subtracted. Once the existence of *three* separate methods of decomposing gross investment is recognised, the argument that measurement errors net out to zero collapses; only by coincidence would tax-allowable depreciation plus the accounting measure of net investment total gross investment, as would be necessary for neutrality.

The choice between debt and equity finance

Despite the tax-deductibility of interest payments, debt does not typically constitute an overwhelming, or even a 'large' proportion of the firm's capital. One answer to the resulting 'puzzle' of financial policy is that the provisions of the personal tax system, particularly the favourable treatment of capital gains, have generally been overlooked (Stiglitz 1973); incorporating these into the analysis considerably reduces the apparent advantage of debt finance. The more usual approach has been to place sole emphasis on bankruptcy or, more generally, on uncertainty. For example, Scott (1976) analyses the effect on the firm's valuation of a positive probability of bankruptcy in a model where, unusually, both creditors and equity-holders are risk-neutral. He shows that under fairly weak conditions there will be an optimal, i.e. market-value-maximising, debt-equity ratio: as the actual ratio increases, the market value of debt rises at a decreasing rate, because of the increasing probability of bankruptcy, but the value of equity falls at a decreasing rate, since '[b]ankruptcy is actually beneficial to stockholders because it provides them with the protection of limited liability' (Scott 1976:45); the optimum occurs where these rates of change are equal (in absolute value). An analysis which is closer to the traditional framework is that of Tambini (1969), who hypothesises that the marginal costs of both debt and equity are an increasing function of the debt-equity ratio, because a higher ratio increases both lenders' and borrowers' risks. In his model, equilibrium occurs when the marginal costs of debt and equity, which differ from their respective average costs on account of these risk premia, are equated. At the equilibrium the average cost of debt, the interest rate, is lower than the average rate of return on equity, consistently with the observed 'puzzle' of financial structure.

   In the models developed by Scott and Tambini, the observed debt-equity ratio is the outcome of an optimising decision. The cost of capital is a weighted average of the corresponding costs under all-equity and all-debt finance, equations [3] and [6] respectively; the equilibrium condition is therefore

$$\frac{\partial Y}{\partial K} = \frac{Q}{P} \frac{(\alpha\rho + (1-\alpha)r(1-t) + \delta)(1-tZ)}{(1-t)} \qquad [7]$$

where $(1-\alpha)/\alpha$ is the optimal debt-equity ratio. In most specialisations of Stiglitz's model, '[t]he actual debt-equity ratio is the fortuitous outcome of the profit and investment history of the firm' (Stiglitz 1973:32), provided the critical inequalities which determine which source of funds is cheapest, and which depend on the personal and corporate tax rates, continue to hold. In the first two models, the optimal (and therefore actual) debt-equity ratio is a continuous function of the corporate tax rate; in Stiglitz's model, a tax change will affect financial policy discretely, if at all, by reversing the relevant inequality. Their common prediction, that the 'average' proportion of debt is an increasing function of the corporate tax rate, is consistent with the evidence for both the UK and USA (King 1977; Peles and Sarnat 1979; HMSO 1975; and Tambini 1969); though the magnitude of the tax incentive is nothing like as large as some of the simpler models suggest.

The dividend pay-out decision

Whether it is determined by deliberate choice or a succession of historical accidents, the debt-equity ratio will obviously determine the proportion of the firm's post-tax income to be paid out in the form of interest. The proportion to be paid out in the form of dividends is much more flexible, and requires explanation.

The form of company taxation, particularly the relative tax burdens imposed on dividends and retentions, has been a political football in the UK and a favourite academic debating ground in the USA (e.g. McLure 1979). An examination of the frequent British changes led one earlier observer to conclude that differential taxation was irrelevant (Rubner 1964), in the sense that dividend pay-out policy was insensitive to the opportunity cost in terms of retentions forgone. The prolonged burst of econometric activity thus provoked demolished this conclusion, generated a qualitative consensus that the major determinants of dividends are corporate income and the degree of fiscal discrimination against distributions, and suggested additional explanatory variables, notably take-over activity (e.g. King 1977:6); but it left unresolved more detailed questions, such as the most appropriate functional form and measure of income, and the magnitude of the fiscal effect on pay-out policy.

At the level of pure theory this econometric evidence is of limited usefulness; it puts the cart before the horse, because it cannot deal with '. . . the central difficulty . . . that in many cases the payments of a dividend is clearly an irrational act' (Kay 1978:866). The difficulty arises because the relatively favourable tax treatment of capital gains is not fully exploited when dividends are paid: the problem is therefore to explain the existence, rather than the magnitude, of dividends. A common approach to this difficulty is to hypothesise a unique role for dividends in 'signalling' information to shareholders; King, who adopts this hypothesis, interprets the significance of his measure of take-over activity in these terms. This explanation is less than fully convincing, for as Kay (p.866) points out, 'adopting a non-optimal financial policy seems a rather expensive means of signalling information'. An alternative explanation has been proposed by Auerbach (1979), but it amounts to treating dividends as a residual: so many constraints are imposed on other potential uses of funds, such as buying back the firm's own shares, buying other firms' shares in the manner of a financial intermediary, or acquiring a majority holding through take-over, that in a situation where profitable investment opportunities are limited there remains no alternative to paying dividends. Repurchase of its own shares by a company, which would be a means of providing equity holders with capital gains, is illegal in the UK and would be deemed to be a dividend distribution for tax purposes in the USA; but the effective prohibition of other activities enforces the payment of dividends *faute de mieux*. Apart from the tautological character of this 'explanation', to treat the dividend decision as a residual is *prima facie* inconsistent with the empirical results, which are derived from a model in which the retention decision is made residually and dividends are deliberately determined.

The constraints imposed by Auerbach on alternative uses of funds are relaxed by Gordon and Bradford (1980), who point out that the lower tax rate on capital gains applies only to personal shareholders. Certain institutional shareholders, notably pension funds and charities, are totally exempt from tax, and so would be indifferent between capital gains and dividends on tax grounds; though the transactions costs of realising capital gains to generate a cash income or to reallocate their portfolios would imply a preference for dividends. Shareholding corporations would have a positive preference for dividends ('franked investment income' in British terminology), on which they are not liable to pay tax, over capital gains, which would be taxed on realisation. The importance of institutional shareholding has increased substantially in the postwar period; and its influence on corporate financial policy is likely to be more than proportionate to its size. In Gordon and Bradford's model, for example, the weight attributed to a shareholder in decision-making depends additionally on attitudes to risk; the less risk-averse an investor, the greater his weight; and institutions might reasonably be presumed to be less risk-averse than the representative individual shareholder. A similar presumption holds in King's model (1977: ch. 5), in which influence depends on the vigour of portfolio management. Thus pay-out decisions may be dominated by the interests of institutions rather than individuals.

At the level of economic policy, the econometric literature on dividend behaviour is valuable, despite its inadequately determined starting point, because it indicates that the aggregate saving of the private sector can be manipulated by variations in the relative taxation of profits and retentions. In turn, savings are of direct interest in their own right, and corporate savings are often linked to corporate investment, though the causal relationships (if any) have been neither clearly articulated nor subjected to discriminating empirical tests.

When macroeconomic conditions require a higher savings rate, a constant-yield increase in the degree of fiscal discrimination against distribution appears to be a feasible means of achieving that objective. One objection to such a policy has been based on qualitative grounds: the larger volume of saving will be allocated less efficiently than if it were channelled through the capital market. More recently, a quantitative objection has been voiced by Feldstein and Fane (1973) for the UK and by Feldstein (1973a) for the USA, who argue that although corporate saving will unambiguously be increased, most of the increase will be offset in the short run, and all of it in the long run, by a decrease in personal saving. The offset occurs less through the decline in the personal sector's disposable income than through a direct link between household consumption and retained earnings, whose postulated role is that of a proxy for the capital gains generated by a higher level of internally financed investment.

The status of these results remains dubious. For the USA, Bhatia (1979) has shown that the estimated response of consumption to a change in retained earnings is extremely sensitive to the choice of estimation period and methods of measurement, collapsing completely when an alternative series for one of the other explanatory variables was substituted. The robustness of the UK results has not been investigated, though a comparison of several of Feldstein and Fane's own equations provides some grounds for suspicion: the addition of a totally insignificant variable produced substantial changes in the other parameter estimates. Their results have been greeted with scepticism by most commentators (e.g. Whittington 1974); but their case remains to be assessed thoroughly.

PRICES AND PRODUCTS

The analysis has so far been confined to conventional forms of corporate tax which, apart from abatement provisions for small firms, are levied at a constant rate. In principle, at least, this feature could be altered, and a number of proposals involving a variable tax rate, determined by some aspect of the firm's behaviour, have been advanced as a means of encouraging particularly desirable forms of conduct. Many of these proposals have been directed towards the maintenance of price stability or, more realistically, the reduction of inflation.

The literature on tax-based incomes (and prices) policies (TIP) mushroomed during the later part of the 1970s, but the essential features can be seen in Scott's (1961) early and neglected proposal, which advocated a schedule of tax rates geared to price increases. To implement such a scheme would require a vast administrative machine: a price index for each firm's output would be needed: and awkward questions of whether, and if so how, to allow for increases in costs and in productivity would arise. In addition to these practical problems, however, there is an important question of how much such a tax could achieve. To illustrate the principles involved, assume that the firm hires a single factor at a cost of F per effective unit (i.e. adjusted for productivity growth), to produce output, Y; the quantity of output it can sell is determined by the price, P, which it sets according to its demand function, $Y = Y(P)$, so its revenue can be written as a function of price, $R(P)$. It seeks to maximise profits net of tax,

$$\pi = [1 - t][R(P) - FY(P)] \qquad [8]$$

where the tax rate is an increasing function of the change in price,

$$t = t(P - P_{-1}).$$

Using primes to denote derivatives, the first-order condition for the profit-maximising price level is

$$\pi' = (1 - t)(R' - FY') - t'(R - FY) = 0 \qquad [9]$$

The first term is the net addition to profit generated by a price increase (which would reduce both revenue and costs); if the tax rate were constant that would be the only term, with a value of zero at the optimal price, say P^*. The second term appears because the tax rate is itself dependent on price; the effect of introducing Scott's scheme while holding price constant at P^* is to make the first-order condition negative.[12] To restore equilibrium the firm will reduce price, since the second-order condition,

$$\pi'' \equiv d\pi'/dP < 0 \qquad [10]$$

means that the value of the first-order condition will change in the opposite direction to that of price.

Scott's proposal would certainly reduce the level of prices, but its effect on the rate of change of prices is the more relevant question. Even its effect on the price level is exaggerated in the previous paragraph, because the firm's time horizon has been limited to a single period by the assumption that its objective is the maximisation of current profits. If it reduces price in the current period, the base from which next period's price increase is calculated will also be reduced, so that the firm's problem can no longer be treated as a static one. In a situation where current choices affect future opportunities a more reasonable objective would be maximisation of net worth, or the present value of current and expected future profits,

$$\sum_{i=0}^{\infty} (1 + r)^{-i} \pi_i$$

The corresponding first-order condition is

$$(1 - t)(R' - FY') - t'(R - FY) + t'_{+1}(R_{+1} - F_{+1}Y_{+1})(1 + r)^{-1} = 0$$

[11]

The effect of adding the third term, which reflects the truism that this period's current price will be next period's lagged price, is to diminish the impact of the tax on the price level considerably. As a first approximation, the effect of this modification is equivalent to multiplying the second term in equation [9] by the discount rate, i.e. reducing it by 80–90 per cent.

A convenient approach to assessing the effect of the scheme on the inflation rate is to characterise, or perhaps caricature, the price level as a mark-up on costs. If in the absence of the tax the mark-up were constant, as it would be if demand elasticity were constant, then price would increase at the same rate as costs. The effect of the tax is to reduce the mark-up; but clearly the mark-up cannot be reduced indefinitely, or profits will become negative. Presumably there will also be feedback effects from a lower rate of price increase to a reduced rate of cost increase; but these do not alter the conclusion that the effects of the tax on inflation will be transitory.

Scott's proposal fails to distinguish clearly between the process of inflation and the level of prices, an allocative problem more usually associated with monopoly. The sole attempt to implement a TIP, the French 'prélèvement conjoncturel' which was based on increases in value added, exhibited the same weakness (Sumner 1975b). Later TIP proposals (e.g. Seidman 1978) have concentrated on penalty or incentive taxes at rates determined by wage increases rather than price increases, because of the practical problems involved in schemes like Scott's. The implied characterisation of the representative firm as a monopsonist is even less plausible than Scott's assumption that it is a monopolist, and the relationship between inflation and the former kind of market failure is even more obscure.

While the implications of monopoly for inflation are at best questionable, it remains an important problem in its own right. Shilling (1969) has shown how sales taxation can be used to reduce the price of a monopolised product. Conventional forms of sales tax, namely specific and *ad valorem* taxes, can be regarded as particular cases of the power tax, levied at rate

$$\tau(P) = aP^{\eta} \qquad [12]$$

The elasticity of the tax rate with respect to price, η, is zero for a specific tax and unity for an *ad valorem* tax; either of these forms would raise price, but they are not the only possibilities. Consider again the condition for maximisation of profit, which is now given by

$$\pi = R(P) - FY(P) - \tau(P)Y(P) \qquad [13]$$

Assume, as before, that the monopolist was maximising profit in the pre-tax situation, and evaluate the first-order condition at the previously optimal price when the tax is imposed:

$$\pi' = 0 - \tau'Y - Y'\tau \qquad [14]$$

More conveniently, multiply the equation by P/Y and by unity $(= \tau/\tau)$ to obtain

$$\pi' \frac{P}{Y} = 0 - \tau' \frac{P}{\tau} \tau - Y' \frac{P}{Y} \tau = 0 - \tau(\eta - \varepsilon) \qquad [15]$$

where ε is the absolute value of the elasticity of demand. If this is smaller than the elasticity of the tax rate, the imposition of the tax reduces the value of the first-order condition below zero. To restore equilibrium the monopolist will therefore reduce price, by the second-order condition. Because the tax base is sales rather than profits, this result is conditional on the firm remaining in business: a sufficiently heavy tax would make it unprofitable to stay in the industry.

Barzel (1976) has drawn attention to another difference between alternative forms of sales tax, in this case specific and *ad valorem* forms only. The difference consists in the incentive for suppliers to change the quality of their product, which is conceptualised as a package of characteristics. An *ad valorem* tax creates a motive to detach characteristics and to market them separately in order to reduce tax liability; thus product quality, defined in terms of the component characteristics, will be reduced, and the imposition of the tax will raise unit supply-price by less than the constant-quality model would predict. In contrast, a specific tax is independent of price and therefore of quality; improvements in quality are thereby rendered more attractive, and so the imposition of a specific tax raises unit supply-price by a greater amount to cover the cost of improvements.

This ingenious analysis serves as a useful reminder that there are more margins of substitution than conventional theory recognises. Barzel's attempt, refined by Johnson (1978), to test the predictions of his analysis is, however, more questionable. In US states which impose a specific tax on cigarettes, the (partial) effect of a tax change on retail price was found to be significantly greater than unity, while in the single state which imposed an *ad valorem* tax the tax effect on price was significantly less than unity. While these results are entirely consistent with the analysis, it is difficult to conceive of a product which offers less scope for quality variation at state level. An alternative explanation of the same data is that changing price is a costly exercise and is therefore performed at discrete intervals; changes in relatively small components of costs are absorbed until a major component, such as the tax, changes, at which time the price is raised by enough to cover the backlog of previous cost increases. The hypothesis is shown by Sumner and Ward (1981) to provide a marginally better fit than the quality hypothesis, as well as imposing less strain on credulity.

The final point to notice concerns the macroeconomic impact of sales taxes. Just as TIP schemes would exert only a transitory influence on the inflation rate, so increases in conventional forms of sales tax would raise the price level but not the inflation rate. Indeed, the impact effect on prices would be mitigated in the longer run by the depressing effect of higher tax revenue on demand, provided the additional proceeds were not reflected in higher government spending. If, however, the results on US cigarette prices are of more general application, attempts to isolate the *ceteris paribus* relationship between tax and price changes will exaggerate even their impact effect.

MANAGERIAL OBJECTIVES AND TAX SHIFTING

Throughout this survey the firm has been assumed to maximise either the current level of profits or, more frequently, the present value of profits. There is, however, a large literature which explores the consequences of alternative objectives and asserts their plausibility in a world where ownership and management are separated. In this final section on the firm, the sensitivity of the earlier results to changes in the assumed objectives is assessed, and the empirical evidence on tax shifting is briefly considered.

Uncertainty

The most fundamental question raised in this literature is concerned not with the behaviour of a firm controlled by its management, but with how a firm should act in the best interests of its shareholders when the simplifying assumption of certainty is discarded. Specifically, King (1977: ch. 5) argues that maximising the expected present value of profits will not necessarily be in the best interests of shareholders, because the firm can influence the prices of the goods they buy (or sell) as well as their income from dividends and capital gains. The connection between uncertainty and monopolistic influence over price stems from the concept of a 'contingent' commodity: a single commodity at a given future date is distinguished according to the then prevailing state of the world; hence, when uncertainty is admitted, the number of commodities, but not the number of firms, is vastly enlarged. The logic of the argument is impeccable, but its significance seems dubious in a setting of diversified consumption; that is presumably the reason for Gordon and Bradford's (1980:113, n.8) 'conjecture that the deviation of firm behaviour from that implied by wealth maximisation will be small in a large system'.

Even if their conjecture turns out to be ill-founded, the significance of

King's argument remains doubtful for another reason, that it precludes any prediction regarding the response to a tax change, or indeed to any other disturbance. Analysis requires a definite objective function, but that does not guarantee definite results. Sumner (1973) incorporates risk-aversion by assuming that the firm considers the variance as well as the expected value of net profits. Output may be higher or lower than under (expected) profit maximisation depending on the form of uncertainty, which in this model relates to the firm's demand curve. If uncertainty takes the form of an additive disturbance term with a fixed variance, which shifts the whole demand curve vertically up or down, output will be lower than under profit maximisation. If the variance of the disturbance depends, more plausibly, on output, the precise character of the relationship determines the sign and size of the departure from the profit-maximising level of output. The response to a tax increase is ambiguous, but always reduces the deviation from profit-maximising output.

Sales and growth objectives

Most of the literature is concerned with a particular form of alternative objective, rather than with uncertainty, and appears to offer more definite conclusions. For instance, a firm which endeavours to maximise sales revenue subject to a minimum profit constraint, an objective suggested by Baumol (1958), will unambiguously produce more than if it were a profit-maximiser. This result is of no predictive value, however, for there is no way of knowing whether a firm's output is 'high' or 'low' in isolation. The only comparisons with any discriminatory power are those between the same firm in two different situations which, in principle at least, permit a predicted change in behaviour to be observed. Attention has therefore been concentrated on isolating differential responses to external stimuli, such as changes in input prices or in tax rates.

Solow (1971) has examined the behaviour of 'orthodox' and 'growth-maximising' firms from this perspective; the former chooses the growth rate which maximises present value, the latter grows as rapidly as possible while maintaining its valuation ratio (of market value to the replacement cost of its capital stock) at a 'safe' level which will not attract a take-over bid. His central conclusion is that their behaviour will be qualitatively similar; consequently '. . . an observer would find it hard to distinguish one kind of firm from the other. But he also might find it unnecessary if his main object were to predict or to control the firm's behaviour' (p.341–2). His specific conclusion regarding the response to a tax increase is that both types of firm will reduce their growth rate. As would be expected in view of our earlier discussion, this conclusion depends on the tax base, which is defined to permit the deduction of economic depreciation, and the method of financing, by retentions; had the tax been neutral or more generous than neutral, the conclusion would have been modified in the obvious way.

Regrettably, Solow diminishes the force of his argument by contrasting the results for these 'dynamic' models with 'what happens in static theory': 'the profit-maximising output is the same with and without the tax. In contrast, a firm which maximises sales or revenue subject to a minimum-profit constraint will respond to a proportional tax on profits by reducing output' (p.338). The first statement is true only under a neutral system; with the tax base and method of financing postulated by Solow, a profit-maximising firm faced with a static demand curve would in the long run reduce its capital stock, through its replacement decisions, in the wake of the tax increase. The second statement, though frequently encountered, is equally misleading (Sumner 1977).

The conventional treatment of a tax increase under constrained sales maximisation is illustrated in Fig. 2.4, where the reduction in net profits at the initial equilibrium output, Y_1, forces the firm to contract output to Y_2 in order to satisfy the minimum profit constraint, $\bar{\pi}$. The critical feature of this argument is that minimum profit is specified net of tax, and hence is unaffected by the tax change; but this specification is quite inconsistent with Baumol's own rationalisation of the constraint. Profits serve a dual purpose in managerially controlled firms, '. . . to provide the retained earnings needed to finance current expansion plans and dividends sufficient to make future issues of stocks attractive to potential purchasers' (Baumol 1958:188). More generally, even if all investment is financed by retentions, shareholder disaffection can be avoided only by paying some dividend[13]; but the necessary level of dividends will be determined by the return available elsewhere. A tax increase will therefore ease the constraint confronting sales-maximisers by depressing the pay-out of profit maximisers. The need for retentions to finance expansion is an odd feature of a static model, particularly when the firm is contracting its output. More seriously, this argument neglects the significance of the tax base. If, for example, capital expenditures can be expensed, the net cost of expansion will fall by the same amount as net retention from a given pre-tax level of earnings, and the planned

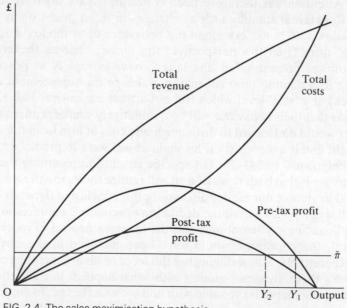

FIG. 2.4 The sales maximisation hypothesis

development can be executed despite the tax increase. Thus, the assumption of an unchanged net profit constraint is questionable on grounds both of internal inconsistency and of neglecting the precise structure of the profits tax. The constraint may fall more or less than actual net profits at the initial level of output, so it is not possible to predict the response of output to a change in the corporate tax rate. If the profit requirement is determined solely by dividend pay-out, it is not clear that any change in behaviour will result. If the firm is committed to financing an investment programme and the tax is less than neutral, a reduction in output and consequent rise in gross profits will be needed to provide the required funds; but a firm pursuing a more conventional objective would also reduce output in those circumstances.

The analysis could be repeated for other models of the managerially controlled firm, but diminishing returns would quickly set in. The modern theory of the firm has provided no general reasons for believing that the analysis of taxation developed under the assumption of wealth maximisation is outmoded or in urgent need of revision. Conversely, the analysis of responses to a tax change raises the important question of whether there is any observable difference between 'conventional' and 'modern' firms; the negative answer proposed by Solow and confirmed here suggests that the numerous exercises in exploring alternative motivational assumptions constitute a set of empty economic boxes.

Empirical studies

It is, of course, possible that some other, as yet unstated, assumption would generate results radically different from the conventional analysis. One way of short-circuiting the search would be to determine whether tax changes do in fact cause changes in behaviour other than those conventionally predicted, and there is a substantial literature which addresses this question. The obvious procedure would be to regress pre-tax profits on tax payments and a vector of other variables to control for non-fiscal influences, and to infer the magnitude of tax-shifting and its statistical significance directly. It is not possible to proceed quite so directly, because tax payments are an endogenous variable through the dependence of the tax base on profits, and so conventional estimation would yield a biased coefficient. Instead an instrumental variable technique, which requires the replacement of tax payments by the exogenously determined statutory tax rate, can be adopted; or the equation (in obvious notation)

$$\pi = a + bt\pi + cX_1 + \cdots$$

can be transformed to

$$\pi = \frac{a}{1 - bt} + \frac{c}{1 - bt} X_1 + \cdots$$

The shifting parameter (b) can then be estimated along with the others by a suitable non-linear technique. Finally, the estimating equation is typically deflated to reduce heteroscedasticity by dividing all variables by assets or sales.

The major specification issue concerns the set of non-fiscal variables, X. The dramatic result of a pioneering study by Krzyzaniak and Musgrave (1963), that corporate tax increases are more than fully shifted in the sense that the *net* rate of return rises with the tax rate, has been attributed by most commentators to an inadequate specification. In particular, Cragg, Harberger and Mieszkowski (1967), among others, argue that the tax coefficient is picking up the effect on profits of cyclical fluctuations for which no suitable control was included. When the employment rate is added to Krzyzaniak and Musgrave's estimating equation, along with a dummy variable to account for the abnormality of the wartime years, the shifting coefficient falls to a small fraction of its former value and becomes statistically insignificant. In contrast to Krzyzaniak and Musgrave's casual approach to specification, Gordon (1967) constructed an explicit model of the firm to account for non-fiscal influences on profits. His results, statistically insignificant shifting in aggregate and both positive and negative shifting in individual industries, confirm the suspicion attached to the earlier and apparently revolutionary results.

The studies cited in the preceding paragraph represent a small sample of the large amount of empirical work performed in the USA. In contrast, there are only two published studies of this question in the UK. In the first, Davis (1972) reports the results of fitting a variety of models, from which he concludes that '... with the exception of the Krzyzaniak-Musgrave model most of the results are consistent with zero or little shifting of the tax' (p. 284). That the contrast between the results of their specification and those of others reappears in a different data set is as remarkable as the general conclusion. A very different inference is drawn by Beath (1979), who postulates a relationship between the mark-up of manufacturing price over expected labour costs and the effective corporate tax rate, and concludes that tax changes over the period 1953–73 were shifted forward into (on average, lower) prices.

One consideration in attempting to arbitrate between these two contradictory studies is that, in a field where specification problems are notorious, the results of Davis are not derived from a single model. Another is that Beath's analysis poses a number of problems of measurement and methodology. The tax deductibility of interest payments is incorporated incorrectly in the earlier part of the estimation period. The hypothesis that, with the effective tax rate constant, prices rise in the same proportion as expected unit labour costs is imposed prior to estimation, yet direct tests of that hypothesis have resulted in refutations (e.g. Laidler and Parkin 1975:768). In the preferred variant of the estimated model, the expected rate of change of unit labour costs is constant, at zero, throughout a period when actual labour costs rose persistently at rates which fluctuated around a rising trend. The attempt to test for cyclical influences on the mark-up is limited to two lagging indicators. No consideration is given to changes in the strength of international competition or in the exposure of the British manufacturing sector. In view of these problems, it is scarcely surprising that the estimated equation fails to exhibit the desirable feature of random residuals, until a separate error process is added to the economic hypothesis to eliminate the autocorrelation. Even if the results were taken at face value, their interpretation would remain ambiguous. As noted in the discussion of Harberger's analysis, the use of an average effective tax rate reduces the number of parameters to be considered, but at the substantial cost of diverting attention from the margin at which decisions are made.

The downward trend in the effective tax rate could have been caused by several factors. The first is a decrease in the 'discriminatory' tax levied on distributed profits, which is included in Beath's calculations. As we have seen, such a change would have no direct influence on a 'traditional' firm's real decisions, and any evidence of shifting would have to be explained in terms of a different behavioural model. The second is a decrease in the statutory tax rate on retained profits. The effect would in general be ambiguous; but provided the tax base did not deviate far from neutrality, the magnitude would be small, whatever its direction, and again marked evidence of shifting would be difficult to reconcile with the traditional model of the firm. If, however, the effective tax rate were reduced by redefinitions of the tax base in relation to accounting profits, as was indeed the case in this period, there would be no inconsistency between traditional theory and evidence of shifting; for the firm would respond to larger capital allowances by expanding its capital input and its output, hence output price would fall relatively to labour costs. In short, Beath's results, if valid, could throw no light on the mechanism of shifting, or therefore on the adequacy or otherwise of traditional theory.

This point does not apply solely to Beath's study; and it cannot, in the present state of econometrics, be resolved by postulating a distinction between shifting in the 'long run', through changes in capital inputs, and in the 'short run', by some other mechanism. Whether the unsatisfactory state of the literature on tax shifting, and on the motivation of the firm, should be treated as a reason for regarding traditional theory as satisfactory, or as a motive for redoubled efforts to supplant it, is a question best left to the reader.

3. Taxation and household behaviour

INTRODUCTION

The framework of analysis and type of question considered in this section differ in several respects from those of the previous section. One relevant difference derives from the nature of the constraints facing households and firms. For example, a household's desired response to an income tax change, of changing the hours worked by one or more of its members, may be frustrated in the short run by the limited possibilities for individual negotiations, and even in the longer term it may require a change of occupation to effect a marginal adjustment of working hours. An alleged difference with similar observable consequences, but which in one respect is more fundamental, is that firms '. . . have a more concrete objective (profits) and a more precise set of tools to measure how well they are doing (balance sheets and income statements) than consumers do. Thus it is reasonable to expect corporate treasurers to calculate the effects of a . . . tax . . .

with a sharper pencil than consumers would and to react accordingly'. Branson (1973:281) made this assertion in the specific context of a variable-rate expenditure tax, but there is no reason why the principle, if valid, should not be applied more generally.

Both differences imply a greater element of inertia in the response of individual households to fiscal stimuli. Less obviously, however, the fact that household performance is not monitored by an external agency, and is of intrinsic interest only to social scientists and the household itself, enlarges the opportunity set to encompass broader possibilities of tax avoidance and evasion than those available to the firm. The distinction between untaxed home production and taxed market production has no direct parallel at the level of the firm; and the distinction between home production, which is untaxed *de jure*, and a secondary job providing services for other households is sufficiently difficult to enforce that the latter is frequently untaxed or under-taxed *de facto*, if conventional wisdom regarding the significance of the 'black economy' is to be believed.[14]

From a welfare perspective, the activities of firms are purely instrumental; it is the satisfaction of households which is of primary interest. That is a matter which involves distributional judgements as well as allocative considerations. Equity and efficiency have traditionally been treated in public finance as two separate criteria, discussed sequentially and with little or no guidance on how they could or should be combined.[15] An important recent development is the integration of these criteria through the medium of an explicit assumption about the social welfare function. This literature, which emphatically does not constitute easy reading and which can be given only the briefest of introductions within the constraints of this survey, does not purport to offer solutions to the traditional problem of trading off distributional justice against allocative efficiency. Its aim is rather to isolate those parameters which are critical to the resolution of that problem, thereby raising a wider variety of empirical questions about behavioural responses than those previously considered, and to draw attention to the special but usually implicit assumptions on which much of the conventional wisdom is based.

THE SUPPLY OF LABOUR

Theory

For most households the supply of labour services is by far the most important source of income. In aggregate, wages and salaries account for around 70 per cent of (pre-tax) personal income in the UK.

Labour supply, typically represented on a single axis of the familiar text-book diagrams, is in fact a multi-dimensional concept. It involves decisions by the household as to which of its members will participate, the skills they will acquire, the number of hours to be offered, the intensity of effort, and the geographical location of the family. These decisions may be made actively or by default, with short- or long-term horizons, and are clearly not taken solely on 'economic' grounds, narrowly defined; their economic dimensions are, however, all influenced by the tax system. The progressivity of the income tax affects the rate of return achieved by postponing entry into the labour market in order to gain the qualifications needed for admission to a better paid occupation. Geographical decisions are presumably not independent of the non-deductibility of commuting expenses incurred by employees, the treatment of overseas earnings and their remittance, or in North America the deductibility of removal expenses; and implementation of a proposal to tax the brain drain (Bhagwati 1976) would have a major effect on migration from poor to rich countries. Child care expenses incurred in consequence of decisions to participate in the labour market are recognised in the North American but not the British income taxes.

Despite the pervasive influence of taxation, most attention has been concentrated on its impact on the subset of labour supply decisions concerning participation and hours of work, partly because the analysis of other dimensions parallels these, and partly because of data availability. The latter constitutes a serious limitation even within the traditional areas of analysis. In particular, it is seldom possible to incorporate fully the interdependence of decisions within the household.

Participation in the labour market involves a binary decision which may be revised at frequent intervals by 'secondary' workers, mainly married women, but which is made by most 'primary' workers in conjunction with decisions concerning initially education and training, and, at a much later stage, retirement. Between these two points, choices may arise about the duration of unemployment after participation has been involuntarily ended. The fiscal system plays some role in all these choices but mainly through transfer payments, such as unemployment benefit and retirement pensions, rather than positive taxes. At the margin, however, this distinction is purely semantic: many transfers are conditional on other income, and it makes little difference to a person of pensionable age whether any earnings are taxed explicitly under the income tax, or implicitly by reducing his pension.[16] The two branches of the fiscal system can be treated as one at the level of the household, though the authorities' choice of administrative arrangements may affect distribution within the household: consider the parental contribution to student grants, or the 'claw-back' of the family allowance paid to a mother through higher income tax levied on her husband's income.[17] These examples suggest that the traditional emphasis on the household as the unit of analysis may be misplaced.

The number of hours worked is in principle a continuous variable, but choices are constrained by negotiated agreements, custom and practice, and social obligation. It is, nevertheless, instructive to ignore these constraints initially, and to focus on the influence of the tax-transfer system on the participation and hours of work decisions in abstraction from other determinants. The budget constraint of a hypothetical family is depicted in Fig. 2.5. The pre-tax standard wage rate of the head of the household is shown by the slope of ACD. The distance H_0B represents family income if the head of the household does not participate in the labour market. Of this, H_0A measures income from property and earnings of other family members, AB is unemployment benefit;

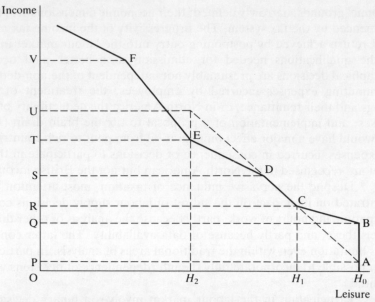

FIG. 2.5 Fiscal effects on the labour market constraint

the two components may, of course, be related through eligibility rules. Along BC, where the head of the household is working a few hours per week, the family receives income-conditioned transfers (e.g. family income supplement, rent or rate rebates, or a more ambitious form of negative income tax). These transfer payments are reduced as income from work increases, and so labour income bears an implicit tax at marginal rate PQ/PR.[18] This rate is considerably higher than the 'basic' rate of income tax which is payable when total income exceeds OS, at marginal rate TU/SU. Along the intermediate segment CD the household neither pays tax nor receives transfers. An overtime premium is introduced when hours in excess of H_0H_2 are worked, and finally a higher rate of income tax is encountered when total income exceeds OV.

The tax-transfer structure assumed in the construction of Fig. 2.5 excludes some of the more bizarre features found in British reality. For example, a decision not to participate in the labour market may yield net income greater than that obtained by working even the standard week, so that point B becomes a 'spike' which projects about the first, (and possibly other) linear segment of the budget constraint. The combined effect of separately administered income-conditioned transfers is capable of producing a marginal tax rate in excess of 100 per cent, so that the segment BC may contain positively-sloped components. Receipts of transfer may overlap with payment of taxes, eliminating segment CD.[19]

It is obvious from inspection that when an indifference map is superimposed on Fig. 2.5, the resulting equilibrium need not involve tangency with the constraint, because of its kinks; hence, despite the assumption that choice of working hours can be exercised freely, a change in the budget constraint need not alter behaviour in the case of a corner solution at B, D or F. Equilibrium need not be unique, for a worker could be indifferent between a point on DE and a point on EF. Equilibrium may be disturbed by a change in either the net income structure available to the head of the household in the labour market, or the net income of other family members. In the latter case the head of the household's constraint shifts vertically; in addition, a change in working hours of other family members will, in this two-dimensional representation, raise the possibility of a shift in the head of the household's indifference map if family leisure hours are complementary (more picnics) or substitutable (baby-sitting?).

The analysis of changes in the constraint of an individual household member is conducted in terms of the familiar decomposition of a price change into income and substitution effects. The latter refers to movements along the original indifference curve: when the tax rate rises the opportunity cost of leisure is reduced, so more of it is chosen. The former relates to movements between indifference curves: presumably leisure is a normal good, at any rate at the margin, so a tax increase reduces consumption of leisure because the individual is now worse off. The net effect on working hours is in general ambiguous, because most tax changes involve both effects.

There are, however, instances where no ambiguity arises. Changes in the tax-free personal allowances or in 'reduced' rates of tax do not alter the marginal wage rate of a 'basic'-rate taxpayer, and so do not activate a substitution effect. Conversely, the income effect may be neutralised for analytical purposes by postulating a particular use of the additional revenue or a particular method of financing a shortfall. For instance, Kosters (1969:302) points out that

> '...if incremental expenditures from tax receipts on services provided by the government have a value to society equal to the incremental value of purchases that individuals would otherwise make for themselves, then, as a first approximation, an incremental change in the tax rate will carry only a substitution effect'.

An alternative, less plausible perspective is presented by Musgrave (1959:240), who suggests that

> 'The worker may view his tax payments as a purchase of public services that he desires. A reduction in wages due to tax, if related to public services received, involves a lesser reduction in the price of leisure than an equivalent wage reduction in the market. Such at least would be the case if a voluntary-exchange solution could be applied to the problem...'

The qualification is, of course, critical.

A more common method of eliminating the income effect is to postulate an equal-yield tax change: differential rather than budget analysis in Musgrave's terminology. The most notable application of this technique is the demonstration that a progressive income tax will cause a greater reduction, or smaller increase, in working hours than an equal-yield proportional tax. The

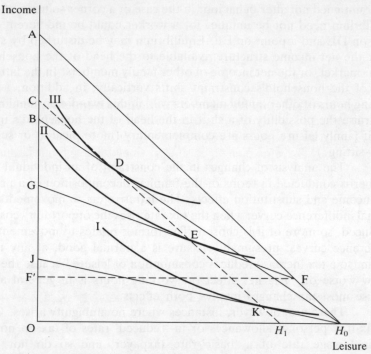

FIG. 2.6 Proportional and progressive taxes: the individual

standard analysis is illustrated in Fig 2.6. When a proportional tax is imposed the budget constraint swivels from H_0A to H_0B with equilibrium at D on indifference curve III. Equal-yield equilibria must lie along H_1C, drawn parallel to H_0A. One such alternative is at E, on indifference curve II. This is achieved under a linearly progressive tax, which exempts income OF' and taxes income above that level at a constant marginal rate, so as to produce the budget constraint H_0FG.[20] The individual in question pays the same tax bill in both cases, but is both worse off, on indifference curve II rather than III, and works shorter hours under the progressive tax. Notice, however, that in general a particular revenue can be extracted from an individual by two proportional tax structures. In this case the alternative produces equilibrium at K on indifference curve I and post-tax budget constraint H_0J, with tax revenue of AC as before. The locus of points like K and D, showing successive equilibria as the net wage-rate changes, is analogous to the price consumption curve of consumer theory; it will intersect the equal-yield line twice, except when the proportional tax rate is set at the unique revenue-maximising level, where the price consumption curve is parallel to the pre-tax constraint. Hence, the standard comparison between progressive and proportional taxes requires careful statement, for if points K and E are compared the standard conclusion is reversed. This perverse possibility has generated a literature of its own which has recently been reviewed by Hemming (1980) in relation to alternative measures of progressivity.

A final case in which, on conventional assumptions, the effects of a tax change on labour supply are unambiguous occurs under negative taxes. When a transfer payment is increased and financed by a higher implicit tax rate on earnings, income and substitution effects operate in the same direction. The effect on incentives may be dampened by the implicit character of the tax, by supplementary rules governing eligibility for benefits, or by the administrative lag between a change in earnings and adjusted entitlement to benefit (Barr and Hall 1975). How far the effect on incentives should be regarded as a matter for concern is itself debateable, but as Culyer (1973:95) observes, 'an obsession with the work-disincentive effects of income maintenance policies runs throughout the discussion of anti-poverty policy'.

Redistribution and labour supply

The effects of income taxation, particularly the comparison of proportional and progressive schedules, on an individual are of limited interest, for the primary rationale of progressivity is the redistribution of income. In aggregate the effects of a switch from proportional to progressive taxation are easily seen to be ambiguous (Musgrave 1959). In Fig. 2.7 the switch from the proportional schedule OX to the linearly progressive schedule OAY involves two sources of difficulty. First, the impact of the tax change on individuals is predictable only for those with initial gross incomes in the range AB: they face an increase in their marginal tax rate, which determines the substitution effect, but a decrease in their average rate, which determines the income effect; both influences therefore operate in the direction of shorter working hours. For initial gross incomes in the range OA, however, both average and marginal rates are

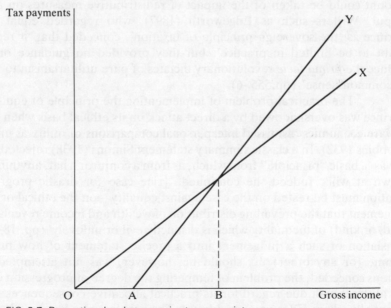

FIG. 2.7 Proportional and progressive taxes: society

reduced; and for gross incomes above B, both are raised, with ambiguous effects in each case. Without making specific assumptions about preferences, there is no reason to suppose that the net effect in these two ranges will be of opposite sign, even if individuals are assumed to have identical tastes and to differ only in earning ability. Secondly, the aggregate effect clearly depends on the numbers in each range and their 'quality' weighting, and on the magnitude as well as the direction of their response. Even if the net 'costs' of the change were known to be positive, there would remain the problem of comparing them with the 'benefits' of a different distribution of income.

This question was traditionally approached in terms of the 'ability to pay' principle, requiring equality of sacrifice in absolute, average or marginal terms. The attractions of the first two forms of the principle are not obvious, and their implications for progressivity are no clearer since the outcome depends on the specific form of utility function assumed; (Musgrave (1959) discusses these aspects at some length. In contrast, provided all individuals were assumed to be equally 'efficient' in maximising utility and the marginal utility of income diminished, equality of marginal sacrifice satisfied the utilitarian objective of maximising the sum of individual utilities. The implication for tax policy was that government expenditure, itself determined on utilitarian principles, should be financed by lopping off income differentials from the top until the required revenue had been raised. Unfortunately, however, there was no reason for stopping there, for total utility could be raised even further by continuing to tax away income differentials at the top and transferring the proceeds to those at the bottom, until complete 'vertical' equality had been achieved. This is described as 'unfortunate' because the process amounts to a *reductio ad absurdum*: no allowance for incentive effects was incorporated in the analysis, so no formal account could be taken of the impact of redistributive measures on aggregate output. Writers such as Edgeworth (1897), who regarded equal marginal sacrifice as 'the sovereign principle of taxation', conceded that 'it requires no doubt to be limited in practice'; but they provided no guidance on how to 'reduce the *prima facie* revolutionary dictates of pure utilitarianism to the limits of common sense' (pp.555–6).

The practical problem of implementing the principle of equi-marginal sacrifice was overshadowed by a direct attack on its ethical basis when the 'new' welfare economics dismissed interpersonal comparisons of utility as unscientific (Robbins 1932). In a classic summary statement Simons (1938) rejected ability to pay as 'a basic "principle" from which, as from a conjuror's hat, anything may be drawn at will'. Indeed, he continued, '[t]he case for drastic progression in taxation must be rested on the case against equality – on the ethical or aesthetic judgement that the prevailing distribution of wealth and income reveals a degree (and/or kind) of inequality which is distinctly evil or unlovely' (pp. 18–19). The translation of such a judgement into a precise statement of how progressive income (or any other) tax should be, however, was not attempted; and as Simons conceded, the problem of tempering the degree of progression desired in the abstract with due regard for its practical allocative consequences remained essentially where Edgeworth had left it. The problem was ignored altogether in a rare attempt to apply the principle of equal absolute sacrifice: Mera (1969), reversing the conventional chain of reasoning, inferred the utility function implicit in the US personal income tax schedule, on the assumption that the legislators had enacted that principle without regard for its costs, in terms of output sacrificed through blunted incentives.

A consistent basis for utilitarianism was finally provided by Mirrlees (1971), who examined the optimal degree of progression in a framework which permits what Simons described as 'the costly luxuries' of 'progress and justice' to be incorporated simultaneously. Individual utility functions are defined on income and leisure, and it is the inclusion of the latter argument which ensures that the incentive effects of taxation are brought into account directly, rather than being tacked on to the traditional formulation as an afterthought. In this model individuals are assumed to differ in their earning ability but not in their tastes. The results of the exercise clearly depend on the assumptions made about the distribution of ability and the utility function, which implies a labour supply function. In this respect there is an important contrast, stressed by Atkinson (1973), with classical utilitarianism, in which the only significant characteristic of the utility function was the postulate of diminishing marginal utility.

Mirrlees' paper might have attracted less attention if his results had been less startling; but his conclusions, that the optimal tax structure is approximately degressive, incorporating a negative income tax at the bottom of the scale, and more particularly that the marginal tax rate should tend to fall with income, generated a spate of literature which explored the sensitivity of the results to alternative assumptions regarding the distribution of earning ability, the objective function, and the form of the utility function. Atkinson (1973) proposed that an explicit social welfare function, defined on individual incomes, be used to represent Simons' 'ethical or aesthetic judgement' in numerical terms. Of the particular forms of SWF examined, the criterion of maximising the welfare of the worst off individual (Rawls 1972) has aroused most interest: examples in which it is applied include Broome (1975) and Phelps (1973). Different objectives and ability distributions have been compared by Cootner and Helpman (1974), using simulation techniques, and analytically by Helpman and Sadka (1978). The partial equilibrium framework adopted in most of these analyses has been relaxed by Feldstein (1973b), who allowed for the repercussions of changes in tax rates and consequently in labour supplies on pre-tax wage rates; although these induced changes were substantial, the bias in the calculation of optimal tax rates which resulted when they were ignored was small. Feldstein also drew attention to the limitations imposed on redistributive tax policies when there is a positive net revenue requirement to finance government expenditure on goods and services: conventional public goods and redistribution, which is itself sometimes characterised as a public good (e.g. by Thurow 1971), are substitutes. Other extensions include the introduction of relative income in the utility function (Boskin and Sheshinski 1978), and of a temporal dimension (e.g. Ordover and Phelps 1979).

The significance of the results reported in this literature clearly does not lie in their immediate policy implications, though Rosen (1976a) used an optimal income tax model as a framework in which to evaluate a number of specific reform proposals, and Boskin (1980) used the same framework to emphasise the interdependence among policy questions which are often examined in isolation. The formalisation of an explicit model does, however, direct attention to critical empirical magnitudes, and it requires that the value judgements concerning distribution be expressed in precise terms. No economist, policy-maker or any other mortal can confidently state the rate at which the social marginal utility of income declines, so in that sense the precision is spurious; but numerical translations of value judgements provide a sharper focus for debate and discussion, and a clearer measure of the extent of disagreement, than purely verbal statements of the kind quoted earlier. The additional stimulus to empirical research will produce more obvious and perhaps less contentious results.

Horizontal equity

One further criticism of the literature on optimal progression should be registered. In their concentration on the balancing of efficiency and vertical equity, contemporary writers have neglected the traditional criterion of horizontal equity, or equal treatment of 'equals'. Musgrave (1976:14) went so far as to complain that 'horizontal equity has been defined out of existence by assuming all individuals to be subject to identical utility functions'. It is certainly true that the translation of horizontal equity into operational terms becomes more difficult when differences in tastes are acknowledged. For instance, the extent to which differences in family size should be reflected in different tax liabilities becomes a two-dimensional problem, in the sense that it bears on both horizontal and vertical equity. Because leisure as such cannot be taxed, an income tax discriminates against those with a pronounced preference for goods and services rather than free time for contemplation. Even in the absence of that kind of complication, however, issues of horizontal equity still arise. In a well-functioning capital market, wealth owners will be indifferent among different assets of a given risk class. Feldstein (1976) notes that the elimination of fiscal distortions in the treatment of different income-producing activities, for example the elimination of the favours granted to home ownership or the oil industry, will impose capital losses on those who happen to be holding their wealth in those forms at the wrong time, and who may not be the beneficiaries of the original distortions which introduced horizontal inequities. He therefore interprets horizontal equity as a constraint on tax reform, and distinguishes sharply between the latter and tax design. Even if tastes are identical and there are no fortuitous differences among individuals of the type which disturbed Feldstein, differences in opportunities raise similar problems. Do labour and property incomes differ in riskiness or in the expenses of earning them in a way which warrants differential tax treatment? If so, should the differences be reflected in the income tax, in social security taxes and benefits, or in a tax which discriminates between human capital and property as sources of income? Clearly, these questions all involve horizontal equity, but the answers cannot be determined solely on that basis. Musgrave's criticism has regenerated interest in horizontal equity, and in the measurement of departures from it. In particular, Atkinson (1980) approaches the latter problem by comparing the ranking of individual units in terms of pre- and post-tax income. The task of integrating this concept into the treatment of optimal progression still remains, however; so far the concept itself has proved elusive. One important source of controversy is a wide range of views concerning the ethical significance of the pre-tax income distribution, and therefore of tax-induced changes in rank order.

Empirical studies of taxation and labour supply

Returning to the positive theme of how households respond to taxation, three sources of information can be distinguished: questionnaires and interviews, econometric analysis of observed behaviour, and experimental schemes for the alleviation of poverty. The last category refers to a number of experiments with negative income taxes in the US. These were of short duration, typically three years, and so the results may provide little guidance on the effects of a permanent scheme, which would exert a stronger income effect and which would not involve the intertemporal substitution effect associated with temporary schemes. The experiments were located in several states, and hence the differences between the experimental and control groups reflected differences among states in pre-experimental provisions for income maintenance, as well as differences in the experimental structures themselves. The interpretation of the results from the best known experiment, in New Jersey, was further complicated by a change in 'standard' welfare arrangements which coincided with the introduction of the experimental scheme. Participation was voluntary, and participants could withdraw from the experiment before the end of the programme The experiments were, of course, confined to a sample drawn from a limited population. Widespread misunderstandings were reported, and the artificiality of the experimental situation may itself have influenced the responses even of those who perceived the new opportunity locus correctly. Because of the difficulties in interpreting the results and the hazards in generalising from them, attention is here confined to the alternative sources of information.[21]

    An interesting illustration of the value of sample surveys is provided by Brown (1968), whose questionnaire study of an admittedly small sample revealed considerable ignorance about the tax structure faced by the respondents. None of the 179 wage earners knew his marginal tax rate, which was typically overestimated; almost all the 53 salaried workers displayed the same bias towards exaggeration, and only three knew the correct figure. The most frequent source of misunderstanding was the earned-income allowance, which (within the relevant range of incomes) reduced the marginal tax rate by the computationally inconvenient fraction of 2/9ths. Whether by coincidence or otherwise, the Inland Revenue distributed a note explaining the operation of the earned-income allowance, and its effect of reducing the tax rate on marginal earnings, shortly after the publication of Brown's findings. When the personal income tax was reformed in 1973, the earned-income allowance was replaced by a surcharge on 'unearned' income as the means of discriminating between the two sources. This example underlines the importance of simplicity in the design of tax structure, and the potential for misinterpreting observed behaviour as a fully informed, carefully calculated response to correctly perceived constraints.

The scope for deriving more positive information from sample surveys is limited. Whatever its effects, the tax system is not a well liked institution, and there is considerable danger that responses will be dictated by emotion. For this reason little reliance can be attached to questionnaires; and the real purpose of interviews designed to elicit information about taxation is often concealed until less emotive topics, which provide a check on the consistency of responses, have been discussed (Brown and Levin 1974). At best, survey results can indicate only the direction, not the magnitude, of response. Finally, samples are typically drawn from groups which have the greatest freedom to vary their working hours in the short run; the results therefore have little bearing on the possible longer-run responses of those whose working hours cannot be altered immediately.

Despite these limitations, the consistency of survey results lends weight to their findings. A good example is the study of tax effects on overtime hours of some 2000 wage earners by Brown and Levin (1974). The vast majority, around 70 per cent, reported insensitivity to tax changes, both in the complete sample and after exclusion of subjects whose claims appeared implausible. Of the remainder, a majority claimed that taxation caused them to work harder than they otherwise would have done, implying that the income effect dominates the substitution effect.

An earlier study by Break (1957) is also worth citing because its replication by Fields and Stanbury (1971) affords a rare opportunity for comparison over time. The sample consisted of British self-employed lawyers and accountants, a group whose knowledge of the tax system and ability to exercise personal choice over working hours and also retirement made them a particularly interesting, albeit atypical, subject. In the earlier study a majority reported a zero effect of income tax on working hours, and among the remainder positive and negative effects were fairly evenly balanced; negative effects appeared more pronounced at higher tax rates. Retirement would be, or had already been, postponed because of taxation. In their replication, Fields and Stanbury detected a similar proportion of positive effects on working hours but a significant increase in the incidence of negative effects; the majority, however, remained insensitive. A particularly interesting result at both dates was the absence of significant differences in actual hours worked by the three categories of respondents; Break suggested that those who claimed disincentive effects were 'by nature more ambitious and hard-working than average' (p.547), but alternative interpretations are, of course, possible!

The survey results strongly suggest that in aggregate, working hours are little influenced by taxation, both because the majority of respondents claim to be totally unresponsive, and because of the fairly even division of the remainder between the positive and negative categories. They cannot, however, determine the magnitude of the net effect, nor can they separate the income and substitution effects.[22] In principle, both these tasks can be accomplished by econometric analysis of time-series or cross-section data, which is typically drawn from a more representative population than that sampled for surveys.

Most investigations have analysed cross-section data, thereby avoiding the need to consider whether the supply function shifts over time, or the awkward problem of whether observations recorded at extreme levels of unemployment reflect involuntary rationing, i.e. points 'off' the supply function. Cross-sectional studies, however, are by no means devoid of problems. The standard specification can be represented as $H = f(W(1-t), Z, D)$ where H denotes working hours, W is the pre-tax wage rate, t the tax rate, Z is non-employment income, and D is a vector of other variables, such as demographic measures and financial commitments, which could influence the hours decision. Assuming away some rather serious measurement problems, the coefficient on Z registers the effect on labour supply of a change in income when the wage rate is held constant. This coefficient can be used to net the income effect out of the coefficient on W to isolate the substitution effect.

The crucial step in the preceding statement was, of course, the assumption that the variables could be measured without error. Non-employment income should include such items as imputed rent of owner-occupied dwellings, but measurement problems invariably lead to its omission. Some forms of non-employment income, such as pensions and some other transfers, are conditional on employment income; these components will affect the hours decision in a very different manner than, say, property income, and they are themselves affected by the hours decision. Changes in the employment incomes and hours of other family members may influence the work-leisure preferences, as well as the non-employment income, of the member under direct scrutiny. These problems have been thoroughly aired in the literature, though that has not made it any easier to circumvent them.[23] More recently, attention has shifted to a different source of difficulty, the measurement of the wage rate.

The point at issue here is the distinction between marginal and average wage rates when the budget constraint is non-linear. The conventional procedure has been to calculate 'the' wage rate by dividing hours worked into income. The problem thereby created is illustrated in Fig. 2.8. Abstracting from other measurement errors, H_0A represents the non-employment income of an individual who works H_0H_2 hours, and earns income $A'Y$; his wage rate is therefore calculated as the slope of line AE. This average wage rate, however, results from a linearly progressive tax schedule which allows him to work H_0H_1 hours before he exhausts his allowances; thereafter he is subject to a constant marginal rate, resulting in the constraint H_0ABE. Assume the marginal tax rate and allowance are both increased in such a way that net income $A'Y$ continues to be paid for H_0H_2 hours, and that net non-employment income, H_0A is unaffected. The worker's net average wage is therefore still represented by the slope of AE, but he is confronted with the new budget constraint H_0ACE. No response will be predicted under an average-wage calculation; but in fact the individual has experienced an income-compensated reduction in the net marginal wage rate, which will induce him to reduce working hours along the CE segment of his

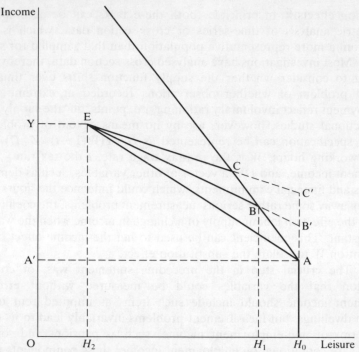

FIG. 2.8 Average and marginal wage rates

constraint.[24] The distortion in the measurement of the net wage rate which is illustrated in this simple example may explain why investigators such as Kosters (1969) have reported incorrectly signed estimates of the substitution effect when using the standard average-wage specification. Consider, for example, two workers with identical preferences and non-employment income who face the same net marginal wage rate but who are credited with different tax allowances. Their budget constraints will be parallel in the range of incomes where both pay tax, but the recipient of the higher tax allowance will be able to enjoy more leisure and more income, and if leisure is a normal good he will choose to work shorter hours than his less fortunate colleague. Because their net marginal wage rates have been assumed identical, the difference in working hours reflects a pure income effect; but the average-wage model cannot ascribe the difference in their working hours to an income effect because their non-employment incomes have also been assumed identical. Instead, the model must attribute the shorter hours of the worker with the higher tax allowance to his higher net average wage rate. In this way the estimated price effect is biased downwards in algebraic value. A labour supply curve which is really upward sloping may even be estimated as backward bending. By reducing the algebraic value of the price effect, the procedure biases the estimated substitution effect downwards, and so may easily yield the incorrect conclusion that an increase in the wage rate reduces hours worked through the substitution effect alone. Moreover, any error in the measurement of hours worked will introduce a spurious negative association between the dependent variable and the net average wage rate. In addition, as Kosters himself noted, data deficiencies mean that non-employment income is likely to be measured with error, and so the estimate of the income effect is likely to be biased towards zero. When this incorrectly estimated income effect is netted out of the price effect, the tendency to underestimate the substitution effect will be reinforced, provided leisure is a normal good.

A simple solution to this problem, suggested first by Hall (1973) and extended by Brown, Levin and Ulph (1976), is to approximate the true, non-linear, initial budget constraint by $H_0AB'E$: the marginal wage rate in the neighbourhood of E is correctly measured by the slope of B'E, and the individual behaves as if this marginal wage rate obtained throughout the range of hours worked, and he enjoyed non-employment income of H_0B' rather than H_0A. The tax change postulated above would shift the constraint 'as if' non-employment income were raised to H_0C' and the net wage were reduced to the slope of C'E. The necessary adjustment to true non-employment income, described as 'virtual' income by Hausman (1980), can be found by subtracting the product of hours worked and the net marginal wage rate from actual employment income.[25]

The study by Brown, Levin and Ulph applies this procedure to a sample of 434 British male workers. Their major departure from the simple model outlined above is that, because of biases in the reported figures for non-employment income and in the way it would influence hours, this variable and virtual income were entered as separate explanatory variables, and the income effect was derived from the latter. Their specification permits both the marginal wage and virtual income to influence hours non-linearly, by including quadratic as well as linear terms, and also permits these two variables to interact, so that the price effect can differ at different levels of income. This initial specification is then augmented by a proxy for job satisfaction, and by a variable which controls for differences among families in size and financial commitments. The sample was also split to distinguish families in which the wife worked, and to exclude workers whose choice of hours was constrained or who were able to influence their marginal wage through bonus schemes. Evaluated at the sample mean, the income effect on hours worked was consistently negative and the substitution effect positive in all the reported regressions; their combination, the price effect, was always negative, implying a backward-bending supply curve. In terms of the standard analysis, the income effect dominates. The elasticities were small in absolute value, ranging from about -0.01 to -0.03 for income, and between -0.01 and -0.3 for price (total effect), depending on which additional variables and which observations were included. As the authors noted, the elasticities tended to rise (in absolute value) as the sample was made more homogeneous through the adjustments noted above. The negatively sloped supply curve is a conventional result for males, in the sense that it has been frequently reported in US studies. In this case, however, the shape of the supply curve was not the conventional 'U' twisted counter-clockwise through 90°, but rather twisted clockwise; the same phenomenon has been reported more recently by Atkinson, Stern and Gomulka (1980). In other words labour supply initially falls as the wage rate rises; but as the wage continues to rise, labour supply ceases to fall and thereafter starts to rise. A final feature of the results was the consistently larger (absolute) effect of virtual income than of non-employment income, an outcome which confirms the practical importance of the measurement problems raised earlier.

An assumption maintained through the study was that taxation influences the supply of hours in the same way as the pre-tax wage, i.e. that there is no tax illusion. In view of Brown's earlier findings, it is some consolation that Rosen (1976b), in a study of US females using the marginal wage and virtual income as the principal variables, split the net wage into its two components, W and tW, and obtained coefficients whose ratio did not differ significantly from the expected value of minus unity. As in most investigations of female labour supply, he also reported a greater degree of responsiveness to fiscal (and other) sources of income change than has typically been found for males.

The investigators who have studied this topic, especially in the UK, would be the first to agree that their work is to be treated as preliminary, and their conclusions as provisional. If optimal tax structures are to be implemented a great deal more information will have to be accumulated! Even the currently available results, however, provide important insights, particularly regarding the significance of the distinction between 'primary' and the much more responsive 'secondary' workers.

SALES TAXATION

The main question to be addressed in this section arises from another branch of the optimal tax problem: how should the relative importance and the structure of commodity taxation be influenced by the characteristics of consumer demand? As a specific illustration consider the claim that the replacement of purchase tax (which was levied on a limited range of goods at markedly differentiated rates) and selective employment tax by value added tax would, 'by removing the economic distortion of selective indirect taxation ... improve the efficiency of our economy' (HMSO 1971:5). In fact the base of VAT covers only about half of consumer expenditure, so it would be difficult to sustain the claim; nevertheless, the question of whether a uniform rate of sales tax would be desirable remains open.

Even in a community of identical individuals where distributional issues do not arise, the answer is not straightforward. More precisely, two very different answers are suggested within the framework of elementary welfare economics.[26]

The Pareto conditions, in their usual two-dimensional form, imply that sales taxes should be levied at equal proportional rates. The consumer price of a commodity, the amount paid by the household, includes any tax levied on that good; while the producer price, the amount received by the firm, excludes the tax. The prices which influence households in their maximisation of utility therefore differ, when sales taxes are levied, from those which determine the outputs of firms. If the rate of tax is the same, in proportionate terms, for all commodities, the ratio between any pair of prices will be the same whether they are measured including or excluding tax. The marginal rate of substitution in consumption, which households equate with the ratio of tax-inclusive prices, will therefore be equal to the marginal rate of transformation in production, which competitive firms equate to the ratio of tax-exclusive prices, and so the optimal conditions are not violated in the post-tax equilibrium. If, on the other hand, different tax rates are levied on different commodities, the relative prices paid by consumers will differ from those received by producers, and there will be a corresponding discrepancy between marginal rates of substitution and trans- formation. The post-tax equilibrium will be characterised by the intersection of the production possibility frontier and a community indifference curve, rather than a point of tangency (e.g. Friedman 1952).

A very different policy for sales taxation is suggested by partial- equilibrium analysis of a single market. As the reader may readily verify, the net loss of surplus suffered by consumers (and, where supply is not infinitely elastic, by producers) when a sales tax is imposed is greater, the greater is the elasticity of demand (and supply). Therefore, to minimise the excess burden of taxation which is entailed in the loss of consumers' (and producers') surplus, tax rates should be differentiated, with the highest rates levied on goods with the least elastic demand (or supply) schedules (e.g. Hicks 1947).[27]

How is this apparent contradiction to be resolved? It turns out that the proportional rule and the inverse elasticity rule are both special cases of a more general formula, whose derivation is clearly explained by Sandmo (1974, 1976). The reason why proportional taxation is implied by the standard two- dimensional representation of the Pareto conditions is that factor supplies are assumed fixed in that framework. The imposition of taxes on factor incomes would therefore follow from the inverse elasticity rule: since the elasticities of factor supplies are zero, no economic surplus is sacrificed when they are taxed. Alternatively, because all incomes are assumed to be spent in this static model, the same result could be achieved by imposing a uniform tax on expenditure, implying equiproportional tax rates on all commodities. Under these circum- stances, therefore, the two formulae clearly reduce to equivalent recommenda- tions. Notice, however, that if the authorities select an income tax rather than equiproportional commodity taxes, they gain an additional degree of freedom, in the form of a tax exemption below specified income levels, which can be applied to distributional objectives when the model is expanded to incorporate differences in the abilities or other circumstances of households.

If the proportional rule were confined to the case where factor supplies are totally inelastic, it would be of very limited interest. There is, however, another set of conditions in which equal-rate taxes are optimal, though it is an equally special case. Assume for simplicity that returns to scale are everywhere constant, so that producer prices cannot change. If commodity preferences are homothetic and are independent of factor supplies, then the optimal tax structure is again uniform. The first of these conditions means that along any ray from the origin, all indifference curves have the same slope. Therefore an exogenous reduction in income would not change the proportions in which commodities are consumed: the income elasticity demand for every commodity is unity. The second condition, described as weak separability, means that a change in a household's factor supplies does not change its commodity indifference map. Intuitively, the imposition of equiproportional taxes on all commodities will shift the production frontier by changing the (real) returns to factors and therefore factor supplies; but, because of the assumption of constant producer prices, the slope of the production frontier, the marginal rate of transformation, will not be affected. Equiproportional changes in consumer prices will not disturb the equality of the marginal rate of substitution with the price ratio. Hence, both households and firms remain in equilibrium, and marginal rates of substitution and transformation remain the same.

If preferences are not homothetic, equiproportional contraction of all commodity demands will not result from equiproportional price changes, and uniform taxation is no longer desirable. If cross-elasticities of demand are all zero, and still assuming given producer prices, equiproportional contraction of demands requires taxes which are inversely proportional to own-price elasticities. Thus, the inverse elasticity rule emerges as another special case.

In the absence of these alternative simplifying assumptions, one other general statement is possible, that complements with leisure should be taxed more heavily than substitutes for leisure. Intuitively, the untaxable good, leisure, is indirectly taxed as a result; again Sandmo (1976) provides an admirably clear and succinct formal statement of this proposition, originally derived by Corlett and Hague (1953). Problems of implementation arise, of course, if labour is not homogeneous in a 'horizontal' sense, so that commodities like hand tools are complementary with work for one group but substitutes for another.

The model has been expanded in various ways, particularly to incorporate 'vertical' differences which introduce a redistributional objective, though as Sandmo (1976:50) observes, it would be 'difficult to claim much in the way of immediate applicability' for the results. One of the more curious assumptions in many discussions of the optimal tax problem is that the government has a fixed revenue requirement for an unspecified purpose which has no bearing on the utility of individuals. The expenditure side of the budget has been incorporated by Atkinson and Stern (1974), and in a neglected contribution, which predates the revival of interest in optimal taxation, by Sen (1966). The former consider the necessary modifications to the conventional rule for the provision of public goods when taxes are distortionary, and the consequential changes in the optimal level of provision. Sen demonstrates the 'efficiency' of differentiated sales tax rates when the optimal outputs of publicly provided goods, for which direct charges cannot be levied, depend on the composition of private expenditure. The problem is similar to the more familiar issue of externalities, which has been considered in an optimal tax setting by Sandmo (1975).

Policy towards sales taxation depends on a broader range of issues than those currently represented in the optimal tax literature. The cost of operating the tax system, both to the authorities who administer it and to the private agents who are required to comply with it, is an important practical consideration for which no adequate analytical framework has yet been developed. Operating costs are related partly to the form of sales tax, especially the number of collection points, and partly to the number of tax rates, particularly the number applying within an individual business unit; neither of these dimensions can be easily accommodated within an analytical model. The level of tax rates seems likely to affect operating costs only through its influence on the incentive to evade. The risk that the present analytical vacuum will result in neglect of administrative and compliance costs is compounded by the difficulty of collecting reliable data, particularly on the latter. Pioneering results in this field have been reported for the UK by Sandford *et al*. (1981).

This strand of the optimal tax literature, like the literature on progression, can offer only conditional prescriptions. It does, however, serve the valuable function of identifying the behavioural parameters and distributional judgements on which optimal tax design hinges, and, in its broader versions, of emphasising the interrelationships among sales and income taxes. Most importantly, perhaps, it makes explicit the special assumptions on which conventional wisdom about sales taxation, of the kind illustrated at the beginning of this section, rests.

REFORM OF THE PERSONAL TAX BASE

The income tax influences not only the household's choices in the labour market, but also its decisions on the timing of consumption, for the net interest rate determines the opportunity cost of future consumption in terms of current consumption forgone. The magnitude of this influence is a topic of interest in its own right, and it has also been invested with significant policy overtones: one of the traditional arguments in favour of substituting an expenditure tax for the income tax is that the latter's distorting effect on intertemporal choice would be abolished. More recently, however, the case for an expenditure tax has been made on wider and more pragmatic grounds, and a macroeconomic argument in favour of distorting intertemporal choice has been added to the arguments in its favour.

The type of expenditure tax at issue here would, like income tax, recognise the existence of differences in family circumstances, through a system of personal allowances or an equivalent mechanism. Expenditure above the threshold level could be taxed at progressive, proportional or for that matter regressive rates. The expenditure tax should therefore be sharply distinguished from a general sales tax, which could differentiate the rates of tax levied on individual commodities, in some relation with their estimated income elasticities for example, but not those levied on individual households. Most specific proposals envisage the collection of expenditure tax through a modified form of the apparatus currently used to collect income tax.

The traditional argument for an expenditure tax has invariably been based on partial equilibrium reasoning. The individual saver, facing a given pre-tax interest rate, will alter his intertemporal consumption pattern when an income tax is introduced, in a manner determined by the familiar balancing of

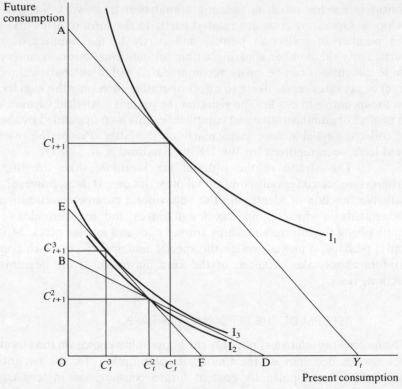

FIG. 2.9 Income and expenditure taxes

income and substitution effects. The analysis is summarised in Fig. 2.9, which shows an individual who earns income Y_t in the 'present' period, retires in the 'future', and dies thereafter. His current income, plus interest on savings carried over to the future, must finance both present and future consumption. In the absence of any taxation he would reach equilibrium on indifference curve I_1 and budget constraint AY_t, whose slope indicates the rate of interest. An income tax is levied on both earned income in the present and interest income in the future. The budget constraint therefore becomes flatter, as shown by BD, because the net interest rate is reduced. In contrast, an expenditure tax changes the position but not the slope of his budget constraint, to EF, thus exerting only an income effect; for a given level of revenue, the individual is better off and saves more than under the income tax.[28] The curious feature of this exercise is the assumption of a given gross interest rate. Suppose that all agents are taxed at a uniform rate, and that borrowers are permitted to deduct interest payments when computing their taxable income. As illustrated in Fig. 2.10, the market-clearing gross interest rate would then rise from r_0 to $r_0/(1-t)$, leaving the net interest rate at the same level as in the period before the introduction of the income tax. This result occurs because the supply curve of loanable funds shifts vertically upwards from S_1 to S_2, so that a given amount is supplied only if lenders receive the same net reward as previously; similarly, the demand curve

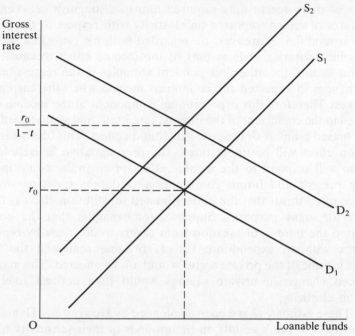

FIG. 2.10   Equilibrium in the capital market

shifts vertically upwards from D_1 to D_2 because borrowers are prepared to pay a given net rate for a given volume of funds. Matters are obviously more complicated if the tax rate is not the same for all potential borrowers and lenders, if there are constraints on the tax deductibility of interest payments, or if the adjustment of the gross interest rate is subject to other influences. Nevertheless, this simple illustration demonstrates that an income tax does not necessarily alter the volume of saving, nor need it violate the welfare condition that marginal rates of substitution and transformation, in this instance between present and future consumption, should be equal in an otherwise first-best world.

The relation between interest rates and tax rates has attracted even less attention at the empirical level, though the interaction between taxes and inflation has generated some recent research (Tanzi 1980a). Casual observation suggests, however, that, for whatever reason, variations in income taxation do not produce sufficiently large adjustments in market interest rates to leave net rates unaffected. Assuming a positive interest elasticity of saving, the conventional view that the income tax depresses saving is therefore probably correct, despite its insecure analytical foundation.

How much is known about the interest elasticity of saving? In the UK, very little; in the USA, not much more. Wright (1969) reported estimates of the substitution elasticity in the range 0.18 to 0.27. These were obtained by regressing consumption on wealth, income and the interest rate; the interest rate coefficient shows the response of consumption (and hence of savings) holding income and wealth constant, isolating the substitution effect. Boskin (1978), whose use of more recent data required him to distinguish between real and nominal rates of return, reported an elasticity with respect to the real rate of return of around 0.4. Moreover, he regarded both his estimates and those of Wright as incorporating at least part of the income effect, because observed income and wealth, the other independent variables in the regressions, cannot register changes in expected future interest income when the current interest rate changes. Therefore this expectational component of the income effect will be reflected in the coefficient of the interest rate itself, and so that coefficient will provide a biased estimate of the pure substitution effect. This bias means that the substitution effect will be understated: the representative household is a net saver, who will respond to the income effect of an interest-rate increase by increasing present and future consumption, and thus reducing saving. The significance of all this is that the understimated substitution effect is the critical parameter for many purposes. Suppose, for example, that the government redistributed the burden of taxation from savers to dissavers by replacing the income tax with an expenditure tax. If revenue remained the same the disposable income of the private sector would not be affected. The magnitude of the induced change in private savings would then depend solely on the substitution elasticity.

These estimates have been challenged by Howrey and Hymans (1978), who questioned Boskin's results on the grounds of their sensitivity to different methods of proxying the real interest rate. They also raised the more general question of what concept of saving should be used as the dependent variable. They argued that 'loanable-funds' saving is a more relevant measure than either the national income accounting measure, which includes owner-occupiers' investment and private pension and insurance contributions, or the flow-of-funds definition, which includes net purchases of consumer durables and therefore corresponds to consumption rather than consumers' expenditure. With their preferred dependent variable, they were unable to isolate any significant effect of the interest rate. A recent conference in which both Boskin and Howrey-Hymans participated failed to resolve the differences or even to define the boundaries of disagreement (Pechman 1980). Commenting on the exchange, Mieszkowski (1980:186) concludes 'it is unlikely that further empirical work with time series will narrow the range of elasticity estimates'.

This may seem an excessively pessimistic view, especially for an advocate of the expenditure tax, but Mieszkowski continues in more positive vein to suggest that 'such refinements may not be very important'. One reason for shifting the grounds of the argument is that the traditional focus on the saving effect is misplaced. In the conventional two-period model the objects of choice are the quantities of present and future consumption; saving is expenditure on future consumption, and is therefore the product of a quantity and a price. When an increase in the net interest rate reduces the price of future consumption, the quantity can increase even if expenditure falls; and it is the quantity responses which determine the effects of a tax change on welfare (Feldstein 1978). Thus a zero or even a negative response of saving to a change in interest rates may divert attention from a substantial change in future consumption. One implication of this point is that even the substitution effect on saving of a tax-induced change in interest rates cannot be signed *a priori*. It depends, as Sandmo (1981) has shown, on the form in which compensation for the change is paid. For instance if a tax on labour income is substituted for a general income tax, the individual necessarily substitutes future for present consumption; but saving, as well as current consumption, may fall because the (compensated) tax change implies heavier taxes during the 'current' period offset by lower (in this case, zero) taxes after retirement. Interpreting Fig. 2.9 in terms of this example, OD represents net income under the general income tax, as before; an equal-yield tax on labour income only would leave a net income of OF. Under the general income tax savings would be $(D - C_t^2)$, which may be greater or less than $(F - C_t^3)$, savings under the labour income tax. The ambiguity arises because the compensation for the increase in the net interest rate is paid in the current period, in the form of an increase in tax payments by $(D - F)$. If compensation were paid in the future period, however, the increase in the net interest rate would unambiguously increase current savings. The reader is invited to illustrate this case, interpreting the compensation for the higher net interest rate as the withdrawal of a tax-exempt retirement pension when interest income is withdrawn from the tax base. When an expenditure tax is substituted for an income tax of equal present value, however, there is an unambiguous increase in savings. In terms of Sandmo's argument, the reason is the shift of tax payments from the current period: compensation for the increase in the net interest rate is paid in the future.[29]

The appropriate framework in which to analyse the welfare consequences of tax changes is the optimal commodity tax model sketched above. Interpreting consumption in different periods as different commodities, the conditions for an expenditure tax to be optimal are analogous to those required for proportional taxation. In other cases, as Atkinson and Sandmo (1980: 547) caution, the optimal tax regime '... may depend on parameters, such as the interest elasticity of labour supply, which have typically been disregarded in empirical studies'. Their warning serves to emphasise the recurrent theme of this literature, that individual tax-induced distortions, in this case of intertemporal choice, can be considered separately only in special cases.

Mieszkowski's view that the traditional substitution effect may be unimportant does not imply that the total effect of a tax change on saving would be negligible. An important part of his argument is that the standard two-period model understates the effect of adopting the expenditure tax on saving, because the individual, who works only in the 'current' period, has a given present value of labour income. In a more general multi-period context, the present value of future wages is reduced by a rise in the net interest rate; current consumption is consequently reduced and saving increased by this indirect wealth effect. An analytically analogous effect is introduced if saving is motivated by considerations, such as the desire to establish a business, additional to those recognised in the life-cycle model. The expenditure tax then discriminates in favour of accumulation (Musgrave 1959). Conversely, the belief that 'the wealthy classes in Britain have ceased to save, and dis-save on a considerable scale' (Kaldor

1955:93) was one of the main arguments put forward in the first modern restatement of the case for an expenditure tax, which is distinguished from an income tax by 'the charge on dissaving, much more than the exemption of savings' (Kaldor 1980:151).

Whatever the magnitude of its effect on total savings, the existing system of income taxation in the UK discriminates among alternative forms of saving 'in what appears to be a totally arbitrary manner' (Meade *et al*. 1978:70). Personal saving through the medium of life insurance, pension funds or owner-occupied dwellings is treated on favourable terms. The bias against entrepreneurial activity implicit in these provisions is to some extent offset by the fiscal treatment of investment expenditures; but the net effect remains distortionary. Kay (1980:49) summarises the consequences as 'the dominance of large financial institutions in the market for personal savings; high levels . . . of investment in property in general and owner-occupied housing in particular; the limited availability of equity finance to incipient small businesses; the absence of a market for the transfer of control of small business; the routine assimilation of the successful new enterprise by an existing larger organisation'. This catalogue of complaints was one reason for the Meade Committee's advocacy of an expenditure tax, which would treat all forms of saving in a similar manner to that currently reserved for particularly favoured components.

An alternative response, which the Committee also considered, would have been to propose that proper income tax treatment of all forms of saving be established. The case for reform of the present system in accordance with an explicit and consistent definition of income could be based on wider considerations than the distorted treatment of savings; for, as the Minority of the Royal Commission on the Taxation of Profits and Income lamented long ago, 'our tax system has not been developed in obedience to . . . general principles' a lament which they justified by quoting the legal interpretation that 'income . . . means such income as is within the Act taxable under the Act' (HMSO 1955:357). This excessively practical foundation contrasts sharply with the comprehensive or accretions concept of income, developed most notably by Simons, who defined personal income for tax purposes '. . . as the algebraic sum of (a) the market value of rights exercised in consumption and (b) the change in the value of the store of property rights between the beginning and end of the period in question' (Simons 1938:30). This definition, which came closest to implementation in Canada after its espousal by the Carter Commission (1966), 'has been accepted by most American specialists as the best available for tax purposes' (Goode 1977:10); but it has attracted little positive support in the UK, and was explicitly rejected by the Meade Committee.[30]

One ground for rejecting comprehensive income as the tax base is the claim by Kaldor (1955:70) that 'the problem of *defining* individual income, quite apart from any problem of practical measurement, appears in principle insoluble'. The source of his problem is the distinction between 'genuine' capital appreciation, due for instance to expectations of higher profits, and the revaluation caused by a change in discount rates. Another perennial problem is the infeasibility of taxing capital gains as they accrue, rather than when they are realised. These and a variety of other conceptual and practical problems have recently been reviewed by Goode (1977). The primary reason for the Meade Committee's rejection of the comprehensive income tax base was not these traditional difficulties, however, but the contemporarily more urgent problem created by inflation. This has also been invoked as an argument against income taxation by advocates of other reforms, including Flemming and Little (1974) in their statement of the case for taxing wealth rather than the income derived from wealth.

Any progressive tax, whatever its base, will be distorted by inflation unless the tax brackets within which a particular tax rate applies are adjusted in line with inflation. The most obvious, and in equity terms the most serious, consequence of failure to index tax brackets occurs at the bottom end of the distribution, where households initially deemed to be below the tax threshold are pushed above it in the intervals between adjustments. The adjustments needed to deal with this problem involve essentially practical questions, such as frequency, the appropriate price index, and the choice between discretionary and automatic correction. These adjustments could be avoided only under a strictly proportional tax structure.

Under an income tax, even if it is strictly proportional, a wholly separate adjustment, described by the Meade Committee as 'indexation for capital income adjustment', would also be necessary to neutralise the effects of inflation. At the household level the most important adjustments are the reduction of nominal capital gains and interest receipts to their real components, and the equivalent adjustment of tax relief granted on interest payments. A survey by Tanzi (1980b) indicates that even partial measures to index for capital income adjustment have been introduced in only a handful of countries, and those measures are frequently characterised by a substantial degree of arbitrariness. A particularly common form of adjusting capital gains, used in Columbia, Mexico, Finland, Spain and Sweden, and considered by the Inland Revenue in the UK, is to reduce the fraction of the nominal gain that is subject to tax, the longer the asset has been held; yet the ratio of the real to the nominal gain *rises* with the holding period, provided a real gain accrues at all, so this form of adjustment is entirely inappropriate (e.g. Brinner 1976). There is no difficulty of principle in calculating the appropriate forms of adjustment for capital income; but they would be administratively expensive, and would not be necessary under an expenditure tax. Moreover, the fact that they are not being effected in practice means that positive taxes are being levied on negative real gains, and the tax on interest income is more accurately described as a tax on real interest income plus an unlegislated tax on the wealth which generates it.

The major arguments for an inflation-proof tax system are based on the allocative and distributional consequences of taxing nominal magnitudes, especially nominal income. The decision to index the tax base would, however, also have macroeconomic implications, for the tax system acts as a built-in stabiliser or, in Dow's (1964) more precise terminology, as a 'built-in disinflator'. Between legislated adjustments, the real yield of an unindexed system varies not only with real income but also with the price level. If excess demand generates price *increases*, real tax revenue will continue to increase as long as excess demand persists, for the price *level* will be persistently rising. In principle, therefore, the automatic flexibility of the tax system could correct disturbances in the level of demand completely, rather than only partially as suggested by fixed-price models which portray built-in flexibility as merely reducing the size of the multiplier. This characteristic of an unindexed tax structure was emphasised by Friedman (1948), but was subsequently neglected. Its consequences are most readily analysed in the framework developed by Phillips (1954 and, more accessibly, 1962), who demonstrated very clearly that an 'integral' corrective mechanism like an unindexed tax system is a mixed blessing. The fiscal response to a disturbance will go on increasing until the disturbance is eliminated, and so if the economy is stable it must eventually return to the initial equilibrium; but the 'stabiliser' may introduce a cyclical adjustment or, even worse, may render the economy unstable. The probability of an unstable response now seems higher in the light of more recent developments in macroeconomics, particularly an expectational factor which prolongs the effect of excess demand on prices.

The effect of indexation on macroeconomic stability is, therefore, an unavoidably empirical question. It has been examined most thoroughly in Canada, under the stimulus of a provision for bracket indexation enacted in 1972. It may be inferred from the simulation experiments reported by Grady and Stephenson (1977) that instability is unlikely, that the relative desirability of the two tax systems depends on the source of the shock, and that the difference is in any case small enough that the macroeconomic consequences of indexation can be assigned a low weight in comparison with its allocative and distributional effects.

The adoption of an expenditure tax would be an administratively cheap method of avoiding the arbitrary redistributional consequences of an unindexed tax system. How does it compare with an income tax when these criteria are interpreted in a more general context than that of inflation?

There are two major issues under the heading of equity. The difference between lifetime income and consumption reduces to the difference between gifts and bequests made and received. The first question is whether these should be treated as a taxable expenditure of the donor, who presumably derives equal pleasure from his act of self-denial as from consumption, as well as a taxable expenditure of the recipient when he spends them. Views were aired at the Brookings conference (Pechman 1980) on this conundrum, as well as on the second and more interesting question of the time perspective appropriate for the tax system. The income tax is based on an annual horizon, supplemented by specific averaging provisions to mitigate the most serious of the penalties that would otherwise be imposed on those with fluctuating incomes. Two individuals with the same earnings profile will pay different tax bills if the timing of their consumption differs, because of the tax levied on their interest income. Under an expenditure tax, however, and ignoring gifts and bequests, they would face the same tax liabilities, in present value terms, whatever the differences in their consumption profiles. While the case against a one-year horizon is overwhelming, the attraction of a lifetime horizon is considerably diminished by uncertainty, including of course uncertainty regarding future tax rates.

The feasibility of an expenditure tax has traditionally been regarded as a major obstacle even by those sympathetic to the principle. That tradition has been subjected to systematic questioning more recently, and considerable attention has been devoted to alternative means of converting the present system to an expenditure base. Detailed discussions will be found in Meade *et al.* (1978) and Pechman (1980). A direct expenditure tax would be administered not by totalling expenditure but by making the necessary adjustments to income; the informational requirements would be similar to, but probably simpler than, those which obtain currently. If the mass of the population faced a proportional structure, as is approximately true under the present system, a two-tier expenditure tax, collected predominantly through sales taxation with a supplementary direct tax on a relatively small number of households whose expenditure exceeded some threshold, would be a low-cost method of collection (Meade *et al.* 1978). Whatever the scope of a direct expenditure tax, its administration would be considerably simplified by the availability of a 'prepayment' option, under which both saving and its proceeds would be ignored for tax purposes. Tax is prepaid in that the usual exemption of saving would not apply; the present value of tax payments would be the same, at the margin, as under the more conventional treatment, provided the saver remained in a given tax bracket. The prepayment option would effectively tax investment opportunities rather than investment outcomes, a feature which was extensively debated at the Brookings conference.

The arguments surrounding the expenditure tax have been predominantly microeconomic in character, but a change of tax base would involve macroeconomic repercussions as well, quite apart from the question of indexation discussed above. A tax on consumer expenditure would display less automatic flexibility (that is, tax revenue would change less for a given change in national income) than the existing income tax because consumers smooth out fluctuations in their disposable income through asset transactions. The same would hold *a fortiori* if the base were not expenditure but consumption, which excludes purchases of durables and includes the service flow from consumers' stocks of durables. A consumption base is, however, effectively ruled out on practical grounds, which dictate that the prepayment 'option' would be compulsory for purchases of durables.

Outside the main currents of debate on the expenditure tax, a spate of literature has argued for explicitly temporary variations in the rates of expenditure or sales taxes as an instrument of countercyclical policy. The basis of the argument, first stated clearly by Kaldor (1955) and subsequently revived by Branson (1973), Eisner (1969), Motley (1973) and many others, is that the announcement of a tax increase for the 'current' period only will add an intertemporal substitution effect against current expenditure to the standard effect of any tax in reducing the present value of resources available for financing expenditure. Outside the confines of the two-period model under certainty, however, the implementation of this proposal poses problems which are not immediately apparent. These have been reviewed by Sumner and Laing (1981), who also infer from the preannounced transition to VAT during 1972–3 that consumers do not always react in a predictable manner to intertemporal fiscal incentives. A similarly agnostic conclusion was reached in a study of the only documented case of an explicitly temporary sales tax reduction which was unencumbered by tax reform (Sumner 1979): consumer expenditure was no higher, in fact insignificantly lower, than the level predicted in the absence of a tax cut. The evidence suggests that the household sector will have to be better informed or given more opportunities for practice if it is to respond as benefits economic man.

DISTRIBUTIONAL IMPACTS

Throughout this section considerably more attention has been devoted to the allocative effect of individual taxes than to their distributional implications. This emphasis is partly a reflection of the behavioural orientation of the survey, and partly a consequence of the fact that the distributional effects of individual taxes are of little importance. Considerably more importance attaches to the redistributional effects of the entire tax system and to changes at the margin. The significance of this question has been fully reflected in the literature. Indeed, the author of an earlier survey (Shoup 1972:3) described calculation of the distribution of taxation by income class as 'the most popular quantitative exercise in public finance'.

Its popularity is indicated by its institutionalisation, in Britain at least, for the Central Statistical Office publishes an annual report on 'the effects of taxes and benefits on household income'. A typical example (HMSO 1980) allocates the main taxes and some expenditures to households by decile, and draws attention to the stability of the post-tax, post-benefit distribution of income during the 1970s. This series of articles provides a considerable amount of information about the fiscal structure, but for present purposes its most interesting feature is methodological. The way in which the calculations are performed illustrates quite strikingly the present limitations of tax analysis.

One perennial target of criticism has been the difficulty of allocating certain budget items at all. This problem is more severe on the expenditure side, where the unallocated proportion, on items like defence and law and order, typically approaches 60 per cent, than on the revenue side, where the corresponding proportion is 'only' about 40 per cent. Peacock ((1974) illustrates the absurdities which can arise in this situation, and criticises some of the procedures that have been suggested for allocating items which have normally been ignored. On the revenue side, the major unallocated receipts are borrowing, which involves questions of equity among successive generations as well as intertemporal efficiency,[31] and the yields of corporation and capital taxes and of expenditure taxes not allocated to consumers. A common procedure in US studies (e.g. Musgrave et al. 1974) is to 'solve' this problem by making several sets of calculations on alternative incidence assumptions; in particular, the corporate income tax is variously assumed to be borne by shareholders, by the owners of all forms of capital, as argued by Harberger, or by consumers, as a result of the forward shifting which Krzyzaniak and Musgrave, inter alios.

claimed to have detected. This procedure amounts to a confession of ignorance about the incidence of some of the major sources of revenue, and the progressivity of the tax system is quite sensitive to the assumptions made. On Pechman and Okner's (1974) least progressive assumption about US corporate tax incidence, for example, the federal tax system scarcely differs from a proportional structure, despite its progressive appearance.

The assumptions used in the allocation of taxes are a second source of controversy. Income taxes are assumed to affect only the proportion of a given gross income received by the taxpayer, and have no effect on hours of work, choice of occupation or any other dimension of labour supply. Sales taxes are assumed to be shifted forward immediately into higher prices, and therefore to operate according to the uses of income; there is no consideration of possible changes in factor prices which would work through the sources of income. The consistency of these assumptions has been questioned by Prest (1968), who argues that the income tax treatment implies perfect inelasticity of factor supplies whereas the sales tax treatment implies perfect elasticity. Another curious feature of the incidence assumptions is the treatment of National Insurance contributions: the employee's portion is treated like an income tax, but the employer's portion is classed as an indirect sales tax which is shifted, through transactions in intermediate goods and services, to consumers. This separation of the two components contrasts sharply with the economic distinction between the method of collecting a tax and its incidence, and with the more specific proposition that both components predominantly affect the labour market (Brittain 1971).[32]

An attempt to assess the significance of some of these criticisms has been made by Devarajan et al. (1980). Recognising that the standard, and mechanistic, methodology, will misstate the magnitude of fiscal redistribution, they use an extended version of Harberger's general equilibrium model to determine the circumstances in which the standard calculation could produce misleading conclusions by incorrectly ordering the tax burdens of groups of taxpayers, who are classified by their ownership of labour and capital. Their analysis demonstrates the importance of the capital intensity of production: when the capital-labour ratio of the taxed industry deviates from the mean, the standard calculation is more likely to deviate from the general-equilibrium prediction. Their results also suggest that, for a sales tax at least, the ownership of productive factors may be unimportant. These conclusions are, however, reached on the special assumptions of Cobb-Douglas production and utility functions. They then turn to a larger-scale and more general numerical model, which is used to compute the results of a variety of tax changes. These simulated results are closest to those of the standard allocation procedure in cases involving income tax; the sales tax comparisons again bring out the significance of variations in the capital intensity of production. This exercise may renew the confidence of those engaged in the tabulation of tax burdens; though as the authors point out, the encouragement to be derived from these comparisons is dependent on the degree of faith attached to the standard of reference. Both the analytical and the numerical models contain restrictive assumptions, such as fixed factor supplies, whose relaxation constitutes an extensive research agenda.

Despite their acknowledged defects, which have by no means been comprehensively catalogued here, calculations of tax burdens by income group are the most readily available source of evidence on the distributive effects of taxation, and it is difficult to believe that they have had no influence on policy proposals. For example, Brown and Dawson (1969:29) described the British tax-cash transfer system as progressive only at the extremes of the income distribution, and 'pretty well proportional for most taxpayers who pay a positive rate of tax'. This characterisation is surely not unrelated to their advocacy of the proposal for a universal guaranteed income coupled with a flat rate of tax on original income. In the USA, the contrast between the ostensibly progressive tax structure and its approximately proportional results has produced demands for reform (e.g. Break and Pechman 1975) to eliminate the 'loopholes' which enable the rich to avoid some of their intended share of the tax burden.

If the calculated distribution of tax burdens is systematically misleading, then of course the policy implications derived from them need reconsideration. Buchanan and Brennan (1980) have argued that a further defect of the computations, their neglect of excess burdens, renders the call for loophole plugging entirely inappropriate. The total burden allocated in these studies is tax revenue, ignoring the indirect costs borne by taxpayers who modify their behaviour to reduce their tax liabilities. These indirect costs fall on those exploiting the loopholes, for at the margin it is worth incurring a pound of excess burden (in the form, say, of less productive activities or investments whose lower pre-tax return is compensated by favourable tax treatment) to save a pound of tax. In consequence, the conventional calculations understate the total burden borne by those able to exploit loopholes, and distort policy perspectives. Instead of focussing on the zero-sum game of redistribution through the elimination of tax preferences, reformers would be better employed in pressing the case for the positive-sum game of lower tax rates: eliminating the misallocation of resources resulting from the present system could make everyone better off. The potential appeal of a programme to diminish the attraction of loopholes by treating taxed income less harshly, rather than engaging in an operation to plug newly created ways of exploiting the rules of the tax system, is obvious. Unfortunately the information needed to determine the relative prospects of these two contrasting policies is simply not available.

Perhaps the most useful way of generating more information would be through the elaboration of numerical general equilibrium models of the kind used by Devarajan et al. Two advantages of this technique are that it permits the consideration of allocative and distributional questions within the same framework, and that it facilitates concentration on the marginal changes which are of primary relevance for policy purposes. In contrast, tax burden computations are often criticised for their implicit adoption of a world without government as their standard of reference (e.g. Prest 1968). British examples include the analysis of the 1973 tax reforms by Whalley (1975), and his study with Piggott (1977) of a radical alternative to those reforms. The reader is warned, however, that this method of analysis still offers considerable scope for further development, as already indicated, and that even in its present state it does not constitute easy reading. The task of outlining the underlying model and reporting the numerical results poses severe presentational problems for the investigators; and the user faces considerable difficulty in evaluating the results. Nevertheless, this avenue of research warrants further exploration, for both analytical and prescriptive purposes.

4. Conclusions

The academic study of the tax system has not only generated wider interest among economists during the last two decades, and a correspondingly larger flow of literature; it has also changed in character, and the boundaries of the subject have become less sharply defined. As this survey has repeatedly emphasised, a wide range of quantitative questions has been addressed, covering both the traditional issues of public finance and the effects of newer fiscal instruments, whose emergence reflects the more ambitious conception of government objectives during much of the postwar period. Empirical studies have been based on firmer and more explicit theoretical foundations. The traditional doctrines of public finance have been absorbed in an expanded and generalised body of theory, which emphasises that many of those doctrines rested on special assumptions. One of the questions which still remain is whether this enlarged and enriched literature has yielded results commensurate with the intellectual resources devoted to it.

A summary answer to that question is precluded by the breadth of the field surveyed, and by the academic equivalent of the belief that it is better to travel hopefully than to arrive: a completed piece of research invariably provokes further questions, and often leaves the investigator acutely aware of the limitations he has accepted in order to reach any conclusions at all. Nevertheless, some general impressions are worth recording.

First, there is at least a qualitative consensus on many quantitative questions. Few would dispute that the labour supply of primary workers is inelastic, much more so than that of secondary workers; though fewer still would state numerical results with confidence. There is little doubt, despite the limited evidence available, that an income tax change has a smaller impact on consumer expenditure if it is announced as temporary (Dolde 1980). There is abundant econometric evidence that investment is influenced by fiscal variables, a conclusion which did not emerge at all clearly from the earlier questionnaire studies.

Consensus, even in qualitative form, does not apply to all quantitative questions, as is amply illustrated by the controversy over the relationship between saving and interest rates; though, as we have seen, this dispute no longer dominates the debate about expenditure taxation, and hence its resolution may have little bearing on proposals for tax reform. Moreover, the consensus does not extend to quantitative magnitudes: as the author of an earlier and more specific survey of fiscal influences on investment concluded, 'Perhaps the most that can be claimed in this particular case is that the ... studies ... do not support any allegation that the incentives have been wholly ineffective. It is difficult to go much further' (Lund 1976:261). But it is not impossible to go somewhat further, in this or other cases. It would be feasible to predict the total effects on investment of a particular fiscal change within tolerable limits, and there would be general agreement that these effects would be spread over a period of several years, whose length would depend on the specific aggregate influenced by the change in question. Whether the period was as short as two and a half years or as long as four years, for a change in the tax treatment of plant and machinery, would be more difficult to determine, and some estimates would lie outside this range. There would be even less agreement about the distribution of the induced investment over this period. Despite these limitations, however, the consensus is broad enough to indicate rather clearly the potential hazards of changing the tax treatment of investment in pursuit of stabilisation objectives, and the macroeconomic implications of a change motivated by allocative considerations.

Secondly, the response to fiscal innovations appears less predictable, again in qualitative terms, than the response to more familiar measures. Reactions to the US corporate tax surcharge of 1968 (Eisner and Lawler 1975), and in the UK to the pre-announced shifts to the imputation system of corporation tax (Sumner 1981) and to VAT (Sumner and Laing 1981) in 1973 were directionally perverse. Less dramatic but still difficult to explain was the effect on investment spending of cash grants in the latter half of the 1960s. These episodes offer potentially valuable insights into economic behaviour, by comparison with conventional time-series data whose discriminating power is notoriously weak; but little progress has been registered to date in exploiting them. In the meantime, these examples give new force to the old adage that an old tax, or a familiar method of altering it, is a good tax, from the perspective of the policy-maker if not from that of the researcher.

The state of the theoretical literature offers less scope for even limited generalisation. At the end of another earlier and more specific survey the author concluded that 'the greatest danger lies in placing too great a load on tax policy' (Williams 1966:464). In the period since then there have appeared further analyses of and proposals for ambitious fiscal initiatives, of which tax-based incomes policies are perhaps the most striking example; but most of the theoretical literature, both positive and normative, has concentrated on the traditional objectives of public finance and has applied traditional criteria. Indeed, theorists have devoted far more attention to considering barriers to change, in the form of horizontal equity requirements (e.g. Feldstein 1976) and the other transitional costs of tax change (e.g. Meade *et al.* 1978), than in the past, and simplicity has figured more prominently among their criteria. In many respects the normative literature, especially in its optimal tax branches, has revived the oldest questions of all, although in a reformulation which permits, or rather requires, the application of analytical tools which would have had little purpose when the questions were first asked.

Perhaps the greatest danger at present lies in the temptation to derive nihilistic conclusions from the latest generation of theoretical results, which have been far more powerful in their negative role, of demonstrating that much of the conventional wisdom rests on special assumptions, than in any more positive respect. When the special assumptions necessary for simple prescriptions are not fulfilled, optimal tax formulae require empirical magnitudes for their implementation. In some cases the relevant questions have simply not been asked in the empirical literature. There is, in any case, little ground for believing that even a qualitative consensus regarding a crucial parameter could be narrowed down to a single point estimate; and even if econometric history furnished reasons for belief in the inevitability of progress along this particular dimension, a uniformly agreed point-estimate would still have a standard error attached to it.

The case against nihilism rests on the argument that ignorance is not an absolute barrier, and on the prospects for further analytical developments. One reason why estimates of some parameters identified as potentially critical in theoretical studies are not readily available may be that they are small enough to be ignored, a conjecture that could readily be checked. Sensitivity analysis is an obvious method of supplementing incomplete or imprecise empirical estimates. An analytical development that might prove particularly useful would be a shift of emphasis from the optimality of tax design to robustness in the face of uncertain parameters. Predicting the future course of intellectual endeavour is not a profitable topic for speculation, but there is no reason to suppose that the endeavour will produce no results; and the history of the second-best theorem suggests that intellectual endeavour is a poweful antidote to nihilism.

Finally, whatever its present and prospective limitations, the economics of taxation offers more advice than governments have been able or willing to absorb. Oversimplified ideas about incentives and the tax structure continue to exert an influence on political opinion which cannot be justified by the available evidence. In the absence of a convincing defence of regionally differentiated investment incentives, successive governments have nevertheless stubbornly adhered to the policy for almost 20 years. While the proposals advanced by Meade *et al.* (1978) were not universally endorsed by the economics profession (e.g. Peacock 1978; Prest 1979), they have been greeted with a surprising silence in official quarters. Indeed, in one important respect, the tax treatment of inventory investment, the 1981 budget has introduced an unnecessarily complicated but still deplorably crude replacement for the previous approximation to cashflow treatment, instead of pursuing the recommended path towards efficiency and simplicity. These examples, while far from exhaustive, indicate that economics has not yet reached the limits of its practical usefulness, and suggest that the political economy of tax reform would be an area worthy of further examination.

Notes

1. This distinction, elaboratcd by Feldstein (1976), is discussed in more detail below.
2. For example, in equal annual amounts or as a fixed proportion of the asset's

written-down value, known as the straight-line and reducing-balance methods respectively.

3. With the CES form of production function and constant returns to scale, the elasticity of substitution appears in equation [4] as an exponent on the marginal product of capital. Production functions and their properties are surveyed in the *Microeconomics* volume of this series.

4. Under the classical system t_p is simply the shareholder's personal rate of income tax. Under the imputation system, t_p is the excess of that rate above the basic rate of income tax.

5. In other words, $d_i = \delta$ for all i; hence

$$Z = \frac{\delta}{1 + r(1 - t)} + \frac{\delta(1 - \delta)}{(1 + r(1 - t))^2} + \cdots = \frac{\delta}{r(1 - t) + \delta}$$

When this expression is substituted in equation [6] the latter reduces to equation [1].

6. Subject to the qualification that a delay will itself reduce the present value of a profitable investment; the net outcome therefore depends on the size of the temporary tax reduction and the expected date of its return to 'normal'.

7. For a full-time adult male worker; lower tax rates applied to women, juvenile and part-time employees. SET was specified in money terms, so the effective tax rate was eroded by inflation in the intervals between adjustments.

8. These references are a small sample of a large literature on the 'Harberger model' by Harberger himself and others. For a comprehensive survey of the model and its applications see McClure (1975).

9. The transformation curve will contain a horizontal or vertical segment if an isoquant of one or other industry becomes horizontal as it cuts AB, indicating that the marginal product of labour has fallen to zero.

10. Consider the problem of maximising the sum of industry outputs, weighted by prices: each industry's output requires inputs of both factors; an industry may be located in one or both regions; there is a fixed supply of the immobile factor in each region, and a fixed supply of the mobile factor in the economy as a whole. Derive the first-order conditions for the factor inputs, and interpret them for the case where the 'maximiser' must operate by setting not factor allocations but factor prices, leaving the cost-minimising firms within each industry to choose factor quantities.

11. For a fuller account, see King (1977:ch. 4). The summary treatment in the text abstracts from the liability to capital gains tax which would be created by such a policy, partly because deferral usually makes the effective rate of capital gains tax on accruals much lower than the nominal rate, which is itself lower than the corresponding rate on ordinary income, and more importantly because such behaviour would be inconceivable in the actual world of uncertainty, as will be shown below.

12. If profits are zero or negative, the firm pays no tax (but does not receive a subsidy), so its behaviour is unaffected.

13. Recall King's results regarding the influence of take-over activity on pay-out ratios.

14. See Dilnot and Morris (1981) for an appraisal of recent attempts to quantify this consequence of taxation.

15. The separation between the allocation and distribution branches of government was institutionalised by Musgrave (1959). For a later defence of what he describes as his 'parochial approach' against Samuelson's criticisms, and the latter's objections, see their contributions to Margolis and Guitton (1969).

16. See Zabalza, Pissarides and Barton (1980) for an analysis of the choices facing pensioners. Under the earnings rule, pensions are implicitly taxed at 50 per cent

when earnings exceed a lower limit, and at 100 per cent when earnings exceed a higher limit.

17. Family allowances, which preceded the current child benefit, were taxed as earned income; in addition, the tax allowance for a child for whom a family allowance was paid was reduced by £52.

18. As hours worked increase from zero (OH_0 hours of leisure) to H_0H_1, labour income increases from zero to PR. The household's *net* income, including transfer receipts, rises by only QR. The difference reflects the withdrawal of transfers which depend on income.

19. Piachaud (1980) quotes an official estimate that about three-quarters of families in receipt of Family Income Supplement, the main means-tested benefit payable to households with an income from full-time work, in 1979 were above the income tax threshold. Around 59,000 families (out of a total of 17 million) were caught in the poverty trap caused by the overlap between the tax and social security systems. When other means-tested benefits, such as rent and rate rebates and free school meals, are taken into account, the net benefits of additional earnings are negative for some types of family over some range of earnings; the annual publication *Social Trends* (HMSO) documents the situation facing a hypothetical low-income family. In less extreme cases the effective marginal tax rate, while less than 100 per cent, remains at levels conventionally associated with the very rich rather than those in the lower ranges of the income distribution.

20. Blum and Kalven (1963) describe the linear progressive income tax as 'degressive', but their terminology has not been widely adopted. Notice that even if the exemption level is set so low that everyone pays the same *marginal* rate, the tax is progressive in the generally accepted sense that the *average* tax rate rises with income.

21. For more extensive discussions of the experiments the interested reader is referred to Pechman and Timpane (1975) on the New Jersey experience, and to Ferber and Hirsch (1978) for a more general review.

22. Though Holland (1969) attempted to do so by asking a sample of business executives how they would adapt to a hypothetical tax based on potential income at a fixed number of hours. Even when faced with a zero marginal tax rate, 80 per cent or more of his total sample claimed they would not alter their behaviour in relation to their primary job or vacations. The responses revealed some ambiguity in interpreting a hypothetical question, even from an experienced interviewer. For a summary of the results, see Holland (1977).

23. See Godfrey (1975) for a fuller survey of these issues and of earlier econometric studies.

24. Compensation in the sense of Slutsky: the individual *could* remain at his original equilibrium after the tax change.

25. Notice that the marginal wage, and therefore virtual income, are not defined for individuals located at a kink in the budget constraint. The marginal wage is influenced by the individual's choice of overtime hours, so simultaneity problems are not eliminated entirely by this procedure.

26. In a community of identical individuals a third, correct, answer would be that lump-sum taxes should be levied; hence the question does not arise. The possible rejoinder that sales taxes have the desirable characteristic, from the government's standpoint, of limited visibility raises even more fundamental questions.

27. Notice that, for a given price increase, loss of consumers' surplus increases with the elasticity of demand; but no loss occurs if demand is perfectly elastic. This apparent inconsistency was resolved by Head and Shoup (1969).

28. Revenue remains the same in present value terms, computed at the given pre-tax interest rate. There will be a change in the pattern of revenue flows, however, for current revenue will be smaller under the expenditure tax; hence there will be consequential changes in money creation or borrowing. This example illustrates the general problem of defining the equivalence of taxes: the 'other things' are seldom equal.
29. To demonstrate the increase in saving diagrammatically, project the ray through the expenditure-tax equilibrium to the no-tax budget constraint, AY_t in Fig. 2.9. The height of this point shows the amount needed to finance consumption and expenditure tax liability in the future. To show the amount needed to finance future consumption and tax payments under the income tax, construct a line through D parallel to AY_t. The required sum is represented by the vertical distance between the constructed line and C_t^2, and is necessarily less than under the expenditure tax. The corresponding amounts saved in the current period are simply the present values of future expenditure and tax payments, computed at the same interest rate (gross of income tax).
30. The comprehensive income tax principle is, theoretically, the standard of reference against which tax expenditures are defined and appraised; to that extent it has attracted some support, but for the negative purpose of criticising existing tax systems, not as a positive proposal. See Willis and Hardwick (1978).
31. For a survey of the early literature see Shoup (1962). Bailey (1972) analyses the choice between tax finance and borrowing in a more general framework which recognises the uncertainty attaching to the future benefits of public investment.
32. Brittain's work was challenged by Feldstein (1972), but not on the point at issue here.

References

Archibald, G. C. (1972) On regional economic policy in the United Kingdom, in Peston, M. and Corry, B. C. (eds), *Essays in Honour of Lord Robbins*, Weidenfeld & Nicholson: London.

Arrow, K. J. (1962) The economic implications of learning by doing, *Review of Economic Studies*, **29**, 155–73.

Atkinson, A. B. (1973) How progressive should income tax be, in Parkin, M. (ed.), *Essays in Modern Economics*, Longman: London.

Atkinson, A. B. (1980) Horizontal equity and the distribution of the tax burden, in Aaron, H. J. & Boskin, M. J. (eds), *The Economics of Taxation*, Brookings Institution: Washington DC.

Atkinson, A. B. and Sandmo, A. (1980) Welfare implications of the taxation of savings, *Economic Journal*, **90**, 529–49.

Atkinson, A. B. and Stern, N. H. (1974) Pigou, taxation and public goods, *Review of Economic Studies*, **41**, 119–28.

Atkinson, A. B., Stern, N. H. and Gomulka, J. (1980) On the switch from direct to indirect taxation, *Journal of Public Economics*, **14**, 195–224.

Auerbach, A. J. (1979) Share valuation and corporate equity policy, *Journal of Public Economics*, **11**, 291–305.

Bailey, M. J. (1972) The optimal full-employment surplus, *Journal of Political Economy*, **80**, 649–61.

Barr, N. A. and Hall, R. E. (1975) The taxation of earnings under public assistance, *Economica*, N. S. **42**, 373–84.

Barzel, Y. (1976) An alternative approach to the analysis of taxation, *Journal of Political Economy*, **84**, 1177–97.

Baumol, W. J. (1958) On the theory of oligopoly, *Economica*, N. S. **25**, 187–98.

Beath, J. (1979) Target profits, cost expectations and the incidence of the corporate tax, *Review of Economic Studies*, **46**, 513–25.

Bhagwati, J. N. (ed.) (1976) *The Brain Drain and Taxation*, North-Holland: Amsterdam.

Bhatia, K. B. (1979) Corporate taxation, retained earnings and capital formation, *Journal of Public Economics*, **11**, 123–34.

Blake, C. (1976) Some economics of investment grants and allowances, in Whiting, A. (ed.), *The Economics of Industrial Subsidies*, HMSO.

Blum, W. J. and Kalven, H. (1963) *The Uneasy Case for Progressive Taxation*, University of Chicago Press.

Boadway, R. W. and Bruce, N. (1979) Depreciation and interest deductions and the effect of the corporation income tax on investment, *Journal of Public Economics*, **11**, 93–105.

Boatwright, B. D. and Eaton, J. R. (1972) The estimation of investment functions for manufacturing industry in the UK, *Economica*, N. S. **39**, 403–18.

Boskin, M. J. (1978) Taxation, saving and the rate of interest, *Journal of Political Economy*, **86**, Suppl. 3–27.

Boskin, M. J. (1980) Factor supply and the relationship among the choice of tax base, tax rates, and the unit of account in the design of an optimal tax system, in Aaron, H. J. and Boskin, M. J. (eds), *The Economics of Taxation*, Brookings Institution: Washington DC.

Boskin, M. H. and Sheshinski, E. (1978) Optimal income distribution when individual welfare depends on relative income, *Quarterly Journal of Economics*, **92**, 589–602.

Branson, W. H. (1973) The use of variable tax rates for stabilisation purposes, in Musgrave, R. A. (ed.), *Broad-Based Taxes*, The Johns Hopkins University Press: Baltimore.

Break, G. F. (1957) Income taxes and incentives to work: an empirical study, *American Economic Review*, **47**, 529–49.

Break, G. F. and Pechman, J. A. (1975) *Federal Tax Reform*, Brookings Institution: Washington DC.

Brechling, F. (1975) *Investment and Employment Decisions*, Manchester University Press.

Brinner, R. E. (1976) Inflation and the definition of taxable personal income, in Aaron, H. J. (ed.), *Inflation and the Income Tax*, Brookings Institution: Washington DC.

Brittain, J. (1971) The incidence of the social security payroll tax, *American Economic Review*, **61**, 110–25.

Broome, J. (1975) An important theorem on income tax, *Review of Economic Studies*, **42**, 649–52.

Brown, C. V. (1968) Misconceptions about income tax and incentives, *Scottish Journal of Political Economy*, **15**, 1–21.

Brown, C. V. and Dawson, D. A. (1969) Personal taxation, incentives and tax reform, *P.E.P. Broadsheet*, 506.

Brown, C. V. and Levin, E. (1974) The effects of income taxation on overtime, *Economic Journal*, **84**, 833–48.

Brown, C. V., Levin, E. and Ulph, D. T. (1976) Estimates of labour hours supplied by male workers in Great Britain, *Scottish Journal of Political Economy*, **23**, 261–77.

Buchanan, J. and Brennan, G. (1980) Tax reform without tears, in Aaron, H. J. and Boskin, M. J. (eds), *The Economics of Taxation*, Brookings Institution: Washington DC.

Buck, T. W. and Atkins, M. H. (1976) Capital subsidies and unemployed labour, a regional production function approach, *Regional Studies*, **10**, 215–22.

Carter, K. L. et al. (1966) *Report of the (Canadian) Royal Commission on Taxation*, Queen's Printer: Ottowa.

Coen, R. M. (1968) Effects of tax policy on investment in manufacturing, *American Economic Review, Papers and Proceedings*, **58**, 200–11.

Coen, R. M. (1975) Investment behaviour, the measurement of depreciation, and tax policy, *American Economic Review*, **65**, 59–74.

Cootner, R. and Helpman, E. (1974) Optimal income taxation for transfer payments, *Quarterly Journal of Economics*, **88**, 656–70.

Corlett, W. J. and Hague, D. C. (1953) Complementarity and the excess burden of taxation, *Review of Economic Studies*, **21**, 21–30.

Cragg, J. G., Harberger, A. C. and Mieszkowski, P. (1967) Empirical evidence on the incidence of the corporation income tax, *Journal of Political Economy*, **75**, 811–21

Culyer, A. J. (1973) *The Economics of Social Policy*, Martin Robertson: London.

Dasgupta, P. S. and Stiglitz, J. E. (1972) On optimal taxation and public production, *Review of Economic Studies*, **39**, 87–103.

Davis, J. M. (1972) An aggregate time-series analysis of the short-run shifting of company taxation in the UK, *Oxford Economic Papers*, N. S. **24**, 259–86.

Devarajan, S., Fullerton, D. and Musgrave, R. A. (1980) Estimating the distribution of tax burdens: a comparison of different approaches, *Journal of Public Economics*, **13**, 155–82.

Dilnot, A. and Morris, C. N. (1981) What do we know about the black economy?, *Fiscal Studies*, **2**, 58–73.

Dolde, W. (1980) Issues and models in empirical research on aggregate consumer expenditure, in Brunner, K. and Meltzer, A. H. (eds), On the state of macroeconomics: *Carnegie-Rochester Conference Series on Public Policy*, **12**.

Dorrington, J. C. and Renton, G. A. (1975) A study of the effects of direct taxation on consumers' expenditure, in Renton, G. A. (ed.), *Modelling the Economy*, Heinemann: London.

Dow, J. C. R. (1964) *The Management of the British Economy, 1945–60*, Cambridge University Press.

Edgeworth, F. Y. (1897) The pure theory of taxation, *Economic Journal*, **7**, 46–70, 226–38, 550–71; partially reprinted in Musgrave, R. A. and Peacock, A. T. (eds) (1958), *Classics in the Theory of Public Finance*, Macmillan: London.

Eisner, R. (1969) Fiscal and monetary policy reconsidered, *American Economic Review*, **59**, 897–905.

Eisner, R. and Lawler, P. J. (1975) Tax policy and investment: an analysis of survey responses, *American Economic Review*, **65**, 206–12.

Feldstein, M. S (1972) The influence of the social security payroll tax: a comment, American Economic Review, **62**, 735–8.

Feldstein, M. S. (1973a) Tax incentives, corporate saving and capital accumulation in the US, *Journal of Public Economics*, **2**, 159–71.

Feldstein, M. S. (1973b) On the optimal progressivity of the income tax, *Journal of Public Economics*, **2**, 357–76.

Feldstein, M. S. (1976) On the theory of tax reform, *Journal of Public Economics*, **6**, 77–104.

Feldstein, M. S. (1978) The welfare cost of capital income taxation, *Journal of Political Economy*, **86**, 529–51.

Feldstein, M. S. and Fane, G. (1973) Taxes, corporate dividend policy and personal savings: the British postwar experience, *Review of Economics & Statistics*, **55**, 399–411.

Ferber, R. and Hirsch, W. Z. (1978) Social experimentation and economic policy: a survey, *Journal of Economic Literature*, **16**, 1379–1414.

Fields, D. B. and Stanbury, W. T. (1971) Income taxes and incentives to work: some additional empirical evidence, *American Economic Review*, **61**, 435–43.

Flemming, J. S. and Little, I. M. D. (1974) *Why We Need a Wealth Tax*, Methuen: London.

Friedman, M. (1948) A monetary and fiscal framework for economic stability, *American Economic Review*, **38**, 245–64.

Friedman, M. (1952) The welfare effects of an income tax and an excise tax, *Journal of Political Economy*, **60**, 25–33.

Godfrey, L. (1975) *Theoretical & Empirical Aspects of the Effects of Taxation on the Supply of Labour*, OECD: Paris.

Goode, R. (1977) The economic definition of income, in Pechman, J. A. (ed.), *Comprehensive Income Taxation*, Brookings Institution: Washington DC.

Gordon, R. H. and Bradford, D. F. (1980) Taxation and the stock market valuation of capital gains and dividends, *Journal of Public Economics*, **14**, 109–37.

Gordon, R. J. (1967) The incidence of the corporation income tax in US manufacturing, 1925–62, *American Economic Review*, **57**, 731–58.

Grady, P. and Stephenson, D. R. (1977) Some macroeconomic effects of tax reform and indexing, *Canadian Journal of Economics*, **10**, 378–92.

Hall, R. E. (1973) Wages, income and hours of work in the US labour force, in Cain, G. C. and Watts, H. W. (eds), *Income Maintenance and Labour Supply*, Rand McNally: Chicago.

Hall, R. E. and Jorgenson, D. W. (1971) Application of the theory of optimum capital accumulation, in Fromm, G. (ed.), *Tax Incentives and Capital Spending*, Brookings Institution: Washington DC.

Harberger, A. C. (1966) Efficiency effects of taxes on income from capital, in Krzyzaniak, M. (ed.), *Effects of Corporation Income Tax*, Wayne State University Press: Detroit.

Harberger, A. C. (1962) The incidence of the corporation income tax, *Journal of Political Economy*, **70**, 215–40.

Hausman, J. A. (1980) The effect of wages, taxes, and fixed costs on women's labour force participation, *Journal of Public Economics*, **14**, 161–94.

Head, J. G. and Shoup, C. S. (1969) Excess burden: the corner case, *American Economic Review*, **59**, 181–3.

Helpman, E. and Sadka, E. (1978) The optimal income tax: some comparative statics results, *Journal of Public Economics*, **9**, 383–93.

Hemming, R. (1980) Income tax progressivity and labour supply, *Journal of Public Economics*, **14**, 95–100.

Hicks, U. K. (1947) *Public Finance*, Nisbet: London.

HMSO (1955) Final Report of the Royal Commission on the Taxation of Profits and Income, Cmnd. **9474**: London.

HMSO (1971) Green Paper on *Value-Added Tax*, Cmnd. **4621**.

HMSO (1975) *Income from Companies and its Distribution*, Second Report of the Royal Commission on the Distribution of Income and Wealth, Cmnd. **6172**: London.

HMSO (1980) The effects of taxes and benefits on household income, 1978, *Economic Trends*, **315**, 99–130.

Holland, D. M. (1969) The effect of taxation on effort: some results for business executives, in *Proceedings of the Sixty-Second Annual Conference of the National Tax Association*.

Holland, D. M. (1977) Effect of taxation on incentives of higher income groups, in *Fiscal Policy and Labour Supply*, Institute for Fiscal Studies: London.

Howrey, E. P. and Hymans, S. H. (1978) The measurement and determination of loanable-funds saving, *Brookings Papers on Economic Activity*, **3**: **1978**, 655–85.

Johansen, L. (1967) Regional economic problems elucidated by linear programming, *International Economic Papers*, **12**, Macmillan: London.

Johnson, H. G. (1966) Factor market distortion and the shape of the transformation curve, *Econometrica*, **34**, 686–95.

Johnson, T. R. (1978) Additional evidence on the effect of alternative taxes on cigarette prices, *Journal of Political Economy*, **86**, 325–9.

Kaldor, N. (1955) *An Expenditure Tax*, Allen & Unwin: London.

Kaldor, N. (1980) Comments on a supplemental personal expenditure tax, in Pechman, J. A. (ed.), *What Should be Taxed: Income or Expenditure*, Brookings Institution: Washington DC.

Kay, J. A. (1978) Review of *Public Policy and the Corporation*, *Economic Journal*, **88**, 865–7.

Kay, J. A. (1980) The Meade report after two years, *Fiscal Studies*, **1**, 47–59.

King, M. A. (1972) Taxation and investment incentives in a vintage investment model, *Journal of Public Economics*, **1**, 121–47.

King, M. A. (1977) *Public Policy and the Corporation*, Chapman and Hall: London.

Kosters, M. (1969) Effects of an income tax on labor supply, in Harberger, A. C. and Bailey, M. J. (eds), *The Taxation of Income from Capital*, Brookings Institution: Washington DC.

Krzyzaniak, M. and Musgrave, R. A. (1963) *The Shifting of the Corporation Income Tax*, The Johns Hopkins University Press: Baltimore.

Laidler, D. and Parkin, M. (1975) Inflation: a survey, *Economic Journal*, **85**, 741–809.

Laury, J. S. E., Lewis, G. R. and Ormerod, P. A. (1978) Properties of macroeconomic models of the UK economy: a comparative study, *National Institute Economic Review*, **83**.

Lewis, G. R. and Ormerod, P. A. (1979) Policy simulations and model characteristics, in Cooke, S. and Jackson, P. M. (eds), *Current Issues in Fiscal Policy*, Martin Robertson: London.

Lipsey, R. G. and Lancaster, K. (1956) The general theory of second best, *Review of Economic Studies*, **24**, 11–32.

Lund, P. J (1976) The econometric assessment of the impact of investment incentives, in Whiting, A. (ed.), *The Economics of Industrial Subsidies*, HMSO: London.

Malcomson, J. M. and Prior, M. J. (1979) The estimation of a vintage model of production for UK manufacturing, *Review of Economic Studies*, **46**, 719–36.

Margolis, J. and Guitton, H. (eds) (1969) *Public Economics*, Macmillan: London.

McClure, C. E. Jr. (1975) General equilibrium analysis: the Harberger model after ten years, *Journal of Public Economics*, **4**, 125–61.

McClure, C. E. Jr. (1979) *Must Corporate Income be Taxed Twice?*, Brookings Institution: Washington DC.

Meade, J. E. et al. (1978) *The Structure and Reform of Direct Taxation*, Allen and Unwin: London.

Mera, K. (1969) Experimental determination of relative marginal utilities, *Quarterly Journal of Economics*, **87**, 464–77.

Mieszkowski, P. (1980) The advisability and feasibility of an expenditure tax system, in Aaron, H. J. and Boskin, M. J. (eds), *The Economics of Taxation*, Brookings Institution: Washington DC.

Mirrlees, J. A. (1971) An Exploration in the theory of optimal income taxation, *Review of Economic Studies*, **38**, 175–208.

Mirrlees, J. A. (1972) On producer taxation, *Review of Economic Studies*, **39**, 105–11.

Modigliani, F. and Miller, M. H. (1958) The cost of capital, corporation finance, and the theory of investment, *American Economic Review*, **48**, 261–97.

Moore, B. and Rhodes, J. (1976) A quantitative analysis of the effects of the regional employment premium and other regional policy instruments, in Whiting, A. (ed.), *The Economics of Industrial Subsidies*, HMSO: London.

Motley, B. (1973) Sales versus income taxes: a pedagogic note, *Oxford Economic Papers*, N. S. **25**, 204–12.

Musgrave, R. A. (1959) *The Theory of Public Finance*, McGraw-Hill: New York.

Musgrave, R. A. (1976) ET, OT and SBT, *Journal of Public Economics*, **6**, 3–16.

Musgrave, R. A., Case, K. E. and Leonard, H. (1974) The distribution of fiscal burdens and benefits, *Public Finance Quarterly*, **2**, 259–311.

Nickell, S. J. (1977) The influence of uncertainty on investment: is it important?, *Economic Journal*, **87**, 47–70.

Ordover, J. A. and Phelps, E. S. (1979) The concept of optimal taxation in an overlapping generations model of capital and wealth, *Journal of Public Economics*, **12**, 1–26.

Ormerod, P. A. (1979) **Economic Modelling**, Heinemann: London.

Peacock, A. T. (1974) The treatment of government expenditure in studies of income distribution, in Smith, W. L. and Culbertson, J. (eds), *Public Finance and Stabilisation Policy: Essays in Honour of R. A. Musgrave*, North-Holland: Amsterdam.

Peacock, A. T. (1978) Do we need to reform direct taxes?, *Lloyds Bank Review*, **129**, 128–40.

Pechman, J. A. (ed.) (1980) *What Should be Taxed: Income or Expenditure*, Brookings Institution: Washington DC.

Pechman, J. A. and Okner, B. A. (1974) *Who Bears the Tax Burden?*, Brookings Institution: Washington DC.

Pechman, J. A. and Timpane, P. M. (eds) (1975) *Work Incentives and Income Guarantees*, Brookings Institution: Washington DC.

Peles, Y. C. and Sarnat, M. (1979) Corporate taxes and capital structure, *Review of Economics and Statistics*, **61**, 118–20.

Phelps, E. S. (1973) The taxation of wage income for economic justice, *Quarterly Journal of Economics*, **87**, 331–54.

Phillips, A. W. (1954) Stabilisation policy in a closed economy, *Economic Journal*, **64**, 290–323.

Phillips, A. W. (1962) Employment, inflation and growth, *Economica*, N. S. **29**, 1–16.

Piachaud, D. (1980) Taxation and social security, in Sandford, C., Pond, C. and Walker R. (eds), *Taxation and Social Policy*, Heinemann: London.

Prest, A. R. (1968) The budget and interpersonal distribution, *Public Finance*, **23**, 80–98.

Prest, A. R. (1979) Review of *The Structure and Reform of Direct Taxation*, *Economic Journal*, **89**, 243–60.

Rawls, J. (1972) *A Theory of Justice*, Harvard University Press: Cambridge, Massachusetts; and Oxford University Press.

Reddaway, W. B. (1970) *Effects of the Selective Employment Tax, First Report, The Distributive Trades*, HMSO: London.

Robbins, L. (1932) *An Essay on the Nature and Significance of Economic Science*, Macmillan: London.

Rosen, H. S. (1976a) A methodology for evaluating tax reform proposals, *Journal of Public Economics*, **6**, 105–21.

Rosen, H. S. (1976b) Taxes in a labour supply model with joint wage-hours determination, *Econometrica*, **44**, 485–507.

Rubner, A. (1964) The irrelevancy of the British differential profits tax, *Economic Journal*, **74**, 347–59.

Sandford, C., Godwin, M., Hardwick, M. and Butterworth, I. (1981) *Costs and Benefits of VAT*, Heinemann: London.

Sandilands, F. et al. (1975) *Inflation Accounting*, Cmnd. **6225**, HMSO: London.

Sandmo, A. (1974) A note on the structure of optimal taxation, *American Economic Review*, **64**, 701–6.

Sandmo, A. (1975) Optimal taxation in the presence of externalities, *Swedish Journal of Economics*, **77**, 86–98.

Sandmo, A. (1976) Optimal taxation: an introduction to the literature, *Journal of Public Economics*, **6**, 37–54.

Sandmo, A. (1979) A note on the neutrality of the cash flow corporation tax, *Economics Letters*, **4**, 173–6.

Sandmo, A. (1981) The rate of return and personal savings, *Economic Journal*, **91**, 536–40.

Scott, J. H. Jr. (1976) A theory of optimal capital structure, *Bell Journal of Economics*, **7**, 33–54.

Scott, M. FG. (1961) A tax on price increases?, *Economic Journal*, **71**, 350–66.

Seidman, L. S. (1978) Tax-based incomes policies, *Brookings Papers on Economic Activity*, **1978**: 2, 301–48.

Sen, A. K. (1966) The efficiency of indirect taxes, in *Problems of Economic Dynamics and Planning: Essays in Honour of Michael Kalecki*, Pergamon: London.

Shilling, N. (1969) *Excise Taxation of Monopoly*, Columbia University Press: New York.

Shoup, C. S. (1962) Debt financing and future generations, *Economic Journal*, **72**, 887–98.

Shoup, C. S. (1972) *Public Expenditure and Taxation*, National Bureau of Economic Research: New York.

Shoven, J. B. and Whalley, J. (1972) A general equilibrium calculation of the effects of differential taxation of income from capital in the US, *Journal of Public Economics*, **1**, 281–321.

Simons, H. C. (1938) *Personal Income Taxation*, University of Chicago Press.

Solow, R. M. (1971) Some implications of alternative criteria for the firm, in Marris, R. and Wood, A. (eds), *The Corporate Economy*, Macmillan: London.

Stiglitz, J. E. (1973) Taxation, corporate financial policy, and the cost of capital, *Journal of Public Economics*, **2**, 1–34.

Sumner, M. T. (1973) Announcement effects of profits taxation, in Parkin, M. (ed.), *Essays in Modern Economics*, Longman: London.

Sumner, M. T. (1975a) Neutrality of corporate taxation, or on not accounting for inflation, *Manchester School*, **43**, 353–61.

Sumner, M. T. (1975b) Le prélèvement conjoncturel, *Public Finance*, **30**, 461–7.

Sumner, M. T. (1977) Taxation and the sales maximisation hypothesis, *Public Finance*, **32**, 92–6.

Sumner, M. T. (1979) A sceptical note on the efficacy of temporary sales tax reductions, *Canadian Public Policy*, **5**, 97–101.

Sumner, M. T. (1981) Investment grants, in Currie, D., Peel, D. and Nobay, R. (eds), *Macroeconomic Analysis*, Croom Helm: London.

Sumner, M. T. and Laing, C. J. (1981) Countercyclical tax changes and consumers' expenditure, *Oxford Bulletin of Economics and Statistics*, **43**, 131–47.

Sumner, M. T. and Ward, R. (1981) Tax changes and cigarette prices, *Journal of Political Economy*, **89**,

Tambini, L. (1969) Financial policy and the corporation income tax, in Harberger, A. C. and Bailey, M. J. (eds), *The Taxation of Income from Capital*, Brookings Institution: Washington DC.

Tanzi, V. (1980a) Inflationary expectations, economic activity, taxes and interest rates, *American Economic Review*, **70**, 12–21.

Tanzi, V. (1980b) *Inflation and the Personal Income Tax*, Cambridge University Press.

Thurow, L. C. (1971) The income distribution as a pure public good, *Quarterly Journal of Economics*, **85**, 327–36.

Tooze, M. J. (1976) Regional elasticities of substitution in the UK in 1968, *Urban Studies*, **13**, 35–44.

Whalley, J. (1975) A general equilibrium assessment of the 1973 UK tax reform, *Economica*, NS **42**, 139–61.

Whalley, J. and Piggott, J. R. (1977) General equilibrium investigations of UK tax-subsidy policy: a progress report, in Artis, M. J. and Nobay, A. R. (eds), *Studies in Modern Economic Analysis*, Blackwell: Oxford.

Whittington. G (1974) *Company Taxation and Dividends*, Institute for Fiscal Studies: London.

Williams, A. (1966) Great Britain, in Keith, E. G. (ed.), *Foreign Tax Policies and Economic Growth*, National Bureau of Economic Research: New York.

Willis, J. R. M. and Hardwick, P. J. W. (1978) *Tax Expenditures in the UK*, Heinemann: London.

Wright, C. (1969) Saving and the rate of interest, in Harberger, A. C. and Bailey, M. J. (eds), *The Taxation of Income from Capital*, Brookings Institution: Washington DC.

Zabalza, A., Pissarides, C. and Barton, M. (1980) Social security and the choice between full-time work, part-time work and retirement, *Journal of Public Economics*, **14**, 245–76.

CHAPTER THREE

Subsidies to the personal sector

Leslie Rosenthal

1. Introduction

This survey is concerned with the analysis and use of one particular form of economic policy tool available to agencies of government; that of subsidies distributed to the personal sector. In this work the term 'subsidy' refers exclusively to policies which work to reduce the relative market price at which goods and services are purchased by consumers. Subsidies are therefore differentiated from general purchasing power transfers of money or income, to which the term subsidy is also sometimes applied.

At this early stage the reader is warned that the definition and concept of subsidies are by no means generally agreed. However, as most of the theoretical and institutional literature is not critically dependent upon technical definition, discussion of the problems involved is postponed until immediately prior to the examination of the applied work on housing and food subsidies.

An economic rationale for the use of subsidies for economic regulation may be made on several grounds. The most common arguments concern the existence of external benefits. Individuals are normally assumed to determine their consumption behaviour on the basis of private, personal benefits received from consumption of goods and services. However, other members of society may also derive benefits from an individual's private actions, and in such circumstances it may be that society as a whole may obtain a net gain from encouraging individuals to consume more of particular goods than they otherwise would. A price reduction in the form of a subsidy is one way of providing such encouragement, and, as we shall see, the existence of externalities of this kind provides an important argument for the use of subsidies over alternative policy possibilities.

Subsidy programmes may clearly be designed to give special aid to special groups and hence may form part of the means by which a general redistribution of income may be accomplished. The relative efficiency and costs involved in the use of subsidy systems for such redistributive purposes form a major thread of argument throughout this survey.

One of the important advantages of the use of subsidies is that they may be applied to very carefully selected goods. Subsidies are, therefore,

* My thanks are due to the editors and other participants in this volume for helpful comments and suggestions.

especially useful for the encouragement of consumption by individuals of commodities considered 'meritorious' *per se* by the community at large. Such a situation presupposes that individuals would, without encouragement, under-provide themselves with such goods, according to the views of others. It may clearly be seen that the idea of 'merit goods' fits very uneasily with the normal liberal presumption of consumer sovereignty. Nevertheless, casual observation tends to the view, at least for this writer, that many subsidies (and other policies) are instituted precisely for such merit good reasons. However, a satisfactory framework for the analysis of merit goods has yet to emerge and, possibly for this reason, the importance of such arguments in the literature remains, in contrast to that of externalities, underemphasised.

Subsidy schemes may also be useful in 'second-best' situations where the primary causes of economic inefficiency cannot be tackled directly. The existence of subsidies for rail and bus transportation is, for example, often justified in this way, as the application of congestion taxes on private usage seems to be unavailable as a policy for regulating road use. Alternatively, subsidies may be applied to encourage public and private monopolies to produce at the economically efficient output level.

Subsidies are often justified in other ways and applied other than to the personal sector. Macroeconomic policy pursuits such as anti-inflation policy may be enhanced by the use of subsidies to private and public enterprises in order to keep prices from rising. Policies to alleviate regional problems and to encourage growth and investment, and international trade may involve subsidies. Subsidies are typically used as a means of resource reallocations within socialist economies.

Subsidies to the personal sector come in many different guises, and section 2 of this survey presents a basic classification of the major types of subsidy system available. As subsidies normally constitute an inducement to alter consumption patterns, the beneficiary valuation of the benefits of the subsidy system will normally be less than the costs of instituting the subsidy. Section 3 is concerned with methods of analysis of the valuation of the benefits derived from subsidies. The major argument favouring subsidy systems over cash transfers is contained in an analysis of interdependent utility externalities and this argument is examined during section 4, while section 5 contains a more general discussion of the possible relative merits of price-related subsidies. The promised discussion of the definitional and conceptual difficulties which arise with empirical investigations of subsidies is postponed to section 6. Finally, section 7 comprises a review of the literature regarding subsidies to food and housing; these two areas containing by far the most important and extensive examples of subsidies in practice.

2. Types of Subsidy

There are many different subsidy systems which may be employed in order to encourage the consumption of specified commodities. In this section the major forms that a subsidy system may take will be introduced and discussed within a simple partial equilibrium setting. The funding of such subsidies must be assumed to arise from some form of non-distortionary general taxation.

It is convenient to look at the different types of in-kind subsidy under three main headings: price-reduction systems; gifts and voucher systems; and all-or-nothing systems. Any of the schemes considered may be 'universal' in nature and therefore available to all no matter their circumstances, or 'selective' and available only to specified individuals and households, possibly to those able to satisfy some form of means-test.

PRICE REDUCTION SYSTEMS

Clearly, one obvious way of encouraging the consumption of a specific commodity would be by a simple price reduction. Such a subsidy could, like indirect taxation, be levied as a specific amount per unit purchased, as an *ad valorem* proportion of value, or in some other way.

We may consider the effects of a specific subsidy on consumer optimisation by means of the indifference map shown as Fig. 3.1. Quantities of the subsidised good are measured along the horizontal axis and, for convenience, money rather than quantities of all goods and services is measured along

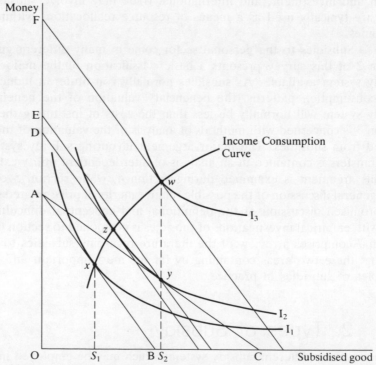

FIG. 3.1 Specific price reduction subsidy system and comparison with cash transfers

the vertical axis. The effect of the price reduction is to move the budget constraint of this typical recipient from AB to AC, causing an increase in the consumption from S_1 to S_2 of the subsidised good. Clearly, 'pathological' cases are possible but we shall only be considering normal goods and 'well-behaved' consumer preferences.

A key point, and one to which we shall often be returning, is to consider whether it is the general welfare of the recipient or his consumption of the specified good that is of prime importance. If an improvement of general welfare is the goal and the subsidy is justified as part of a redistributional programme, then the partial equilibrium analysis can be made to show that a price reduction subsidy is a more costly method of achieving this goal than a simple cash transfer. On the diagram, the cost to the economy of the extra goods consumed at point y is AE. This is the total subsidy, and allows a utility level of I_2 to be obtained. However, the same utility level could be induced by providing an amount of money, AD, keeping prices unchanged, and allowing optimisation to point z. The price reduction subsidy is therefore relatively inefficient for general welfare goals.

If the intention of the subsidy programme is to achieve a target level of consumption of the subsidised product, perhaps a minimum acceptable consumption, then this result may be turned on its head. Let us assume that S_2 is the target level on Fig. 3.1. We have already seen that the cost to taxpayers of inducing this level of consumption by means of a price reduction subsidy is AE. In order to induce the same consumption level of the subsidised good without a price change, but only through income transfers, would entail a cash grant of amount AF to enable the recipient to optimise at point w. In this case it seems clear that the price reduction subsidy is a less costly method of inducing the desired consumption level. That general welfare goals are better served by general purchasing power transfers and specific good consumption levels by particular good price reductions seems a logical result. But the analysis can be taken rather further. It may be that beneficial external effects arise from the consumption of particular goods so that consumption resultant from optimisation subject to private costs and benefits differs from that consumption which would be optimal from consideration of social benefits. In such cases cash transfers simply may not be able to induce the socially optimal consumption pattern. We shall be returning to the debate between income and in-kind transfers at length as the argument develops.

GIFTS AND VOUCHER SYSTEMS

If we are concerned to see individuals or households consuming at least some minimum standard of a specified good the minimum cost price-reduction system requires some basic knowledge of consumer preferences and demand relationships. A more straightforward method, it may be thought, would be to transfer amounts of the designated good directly rather than through reducing price or increasing income.

Lump-sum gifts and grants

Lump-sum gifts refer to systems where recipients receive, at no direct charge, specific fixed quantities of a designated good. Examples of such programmes are the School Lunch Program in the US, and the free school milk and lunch programmes in the UK. These systems in particular are means-tested and therefore selective, but free school milk was a universal provision in the UK for more than twenty-five years.

The receipt of a lump-sum gift will have the effect of shifting the budget constraint of the recipient to the right by an amount equal to the quantity of the commodity transferred. In Fig. 3.2 the gift is of an amount AC or xz or S_1S_3 of the designated good, and after receipt the recipient unit may consume along a new budget constraint ACD. The cost of such and system is shown as amount AE. However, if there exists the possibility of the recipient reselling the gift on the open market – if the gift is marketable – the relevant budget constraint is not ACD but ECD. Such a marketable gift is then equivalent to a simple income transfer of the open market value of the gift in kind, but, if marketing and transactions costs exist, will be less desirable than the income transfer. Clearly, therefore, if the gift were marketable then we would see extra consumption of the subsidised commodity of an amount determined by the income elasticity of demand for the product (S_1S_2) rather than extra consumption of the amount of the gift itself (S_1S_3).

The point, however, is that for the initial case under consideration and diagrammed it is also true that when the gift is *not* marketable there will be the

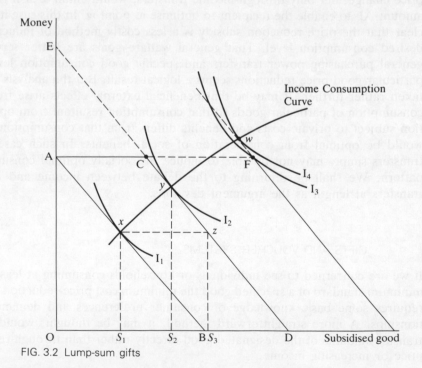

FIG. 3.2 Lump-sum gifts

same result, with the increase in consumption less than the amount of the gift. The reason for this is the 'crowding-out' of private consumption, with the gift being substituted for what would otherwise be privately purchased anyway (Pauly 1970; Peltzman 1973). Thus when the amount of the gift is small relative to private consumption, the increased consumption only takes place according to the income effect of the value of the gift. This analysis implies not only that the result for a small lump-sum gift and an equivalent money transfer are identical, but also that an equal change in consumption could be accomplished by a direct equal-value gift of *any* consumed commodity. As Pauly notes, 'one may as well give the poor person cigarettes as warm clothes'.

Only where the gift is non-marketable and large enough to crowd out all private purchases will a lump-sum gift drive the consumer from his income consumption curve and induce a result different from an equivalent money transfer. On Fig. 3.2 with a non-marketable gift of amount AF our consumer will be unable to reach his preferred position at *w* as he is unable to reduce his private purchases below zero. The gift has crowded out all his private purchases of the good, and the total consumption of the good is equal to the amount of the gift.

This simple analysis raises some interesting points. The possibility of the marketing of the gift by recipients is an important factor. When private purchase and a free market exist side by side with lump-sum gifts, the difficulty and cost of ensuring non-marketability contribute to the argument that where minimum standards are the goal and where in-kind transfers are deemed appropriate, it may be best to replace the private market and allocate entirely on grounds other than those of a market system.

Although examples of lump-sum gifts are certainly not absent within western industrial societies – primary education may be prime example – arguments about marketability and crowding out normally seem to be reserved for criticism of international and disaster aid to the Third World.

Voucher Systems

The schemes considered here as voucher systems have a common theme in that eligible recipients do not receive goods directly, but must purchase vouchers which then entitle them to obtain specified goods in exchange. There are any number of possible voucher schemes available dependent upon (a) the charge made for entry to the scheme, (b) whether vouchers obtained may be directly exchanged for goods or whether they give entitlement to a reduced price, and (c) any limits or constraints imposed upon quantities available within the scheme. A system of free entry and direct exchange of vouchers for a fixed amount of a good would be identical to a lump-sum gift system. Free entry, entitlement to a reduced price and no limit to purchases would be equivalent to a price-reduction subsidy system.

Voucher systems are not in practice particularly common, in spite of the large variety of possibilities available from variations of entry charges, price reductions and limits. In theory, voucher systems are capable of inducing any consumption pattern that results in a higher welfare level for recipients compatible with adequate voluntary take-up rates.

Two actual examples of voucher schemes are illustrated by Fig. 3.3(a) and 3.3(b). Fig. 3.3(a) illustrates the Rail Card voucher system introduced by British Rail as part of a discriminatory pricing structure. Rail Cards, which are available to old age pensioners, full-time students and to other special groups, carry a fixed annual charge and give entitlement to greatly reduced rail fares.

On Fig. 3.3(a) the effect of the scheme is to shift the budget constraint of the eligible recipient from AB to CD, where AC is the fixed entry charge and the per unit reduced price is shown by the reduced slope of the final budget constraint. However, the Rail Card scheme exists as a revenue-raising exercise for British Rail rather than as a redistributional programme or for the encouragement of external benefits. Often more explicitly redistributional in intention are similar schemes for lowering fares to old age pensioners on local buses in the UK funded by local authorities.

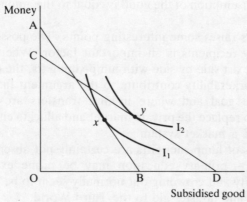

FIG. 3.3(a) Voucher systems with entry charge, price reduction entitlement and unconstrained quantity (British Rail 'Rail Cards')

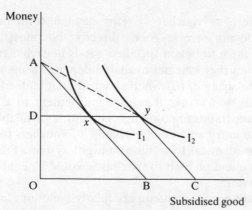

FIG. 3.3(b) Voucher systems with entry charge, direct exchange entitlement and constrained quantity (US food stamps)

However, the classic example of a voucher system is that of the Food Stamp Program in the US from 1964. In its simplest form entry to the scheme was selective and a charge levied roughly equal to normal food expenditure. In return participants received food stamps (vouchers) which could be directly exchanged at designated stores for a wide selection of foodstuffs of higher market value than the entry charge. The situation may be shown as Fig. 3.3(b). The entry charge is amount AD and the amount of the good that may be obtained by use of the voucher is Dy. Any amount of food purchased above this can only be obtained by going to the open market, so that the new budget constraint becomes DyC, and given the indifference map as shown, the consumer optimises at point y. Changes to the Food Stamp Program in the mid-1970s now allow participants to purchase 'fractional' amounts of the food stamp (Clarkson 1976) and if this process is taken to its limit the budget constraint would become AyC, a scheme identical to a reduced-price subsidy up to a purchasing limit. In 1977 an amendment was proposed whereby the food stamp is available without direct charge (Giertz and Sullivan 1978) which would convert the system into a simple application of a free gift system. Olsen (1969, 1971) contain some discussion of the possible effects of voucher systems.

Examples of voucher systems in practice do seem to be quite rare, and in spite of their potentialities for the pursuit of economic efficiency, voucher schemes tend to be advocated more on liberal 'choice' grounds as an alternative to direct governmental provision or intervention. For example, in the UK, voucher schemes are commonly put forward as an alternative to direct state provision of education (Peacock and Wiseman 1964; Rowley and Peacock, 1975). The system would work by the state making the education of children compulsory and supervising standards but the state would not provide education. It would be 'produced' in privately owned institutions. Parents would receive vouchers for the education of each child to the value of a minimum acceptable level, which could be used to purchase education at an institution of their own choice. Parents are of course free to supplement this minimum value and send their children to more expensive and presumably better schools. The major advantages of such a scheme are said to be that the influence of the State would be reduced, a greater degree of choice of schooling available, and an element of competition introduced which would raise the standards of educational provision. Olsen (1969) argues for the introduction of a similar scheme for housing provision.

ALL-OR-NOTHING SUBSIDY SYSTEMS

The third major type of subsidy system that we examine is that of all-or-nothing systems. The distinguishing feature here is that, so long as non-marketability is assured, there exists no possibility of any substitution along the new budget constraint. The potential recipient must either accept the offered package of a given fixed quantity of the good at a fixed price or reject it. There exists no possibility of consuming more or less than the offered quantity within the scheme and the system is therefore well-described as all-or-nothing. Such a subsidy

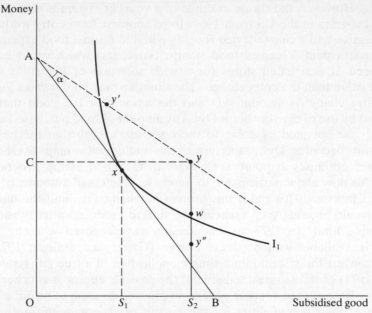

FIG. 3.4 All-or-nothng subsidy system

system may be demonstrated on a diagram as Fig. 3.4.

The quantity offered is S_2 at a total charge of AC to the recipient, and therefore the subsidy offer constitutes an extra point or 'spike' of possible consumption shown as point y, where the implied subsidy per unit is α. So long as y lies above the indifference curve I_1 on which utility was maximised subject to market prices alone, then the subsidy offer should be accepted. If the subsidy point does not lie above I_1, as at y'', then the offer will be rejected even though at y'' an implied subsidy still exists.

If target levels of consumption are not carefully chosen then the impossibility of substituting along a new higher budget constraint line can result in packages containing reduced levels of the subsidised product being accepted. One such acceptable package is shown as y', which involves less of the subsidised product being consumed than at the pre-subsidy position x. Thus, unlike the price reduction system, highly constrained choice can lead to unfortunate results, and the mere observation that a subsidy exists is not enough to imply the increased consumption of the subsidised product.

All-or-nothing subsidies allow systems to be built up which can pinpoint post-subsidy consumption patterns exactly. The absence of substitutability can enable the donor to constrain the effects on general welfare and maximise any external benefit at minimum cost by ensuring as low a level of post-subsidy recipient welfare as possible, consistent with adequate take-up. Clearly, one can offer acceptable target packages such as w which may be only marginally more desirable than the initial consumption mix at x. Such a package would prove relatively cheap to provide and will not usually be able to be induced by a simple price reduction. Similarly, an all-or-nothing package may be chosen to result in exactly that consumption mix that would have resulted from an equal cost cash transfer. This possibility is important because, as we have seen, cash transfers are often argued to be superior to subsidy systems on the grounds that an equal cost cash transfer will enable a higher welfare level to be attained. However, the possibility mentioned here implies that the mere observation of the existence of a subsidy system is not enough to presume relative inefficiency of this kind.

All-or-nothing subsidies are in practice quite common but are mostly confined to one important area; that of public housing schemes where dwelling units are made available at less than market prices. Typically in such schemes the quantity of housing on offer is fixed, and difficult to alter or supplement through additional purchases on the open market. Rents are normally fixed in accordance with legal or financial accounting constraints and entry into the schemes is selective and voluntary.

Direct comparison of all the subsidy systems described in this section is difficult because, as has been shown, both the voucher system and the all-or-nothing system can be used to induce any consumption pattern in potential recipients so long as a higher utility level than that available without the subsidy results. Comparison of the effects and costs of different subsidy systems therefore depends upon the particular form of voucher and all-or-nothing system chosen. One of the more interesting forms is that of the minimum cost all-or-nothing system introduced above, which constrains post-subsidy recipient welfare levels as closely as possible to the pre-subsidy level. It is clear from the analysis above that from the point of view of the recipient, for a given total subsidy cost to the taxpayer, a cash grant (or a 'small' lump-sum gift) will normally be preferred to a price-reduction subsidy which in turn will be preferred to the minimum cost all-or-nothing scheme. From the point of view of the taxpayer wishing to minimise the cost of inducing some target level of consumption of a particular good in recipients, this result is reversed, and the minimum cost all-or-nothing subsidy is preferred to the price-reduction system which in turn is superior to the cash grant. There is therefore something of a conflict of interest between donor and recipient. Further analysis of, in particular, the comparative advantages of cash grants and in-kind subsidy systems in general is contained in the following sections.

3. Subsidies, Benefits and Consumer Surplus

The advantage received by the individual consumer from a subsidy system arises from the obvious fact that the price that he faces and which determines his market behaviour is below that which would rule from market forces alone. The subsidy per unit is simply the difference between the market price and the actual price resulting from the workings of the scheme; and the total subsidy received is this difference multiplied by the number of units of the subsidised product purchased. The total subsidy as measured in this way is clearly a cost to society of providing the subsidy, but will not usually measure the individual's valuation of the benefits received from the scheme.

Consideration of the subsidy cost to society, the valuation of the benefits received, and the associated 'excess burden' of subsidy systems (and, indeed, of indirect taxation) is usually approached through consideration of consumer surplus. There are two major approaches to consumer surplus; those of Marshall and of Hicks.

MARSHALLIAN APPROACHES

The Marshallian approach takes the demand curve for a commodity as being a measure of willingness to pay and, therefore, a measure of the addition to utility of incremental units of the commodity. The area under the demand curve is therefore a measure of the total utility derived from consumption of a given amount of a commodity. Consider a subsidy scheme introduced in a constant cost industry which reduces the price from l to m, and increases the quantity demanded from x to y as shown on Fig. 3.5.

Initially consumer surplus may be considered as the difference between the total area under the demand curve for quantity x (*daxo*) less the charge made to consumers for this quantity (*laxo*). Thus consumer surplus is

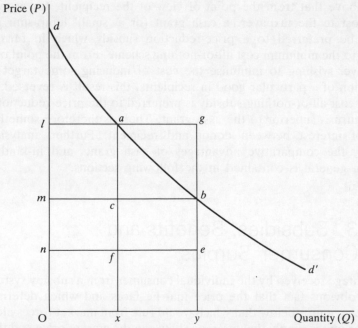

FIG. 3.5 Benefits and deadweight welfare loss of subsidy systems applying Marshallian demand curve methods

originally area *dal*. After the subsidy is introduced, consumer surplus increases to area *dbm*. Therefore the benefit received by consumers as a result of the introduction of the subsidy may be measured as area *labm*. This increase in benefit is made up of two parts; one (area *lacm*) comes from the fact that less is charged for the amount of the commodity originally purchased; and the other comes from the fact that a surplus above the amount charged is obtained from the extra commodity then purchased (area *abc*).

This valuation of the *benefit* of the subsidy scheme is less, however, than the costs of implementing the scheme. This cost of implementation, the total subsidy, as measured by the subsidy per unit multiplied by the number of units consumed is equal to the area of the rectangle *lgbm*. The excess of cost over benefit has been alternatively termed the 'waste', 'deadweight loss', 'welfare loss', 'excess burden' or 'inefficiency' of the subsidy system, and is equal to area *agb* on our diagram.

This simple Marshallian scheme has been quite extensively employed in the literature concerning subsidies both as a means of examining the benefit that consumers derive from subsidy schemes and its distribution over income classes and other household characteristics, as well as for examination of the size of the welfare loss resultant. The application of the Marshallian analysis is computationally simple. For the case of a linear demand function and constant cost of provision, the amount of the benefit of an unconstrained price reduction system is simply the total subsidy (*lgbm*) less the deadweight welfare loss (*agb*), which is one-half of the subsidy per unit multiplied by the increased quantity demanded due to the price reduction, i.e. half *agbc*. The major requirements are therefore a measure of the constant marginal social or, more usually, private costs of provision, the size or amount of the per unit subsidy, existing demand, and a measure of the responsiveness of demand to price charges, normally given as a price elasticity. The classic study using this method for the study of the unconstrained owner-occupier housing subsidy is Laidler (1969).

This approach is also relatively simple to apply for constrained subsidies where there exists a limit to the amount of the good offered or available for purchase at the subsidised price. In this case, the after-subsidy position of the consumers might be a point off the demand curve, such as point *e* on the diagram. Olsen (1972) presents, and applies, a model for the estimation of such a constrained off-the-demand-curve subsidy allocation, where the demand curve is assumed to be a rectangular hyperbola and therefore displays unitary price elasticity of demand. From Fig. 3.5, the consumer surplus obtained from the move from point *a* to point *e* can be seen to equal:

$$laxo - neyo + \text{area } agyx$$

Now for a rectangular hyperbola of the form $P = laxo/Q$ the area *agyx* will be:

$$\int_x^y \frac{laxo}{Q} dQ = laxo[\ln oy - \ln ox]$$
$$= laxo[\ln lgyo - \ln laxo]$$

Thus, Benefit $= laxo - neyo + laxo[\ln lgyo - \ln laxo]$

All the arguments here are observables. We require the expenditure on the subsidised commodity after the acceptance of the subsidy (*neyo*), the open market valuation of the quantity accepted (*lgyo*) and total expenditure on the commodity in the absence of the subsidy (*laxo*). The market valuation and the expenditure on the commodity in the absence of the programme will normally be estimated from observations of the non-subsidised or pre-subsidy market for the good.

Analyses of rent control (Olsen 1972) and public housing programmes (Kraft and Kraft 1979) for the US have been presented which assume constant, unit-price-elastic demand curves for housing and which estimate the market price of the housing in question from the relationship between market price (or rental) and housing characteristics in the free or market sectors.

Use of the Marshallian approach to consumer surplus, though relatively simple to apply to the estimation of the benefits of subsidy schemes, is subject to a good deal of criticism because the valuation of benefits using the Marshallian money-income-constant demand curve takes no account of the effects on real income of differing prices and the associated income effects on demand.[1]

HICKSIAN APPROACHES

The Hicksian analysis of consumer surplus and the valuation of consumer benefit does take the income effects of a price change into account and may be illustrated on an indifference map as shown on Fig. 3.6.

Our consumer is originally at point x along the budget constraint line AA', the slope of which shows the ratio of relative prices in the open unsubsidised market. After the imposition of the subsidy (of whatever kind) the individual moves to point z on the higher indifference curve II. Now the money value of the increase in utility of moving from indifference curve I to indifference curve II would be a measure of the benefit derived by the individual from the existence of the subsidy. There are several such measures of consumer surplus available (Hicks 1956, Machlup 1957) but the most attractive as regards subsidies, is that termed the equivalent variation. Hicks's equivalent variation is that sum of money, or increase in income, which would in the absence of the subsidy system make the consumer as well off as he would have been with the scheme. On the Figure below, starting from point x, the sum of money which would in lieu of the subsidy allow our individual to obtain a level of utility equal to that obtained with the subsidy at point z would be the amount AB. This increase in income would allow the attainment, with unsubsidised market prices, of point y which lies on the same indifference curve as point z. So AB measures, at market prices, the benefit to the consumer of taking advantage of the existence of the subsidy.

The cost to society of allowing the consumer to consume at point z may similarly be measured in terms of market prices as AC, the total subsidy, which is simply the difference in the market valuations of the bundles of goods represented by points x and z. The deadweight loss or welfare loss of the excess

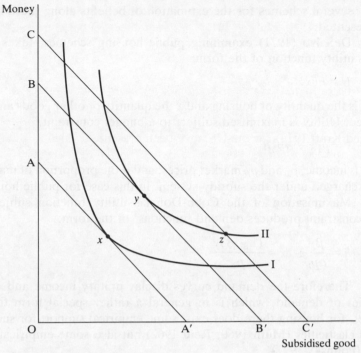

FIG. 3.6 Benefits and deadweight welfare loss of subsidy systems applying Hicksian equivalent variation

of cost over perceived benefit is therefore the amount BC.

The relationship between the Marshallian measure and Hicks's equivalent variation for a price fall is that the Marshallian measure is of an area below the uncompensated, money-income-constant demand curve, whereas the Hicks measure is of an area below the compensated, real-income-constant or welfare-constant demand curve.[2] The uncompensated and compensated demand curves differ by the amount of the income effect of a price change so that the difference between the two measures of benefit depends upon the income elasticity of demand for the product. The more nearly zero the income elasticity of demand the closer will be the Marshallian measure as an approximation to the Hicksian. For bounds on the errors of such an approximation see Willig (1976). However, Murray (1978) points out that such an argument may only be made for unconstrained subsidies, which are identical with the price reductions which form the basis for the original analysis of consumer surplus. Where choices under a subsidy system are constrained, as, for example, with all-or-nothing subsidies, the consumer will not usually be able to optimise fully and will consequently be off the demand curve. Under such circumstances the Marshallian measure may not be a good approximation to the Hicksian.

For direct estimation of the benefits of a subsidy in equivalent variation terms the parameters of the utility function are required. Nothing daunted, several schemes for the estimation of benefits along these lines have been presented.

DeSalvo (1971) examining public housing schemes, takes a Cobb–Douglas utility function of the form:

$$U = h^\beta x^{1-\beta} \tag{1}$$

where h is the quantity of housing and x the quantity of other goods and services consumed. Utility is maximised subject to a budget constraint:

$$y = p_x x + \alpha p_h h \tag{2}$$

where y is income, p_x and p_h market prices, and α the proportion of market price actually charged under the subsidy system, in this case for public housing.

Maximisation of the Cobb-Douglas utility function subject to the budget constraint produces demand functions[3] of the form:

$$h = \frac{\beta y}{\alpha p_h}; \quad x = \frac{(1-\beta)y}{p_x} \tag{3}$$

Therefore the demand curves display unitary income and own price elasticities of demand, which is in general a rather special form to assume. However, for housing there does exist some empirical support for such unitary demand elasticities (Muth 1960; Reid 1962) but also some empirical evidence against (Polinsky 1977).

If the consumer decides to accept the all-or-nothing constrained subsidy programme offer of a fixed quantity h_1 of public housing and x_1 of other goods and services, with an original income of y_0, the resultant utility level will be

$$U_1 = h_1^\beta x_1^{1-\beta} = [h_1]^\beta \left[\frac{y_0 - \alpha p_h h_1}{p_x} \right]^{1-\beta} \tag{4}$$

where the final expression utilises the budget constraint equation [2].

In order to obtain the equivalent variation we require that income change which will result in this level of utility when the consumer is required to face market, unsubsidised, prices. The income, y, required to obtain U_1 subject to market prices is found by substituting the demand relationships of equation [3] into the utility function [1] with $\alpha = 1$, setting $U = U_1$ and solving for y. We therefore require that y which solves:

$$[h_1]^\beta \left[\frac{y_0 - \alpha p_h h_1}{p_x} \right]^{1-\beta} = \left[\frac{\beta y}{p_h} \right]^\beta \left[\frac{(1-\beta)y}{p_x} \right]^{1-\beta} \tag{5}$$

$$\therefore \quad y = \left[\frac{h_1 p_h}{\beta} \right]^\beta \left[\frac{y_0 - \alpha p_h h_1}{1-\beta} \right]^{1-\beta} \tag{6}$$

The equivalent variation benefit of the subsidy is the change in income required so that

$$\text{Benefit} = y - y_0 \tag{7}$$

For estimation of benefit all that is required is original income (y_0), total expenditure on the subsidised good within the scheme ($\alpha p_h h_1$), the market price of the constrained quantity offered ($p_h h_1$) and the utility parameter (β). The first two requirements are directly observable, and market price may be estimated from the open market relationship between characteristics and price, or by knowledge of the value of α. The value of β may again be estimated quite easily, as it is clear from re-arrangement of the demand relationships of equations [2, 3] that β is simply the proportion of total income spent on the subsidised commodity in the absence of the subsidy.

The DeSalvo methodology has been applied to the distribution of benefits from public housing for the US by Murray (1975) and for the distribution of benefits from the Food Stamp program by Clarkson (1976).

If the subsidy program is an unconstrained price reduction rather than a constrained one, then the analysis proceeds by substituting the demand relationships of equation [3] into equation [4] and the left-hand side of equation [5] with the subsidised price αp_h and original income y_0.

The solution for y becomes:

$$y = y_0 \alpha^{-\beta}$$
and Benefit $= y_0 \alpha^{-\beta} - y_0$

This solution was also found by Ricketts (1976).

The use of the Cobb-Douglas utility function is clearly a very restrictive one given the implied unit elasticities. In an examination of housing subsidies, Aaron and von Furstenberg (1971), whilst accepting the supportive empirical findings for a unitary income elasticity of demand for housing are much less convinced of the unit price elasticity. They argue that rather than a Cobb-Douglas utility function, a constant elasticity of substitution (CES) utility function is appropriate. The CES utility function whilst displaying constant unitary income elasticities, can accommodate various values for the price elasticity. The CES utility function used is of the form:

$$U = [Dh^{-r} + (1-D)x^{-r}]^{-1/r} \qquad [8]$$

where h is housing quantity consumed and x is other goods and services. D is a distributional parameter which in this instance is chosen to vary with r such that a given proportion of income is always originally spent on housing. The parameter r is related to the elasticity of substitution (s) such that

$$s = \frac{1}{1+r}$$

The elasticity of substitution is defined as the proportionate change in the proportions of housing and other goods consumed per proportional change in relative prices along a given indifference curve. There is a relationship between the elasticity of substitution and the price elasticity of both the compensated Hicksian demand curve and, given the constant proportion of income assumed spent on housing in the absence of the subsidy, the uncompensated Marshallian demand curve. It may be shown that as the elasticity of substitution approaches unity $(r \rightarrow 0)$ the CES function approaches the Cobb-Douglas form.

Aaron and von Furstenberg take various values of the constant proportion of income spent on housing in the absence of subsidies, the proportion of market price subsidised, and the elasticity of substitution and simulate for the equivalent variation as a proportion of total subsidy for unconstrained subsidies. Their findings show that the higher the elasticity of substitution (and therefore the implied price elasticity) the lower the proportion of the total subsidy valued as benefit and the higher the proportion of deadweight welfare loss. They find also that the welfare loss as a proportion grows with the size of the percentage reduction in price due to the subsidy, but that the original proportion of income spent on the yet-to-be-subsidised commodity is relatively unimportant.

Aaron and von Furstenberg's analysis is carried out in application to the US Federal low rent public housing program, but as their analysis clearly allows unconstrained optimisation by consumers in face of the subsidy and as such optimisation cannot be assumed for public housing, how far their results are applicable to public housing is moot. As they themselves point out, for constrained, quantity-tied subsidy programmes it is possible that the institutional arrangements are such that recipients may be induced to consume exactly that quantity which they would when faced with an equal-value cash transfer. In such a case the equivalent variation benefit does equal the total subsidy and there is no deadweight loss. Only where the constrained quantity is, by chance or possibly by careful design, exactly equal to the quantity which would have been chosen in the unconstrained mode will the measure of benefit be the same for both the subsidy methods.

Murray (1975, 1978) has taken the analysis one stage further by use of a generalised CES utility function specified as

$$U = (ah^b + x^c)^d \qquad a > 0; \ b, \ c, \ d. \ \text{of equal sign.} \qquad [9]$$

where h and x are housing and other goods and services respectively and a is a distributional parameter. This specification contains both the Cobb-Douglas form which appears as a limiting case, and the CES form when $b = c = 1/d$. The generalised CES function has the additional attraction of imposing neither unitary price nor income elasticities, but, unfortunately, the equations for the benefit estimates are not 'closed' and have to be estimated via an iterative process.

Murray (1975) applies the generalised CES utility function to the distribution of benefits of US public housing. In an attempt to estimate equation [9] from data from applications to enter public housing schemes for nine different family compositions, Murray is able to test the three Cobb-Douglas, CES, and generalised CES specifications. He is able to reject the Cobb-Douglas but not, in general, the CES specification, in favour of the generalised CES formulation. This may be interpreted as rejecting the hypothesis of unit price elasticity for housing but not that of unit income elasticity. However, he does find that the Cobb-Douglas specification does not do too badly in estimating aggregate overall benefits though it performs much less well for computing the distribution of benefits over household characteristics.

However one goes about measuring the benefits derived from subsidy systems, the realisation that the benefit derived will be different from, and usually less than, the cost to the community of providing the subsidy, given the attendant deadweight welfare loss, leads to a search for a more efficient means of transferring resources around the economy. There does exist an obvious alternative device that will result in zero deadweight welfare loss using the analysis of Fig. 3.6. This device is a cash transfer.

The reader may well be now experiencing a severe case of *déjà vu* as the presumed superiority of income taxation (cash transfer) over commodity taxation (subsidies or in-kind transfer) on the basis of the excess burden of the latter over the former is a well tried and tested feature of introductory public finance courses. The argument usually proceeds by further demonstrating the superiority of poll taxes (non-means tested transfers) over income taxes (means-tested transfers) by introducing leisure as a good and concludes by arguing that there exists no reasonable means of distributing taxes (transfers) which simultaneously achieve the conflicting ends of efficiency, including the avoidance of excess burden, and equity or the achievement of a desired distributional objective (Allan 1971; Musgrave and Musgrave 1980). Within this framework one traditional view has tended to argue that direct income taxation (transfers) be used in pursuit of equity considerations, and indirect taxation (subsidies) be used in pursuence of revenue or of efficiency considerations, here best thought of as the encouragement of those goods capable of producing external benefits. This argument has much to do with an assignment of targets to instruments approach to public policy, but, as Atkinson (1977) shows, it is possible, within an optimal tax framework with a variable labour supply, for indirect taxes to be associated with the equity objective and direct taxes with efficiency.

What we have seen so far may usefully be summarised here. Of the many different institutional arrangements of subsidies, it appears that none can improve upon the equal-cost cash transfer in terms of *beneficiary* valuation of the benefits derived. In fact, the presumed superiority of cash transfers over in-kind subsidies because of the excess burden argument has left some writers in something of a quandary. After all, if they are inferior, why do we so extensively use subsidy systems as redistributionary devices? Clearly a possible answer may lie in the motives of the putative *donors* to the redistributional process, and it is to this area of the literature on cash versus in-kind transfers that we now turn.

4. Redistribution and interdependence

As we have seen, the recipients or beneficiaries of subsidy systems will likely prefer the least restrictive of possible systems whilst donors will usually prefer the least costly. There is, however, a more fundamental question to be posed: that is, why have any redistributional system at all?

Within the framework of Paretian Welfare theory, policy changes should only be introduced if at least one member of the community gains from the change and none lose. According to taste, this rather strict criterion may be loosened by acceptance of the Hicks-Kaldor-Scitovsky criterion which argues basically that gains and losses may be made but that policy change may only be recommended if the gainers gain more and are therefore potentially able to compensate the losers by more than the losers lose. Alternatively one may argue that there is a higher arbiter for consideration of policy changes than the individual, in the form of a Social Welfare function derived from political, moral or ethical considerations pertaining to society as a whole. There are, therefore, several possible approaches to the examination of redistributional policies.

Rodgers (1974) has surveyed the field of models attempting to explain why redistribution occurs at all in a community of self-interested individuals. He finds three major strands or models. The first concerns the political process whereby decisions are made in a democratic system and follows Downs (1957) and Buchanan and Tullock (1962). With Downs, political parties are able to obtain votes by promising redistributional policies. If voting behaviour is only affected by the income level of voters, then a mandate which promises the poorest 51 per cent of voters a redistribution of income to them from the remaining 49 per cent of rich voters will be a winning coalition, and redistribution will occur. The second major model is that termed the Insurance Model. Here transfers are made willingly at least, on the presumption that any individual faces some risk that at some time he will find himself subject to the misfortune of a large fall in his income level. For risk-averse individuals it will pay to hedge against such a risk and redistributional policies may be viewed as insurance (Friedman and Savage 1948). Finally there is the interdependent utility model where altruism and benevolence on the part of the rich towards the poor is built into individual utilities. When the welfare of the poor is an argument of the utility functions of the rich, it should not come as too much of a surprise that redistributional policies may emerge. Interdependent utility models deserve closer attention since they contain the major arguments in favour of in-kind redistribution over cash transfers.

The power of the interdependent utility model is such that redistributional policies may emerge even using the strict Pareto criterion, which is otherwise normally reserved for efficiency rather than equity considerations. When the utility of one unit of money obtained by seeing someone else enjoying it is greater than that which would be obtained by one's own enjoyment of it, the transfer of the one unit is justified on the grounds of the Pareto principle. This is the line of argument used by Hochman and Rodgers (1969) in providing a justification for the existence of voluntary redistributional activities, and it now becomes 'efficient' to promote 'equity'.

For redistributional policies to pass the weaker potential compensation test of Hicks-Kaldor-Scitovsky it is only required that the utility gained by the donor be positive, but not necessarily greater than that obtained by the donor's own consumption. Mishan (1975) argues that the analysis of Thurow (1971) which views the income distribution as a 'public' good which therefore enters every individual's utility function equally is an example of such use of the weaker criterion. Breit (1974) also sees the degree of equality of incomes, expressed as a Gini coefficient, entering directly into all utility functions.

Recent analyses of models of benevolence in which it may be shown that in-kind subsidies are superior to cash transfers are contained in Daly and Giertz (1972a, 1972b, 1976), Rodgers (1973), Pauly (1970) and Garfinkel (1973). The key is the examination of the form the interdependence between individuals takes. Individuals may be concerned with the general welfare of others, or their consumption levels of specific goods. It is when the consumption of specific goods enters the utility functions of others and there exist 'goods-specific externalities' that the superiority of subsidy systems emerges.[4]

Following Daly and Giertz (1972a, 1972b) consider a two-person, two-good exchange economy, where the utility of A depends not only upon the amount of goods (x_1, x_2) that A consumes but also upon the amount of goods and the utility level that B enjoys. For simplicity B is a purely self-interested individual. Thus

$$U_A = U_A[x_1^A; x_2^A; x_1^B; x_2^B; U_B] \qquad [10]$$
$$U_B = U_B[x_1^B; x_2^B] \qquad [11]$$

where the superscripts refer to whether good x_i is consumed by A or by B. Consider equation [10]. The presence in A's utility function of B's consumption of goods x_1 and x_2 implies goods-specific externalities, while the presence there of B's utility level, U_B, implies a general welfare externality or utility interdependence. Following Buchanan and Stubblebine (1962) we may distinguish marginal and infra-marginal externalities, and it is the existence of externalities at the margin which determines the effect of externalities on behaviour. A marginal benevolent goods-specific externality will exist if $dU_A/dx_i^B > 0$, and a marginal benevolent utility-externality will exist if $dU_A/dU_B > 0$.

Under the simple model presented here there clearly exists the possibility of *voluntary* mutually advantageous redistribution of goods from A to B, where under the strict Pareto criterion, both parties may gain. As we have argued, A will transfer units of a good to B so long as the utility he receives from B's consumption of units of the good in question is greater than the utility he receives from his own consumption of the units. A will voluntarily transfer so long as:

$$\frac{dU_A}{dx_i^A} < \frac{dU_A}{dx_i^B} + \frac{dU_A}{dU_B}\frac{dU_B}{dx_i^B} \quad i = 1, 2. \qquad [12]$$

Here the right-hand side represents the marginal utility received from the transfer of the good and comprises firstly the direct effect on A's utility of B's extra consumption, and secondly the indirect effect of B's extra consumption x_i on B's utility level, which then effects A's utility level through the utility interdependence.

It should be noted that voluntary transfer does not necessarily follow from the existence of externalities, for we may have situations in which marginal

externalities exist but where inequality [12] does not hold. In these circumstances the weaker potential compensation test may well recommend transfer
but it would not be forthcoming voluntarily.

For the model as above, a Pareto optimum will exist when the
marginal rates of substitution between commodities for each individual are
equal. Given the interdependencies and the fixed commodity levels, the first
order conditions for utility maximisation require

$$\frac{\dfrac{dU_A}{dx_1^A} - \dfrac{dU_A}{dx_1^B} - \dfrac{dU_A}{dU_B}\dfrac{dU_B}{dx_1^B} - \dfrac{dU_B}{dx_1^B}}{\dfrac{dU_A}{dx_2^A} - \dfrac{dU_A}{dx_2^B} - \dfrac{dU_A}{dU_B}\dfrac{dU_B}{dx_2^B}} = \frac{\dfrac{dU_B}{dx_1^B}}{\dfrac{dU_B}{dx_2^B}} \tag{13}$$

Now the question to be asked is whether equation [13] will hold under
circumstances of pure transfer with market prices facing both individuals or
whether it is necessary in order to attain a Pareto-optimum that our two
individuals have to face other than market prices. Here the necessity for other
than market prices would be equivalent to requiring a subsidy system of some
kind, while pure transfer under market prices for both would not require a
subsidy system but only 'cash' transfers.

One way of approaching the problem is to compare equation [13] with
the condition necessary for Pareto optimality for purely selfish individuals in the
absence of externalities. In these circumstances we require the ratio of prices to
be equal for both individuals so that the condition of equation [14] holds:

$$\frac{\dfrac{dU_A}{dx_1^A}}{\dfrac{dU_A}{dx_2^A}} = \frac{\dfrac{dU_B}{dx_1^B}}{\dfrac{dU_B}{dx_2^B}} \tag{14}$$

It may be shown (Daly and Giertz 1972a) that equation [13] and
equation [14] are equivalent so long as

$$\frac{dU_A}{dx_1^B}\frac{dU_B}{dx_2^B} = \frac{dU_A}{dx_2^B}\frac{dU_B}{dx_1^B} \tag{15}$$

and a sufficient (but not necessary) condition for equation [15] to hold is that

$$\frac{dU_A}{dx_1^B} = \frac{dU_A}{dx_2^B} = 0$$

This final condition implies, of course, that there exist no marginal
goods-specific externalities.

Our conclusion is therefore that in the presence of utility externalities
alone, Pareto optimality may be achieved with market-determined trade plus
financial transfers. Only where goods-specific externalities occur does interdependence lead to a requirement for subsidies or differentiated and 'non-
market' prices for consumers.

It should be noted that this result is not quite as modern as implied. Collard (1975, 1978) shows that Edgeworth (1881) was well aware of the effects of the introduction of such interdependent benevolence on the private trading or contract curve in what is now termed the Edgeworth-Bowley exchange diagram. In Collard's terms, the introduction of utility-externalities 'shrinks' the selfish contract curve, while the introduction of goods-specific externalities 'twists' it. Only when the contract curve is 'twisted' will there be a need for changing market prices to attain an optimum.

It is a matter of personal preference whether or not one is willing to be bound by application of the strict Paretian approach to such redistributional problems (Buchanan 1968). If one is willing to apply a Social Welfare Function framework then individual utility functions may be allowed to continue to be independent, and redistributional results arise from differential weights attached to individual utilities as they enter the social welfare function. It is this approach which has lead to the Optimal Taxation literature which attempts to simultaneously consider efficiency and equity considerations.

It is within this framework that Le Grand (1975), following Feldstein (1972) and Diamond and Mirrlees (1971), considers optimal public sector price discrimination amongst consumers. Here the explicit assumption is that cash transfers are not available. Le Grand finds that the product should be priced differentially between any two consumers A and B depending upon the consumer's own-price elasticities of demand and the social welfare weights given by the social welfare function to changes in household income.

Where there are many persons in an economy displaying interdependence characteristics several complications arise. Firstly, and fundamentally, the action of the competitive market and trade, with the implication of large numbers of participants facing a single unified price ratio, cannot bring about social welfare maximisation with differentiated social welfare weights, or a Pareto optimum in the presence of goods-specific externalities where the intensities of the externality differs amongst pairs of individuals. Larger amounts of consumption must be induced from those individuals whose consumption extends the larger external benefit and a lower price ratio must be offered to them. Such a discriminatory system is incompatable with a market system of competitive trading. Setting appropriate discriminatory prices would be, need it be said, hardly the simplest of processes for governmental agencies.

Secondly, in a world of interdependent utility externalities it is not clear that voluntary redistribution of the amount necessary to obtain a Pareto optimum will be forthcoming even though, as we have argued, only direct 'cash' transfers are necessary. This is because any redistribution made to those whose utilities confer external benefits on others is a public good in that all 'benevolent' individuals will gain from such action. As with any public good there arises a basic problem of strategic behaviour on the part of the potential donors normally called free-riding. It is argued that rational behaviour dictates that potential donors, rather than voluntarily donate, will refrain from instituting a transfer in the hope of obtaining an external benefit from others' actions without cost to themselves. If free-riding occurs the Pareto optimum will not be attained.

We ended the previous section of this survey by noting that consideration of the beneficiary of a redistributional transfer alone may lead to a presumption of superiority of cash transfers over in-kind subsidies. In this section it has been argued that when the situation of the donor as well as the beneficiary is considered, then a case may be made for subsidy systems where goods-specific externalities exist. Here, voluntary transfers under competitive prices cannot achieve an optimum and there arises a case for interference with market price signals.

5. Subsidies versus cash transfers

Although the above arguments may be read as a case for general governmental intervention in the redistributive system, the strongest case for subsidies as the means of redistribution does tend to rest upon the existence of goods-specific externalities. At the risk of some overkill, and as an introduction to some other arguments concerning the subsidy versus cash transfer debate, the simplest case is here again presented (Rodgers 1973).

In a two-person world where A receives a goods-specific externality from B's consumption of the single good (x), the socially optimal amount of consumption by B would be that amount such that marginal *social* benefit (MSB_x) is equal to marginal cost. Marginal social benefit here is the sum of B's marginal private benefit (MPB_x) plus marginal external benefit to A (MEB_x). A social optimum requires

$$MSB_x = MPB_x + MEB_x = MC_x = P_x \qquad [16]$$

where MC_x is the marginal cost of x, and P_x its competitive market price. However, as B will not take account of the external benefit that his increased consumption would have on A, B will consume that amount of x such that

$$MPB_x = P_x \qquad [17]$$

As for an external benefit $MEB > O$, equations [16] and [17] cannot hold simultaneously and the initial situation is not socially optimal. We may show this on Fig. 3.7, which shows diminishing marginal benefits and the vertical summation of marginal private benefit and marginal external benefit into marginal social benefit.

Here we have a constant marginal cost (OP) and we assume no income effects of price changes. B's private optimum is x_0 where equation [17] holds, whereas the social optimum is x_1 where equation [16] holds.

B's consumption of x may be encouraged by reducing the price he faces, and a price of P^1 would induce the socially optimal level x_1 where

$$MPB_x = P_x^1 < P_x$$

which would allow equation [16] to hold. But a cash transfer to B would not disturb the equality of equation [17] so that [16] cannot hold so long as any positive external benefit exists. In terms of the diagram a cash transfer will shift

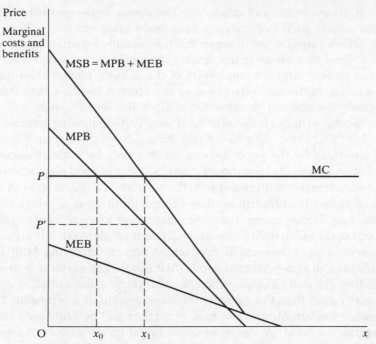

FIG. 3.7 Comparison of price reduction subsidy and cash transfer where external benefits exist

the MPB curve to the right. But this will also shift the MSB curve, as this is derived from the vertical addition of the private and external benefit curves, and the social optimum level of x will increase. We can only obtain the social optimum by means of a cash transfer by shifting the private benefit curve enough to reduce the marginal external benefit to zero. If marginal external benefits never fall to zero, cash transfers cannot achieve an optimum.

This argument has been coupled together with the observation that a large proportion of the assistance made available to the poor is, in fact, in the form of goods-specific subsidies rather than as cash transfers. The implication is then that goods-specific externalities are indeed important and widespread in order to justify such subsidy systems.

Browning (1975) has made a major attack upon the externalities case for subsidies over cash grants, as well as upon the implications that such externalities are large and extensive. As we have seen, the optimal subsidy system requires differential prices for different households according to the different external benefits generated. These external benefits are typically rather vague, difficult to evaluate, and display public good characteristics. As the information necessary to achieve optimal subsidisation is either unavailable or very costly to collect, subsidy systems in practice at the very most only take very crude account of private demands and circumstances. Many subsidy systems use no information on household situations at all. Thus, for practical purposes, the choice between subsidies and cash grants is a choice between methods neither of which can always attain full efficiency. The choice between such 'second-best' measures clearly then becomes a rather more open one.

Browning goes on to argue that it is possible for an inappropriate price subsidy to lead to such an inappropriate consumption level that a welfare loss accrues to society after the imposition of the subsidy greater than the welfare loss due to the initial non-attainment of the optimal level. A cash transfer will not normally be able to increase the welfare loss in this way.

Some writers (Johnson 1978; Pauly 1970) following Lancaster (1966) and Becker (1965) have pointed out that the goods-specific external benefits may not be generated by the goods themselves, but only by some characteristics of goods. For example, the 'nutritional' characteristics of food may be important as a source of external benefit rather than the 'palatability' characteristics. If food is subsidised rather than 'nutrition' then changes in the way in which nutrition is achieved may occur rather than the amount produced. The characteristics (nutrition) upon which utility ultimately depends are derived, it is argued, within the household by a household production process involving both marketed goods (food) and non-marketed goods (like time). The easier it is to substitute food for time the more likely it is that the method by which nutrition is produced will change rather than the amount. If food is subsidised it is possible that more convenience foods requiring less time to prepare will be purchased rather than more nutritional food. A simple example might be the effects of a subsidy on education reducing the efforts made by parents in providing instruction at home. The pattern of provision and production of education has changed while the total provided may remain constant.

As regards administration costs, it may be argued that there are likely to be very high administrative and policing costs in providing in-kind subsidies compared to providing cash transfers through, say, a negative income tax. Especially important here is the consideration of ensuring the non-marketability of goods differentially priced amongst the community which is required for in-kind subsidies not to be converted into cash equivalents. Tullock (1970) argues that insistence upon the non-marketability of subsidised vouchers creates a 'crime without a victim' and that the difficulties and costs of enforcement create a strong presumption in favour of cash. Olsen (1970) in reply points out that there is a 'victim' to the crime, the donor, who in the absence of a first-best subsidy system may prefer the initial non-optimum to one in which a cash grant equivalent (resultant from marketability) is provided. There can be a preference for enforced subsidy systems even where enforcement costs are high, and the case for subsidies depends upon the magnitude of these costs.

Browning also takes issue with the presumption that the empirical observation of the large numbers and importance of in-kind subsidies in existence is evidence to support the contention that there are widespread goods-specific externalities which give justification for such subsidies. He argues the political process is biased towards large-scale provision of subsidies and that the external benefits presumed may either not exist or be grossly overestimated. Recipients of the subsidy will prefer large subsidies regardless of any external benefits that might be resultant. Producers of subsidised goods will prefer subsidies favouring their goods to general cash transfers with a lower impact on the sales of their products. Bureaucrats will also prefer, it may be argued, the relatively large staffs and high budgets associated with in-kind programmes. On the other hand, other voters and pressure groups are provided with little information about the effects and costs of the complex in-kind subsidy systems about which they must choose. Cash transfers would be more readily understood and more easily analysed. For all these reasons then, it would be misleading to view the large-scale provision by the political system of in-kind subsidies as evidence of the existence of substantial goods-specific externalities.

As regards the complexity and lack of information about subsidies the argument of Tullock (1966) may be relevant. Here it is the perception of the donor about the effects of the transfer rather than the actuality that induces external benefits. An increase in the amount of information may then actually reduce the welfare of the donor if expectations are not realised (Giertz and Sullivan 1977; Marshall 1980).

Finally there is an argument against subsidies on the ethical and moral grounds often termed 'liberalism'. Although the liberal may support redistributional transfers, the paternalism implicit in subsidies designed to induce households to consume amounts and types of commodities they otherwise would not, has drawn no little fire from liberal economists (Rowley and Peacock 1975; Mishan 1972, 1975). Mishan argues that the liberal economist sees it as 'morally appropriate' that, as regards market goods, all adults should be treated as if they know their own interests best. The meddlesome, paternalistic interference in the liberty of the market place associated with in-kind transfers is therefore an indignity perpetrated on the poor. The liberal supports cash transfers as a means of redistribution not only because subsidies are·patronising but also because choice resides in the hands of the individual and not in the hands of an (overgrown) state bureaucracy.

There are, then, some important as well as emotionally strong arguments in favour of cash transfers over transfers by means of subsidy. Income transfers have advantages of simplicity and efficiency and are less open to charges of paternalism and arrogance on the part of donors. Nevertheless the existence of goods-specific externalities does give firm theoretical substance for the use of subsidy systems.

6. The measurement of subsidies

So far, the use of the term 'subsidy' has carried a specific and, it is to be hoped, a consistent idea of what constitutes a subsidy rather than some other form of governmental policy. It seems most useful, at least to this writer, to reserve the term subsidy for the intervention of government in the form of a reduced (relative) price of a *marketed* commodity which does not reduce the (absolute) price of that commodity to zero. This definition is by no means perfect but serves the useful purpose of differentiating subsidies from two other major forms of government action, namely cash/income transfers and supplements, and provision of goods through non-marketed modes at a zero direct price, for which the term subsidy has often been applied.

That the literature contains other, both broader and narrower, definitions and ideas of a subsidy should come as no surprise to the reader, and this section is devoted to an examination of various possible definitions and the problems which arise in applying them. An especially valuable and interesting survey of the concept and definition of subsidies is contained in Prest (1974).

The national accounting conventions define subsidies to be 'payments to a producer or trader having the effect of reducing selling prices below the factor costs of production, including the financing of deficits on public trading services deliberately run at a loss' (CSO 1968). Such a view of subsidies clearly excludes the receipt of subsidies *directly* by the personal sector. Subsidies will only benefit households to the extent that shifting and a reduced market price occurs. Within the national accounting system direct payments to individuals and households will come under the heading of 'grants to persons' whether they are cash grants or commodity-tied subsidies. There is obviously much scope for confusion. In an official study of subsidies in the UK, Stephenson and Harris (1977) explicitly include payments for rent rebates and allowances, even though on the above definition they are clearly not subsidies.

The internationally approved national accounting definition, dealing as it does with book-keeping flows of actual payments has two other striking drawbacks. Firstly much of the accounting procedure is concerned only with historic cost. When assets are long-lived, calculation of values of annual flows of services based on the historic cost of provision of the assets will be, in the absence of indexation or use of replacement cost, a misleading estimate of marketable value. The resulting view of a subsidy as a payment to reduce selling price below factor cost, when that factor cost is itself underestimated due to the use of historic costs, will be an underestimate of the subsidy to the consumer. This point will be taken up again when we consider housing subsidies.

Secondly there is the problem of 'imputation', a term which is often used for a situation where the reduction of price is achieved not through the positive action of use of existing government revenues, but by the negative action of, for example, not imposing taxation. The effects of the zero rating for value added tax on books, food and children's clothes in the UK can clearly be viewed as a subsidy, but because taxation funds are not actually received and transferred by government, the existence of such subsidies will not appear in national income accounts.

For the above reasons then, it is apparent that the existing conventions concerning subsidies within the accepted national accounts may grossly underestimate the extent and importance of subsidies within the economy.

Rather than the very narrow conventional view and definition of subsidies some writers have taken an overly broad view of the topic and have applied the term subsidy to any net benefit received by individuals resultant from governmental activities. This would include services provided by the state at zero direct cost to consumers, so that pure public goods publicly provided are included as a limiting case of good subsidised by 100 per cent. There is however, as Prest argues, a basic theoretical difference between pure public goods which are basically non-marketable and private goods which are marketable and whose market price may be managed. Although there do in practice exist goods and services which while clearly marketable have been largely removed from the market sector and provided by the state at zero direct charge (primary education, health services in the UK), it remains a useful exercise to reserve a special term for the management of goods and services which still retain their marketed characteristics. If subsidies are to be reserved for the means of management of private goods (possibly those displaying external effects) then the problem of whether goods provided at zero direct cost should be considered subsidised is an analogue to the debate whether pure public goods should be simply considered as a special case of goods displaying external effects. So long as a distinction is made between public goods and goods displaying externalities then a distinction between subsidised goods and goods provided at zero direct charge may be made.

It is tempting and common in the literature to view, and often to dismiss, subsidies as a form of negative indirect taxation. After all, an indirect tax must be paid according to the amount or value consumed and a price subsidy will be received in precisely the same way. In the long run under perfect competition and constant costs the market price of a good subject to an indirect specific tax will rise by precisely the amount of the per unit tax; a per unit subsidy will reduce the market price by the amount of the per unit subsidy. Analysis of the extent of incidence and shifting will normally be symmetric between indirect specific taxes and per unit price subsidies. Treatment is similar in many other ways also. For an indirect tax to be progressive in its impact on the distribution of income it is necessary that the average effective tax rate rise as income rises; for a subsidy it is required to fall with income. Indirect taxes lead to an excess burden which may be minimised by setting the amount of indirect tax on any commodity such that the proportional reduction in real-income-compensated demand is the same for all commodities or, where there are zero cross-price elasticities, set the tax per cent as proportional to the inverse of the own-price elasticities of demand.[5] With suitable changes this, the Ramsey Rule, holds for price subsidies also.

Once subsidies are accepted as the negative counterpart of indirect taxes then cash transfers may be similarly viewed as the negative counterpart of direct taxes. In their effects upon consumption patterns indirect taxes will normally involve both an income and a substitution effect, whereas direct taxes which do not change relative prices will normally only involve an income effect. The absence of a substitution effect for direct taxes and cash grants could prove to be a useful means of distinguishing between cash grants and price or other in-kind subsidies. As we have seen, the in-kind subsidy versus cash grant debate is very much along the same lines as the direct versus indirect tax debate.

However, there are several reasons why the superficially rather attractive notion of subsidies as negative taxes must be viewed with some care. The association between direct taxes and cash grants and indirect taxes with subsidies depends upon there being a clear and unambiguous distinction between direct and indirect taxation. The idea that they may be distinguished by the absence of substitution effects in the case of direct taxes is clearly untenable, as direct taxes will have a crucial effect upon the relative price of leisure and, therefore, a substitution effect appears within the work/leisure choice.

The very definitions of direct and indirect taxes are by no means either clear or generally accepted. The most common definitions are usually related to some idea of the final incidence of the tax, with the formal and effective incidence of the tax being presumed to be identical for direct taxes but differing (through shifting) for indirect taxes. It remains a dubious proposition that, for example, income tax cannot be shifted by means of wage bargaining or taxes on profits by means of pricing adjustments. The difficulties inherent in this approach have been such that some writers (Rolph 1968; Atkinson 1977) have concentrated upon the idea that direct taxes may be differentiated in that they may be adjusted or tailored to the individual circumstances of the taxpayer, whereas indirect taxes on transactions are independent of individual circumstances. The only way to relate indirect taxes to individual characteristics is *indirectly* through differing consumption patterns.

If this 'means-tested' approach is accepted then some rather curious results arise. For the subsidy systems described in section 2 above it is typically true that there exist means-tested entry to the schemes and sometimes means-tested price reductions. The only commonly non-means-tested subsidy system is the universal price-reduction subsidy, but for all others some measure of direct albeit crude tailoring to individual circumstances is normally available and applied. Thus subsidy systems other than universal do not involve negative indirect taxes but negative direct taxes; and universal fixed-sum cash grants or vouchers become negative indirect taxes.

There are other ways too in which the view of subsidies as negative taxes is not quite the simplification that it first appears. For many of the possible subsidy systems there is no obvious positive tax equivalent nor ever could be, except of the most arbitrary kind. There is, further, a measure of legal compulsion in taxation which is absent in subsidy systems, entry to which are, without fail, purely voluntary; a point which examination of the take-up rates for some subsidy systems makes obvious.[6]

When subsidies are viewed empirically, several of these conceptual problems arise. It is clear that consideration of subsidies resulting from a reduced price involves a counterfactual argument as regards the situation which would occur in the absence of the subsidy. If the subsidy per unit received by the consumer is the difference between the market price in the absence of the subsidy and the price actually paid, we obviously need to know that counterfactual market price. Even where the subsidy is measurable in flows of governmental finance the existence of shifting and the divergence of formal and effective incidence will normally mean that prices actually charged will not be below the non-subsidised market price by exactly the amount of the subsidy per unit. The possibility of shifting is normally explicitly ignored in such cases.

Even more intractable is the problem of subsidies which are not measurable as flows of governmental finance and which arise not out of action but rather out of non-action on the part of the State. This is a contentious area. Subsidies in this area often arise from the non-taxation or reduced taxation of certain goods and services, which clearly reduce relative prices compared with the situation which would arise were full taxes to be levied. The reduced tax revenues will not normally be recorded, and it must be decided what must be considered 'the generally accepted structure of a . . . tax that would exist in the absence of the use of tax incentives or tax reliefs'[7] for measurement to take place. Such tax exemptions have been called 'tax expenditures' (Willis and Hardwick 1978; Surrey 1973) and may occur for many reasons other than for the explicit encouragement of consumption of certain goods and services.

The criterion of 'generally accepted structure' is not too solid a foundation against which to judge tax expenditures. Questions whether, for example, the existence of a child allowance as part of the personal allowance within an income tax represents part of the normal structure of the tax, or whether it constitutes an incentive to reproduce (a subsidy on children) and, therefore, a tax expenditure, are moot. In fact the tax expenditure literature normally considers personal, married, and child allowances as part of the structure and not as tax expenditures. However, there clearly are some elements of the tax system the existence of which, whatever the reason for their introduction, constitute an inducement to rearrange consumption patterns. One of the most important of these tax expenditure subsidies is the reduction of the cost of owner-occupied housing due to non-taxation of the income-in-kind derived from owner-occupation, which is characteristic of many but not all western industrial economies. Similar subsidies commonly exist due to the preferential tax treatment of other kind of savings such as life assurance and pension schemes.

In the examination of the literature on food and housing subsidies that follows, many of the conceptual problems involved in identifying and measuring subsidies that have been discussed above arise.

7. Applications: subsidies on housing and food

Within the context of the mixed economy, by far the most common applications of subsidies to consumers as a strategy for manipulation of market prices lie in the two fields of housing and food. The following sections of this survey are concerned with the analysis of subsidies on these commodities, expenditure on which comprise a substantial proportion of household disposable income and consumption expenditure.

The different works cited are often concerned with different aspects of analysis, and the reader should bear in mind at least three of the more common threads that have run through the debate on subsidies:

(a) Considerations of the incidence and equity of the subsidy, including how the subsidy is distributed over different income classes and how important the subsidy is as a proportion of income. If the subsidy is a source of increasing equality of income, the proportion of the subsidy to income should fall as income increases.

(b) Consideration of the economic or allocative efficiency of the subsidy. As we have seen, the benefits derived from the subsidy system will differ from the amount of the subsidy itself, so that the size of the deadweight loss of a subsidy is, as far as it can be measured, an important aspect.

(c) Consideration of the effects of the subsidy system on consumption patterns. It is to be assumed that subsidy systems are, at least partly, imposed in order to increase the consumption of the goods subsidised, so that the effectiveness of the subsidy in doing so is an important factor.

As we shall see, all the analyses deal for the most part with the effects and distribution of particular subsidies in the isolation of a partial equilibrium setting. It has proved difficult to model and plot the effects of such subsidy systems within a general equilibrium framework, though such an approach is clearly not an impossible task (see, for example, Whalley 1975).

Also, most of the analyses deal with particular subsidies on their own, rather than as part of a total package of different subsidies and other redistributional policies. The total impact of all subsidies received by, for example, the poor may be very different from the impact of the particular subsidy under consideration. Similarly, it is difficult in practice to separate such effects upon individuals who benefit from many schemes.

HOUSING SUBSIDIES

Housing is a prime target for governmental intervention in the form of subsidies. Housing expenditure takes a large proportion of income, often around 30 per cent; it is easy to prevent the marketing of subsidised housing and therefore housing schemes are easily policed and administered. But probably the most important factor is that housing is an obvious, highly visible, solid and relatively permanent indication of poverty where it exists. It should therefore come as little surprise that housing subsidies tend to be extensive and substantial.

Subsidy policies towards housing prove to be variable and quite complex. Typically governments maintain a general supervisory role over housing through public health measures and standards, and they regulate land use through local zoning and planning regulations. Apart from this general supervision, governmental policy usually treats housing in different ways according to the tenure under which the dwelling is held. The major tenure groups comprise the publicly owned rental sector, and the private sectors of owner-occupied housing and private landlord rental housing, and we shall be considering subsidies in each of these areas in turn.

Subsidies in the private housing sector

Owner-occupation as a tenure has experienced a large increase in popularity in the post-war period. In the UK, in 1951 owner-occupied dwellings comprised under 30 per cent of all dwellings, but by 1977 this proportion had risen to about 56 per cent. The reasons for this phenomenon have been variously ascribed, but one reason is certainly the encouragement of a large subsidy given owner-occupation in the form of the favourable taxation of assets held in this manner.

The most obvious and important such aid for the owner-occupier has been the exemption from taxation of the income received in kind rather than as a flow of cash from owner-occupation. An individual who owns a house may either let it to others or occupy it himself. If he lets the dwelling, the net income he receives is subject to income tax. If he occupies it himself, he receives a non-monetary return from the dwelling equal to the market rental value of the property but this will not be subject to income taxation.

It should be noted that some nations do attempt some taxation of the return to owner-occupation and examples include West Germany, Italy, the Low Countries and Scandinavia, but the tax base is usually significantly less than the open market rental value (Willis and Hardwick 1978). The UK (since 1963), France, Ireland, US, Canada, Australia and New Zealand all exempt owner-occupier returns from income taxation.

The situation is confused by the position of owner-occupiers who still have mortgages or home loans outstanding. If income is defined as the net return to capital then only that part of the return from housing that results from the equity owned in the property should be counted as part of taxable income. In the US and UK,[8] but not in Australia, for example, interest payments on mortgages raised for the finance of owner-occupation are exempt from income taxation. The existence of such exemptions on mortgage interest payments in fact rather simplifies the situation, as it may be shown that the ability to offset mortgage interest is a device by which the owner-occupier, whether a mortgage holder or not, obtains the same tax exemption subsidy.

Following Rosenthal (1975), we may compare the situation of the owner-occupier under the UK tax laws with the situation in which he would find himself as a renter facing a free market rent, to show the advantage accruing from favourable tax treatment.

For the simplest case, assume that the rate of return on all forms of capital is equal to the mortgage interest rate (i), and that the owner-occupier and renter live in identical houses with a market sale value of P. If M is the total of maintenance and other running costs then the competitive equilibrium rent charged for the property will be ($iP + M$), and if t is the tax rate and Y_r the gross income of the renter the disposable income after tax and housing costs of the renter will be

$$Y'_r = Y_r(1 - t) - M - iP \qquad [18]$$

If E is the equity held as housing then the amount of any mortgage held by the owner-occupier will be $(P - E)$ with interest payments of $i(P - E)$. If the owner-occupier with pecuniary income of Y_0 receives a tax rebate on mortgage interest then after tax, rebate, interest payments and running costs his disposable income will be

$$Y'_0 = Y_0(1 - t) - M - i(P - E)(1 - t) \qquad [19]$$

Now the intention is of course to compare the final disposable incomes of the renter and the owner-occupier, but in order to compare like with like we must ensure that initial gross incomes are equal. As the owner-occupier receives a gross money income of Y_0, plus non-pecuniary income-in-kind from owner-occupation of iE, we require:

$$Y_r = Y_0 + iE \qquad [20]$$

The difference between the after tax and housing costs income of owner-occupier and renter will be the subsidy accruing to the owner-occupier through the tax system. Subtracting [18] from [19]

$$Y'_0 - Y'_r = (Y_0 - Y_r)(1 - t) + iE(1 - t) + tiP \qquad [21]$$

But from equation [20]

$$Y_0 - Y_r = -iE$$

Therefore, subsidy

$$= Y'_0 - Y'_r = tiP \qquad [22]$$

Thus the owner-occupier subsidy is equal to the amount of tax not paid on the annual rental value of the property occupied, which is independent of equity held. Were mortgage interest payments not tax deductible, the same procedure indicates that the subsidy would be tiE, which does depend upon equity held. Far from being the total subsidy received by the owner-occupier, as believed by many writers, the amount of the non-payment of tax on mortgage interest is only that part which ensures the subsidy received by the mortgage holder is equal to that received by the outright owner; but this only strictly holds for competitive equilibrium, and where the mortgage rate accurately reflects rates of return on all capital.

As has been commonly noted, the amount of the tax forgone by the authorities will normally be expected to rise with income. This is because both the tax rate (t) and the market value of housing consumed (P), as well as the probability of becoming an owner-occupier, all tend to rise with income. The owner-occupier imputed rent tax exemption subsidy seems to be an *ad valorem* price-reduction subsidy system. Except for an upper limit imposed in the UK, it is unconstrained and entry to the scheme is not restricted by the authorities.

Consideration of the effects of the tax exemption of the imputed return from owner-occupation in the US followed the work of Goode (1960), who considers the distribution of the subsidy over income classes. His general findings, that the subsidy discriminates against renters, favours high income groups and stimulates home ownership have seldom since been challenged. Aaron (1970, 1972) using data on the tax position of households, computes the changes in tax liabilities that would result from modifications in the tax laws relating to housing. A major finding is that if the tax exemption of imputed net rent on owner-occupied housing were disallowed, the increase in tax as a percentage of income would vary considerably with income. Although the percentage does tend to increase with income the trend is very variable. Aaron argues that the effect on housing consumption is substantial, and makes special note of the possibility of consumers switching between the rental sector and owner-occupation. His argument that rents in the rental sector would fall, presumably as a result of a decrease in the number of renters and imperfect substitutability between rental and owner dwellings, has caused some confusion (Rolph 1973) and alternative results have appeared. Aaron estimates the total cost to the tax authorities of the exemption to be of the order of $7–9 billion in 1966, which may be compared to a $42 billion total collected from income tax overall.

Laidler (1969) attempts to measure the deadweight welfare loss due to the owner-occupier subsidy on the Marshallian basis of excess burden described above and illustrated on Fig. 3.5 (p.88). The method is as follows. For each of several income groups the proportionate reduction in private cost per unit below constant marginal social cost due to the subsidy is derived. It will be remembered that the owner-occupier subsidy depends upon the tax rate and therefore upon the income band. Taking a single price elasticity of -1.5 along with information on the quantity of housing consumed by each income band the change in housing consumed because of the subsidy may be calculated. All the information required for evaluating the difference between the total social and private cost of the overinvestment in housing is now available, and assuming linear demand functions the area of the welfare loss triangle (*agb* in Fig. 3.5) may be simply derived for each income group and overall. Laidler's result shows that the deadweight loss is relatively small per capita ($2.50 per annum) but really relatively large in total.

The framework used by Aaron and Laidler includes an assumption of a perfectly price-elastic supply of housing in the long run, at least over the relevant range, which is a common assumption always justified by reference to the work of Muth (1960). In such circumstances the subsidy causes no change in the market price of housing, and a flow of benefits will be generated to new and existing homeowners.

However, this assumption has not met with general approval. Rolph (1973) presents some results for a housing model using the alternative extreme version of the supply curve, that of fixed supply or perfect inelasticity. Here the subsidy will be fully capitalised into the value of property as consumers bid up the price of housing until the perceived price of owner-occupied housing, including the subsidy, is again just equal to the opportunity cost of renting. Existing owners obtain a capital gain but potential buyers find that the increase in house prices fully offsets the value of the subsidy, so they receive no benefit from the scheme. This view is also taken by Kay and King (1978).

When the supply curve is no longer taken as horizontal there arises the possibility of discriminatory effects not only between owners and non-owners, but also among owners themselves. If the effect of the owner-occupier subsidy is to increase the price of housing overall, but the cost of housing is differentially reduced amongst income classes because of the subsidy, then the overall rise in price for the relatively poor may more than outweigh the savings made because of the subsidy. Shreiber (1978) presents an illustrative numerical example of such a situation where the introduction of an imputed rental subsidy is not only discriminatory against the poorer owner-occupier but positively harmful.

When alternative supply elasticities and the movement of dwellings from the rental to the owner-occupier sector are allowed, the calculation of the consumer surplus benefit and the deadweight welfare loss of the subsidy, even using the Marshallian method, becomes rather more problematic. White and White (1977) attempt a re-estimate of the Laidler model employing a positive supply elasticity and substitutability between rental and owner-occupied dwellings, but without the possibility of renters changing their tenure to owners.

Considering just the effect of the introduction of a finite supply elasticity a diagram such as Fig. 3.8 results. If before the introduction of the subsidy the demand curve is $d_0 d_0$ and the supply curve SS then the initial price per unit is P_0.

The most useful way of introducing the effect of the subsidy in these circumstances is to represent it as shifting the demand curve to the right, to $d_0' d_0'$. This will increase the market price of housing to P_1, but, net of the subsidy, the perceived price to the owner-occupier will be only P_2 and demand will therefore increase from Q_0 to Q_2. The total cost of the subsidy is clearly equal to the area $P_1 b c P_2$. There will be an increase in consumer surplus shown by area $P_0 a c P_2$ and an increase in producer surplus of area $P_1 b a P_0$. There are

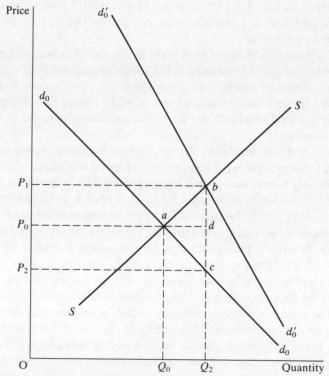

FIG. 3.8 Welfare gains and losses of owner-occupier housing subsidy with finite supply elasticity

clearly now two sources of welfare loss; a deadweight loss on new resources drafted into housing (triangle *abd*) in addition to the traditional welfare loss measure (triangle *adc*). It may be seen that as the elasticity of the supply curve passing through point *a* is altered so the relative and absolute sizes of these welfare loss triangles alter. When the supply curve is horizontal, as with Laidler, only the traditional consumer surplus loss remains positive; and when the supply curve is vertical both triangles disappear.

However, White and White are concerned to introduce the effects of the owner-occupier subsidy on the rental market sector of the housing market. As the overall market price of housing rises, so the price within the rental sector will rise. This price rise will lead to a third source of deadweight welfare loss, that of a consumer surplus loss to renters. This particular source of welfare loss will remain positive with a vertical supply curve even though the other two measures are reduced to zero. There is therefore an important conclusion that when a subsidy applies only to part of the market or differentially to sub-sections, then analyses carried out on the aggregate structure only will be misleading. In addition to a deadweight welfare loss, renters incur direct losses from the introduction of the owner-occupier subsidy in the form of increased rents.

White and White replicate Laidler's model for the tax allowance subsidy to owner-occupiers in the US for 1970, using a price elasticity of -1.5 and a supply elasticity of unity (amongst others). Of the total $10.23 billion programme cost, they find that only 53 per cent accrues to owner-occupiers as consumers, with 38 per cent coming in the form of capital gains. Of the rest, 7 per cent is total deadweight loss and the remainder accrues to landlords and producers transferring resources into the owner-occupied sector. One important result is the impact upon the rental sector. Renters' higher rentals plus their deadweight loss amount to some 18 per cent of the programme cost so that the cost to renters of the owner-occupier subsidy is therefore substantial.

Although the actual value of the price elasticity of supply (and, indeed, demand) remains unresolved, Rosen (1979) has examined empirically one of the other pieces in the jigsaw required for a complete analysis of the imputed rental subsidy; that of the possible switching of consumers between the rental and owner-occupier sectors in response to the subsidy. Rosen's study again re-estimates the Laidler model but allowing tenure choice changes as well as increased consumption by owner-occupiers themselves. The econometric analysis is made in two stages. Firstly he presents a regression analysis of owner-occupied housing demand which allows for the possibility of different price elasticities at different income levels, and secondly a probit analysis of tenure choice where the probability of being an owner depends upon income, relative prices in the two sectors, and a series of household characteristics. The results indicate a central estimate of an income elasticity of demand of about 0.76 and a price elasticity which increases with income and centres around unity. Estimates of the welfare loss in the Laidler model using these results, which therefore allow for tenure choice changes but not for finite supply elasticities, show that distributed over income classes the excess burden rises, then falls with income.

Rosen goes on to simulate the induced changes in income and tenure choice from different possible tax regimes. As the tax exemptions are removed there is a substantial decrease in owner-occupied housing demand and in the proportions of owners, and there seems to be a clear effect of redistribution of disposable income away from higher income groups.

Much of the debate on the incidence and effect of the imputed rental tax exemption subsidy has taken place within the US context, although the position in the UK and other countries is very similar. In Britain there has been a noticeable reluctance to admit even the existence of such a subsidy (exemplified by the official policy document, the Housing Policy Review (1977), which finally admitted only mortgage interest tax relief as an owner-occupier subsidy) let alone any significant analysis of incidence, effect, benefit and efficiency. This is possibly due to the complete absence in Britain of any major housing sector that could serve as an approximation to an open or free market as a 'control' against which the owner-occupied subsidy could be judged. Honourable exceptions are Hughes (1979), King and Atkinson (1980) and Willis and Hardwick (1978), all of whom attempt a comparison between the existing system and some form of 'normal' or 'neutral' tax base, but only Hughes attempts an analysis of the distribution over income classes using data on household income and expenditure. His findings, for 1973, show that the amount of the subsidy tends to rise with income, varies little for the middle income groups and changes dramatically only for very low and very high incomes.

The Laidler welfare loss model of the owner-occupier tax exemption subsidy has been applied to the situation in Australia by Reece (1975). He argues that the actual amount of the per capita deadweight welfare loss is so small as to challenge the power of the economic and allocative efficiency case for reform of the owner-occupier subsidy system. His argument is that it is the effects on equity and the distribution of disposable income that provide much the stronger case for reform given the substantial tax savings accruing to high income groups.

This argument is indicative of general opinion within the literature about the general efficacy of the tax exemption of the imputed income in kind from owner-occupation, which accrues mainly to high income sectors in large amounts that increase with income. 'Such inequitable subsidies are defensible ... only if the national goal is to encourage the relatively well-to-do to buy even better housing than they would buy without a subsidy' (Aaron, 1972:163), '... to continue a policy that enables wealthy businessmen, lawyers, doctors, engineers and university professors to buy large quantities of housing services at bargain prices remains an obstacle to the goal of reducing the cost of housing to lower income groups' (Rolph 1973:484), ' ... a system of housing finance which is greatly distorted by taxation ... and leads both to patent inequalities and to a bizarre pattern of incentives' (King and Atkinson 1980:15).

Although the exemption from taxation of the imputed net income from owner-occupation is probably the most important, it is by no means the only advantage gained by holding wealth in the form of owner-occupied housing rather than in some other way. In Britain, and in other countries, owner-occupiers are exempt from payment on any capital gain that accrues from appreciation of the market value of the occupied property.

In fact much attention has been paid to this tax exemption, at least at a casual level. In practice the tax laws make tax payable on money capital gains rather than on real capital gains. In a time of general inflation a rise in the monetary value of an asset will attract taxation even when there has been no real capital gain, unless of course there is allowance for indexation or for the use of replacement cost rather than historic cost in tax accounting exercises. Therefore, in a time of high inflation, the exemption of owner-occupier housing from the taxation of capital gains has proved of great value to owner-occupiers, as demonstrated by the estimates of Willis and Hardwick.[9] However, that money rather than real capital gains be taxable seems an extremely dubious proposition for any logically-based tax structure of any 'neutral' character. In addition, at least in the UK, the real capital gain on owner-occupied housing, once an allowance is made for the continuing increase in the quality of the housing stock since the Second World War, seems to be either very small or negligible (see, for example, King and Atkinson 1980). However, the existence of discriminatory taxation as regards capital gains in practice may have important effects on tenure choice (Weiss 1978).

Within the private housing market sector there does exist a form of subsidisation of consumers which does not arise directly from government, but indirectly through the imposition of rent controls and regulation on the privately rented landlord sector. If, as is normal, rent is controlled at less than market rates then a reduction in price results in an in-kind subsidy, the costs of which are borne primarily by those landlords who own assets when controls are introduced.

Rent control has been picked out as a major cause of the decline and predicament of the privately rented sector of the housing market where such control exists, although, as we have seen, the spill-over effects from the subsidisation of owner-occupation must also have played a part. One of the more curious aspects of the situation is that the private rental sector is often that sector which contains the least well-off of the community, yet it is this tenure group that receives least direct aid from government. The reaction on the part of private landlords, at least in Britain where rent control has existed in various degrees and to a varying extent since 1915, has been to run down their investments by failure to maintain or by sale into the owner-occupier sector (see Robinson 1979: ch.6). The private rental sector in Britain has declined from over 90 per cent of the total housing stock before the First World War to about 15 per cent in 1977, and now contains by far the worst quality housing of any sector (Housing Policy Review 1977: ch.8).

The major economic analysis of the effects and distribution of benefits of rent control is again American, that of Olsen (1972) who examines rent control in New York in 1968. This study which estimated firstly the open market rental which would obtain for dwellings in the absence of rent control, and secondly the quantity of housing which households would demand within the open market, concludes that rent controlled tenants consume about 4 per cent *less* housing than they otherwise would. This is because the availability of controlled dwellings does not allow optimisation subject to the lower price, so the subsidy is of a highly constrained variety. Of the estimated $514 million cost incurred by landlords only $270 million accrues to tenants in the form of Marshallian benefit, equivalent to a 3.4 per cent increase in income which leaves a sizable excess burden of deadweight welfare loss. As far as redistributive effects are concerned, there does seems to be some relative redistribution to the poorer tenant, but Olsen concludes that rent control is a 'poorly (*sic*) focused redistributive device'.

Even though rent control is much more important in Britain, no such detailed analysis has appeared, probably due to the lack of an open sector of the rental market which could serve in order to obtain the necessary estimates of market prices and demand. Hughes (1979) attempts to use the owner-occupier sector as a basis for estimation of the market value of rental accommodation, but the results of the procedure are not presented as a distribution over income classes. Hughes does make the nice point that the subsidy received from landlords by private tenants (and by local authority tenants) is not counted as part of tenants' taxable income and hence constitutes a tax expenditure subsidy on the part of government.

Subsidies in the public housing sector

The other major sector of housing tenure is that constituting public housing schemes, which in Britain, where the term 'public house' has a rather different meaning, is normally called council or local authority housing. In Britain 30 per cent of dwellings are owned by local housing authorities whilst in the US public housing schemes constitute barely 1 per cent of the housing stock.

Public housing schemes in general work quite simply in an all-or-nothing manner. Governmental agencies offer particular dwelling units to selected households at rentals which are implicitly or explicitly below that which would be charged by the market. Households are free to accept or reject the offer but once accepted will find it difficult to alter the quantity of housing consumed so long as they stay within the scheme. The difference between market rentals and the actual rent charged is, of course, the amount of the total subsidy per unit time to the beneficiaries of the system. As the actual rents charged are directly observable, the basic problem in attempting to estimate the subsidy amount is in providing an adequate measure of 'notional' open market rental values.

In the US, studies by Bish (1969) and Aaron (1972) make use of legal restrictions on the relationship between the possible rent chargeable for a public housing unit and its private market value. A 20 per cent gap must exist, by law, between the private market rent and the maximum rent chargeable for a particular type of dwelling unit. From data on maximum chargeable rents, private market rents are determined and the difference between this amount and the actual rent paid is then the subsidy. For 1965 Bish finds that the amount of the subsidy is large as a percentage of the income of recipients, falls as income rises and implies a large increase in housing consumption for the relatively poor.

Calculation of open market rentals based on such legal restrictions relies perhaps a little too much on the discretion of local housing authority managers in determining the 'gap rents', and a more objective, but not necessarily more accurate, method is to use empirical relationships between housing characteristics and rentals in the open market sectors. Once a reliable relationship is established, the characteristics of public housing dwellings may be 'plugged in' to obtain a market rental estimate. This is the technique employed by Murray (1975) and by Kraft and Kraft (1979). Both these studies go on to estimate the consumer-surplus-based benefits of the subsidy to recipients, Kraft and Kraft using the Marshallian model of Olsen (1972), whilst Murray uses the Hicksian equivalent variation method based upon three different forms of utility function. These methods have already been outlined above.

Murray's application is to public housing in 1968 and his 'best' estimates, using the generalised constant elasticity of substitution utility function, are that benefits amount to about 84 per cent of the total subsidy which increases participants' income by about 35 per cent on average. Benefits tend to fall as income rises. Kraft and Kraft's Marshallian-based estimates assume a unitary price elasticity of demand (which Murray's work rejects) and find that, for 1971, benefits were on average about 68 per cent of the subsidy, contributed 22 per cent to participants' income and again tended to fall as income rose. They also find that public housing schemes were quite efficient at increasing housing consumed (by 59%) whilst consumption of other goods increased relatively little (by 5%).

In the UK, publicly-owned housing is mostly administered by local authorities and councils. Entry to local authority housing is much less determined by means-testing than in the US, and is normally conditioned by family circumstances such as family size and existing housing conditions.

Rents of council dwellings are usually set such that the Housing Revenue Account of each authority balances. The income side of the account is mainly composed of the total of rents received plus payments directly from central government. There may also be contributions from local taxation funds. The expenditure side consists mainly of costs of supervision, maintenance and repairs and the loan charges accruing from the costs incurred in the initial provision of the dwellings. A major source of confusion arises because, under the national accounting conventions the fixed payments into the account from central and local tax funds are recorded as subsidies, respectively termed the Exchequer Subsidy and the Rate Subsidy, and these amounts are often used as measuring the subsidy received by local authority tenants. This would be correct only if the expenditure side of the accounts properly measured the market value of the services derived from the local authority housing stock. As it stands, however, the loan charges recorded are the costs of servicing the loans raised to build dwellings sometimes 40 or 50 years into the past. These loan charges are, therefore, a reflection of historic cost which because of inflation grossly understate market value or replacement cost. Only on newly constructed dwellings financed at a market rate of interest will the Exchequer plus Rate Subsidy method accurately reflect the difference between market value and actual rent which properly measures the subsidy to tenants.

The literature on the British housing market contains numerous examples of work which equates the subsidy to council house tenants with the Exchequer and the Rate financial assistance to local authorities (Housing Policy Review 1977; Nevitt 1966, for example), but very few which attempt to develop a procedure by which the subsidy to council tenants may be derived from market valuations of the services obtained.

Rosenthal (1975, 1977) uses the owner-occupier sector as a proxy through which council dwellings may be priced. In Britain each dwelling, no matter the tenure, is assessed for local taxation purposes and this assessment, termed rateable value, is generally an increasing function of the services derived from the dwelling. Dwellings with equal rateable values may be treated as embodying identical amounts of housing. The relationship between rateable value and purchase price in the owner-occupier sector is determined, and may be used to predict, from the rateable value of council tenancies, a notional market selling price. The value of the flow of services from the council dwelling may then be derived by application of an appropriate rate of return on assets to obtain an estimated market rent and hence, by subtraction of actual rents paid, the subsidy to council tenants. Rosenthal's findings, for selected towns in 1968 and for the whole country in 1969, show that the sum of Exchequer and Rate Subsidies understates the subsidy received by council tenants by a factor of about four or five. He finds that the amount of the subsidy is large, amounting to about 14 per cent of the measured income of participants on average but much more for lower incomes. The amount of the subsidy tends to rise mildly with income but to fall sharply as a percentage of income as income rises. He is able to find at most only a mildly positive effect on housing consumption. Hughes (1979), as we have seen, uses a similar method to estimate housing subsidies, and finds that over all members of an income group the council house subsidy tends to fall with income, but this may be due to the declining proportion of council tenants in relatively high income classes.

This survey of the literature by no means exhausts the current discussion on the existence of housing subsidies. Interesting problems arise with, for example, housing allowances and rent rebates where the state finances means-tested rent reduction systems on private rental tenancies (Ricketts 1976; Carlton and Ferreira 1977; Murray 1977). These have not been explicitly examined. However, something at least has been shown of the conceptual and empirical problems which arise in an examination of the role of housing subsidies in the economy, and we move on to an examination of subsidies on food.

FOOD SUBSIDIES

Policies on the subsidisation of food consumption also illustrate many of the points previously made about consumer subsidies in a more general context. As expenditure on food comprises a large proportion of total expenditure as well as being a socially 'meritorious' expenditure, food becomes a strong candidate for in-kind subsidies for social aims. As the proportion of total income spent on food normally decreases as income rises, universal price-reduction schemes should have an effect similar to that of progressively distributed direct aid, in that the value of the subsidy as a proportion of income falls as income rises. Such a result is progressive even though the absolute amount of subsidy rises as income rises, because the relative difference between highest and lowest incomes is reduced.

In the UK, there has recently been a large-scale universal price-reduction scheme for the subsidisation of some food products. This began in 1974, introduced by the then Labour Government as part of the social contract with the trade unions. The explicit stated aim of the food subsidy scheme was to 'maintain the living standards of lower income household'[10] within a period of rising inflation. The scheme that was introduced augmented and extended food subsidies which were already being paid from EEC funds, though we shall only consider those subsidies financed by the UK government. The dominant item in the system was milk, but included were bread, cheese, butter, flour and tea. Table 3.1 shows the cost to the Exchequer of these food subsidies for 1974–78. The method of payment of the subsidies was one of direct reimbursement to food distributors of specific amounts per unit sold, so that both households and caterers would benefit. The final row of the table shows the estimated amount of the subsidy allocated to households rather than directly to caterers. These figures make no allowance for any possible non-complete shifting of incidence to consumers, which may be justified because of the large-scale statutory intervention by the government into food prices introduced alongside the subsidy scheme.

Stephenson and Harris (1977) present an analysis of the redistributional effects of the subsidy scheme for 1975, which shows that the food subsidy amounted to about 1 per cent of household disposable income on average, and fell as a proportion of income as income rises. The method used is to

TABLE 3.1   Cost of food subsidies on specific items finance by the UK Government 1974–78 (£ million)

	1974	1975	1976	1977	1978
Bread	41	83	58	19	—
Butter	43	89	80	13	22
Cheese	22	64	49	12	—
Milk	277	359	229	182	—
Flour	2	8	8	4	—
Tea	10	30	24	—	—
Total:	395	633	448	230	22
Allocated to households:	371	575	407	213	20

Sources: 1974–75, Stephenson and Harris 1977 : 100/Table b; 1976–78, Personal correspondence with Central Statistical Office 1980.

calculate the subsidy on each food category as a proportion of total consumer expenditure on that category. The factors obtained are then applied to information on household types, income and expenditure obtained from the Family Expenditure Survey.

This study draws insufficient attention to the fact that, in absolute terms, higher income groups benefited to a much greater extent than lower income groups, resulting from their relatively higher general consumption of all subsidised categories of food. Witt and Newbould (1976), whose calculations for 1974 were based upon a similar approach to that of Stephenson and Harris, concentrate on this point. They conclude that 63 per cent of food subsidy expenditure was received by higher than average income households. This conclusion, though surprising, is consistent with a falling average subsidy rate, and clearly demonstrates the high cost of redistributing income through a universal subsidy system. Because all households benefit, universal schemes are relatively inefficient at directing aid to a specific group. Still, McClements (1978), argues that food subsidies are in practice more progressive than some other measures which have more explicitly redistributional aims.

Dodgson (1980) examines these food subsidies from the point of view of their effect upon an assumed social welfare function, where the weights given the income of households fall as income rises. Using this system he notes that some food subsidy components notably tea, bread and flour are more effective at increasing the value of the social welfare function than others. He also notes, however, that the same resources put into social security supplementary benefit payments would have had a much greater impact on the value of the social welfare function.

Whether the limited results of the 1974–78 food subsidy programme in the UK, which included an estimated 1 per cent lowering of the Retail Price Index (Stephenson and Harris), can justify the cost of the scheme, even without consideration of administrative costs and deadweight welfare loss, is doubtful. In 1977, except for butter, the scheme was phased out.

Another source of universal food subsidisation in the UK comes in the form of a tax expenditure due to the zero-rating of food, amongst others, for value added tax. Value added tax is a tax on the value of all output, with the important provision that sellers may recoup any tax that has already been paid on inputs to their production processes. As intermediate goods do not carry the tax, it becomes a general consumption tax. Since inception in Britain in 1973, various standard rates and higher, 'luxury' rates have been chargeable, but at the time of writing a uniform 15 per cent applies. However, as well as the standard rate, some commodities are exempt and some are zero rated. Neither of these types of goods charges tax, but only zero-rated goods may have the VAT paid on inputs reclaimed. Zero-rated commodities include food, books, water, fuel and power, transport, children's clothes and exports.

Although VAT is a proportional tax, the proportion of income used on consumption in general falls with income, so it might be expected that VAT would be regressive in its impact upon the income distribution. However, the existence and importance of the zero-rated items makes VAT one of the more progressive of the UK indirect taxes,[11] acting rather like a personal allowance for income taxes (Adams 1980).

The UK is not alone in giving preferential tax treatment to expenditure on food. In the nations of the EEC it is normal for a reduced rate of VAT to be applied to food, though not normally one of zero. In the US there is, typically, exemption of food from sales taxation and there is general agreement that this exemption increases the progressivity of the sales tax (Schaefer 1969). One interesting aspect of the US literature is that Schaefer, and Davies (1969), show that another exempted commodity, that of clothing, seems to reduce the degree of progressivity of the sales tax. In Canada too the exemption of food from sales taxation is a major element contributing to the lessening of the basically regressive structure of such a tax (Ruggeri 1978).

Indeed, the subsidisation of food through exemptions to general consumption taxes is now often justified on the grounds of lessening the regressive impact of indirect taxes rather than on any efficiency grounds (Kay and King 1978, for example). This seems, at least to this writer, a rather roundabout way of introducing a progressive element to the tax structure, and implicitly raises the subsidy versus cash transfer issue yet again. It is true to say however that what literature that exists on universal food subsidies has certainly concentrated upon the redistributional elements.

Means-tested or other directly discriminatory food subsidies concentrating upon specific groups tend to be much less common than the universal systems described above (see Davis 1977).

The most apparent and by far the most extensive and important example of a selective, means-tested food subsidy scheme is the Food Stamp Program initiated in the US by the Food Stamp Act of 1964. Entitlement to entry to the scheme is based on income and family size criteria, and the system works by participants buying a determined amount of food stamps at a cost roughly equal to the household's normal monthly expenditure on food. The average price charged per stamp therefore varies with income (Bryant 1972). These stamps may then be exchanged for food with a market value well above their price, which is meant to enable the attainment of an adequate diet. Food stamps in this form are a classic example of a voucher system.

Clarkson (1975, 1976) contains the most ambitious empirical analysis, and attempts to measure the consumer surplus benefits derivable from the Food Stamp Program in its 1973 form. This benefit estimate is obtained from the procedure developed by DeSalvo (1971) for evaluating public housing schemes, described above, which assumes a Cobb-Douglas utility function specification and which, crucially, implies constant unitary price and income elasticities of demand. This is much more difficult to justify for food than for housing expenditure. Also required are identical preference patterns for all, constancy of the work/leisure choice and non-marketability of the stamps.

Clarkson presents the costs of the food stamp subsidy, the 'bonus value', as $2.1 billion in 1973 and at $3.6 billion in 1975. For 1972–73, he estimates both the amount of the subsidy and benefit received by beneficiaries distributed over income classes. The amount of the subsidy clearly falls as income rises, whereas the benefit rises over the lowest classes of income before declining. He estimates that, on average, each $1.00 provided through food stamps was worth less than 83 cents in terms of benefit to recipients. In addition to this welfare loss there were also administrative costs of over 9 cents per dollar of subsidy. However, Clarkson does argue that the food stamps were more effective in increasing food consumption than an equal cost cash transfer would be.

Although Clarkson stresses that food stamps seem not to be a particularly efficient means of redistributing income, the work of Benus, Kmenta and Shapiro (1976) also seems to indicate that food stamps have a different impact on food consumption than cash grants. The marginal propensity to consume food out of food subsidies they estimate at over ten times as great as the propensity to consume food out of income or general transfers.

Clarkson makes some other interesting observations. Participation in the scheme, for which over twelve million households are eligible, is low (only 31 per cent of eligible households) and variable among income and household size characteristics; but participation rates are explained better by the estimated value of net benefit than by the amount of the gross subsidy itself. As the benefits to consumers are less than the market value of the stamps, there is a clear temptation fraudulently to convert stamps into general purchasing power, and cases of fraud run into thousands annually. Giertz and Sullivan (1978) report that journalistic accounts cite a going price of about 75 cents per dollar of stamps; and Clarkson reports a 50 per cent rate, as well as that stamps have been used to purchase such diverse non-food products as automobiles and marijuana. Other works on the food stamp subsidy programme in the US are contained in Galatin (1973), Storey (1976), Giertz and Sullivan (1977), MacDonald (1977), and Browning (1978).

That, with the glaring exception of the food stamp programme in the US, food subsidy systems have been mostly universal in nature rather than selective should not come as too much of a surprise. Selective systems do get the resources where they are most required, but food is an easily marketed commodity. The organisational, administrative and enforcement costs are high, and fraud is encouraged. Finally, unless carefully constructed, selective schemes may extend the poverty trap and, certainly in Britain, the necessary means-testing will often be considered an unwarranted and unacceptable intrusion.

8. Concluding remarks

Subsidies as a means of governmental intervention into the workings of market economies are in practice of major importance as a tool for regulation and income redistribution. The analysis of the role and impact of subsidy systems involves considerations which are unique in public policy evaluation, and which are badly served by the dismissal of subsidies as merely negative taxes.

The difficulties which must be faced in order properly to identify and evaluate subsidy systems are not, however, to be underestimated. This is of course true for all empirical and applied work. Nevertheless, we do well to bear in mind that 'there is more to be said for rough estimates of the precise concept than precise estimates of economically irrelevant concepts' (Mishan 1971).

Notes

1. For a textbook exposition of Marshallian consumer surplus and the strict assumptions necessary for its validity see, for example, Laidler (1974:49–57).
2. For an exposition of the derivation of the compensated real-income-constant demand curve and the associated Hicksian measures of consumer surplus see, for example, Winch (1971:135–43) and Bilas (1971:97–107).
3. These demand functions may be derived as follows:

   From equation [2]

   $$x = \frac{y - \alpha p_h h}{p_x}$$

   Substituting into [1]

   $$U = h^\beta \left[\frac{y - \alpha p_h h}{p_x} \right]^{1-\beta}$$

   Differentiating, optimising and noting that the second order conditions for a utility maximum hold,

   $$\frac{dU}{dh} = \left[\frac{y - \alpha p_h h}{p_x} \right]^{1-\beta} [\beta h^{\beta-1}] - h^\beta \left[\frac{(1-\beta)\alpha p_h}{p_x} \left(\frac{y - \alpha p_h h}{p_x} \right)^{-\beta} \right] = 0$$

   This expression conveniently simplified to

   $$\frac{dU}{dh} = \frac{\beta y}{h} - \alpha p_h = 0$$

   Hence

   $$h = \beta y / \alpha p_h$$

   And symmetrically

   $$x = (1 - \beta) y / p_x$$

4. Rather than benevolence, malevolence to others can also be incorporated into models of this kind and may similarly lead to voluntary redistribution, in this case 'away from' the rich rather than 'towards' the poor (Brennan 1973).
5. For derivation of these and other optimal indirect tax rules, see Diamond and Mirrlees (1971) and Atkinson and Stiglitz (1980, lecture 12:366–93).
6. Estimated non-take-up rates for some UK means-tested benefits in 1975 were as follows:

	Estimated number eligible	Non-claimers	
		No:	%
Rent rebates and allowances	1,775,000	798,333	45.0%
Rate rebates	3,500,000	1,050,000	30.0%
Free school meals	940,800	156,800	16.67%

Source: Field, Meacher and Pond (1977 Table 11: 87).

MacDonald (1977) estimates the take-up rate for Food Stamps in the US at 37 per cent, Table 6.1:94.

7. Willis and Hardwick (1978:2).
8. In the UK currently, interest payments on the first £25,000 of a mortgage only are so tax exempt.
9. Willis and Hardwick present estimates of the tax loss from the non-taxation of the capital gains on owner-occupier housing in the UK of

1973/4	1974/5	1975/6
£3987 m.	£1822 m.	£1465 m.

These figures are considerably in excess of their figures for the tax loss resultant from exclusion from charge of the annual value of owner-occupied housing (see Willis and Hardwick, 1978:93), but do refer to a period of exceptional house price inflation.

10. Stephenson and Harris (1977:100).
11. For general evidence as to the impact of indirect taxes on household income see the continuing CSO series 'The effects of taxes and benefits on household income', of which the latest is CSO (1980). The reader is warned that the 'subsidies' included there strictly follow the national income accounting conventions.

References

Aaron, H. J. (1970) Income taxes and housing, *American Economic Review*, **60**, 789–804.

Aaron, H. J. (1972) *Shelter and Subsidies*, Brookings Institution: Washington, DC.

Aaron, H. J., and von Furstenberg, G. M. (1971) The inefficiency of transfers in kind: the case of housing assistance, *Western Economic Journal*, **9**, 184–91.

Adams, D. W. (1980) The distributive effects of VAT in the United Kingdom, Ireland, Belgium and Germany, The *Three Banks Review*, **No: 128**, December 21–37.

Allan, C. M. (1971) *The Theory of Taxation*, Penguin: London.

Atkinson, A. B. (1977) Optimal taxation and the direct versus indirect tax controversy, *Canadian Journal of Economics,* **10**, 590–606.

Atkinson, A. B. and Stiglitz, J. E. (1980) *Lectures on Public Economics*, McGraw Hill: London.

Becker, G. S. (1965) A theory of the allocation of time, *Economic Journal*, **299**, 493–518.

Benus, J., Kmenta, J., and Shapiro, H. (1976) The dynamics of household budget allocation to food expenditures, *Review of Economics and Statistics,* **58**, 129–38.

Bilas, R. A. (1971) *Microeconomic Theory*, 2nd edn, McGraw Hill: New York.

Bish, R. L. (1969) Public housing: the magnitude and distribution of direct benefits and effects on housing consumption, *Journal of Regional Science*, **9**, 425–38.

Breit, W. (1974) Income redistribution and efficiency norms, ch. 1 in Hochman, M. H. and Peterson, G. E. (eds) *Redistribution through Public Choice*, Columbia University Press: New York and London, 3–21.

Brennan, G. (1973) Pareto-optimal redistribution: the case of malice and envy, *Journal of Public Economics*, **2**, 173–83.

Browning, E. K. (1975) The externally argument for in-kind transfers: some critical remarks, *Kyklos*, **28**, 526–44.

Browning, E. K. (1978) Donor optimization and the food stamp program: comment, *Public Choice*, **30**, 107–11.

Bryant, W. (1972) An analysis of the market for food stamps, *American Journal of Agricultural Economics*, **54**, 305–14.

Buchanan, J. M. (1968) What kind of redistribution do we want? *Economica*, **40**, 185–90.

Buchanan, J. M. and Stubblebine, W. C. (1962) Externality, *Economica*, **34**, 371–84.

Buchanan, J. M. and Tullock, G. (1962) *The Calculus of Consent*, University of Michigan, Ann Arbor.

Carlton, D. W., and Ferreira, J. (1977) Selecting subsidy strategies for housing allowance programs, *Journal of Urban Economics*, **4**, 221–47.

CSO (1968) *National Accounts Statistics: Sources and Methods*, Central Statistical Office, Maurice, R. (ed.), HMSO: London.

CSO (1980) The effects of taxes and benefits on household income 1978, *Economic Trends*, No: **315**, January 1980, 99–130.

Clarkson, K. W. (1975) *Food Stamps and Nutrition*, American Enterprise Institute for Public Policy Research: Washington, DC.

Clarkson, K. W. (1976) Welfare benefits of the food stamp program, *Southern Economic Journal*, **43**, 864–78.

Collard, D. (1975) Edgeworth's propositions on altruism, *Economic Journal*, **85**, 355–60.

Collard, D. (1978) *Altruism and Economy*, Martin Robertson: Oxford.

Daly, G., and Giertz, F. (1972a) Welfare economics and welfare reform, *American Economic Review*, **62**, 131–38.

Daly, G., and Giertz, F. (1972b) Benevolence, malevolence, and economic theory, *Public Choice*, **13**, 1–19.

Daly, G., and Giertz, F. (1976) Transfers and Pareto optimality, *Journal of Public Economics*, **5**, 176–82.

Davies, D. G. (1969) Clothing exemptions and sales tax regressivity: note, *American Economic Review*, **59**, 187–89.

Davis, J. M. (1977) The fiscal role of food subsidy programs, *IMF Staff Papers*, **24**, 100–27.

DeSalvo, J. S. (1971) A methodology for evaluating housing programs, *Journal of Regional Science*, **11**, 173–86.

Diamond, P. A. and Mirrlees, J. A. (1971) Optimal taxation and public production II: tax rules, *American Economic Review*, **61**, 261–78.

Dodgson, J. S. (1980) Social welfare functions, income distribution, and welfare weights in the United Kingdom, *Manchester School*, **48**, 1–16.

Downs, A. (1957) *An Economic Theory of Democracy*, Harper and Row: New York.

Edgeworth, F. Y. (1881) *Mathematical Psychics*, London School of Economics reprint (1932).

Feldstein, M. S. (1972) Distributional equity and the optimal structure of public prices, *American Economic Review*, **62**, 32–36.

Field, F., Meacher, M., and Pond, C. (1977) *To Him Who Hath*, Penguin; Harmondsworth.

Friedman, M., and Savage, L. J. (1948) The utility analysis of choices involving risk, *Journal of Political Economy*, **56**, 279–304.

Garfinkel, I. (1973) Is in-kind redistribution efficient?, *Quarterly Journal of Economics*, **87**, 320–30.

Galatin, M. (1973) A comparison of the benefits of the food stamp program, free food stamps and an equivalent cash payment, *Public Policy*, 291–302.

Giertz, F., and Sullivan, D. H. (1977) Donor optimization and the food stamp program, *Public Choice*, **29**, 18–35.

Giertz, F., and Sullivan, D. H. (1978) On the political economy of food stamps, *Public Choice*, **30**, 113–17.

Goode, R. (1960) Imputed rent of owner-occupied dwellings under the income tax, *Journal of Finance*, **15**, 504–30.

Hicks, J. R. (1956) *A Revision of Demand Theory*, Clarendon: Oxford.

Hochman, H. and Rodgers, J. (1969), Pareto optimal redistribution, *American Economic Review*, **59**, 542–57.

Housing Policy Review (1977) *Housing Policy – A Consultative Document*, **Cmnd. 6851**, HMSO: London.

Hughes, G. A. (1979) Housing income and subsidies, *Fiscal Studies*, **1**, 20–38.

Johnson W. R. (1978) Substitution in household production and the efficiency of in-kind transfers, *Public Finance Quarterly*, **6**, 204–10.

Kay, J. A., and King, M. A. (1978) *The British Tax System*, OUP: Oxford.

King, M. A and Atkinson, A. B. (1980) Housing policy taxation and reform, *Midland Bank Review*, Spring, 7–15.

Kraft, J., and Kraft, A. (1979) Benefits and costs of low rent public housing, *Journal of Regional Science*, **19**, 309–17.

Laidler, D. E. (1969) Income tax incentives for owner occupied housing, in Harberger, A. C. and Bailey, M. J. (eds) *The Taxation of Income from Capital*, Brookings Institution: Washington, DC.

Laidler, D. E. (1974) *Introduction to Microeconomics*, Philip Allan: Oxford.

Lancaster, K. (1966) A new approach to consumer theory, *Journal of Political Economy*, **74**, 132–57.

Le Grand, J. (1975) Public price discrimination and aid to low income groups, *Economica*, **42**, 32–42.

McClements, L. D. (1978) *The Economics of Social Security*, Heinemann: London.

MacDonald, M. (1977) *Food, Stamps and Income Maintenance*, Academic Press: New York and London.

Machlup, F. (1957) Professor Hicks' Revision of Demand Theory, *American Economic Review*, 47.

Marshall, G. P. (1980) *Social Goals and Economic Perspectives*, Penguin: Harmondsworth.

Mishan, E. J. (1971) Evaluation of life and limb: a theoretical approach, *Journal of Political Economy*, **79**, 687–705.

Mishan, E. J. (1972) The futility of Pareto efficient distribution, *American Economic Review*, **62**, 974–76.

Mishan, E. J. (1975) The folklore of the market: an inquiry into the economic doctrine of the Chicago School, *Journal of Economic Issues*, **9**, 681–752.

Murray, M. P. (1975) The distribution of tenant benefits in public housing, *Econometrica*, **43**, 771–88.

Murray, M. P. (1977) A potential hazard of housing allowances for public housing, *Journal of Urban Economics*, **4**, 119–34.

Murray, M. P. (1978) Methodologies for estimating housing subsidy benefits, *Public Finance Quarterly*, **6**, 161–92.

Musgrave, R. A. and Musgrave, P. B. (1980) *Public Finance in Theory and Practice*, (3rd edn), McGraw-Hill: New York.

Muth, R. F. (1960) The demand for non-farm housing, in Harberger, A. C. (ed.) *The Demand for Durable Goods*, University of Chicago Press: Chicago.

Nevitt, A. A. (1966) *Housing, Taxation and Subsidies*, Nelson: London.

Olsen, E. O. (1969) A competitive theory of the housing market, *American Economic Review*, **59**, 612–22.

Olsen, E. O. (1970) Subsidized housing in a competitive market: reply, *American Economic Review*, **60**, 220–24.

Olsen, E. O. (1971) Some theorems in the theory of efficient transfers, *Journal of Political Economy*, **79**, 166–76.

Olsen, E. O. (1972) An econometric analysis of rent control, *Journal of Political Economy*, **80**, 1081–1100.

Pauly, M. V. (1970) Efficiency in the provision of consumption subsidies, *Kyklos*, **23**, 35–57.

Peacock, A. T., and Wiseman, J. (1964) *Education for Democrats*, Institute for Economic Affairs: London.

Peltzman, S. (1973) The effect of government subsidies-in-kind on private expenditures: the case of higher education, *Journal of Political Economy*, **81**, 1–27.

Polinsky, A. M. (1977) The demand for housing: a study in specification and grouping, *Econometrica*, **45**, 447–61.

Prest, A. R. (1974) *How Much Subsidy?*, Institute of Economic Affairs: London.

Reece, B. F. (1975) The income tax incentive to owner-occupied housing in Australia, *Economic Record*, **51**, 218–31.

Reid, M. G. (1962) *Housing and Income*, University of Chicago Press.

Ricketts, M. (1976) The economics of the rent allowance, *Scottish Journal of Political Economy*, **23**, 235–60.

Robinson, R. (1979) *Housing Economics and Public Policy*, Macmillan: London.

Rodgers, J. D. (1973) Distributional externalities and the optimal form of income transfers, *Public Finance Quarterly*, **3**, 266–99.

Rodgers, J. D. (1974) Explaining income redistribution, ch. 7 in Hochman, M. H. and Peterson, C. E. (eds). *Redistribution through Public Choice*, 165–205, Columbia University Press: New York and London.

Rolph, E. R. (1968) Taxation, *International Encyclopedia of the Social Sciences*.

Rolph, E. R. (1973) Discriminating effects of the income tax treatment of owner-occupants, *National Tax Journal*, **26**, 471–84.

Rosen, H. S. (1979) Housing decision and the US income tax, *Journal of Public Economics*, **11**, 1–23.

Rosenthal, L. (1975) The nature of council house subsidies, unpublished Ph. D. thesis, University of Essex.

Rosenthal, L. (1977) The regional and income distribution of the council house subsidy in the United Kingdom, *Manchester School*, **45**, 127–40.

Rowley, C. K. and Peacock, A. T. (1975) *Welfare Economics: A Liberal Restatement*, Martin Robertson: London.

Ruggeri, G. H. (1978) On the incidence of Canada's provincial sales taxation, *Public Finance Quarterly*, **6**, 473–84.

Schaefer, J. M. (1969) Clothing exemptions and sales tax regressivity, *American Economic Review*, **59**, 596–99.

Shreiber, C. (1978) Inequality in the tax treatment of owner-occupied homes, *National Tax Journal*, **31**, 101–04.

Stephenson, G. A., and Harris, R. P. (1977) The redistributional effect of subsidies on households, *Economic Trends*, **No: 289**, 99–108, Central Statistical Office, HMSO: London.

Storey, J. R. (1976) The social policy role of food assistance programs, *American Journal of Agricultural Economics*, **56**, 1010–16.

Surrey, S. S. (1973) *Pathways to Tax Reform*, Harvard University Press.

Thurow, L. (1971) The income distribution as a pure public good, *Quarterly Journal of Economics*, **85**, 327–36.

Tullock, G. (1970) Subsidized housing in a competitive market: comment, *American Economic Review*, **60**, 218–19.

Tullock, G. (1966) Information without profit, *Papers on Non-Market Decision Making*, **1**, 140–59, repr. in Lamberton, D. M. (ed) (1971) *Economics of Information and Knowledge*, 119–38, Penguin, Harmondsworth.

Weiss, Y. (1978) Capital gains, discriminatory taxes, and the choice between renting and owning a house, *Journal of Public Economics*, **10**, 45–55.

Whalley, J. (1975) A general equilibrium assessment of the 1973 United Kingdom tax reform, *Economica*, **47**, 139–61.

White, M. J. and White, L. J. (1977) The tax subsidy to owner occupied housing: who benefits? *Journal of Public Economics*, **3**, 111–26.

Willig, R. (1976) Consumers' surplus without apology, *American Economic Review*, **66**, 589–97.

Willis, J. R. and Hardwick, P. J. W. (1978) *Tax Expenditures in the United Kingdom*, Institute for Fiscal Studies, Heinemann: London.

Winch, D. M. (1971) *Analytical Welfare Economics*, Penguin: Harmondsworth.

Witt, S. F., and Newbould, G. D. (1976) The impact of food subsidies, *National Westminster Bank Review*, August, 29–36.

CHAPTER FOUR

Local government economics

Neville Topham*

1. Introduction

Idiom is an autocrat with whom it is always well to keep on good terms; so although the author prefers to call the subject matter of this survey Fiscal Federalism, following American usage, the constitutional position in Britain has led to a popular preference for his more prosaic title. In an economic context, the generic meaning of federalism is decentralisation, and the fiscal implications of a decentralised system of government – Fiscal Decentralisation – provides most of the problems the literature wrestles with.

Parliament is sovereign in a unitary system of government, and such powers as local governments possess are defined by its statutes. If Parliament were so foolish, local government could be abolished tomorrow. But so far as economics is concerned, the differences that exist between federal and unitary governmental systems do not signify. The rights of both the central government and the constituent state governments in a federal structure are enshrined in a constitution, which when doubts and arguments occur is given specific interpretation by a supreme court. However, whilst state government boundaries in the United States are constitutionally inviolate, local government boundaries can be and are changed. Moreover, state constitutions – witness Proposition 13 – can be changed and local governments abolished or extended or their powers altered, as the case may be. Thus the literature on which attention is focused has a general relevance for any decentralised system of governments.

Local governments introduce spatial considerations. Tax-benefit baskets have unique locations, and baskets will differ, for a variety of reasons, as one moves from one community to another. But before a move is possible, communities have to be established. The first problem to be dealt with in this survey concerns the size of local 'clubs' and the assignment of individuals to them. This is section 2 and it concludes with a proof of the decentralisation theorem – a demonstration of how welfare losses are minimised with a decentralised governmental structure.

* I am grateful to Ronald Barback, Richard Barnett, Christopher Foster, John Gibson, Richard Jackman, the general editors, and an anonymous referee for many helpful comments on an earlier draft. I have accepted most but not all of the advice I was given, and therefore accept full responsibility for what is written.

Section 3 is concerned with movement between jurisdictions once they have been established. Tiebout (1956) argued that through the process of voting with feet, local governments could provide a shopping analogue. This is a seminal paper that has generated much discussion. Other issues discussed in this section concern spillovers of benefits from one locality to another and problems that arise when Tiebout voting-with-feet is not possible because local (or state) governments are too large spatially. If fiscal baskets are important, that fact should be reflected in property prices, and section 3 closes with examination of the capitalisation literature.

The main source of local finance is the property tax, which can be levied on the capital value of property or its rental income (as in this country). Economists have recently revised their view of the incidence of this tax, and both old and new views are examined in section 4. If the property tax is a benefit tax, a user price, as would occur with a Tiebout shopping analogue, these views of incidence are inappropriate. The section closes reviewing the conditions under which a property tax turns out to be a benefit tax.

Grants-in-aid are another important source of local finance. Their incidence can be understood only if the incidence of the tax burdens they alleviate is understood. Various distributional problems are discussed in section 5. The impact of grants on local spending has been examined at great length in econometric exercises and these also are reviewed.

Further econometric work is discussed in section 6. Local governments provide observations for testing various public choice models. The survey closes with a consideration of a number of median voter models, using these findings to refer back to earlier discussion, particularly in section 4.

As will be apparent now, there are a number of gaps. Discussion of urban economics is not attempted and space considerations did not allow the literature on local debt and investment to be included. But perhaps the major gap is the absence of much institutional material: the survey is largely analytical in focus.

2. The assignment problem

THE THEORY OF CLUBS

We start by considering a fundamental question. What factors should be taken into account in determining the degree of decentralisation in the structure of government? Should public services be centrally, regionally, or locally supplied? For economists the response is simple: they should be supplied in the cheapest and most efficient way. By cheapest the author means the smallest resource cost, and by efficient means that public services accord with consumers' preferences. In addition, it is assumed that local governments do not discriminate between households when delivering local services.

As intuition suggests, pure public goods should be supplied over as large a population as possible. Public goods are defined conventionally as those for which consumption is non-exhaustive; if one individual consumes the service it does not detract from the benefits available to others. A community could provide a local radio service for itself. Reception by one consumer would not weaken the radio signal available to another if he wanted to hear the programme. 'Clean air' provides another example. Such goods are freely available to all who live within its jurisdictional boundaries. The more people that contribute to their cost the better; they reduce the tax bills of other contributors thereby, and yet such consumption by additional taxpayers does not detract from the consumption of these public goods by existing members of the society.

But not all public services are pure public goods; some are impure in the sense that they can be crowded and congested. The more people that share a given facility which is crowdable, the lower the benefit any individual derives from it. There are many examples: roads become congested, classrooms crowded, and swimming pools polluted as the numbers of people using them increase. Replication is possible of course, but ultimately jurisdictional boundaries constrain further supply. On the other hand, additional users reduce tax bills at the same time as they increase demand on facilities. The central problem for the theory of clubs is to find the optimal balance between these two forces.

In designing a system of local governments, we are concerned with the formation of clubs in a spatial context.[1] To prevent the possibility of everyone being his own local government, we assume a fixed factor. It may be space (land); for there is a limited amount of 'commutable' land over which a suburban population may spread itself. Or it may be a local beach, to use the example of Tiebout (1956), which cannot be replicated. Associated with it is some optimal club size. Imagine then a number of geographical areas, located in space, producing a public service. With each production unit, we associate the usual cost curves for the provision of public services. By and large, we assume that over the relevant range there are constant costs of production obtaining for the local government's inputs.[2] For example, in the case of transport a local government is a 'price taker' in its purchase of buses and fuel, and wages of crew are fixed at a national level. However, what we are interested in is consumption rather than production, outputs rather than inputs. It is necessary to take into account congestion costs as well as production costs.

The analysis which follows is in the main stream of the economic theory of clubs.[3] But naturally in this context, we are concerned with applications to local-government economics. Specifically, we base ourselves on the analysis of Litvak and Oates (1970), which is an excellent but somewhat neglected paper. However, their framework is used rather freely here.

The question Litvak and Oates pose is 'What factors suggest a high degree of centralisation of governmental activity?' They point out that for pure national public goods, an increase in the population who benefit from and contribute to their financing reduces the tax price per unit of existing consumers. Denote the utility function of a consumer with income Y (y-man) as $U = u(y, z)$, where y is his consumption of the numeraire private good and z is the community's and his consumption of the public good. His disposable income is given by $y = Y - t(z)$, where his tax payment is some function of z. Under equal tax sharing arrangements $t = pz/N$ with N signifying the population and p the marginal resource cost of supplying a unit of z. The y-man maximises his utility function $U = u(Y - t(z), z)$ with respect to z:

$$dU/dz = -u_y t'(z) + u_z = 0 \qquad [1]$$

where $u_y = \partial u/\partial y$ is the partial derivative and $t'(z) = dt(z)/dz$ is the marginal change in his tax bill as a result of the change in the provision of the public good. Assuming constant costs of production, $t'(z) = p/N$ and the individual's marginal subjective rate of substitution between y and z is:

$$MRS = u_z/u_y = p/N \qquad [2]$$

Since there are N identical y-men in the community and all consumers are in equilibrium at the same level of z as determined by [2], we can multiply both sides of [2] by N and satisfy the Samuelson (1954) conditions for the optimal supply of public goods: $N . MRS = p$.

Equation [2] is the first condition that has to be satisfied. It determines the optimal amount of z to be provided. Having determined the size of the facility, we must now discover the rule for the associated optimal club size. Obviously it is the one that minimises what each individual effectively pays for each unit of the public good. This is known as the tax price. In the present context, it is equal to p/N and $d(p/N)/dN = -p/N^2$. As N gets larger, this derivative approaches zero. The answer to part two is: make N as large as possible, which was always going to be the case because a pure public good is not crowdable.

If this was all there was to it, efficiency considerations would require that all public services be provided centrally. However, not all public goods are national in scope and many services the public sector supplies are easily congested. If the output of a public service is z, for an impure public good let the quantity of z consumed by y-man be z^*. The relationship between z and z^* (that is, the degree of crowding of the facility producing z) is given by $z^* = (1/\alpha)z$, where α is an increasing function of N after some threshold level of N is achieved. Each unit of z costs p; so that for a given N the marginal cost of z^* is αp. For example, if α is 2, two units of z are required to produce one unit of z^*, and hence a unit of z^* costs $2p$. Moreover, as N increases the number of units of z required to generate a unit of z^* increases. Since it is z^* rather than z that is being consumed, we rewrite the utility function as $u(Y - t, z^*)$. Note that $t = \alpha p z^*/N$, and changing z^* will not affect p, or N. Maximising the new utility function with respect to z^*, we have as equivalent to [2]:

$$u_{z^*}/u_y = \alpha p/N \qquad [3]$$

This is the adapted Samuelson condition,[4] and it determines the optimal level of z^*. Having determined the size of the facility, we again have to discover the optimal population to associate with it. Bearing in mind that α is a function of N, we differentiate the tax price, $\alpha p/N$, with respect to N to determine its minimum. Denoting the tax price by p^* we have:

$$\frac{\mathrm{d}p^*}{\mathrm{d}N} = \frac{p}{N}\frac{\partial\alpha}{\partial N} - \frac{\alpha p}{N^2} = 0$$

Now $(\partial\alpha/\partial N)(N/\alpha)$ is the elasticity of α with respect to a change in N. Denoting this by r we have[5]:

$$\frac{\mathrm{d}p^*}{\mathrm{d}N} = \frac{\alpha p}{N^2}(r-1) = 0 \qquad\qquad [4]$$

where r is the elasticity of α with respect to a change in N. Obviously p^* is minimised when $r = 1$. At this point, the reduction in p^* from more sharing the tax burden is precisely offset by the addition to tax prices from congestion, via the α function.

Group size is optimised when $r = 1$. If we write r as:

$$r = \frac{\mathrm{d}\alpha/\mathrm{d}N}{\alpha/N}$$

we see that the numerator is the marginal change whilst the denominator is the average relation. For r to equal unity requires numerator and denominator to be equal; and since α is an increasing function of N this occurs where α/N is minimised – by analogy with cost functions. The shape of the $\alpha(N)$ function determines the degree of decentralisation of the governmental structure. For private goods such as chocolate, sharing is not possible: either you eat it or someone else does, which is just another way of saying that after the threshold $N = 1$ is reached $\alpha = \infty$. The α function is more relaxed for services such as education and roads and police. It will differ from service to service.

What lessons do we learn from this analysis? First, we learn the obvious: pure public goods should be provided centrally. Second, impure public goods should be assigned to lower levels of government according to the degree of crowding of a given facility additional population generates. Litvak and Oates enquired whether assignments were in practice like this; they tested their hypotheses somewhat crudely and found some support in their findings. Other writers – (Giertz 1976) and (Mullen 1980) – have looked at the same evidence, used additional explanatory variables, and drawn different conclusions. As so often in economics, the data available are unsatisfactory and do not justify rejection or acceptance of the hypothesis, no matter what the signs or regression coefficients and values of R^2 might be.

In this indirect way, we have outlined the standard (Buchanan 1965) approach to the theory of clubs. From the point of view of existing members, optimal club size occurs when the marginal cost of an additional member, via congestion, is equated with the marginal benefit he confers through lower tax prices and hence an associated consumer surplus. McGuire (1972, 1974) has suggested additionally that optimal club size occurs when marginal and average cost are equal. Costs include congestion costs, and this requirement is met when $r = 1$, which as we know is the value associated with an optimal value for N.

Equal sharing arrangements are not common in public finance generally, and it is on property taxes that the real world confers salience in local finance. When all consumers are identical, as here, tax shares are always equal whether poll, income, or property taxes finance the facility. However, if either property or income taxes were analysed we should find that levels of z^* were different under such tax regimes because of the distortionary nature and consequent deadweight losses associated with those forms of taxation.

Finally, note that since N is a determinant of tax prices, the level of public spending will differ for the same facility depending on the size of club it is assigned to. Tax prices are minimised when p^* takes its optimal value. Suppose society is composed of JN individuals, where J is the number of jurisdictions. If a facility that is optimally provided under population N is assigned to a club with population JN, its tax price will rise, and hence levels of z^* will be lower unless the jurisdiction's price elasticity of demand is zero. In this latter event, z^* would be the same in each location, but public spending would be higher at a central than local level. Other than when price elasticity equals zero, benefit levels will always be higher for impure public goods if they are localised. It is only then that the Samuelson condition will be met.

Implicit in the discussion of clubs is an assumption that any benefits (and costs) from supplying z or z^* are confined to club members. This may not be so. For pure local public goods and for some other services, the correspondence between club boundaries and the geographical area over which benefits extend may not be perfect. In this case, it would be necessary to amend previous formulae to take account of this fact. For example, if a fifth of all output benefits spilt over to the benefit of members of some contiguous club, this implies that to produce 80 units of a service it is necessary to produce an output of 100. This is tantamount to a price increase. However, it would not affect club size (i.e. the value of N) although it would affect the level of club provision. Spillovers would affect club size only if they were a function of N in some way. The same is true for spillins. Each problem would have to be investigated on its merits.

Since externalities are discussed in more detail on p.148, there is no need to make extensive reference here. However, a word of warning is appropriate. Many so-called externalities are not externalities. If a city decides to sanction the building of office blocks in order to maximise benefits for its members, some of these benefits are better employment prospects, enhanced yields from the property tax; but a rational jurisdiction would also take account of the fact that it would incur costs as workers from neighbouring jurisdictions commute to work in its office blocks, use its central business district, and so on. These costs are a direct result of its own planning decisions; they are not what economists would normally denote as externalities, and should not be seen as such.

DECENTRALISATION

The theory of clubs assumes, for the most part, a world of identical individuals. As will become clear when the Tiebout process is discussed, the relaxation of this assumption provides a justification for a system of local governments: according to taste and income individuals can allocate themselves amongst the various clubs providing different levels of club goods.

Suppose the optimal size of club for an impure (congestible) local public good is N and the total population is JN. The theory of clubs implies that in these circumstances it is better to have J clubs of size N rather than one of size JN. However, if the club good is a pure public good, theory says have one club of size JN.

Now it is necessary to refocus. The assumption of identical tastes is dropped. Let the population of society now be KJN, where K is a large number. A different but equally fundamental question is posed: should the structure of government be democratically decentralised? That is, should there be local as well as central government? In their response to this question, economists habitually adopt an important assumption about governmental behaviour. Governments are assumed to treat individuals within their jurisdiction equally, regardless of tastes and incomes. The fact that one man wants more of z than another man, and is willing to pay for the privilege of receiving more, does not entitle him to receive more. This accords with everyday governmental practice. But Foster *et al.* (1980) point out that the assumption is not mandatory on economists, since it is possible to imagine central governments who conceive localities as agents rather than as local democracies. However, this point is not an issue to pursue here, since both systems of government are theoretically underpinned by the decentralisation theorem, which is now outlined.

Assume that over some range, local services can be provided at constant costs and suppose that the service is, to all intents and purposes, a private good – i.e. $\alpha = N$. The price is now independent of club size.

Consider a group of individuals with identical demand functions for the local service. Let the demand curves be linear and exhibit zero income elasticity of demand.[6] In Fig. 4.1, the demand curve for an individual is shown. At 'price' $\bar{p}$, he demands z of the local service; but quantity $\hat{z}$ is supplied. Let the individual's demand curve be characterised by the equation $p = 2az + b$, where b is positive and represents the intercept term and a is negative. The consumer wishes to be at r but is taken off his demand curve to s, and there is a subsequent loss of consumer surplus of the triangle rst. The area of this triangle is:

$$d = \tfrac{1}{2}(\hat{z} - z) \cdot st$$

The slope of the demand curve is:

$$2a = st/(\hat{z} - z)$$
$$\therefore d = a(\hat{z} - z)^2 \qquad [5]$$

This is the welfare loss suffered by a person not in equilibrium. If we assume, as in Bowen (1943) and Barzel (1969), that the slope of the demand curve is common to all individuals, then [5] will characterise the loss of those who want more of the good z as well as those who want less.

Assume now that whilst $2a$ (the slope of demand curves) is the same across individuals, in any given community b (the intercept term) is distributed

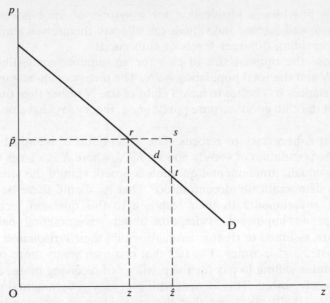

FIG. 4.1 Collective choice and welfare losses

normally – again this ·is implicit in Bowen and Barzel. That is, whatever the price, there is a normal distribution across the population of demands for the good. Demands for quantities of z are distributed normally – with mean μ and variance ψ^2:

$$z \sim N(\mu, \psi^2) \qquad [6]$$

As described below, in a pure Tiebout world, jurisdictions will be homogeneous with $\psi^2 = 0$. There is no need to impose that restriction here, but we assume ψ^2 is common to all jurisdictions. The situation in a single jurisdiction is given by the left-hand diagram of Fig. 4.2. The vertical axis represents the probability of people in a jurisdiction with an output of μ demanding that quantity. Note that the local output is the quantity that would be chosen by a median voter. The output preferences of individuals in a jurisdiction with output μ are shown on the horizontal. Output μ is the median of these preferences. The conditions under which the median preferences dominate are described in most textbooks on public finance.

Since, in the world being described, individuals have assigned them-selves to jurisdictions and taken outputs into account in making this choice, there will be variations in tax-spending decisions. Now we assume, as in the central diagram in Fig 4.2, that the outputs are normally distributed with mean m and variance σ^2:

$$\mu \sim N(m, \sigma^2) \qquad [7]$$

Distribution of personal
preferences in a single
jurisdiction

Distribution of outputs
across jurisdictions

Distribution of personal
preferences across all
jurisdictions

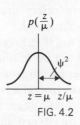

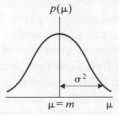

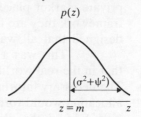

FIG. 4.2

From [6] and [7], it can be shown[7] that the distribution of individual preferences is also normally distributed with mean m and variance $(\psi^2 + \sigma^2)$:

$$z \sim N(m,\ \psi^2 + \sigma^2) \qquad [8]$$

as in the right-hand diagram of Fig. 4.2.

We can now use equations [6] and [8] to consider welfare losses arising from centralisation. In [6], the dispersions about the average of z are on *average* equal to $(\hat{z} - z)^2$, by the definition of a variance. Hence the average loss in a decentralised world is: $d = a\psi^2$. If all clubs are consolidated the variance is given by [8] and thus the welfare loss is: $d = a(\psi^2 + \sigma^2)$. Hence the increase in *average* loss for individuals in society resulting from a decision to dispense with local governments, in the world described by Fig. 4.2, is $a\sigma^2$. This is another way of presenting the decentralisation theorem of Barzel (1969) as described by Oates (1972).

3. Tiebout and non-Tiebout worlds

LOCAL GOVERNMENT AS A SHOPPING ANALOGUE

Public goods are indivisible and collectively consumed. Exclusion is not possible – or at least it is taken to be prohibitively costly. If we assume no crowding and tax prices that take the form of lump-sum taxes, the optimal allocation of goods to the public sector is achieved when $\Sigma MRS = MC$. The Bowen-Lindahl-Samuelson model determines lump-sum taxes on the basis of individual marginal rates of substitution; in this model, the tax price facing individuals in society is $(MRS/\Sigma MRS)$ MC, where MC is the resource cost at the margin. But it is not operational. Each MRS schedule is known only to the person to whom it refers, and being a rational individual he will understate his marginal evaluation of the public good if asked; for in that way, he lowers the fraction of MC he is financially responsible for and thus his tax price. Faced with free-riding of this nature, Samuelson (1954) suggested the intriguing possibility of an omniscient referee who knows all MRS schedules and can thus devise a set of individual lump-sum taxes to satisfy the $\Sigma MRS = MC$ criterion. The basis of these taxes is not made known to an ignorant populace, each of whom is unaware of the *MRS* schedule of anyone else but himself.[8] Thus whereas individuals operating in private market places are typically price takers and quantity choosers, in this framework they are both price and quantity takers. However, the 'prices' are so designed that all want and take the same quantity of the public good.

This was a depressing contribution to the literature; for it suggested that in the real world such conditions would not, perhaps could not be fulfilled. The necessary information would not be available to a government and resource allocation would forever be non-optimal. A seminal contribution from Tiebout (1956) lifted the gloom. He pointed out that some public goods were not national public goods and indeed that many services supplied by governments were neither public goods nor nationally nor uniformly provided. They were supplied by local governments. If tax prices were known in advance, and if local governments were small in size and large in number, individuals could shop around spatially and vote with their feet to achieve an output of public goods that corresponded closely to their preferences.

The Tiebout model assumes voters are mobile and move to a community where their preference patterns come nearest to being satisfied. Individuals have full information of community outputs and there are a large number of communities to choose from. There are no employment restrictions; Tiebout peoples his world only with a rentier class, who live off income from capital. There are no spillovers between jurisdictions. There are fixed factors of production, and jurisdictions have U-shaped cost curves. Zoning (planning) laws prevent population size exceeding the minimum-cost level. City managers in this scenario charge the same 'prices' as would occur in private market places; that is, a poll tax is implicit in the model. The choice between one jurisdiction and another is wholly akin to the choice individuals face in private market places. One cannot within the model contest Tiebout's proposition: 'the greater the number of communities and the greater the variance among them, the closer the consumer will come to fully realising his preference position'. As in private market places, the mobile consumer is a price taker and quantity adjuster.

The Tiebout model has drawn many comments. Samuelson (1958) said that as a solution to the public goods problem it holds some difficulties. Individuals are often prepared to take a little welfare loss rather than live with their own. People like heterogeneity – for example, the old do not want to live with the old all the time.

Pauly (1967) has pointed out that if optimal jurisdiction size is N and society's population is S, S/N may not be an integer. If this is the case, one can change club size up or down to the nearest integer.

Some practical difficulties concern the number of clubs required. Jurisdictions produce more than one service. Mueller (1979) raised the example of a town square that has a flowerbed and trees. Ignore the trees and consider the question of tulips in the flowerbed. Shall we have zero, one per cent of tulips, 100 per cent, or something in between? People will have ideas about the spacing of the tulips and some will not like them at all. Considering the percentile changes only, we see that 101 different clubs are required to satisfy all possible preferences for tulip plantings in a flowerbed. When we go on to consider trees as well, the problem becomes yet more complex. Trees can be used to substitute or complement the tulips. Taking all possible combinations into account requires 101^2 clubs.

There is an extension to this argument that seriously erodes the Tiebout process. Oates (1969) has shown that people do in fact take account of fiscal variables when deciding where to locate. But they take account of other factors also, and the number of local communities has to be large enough to take account of these other considerations. However, there is little a government can do to enlarge choice in those community attributes of life that are not governmentally provided. Left to themselves, individuals will trade-off community attributes against fiscal advantages, and homogeneous communities, in the Tiebout sense, might not emerge.[9] What a central government creates, it can modify. In creating for themselves local governments, the individuals that people society become members of two clubs conjointly – the national and the local one. But if the legislatively superior government functions on the basis of a simple majority voting rule, the majority may wish to eliminate provision for minority tastes so as to allow greater room for exercising their own tastes in respect of both fiscal and community attributers. The pattern of jurisdictional outputs that emerges from the Tiebout process is not necessarily optimal from any one individual's standpoint. The reason is an individual does not want only one jurisdiction to provide the fiscal basket he requires, but a large number so that he can freely maximise his preference function, which contains community attributes as arguments. A superior government, acting on behalf of those it represents, may seek to curtail minority tastes in local public goods so as to allow room for the majority to shop for community attributes. If voting takes place from a position where jurisdictions are homogeneous in the fiscal plane, Topham (1977) shows that there will ensue a severe erosion of the Tiebout shopping analogue as the central government imposes tax rate ceilings and floors. On the other hand, if jurisdictions are already highly heterogeneous, there will be little change. But in the latter case, the Tiebout process would not have generated a situation that provides a solution for Samuelson's problem, which was Tiebout's intention.

A more fundamental attack on the Tiebout shopping analogue has been launched by Buchanan and Wagner (1970), Buchanan and Goetz (1972), and by Flatters, Henderson and Mieszkowski (1974). They advance the proposition that free mobility between jurisdictions may not be Pareto optimal, and their line of argument has begun to enter the better textbooks – see Boadway (1979) and Atkinson and Stiglitz (1980).

The argument is as follows. Consider two regions, A and B. Region A is the larger of the two. They each produce a pure local public good without spillovers. Two considerations give rise to a movement of population from B to A if we were to start them off with identical populations. First, because labour and capital have more land to work with, factor returns are higher in region A; factor mobility will lead to equalisation at the margin, of course, but by the time this occurs, the population of A will exceed that of B. Factor incomes per head will thus be the same before tax, but in aggregate they will be higher in A. So far so good: optimality in production requires mobility so motivated.

But there is a second consideration to contend with. The tax price of a *pure* public good is inversely related to the size of the population. Both the population and its aggregate income – and hence the tax base – are higher in A than in B. Consequently, migration will take place from B to A as individuals attempt to secure the consumers' surplus gain associated with the lower tax prices confronting equivalent houses in A. And this migration, argue Buchanan and associates and Flatters *et al.*, is non-optimal.

It need not even be the case that one region is richer or larger than another. Consider a society composed of *N* identical individuals and just two identical regions: that is, land is of the same acreage and has the same mineral and other properties in both communities. How shall we divide the population between the two regions? Land is the fixed factor in both communities. As more and more of the variable factor, say labour, is applied to land, its marginal product will eventually decline. Obviously, in these circumstances, the appropriate strategy is to divide the population equally between the two communities – for then, marginal products are equal in each community and national income is maximised. But this income is spent on public goods as well as private goods, and a pure public good is delivered cheapest when all individuals are in one community. There are therefore two opposing forces to contend with. As Helpman (1978) points out, it may be beneficial to society as a whole to have unequal community sizes. Atkinson and Stiglitz (1980: 529) emphasise that if this is the case, equals will not be treated equally: welfare maximisation requires allowing a majority to achieve a higher level of utility, leaving a minority behind. They point out also that strong complementarity in both production and consumption alleviates this problem; for such complementarity implies shallow budget lines and steeply-sloped indifference curves; multiple equilibria are unlikely to occur, and given symmetry an equal division of the population between the two communities is optimal.

However, all these arguments suffer from a serious omission. If, for one reason or another, region A were to turn out to be a tax haven, then in the long run that fact would be reflected in its land prices. If property and land constitute the tax base, and if capital is mobile in the long run, then the lower tax price associated with larger population will be reflected in land prices. In a spatial context, what individuals seek to equalise is the joint price for land and public goods; for it is residence on land in A that allows consumption of the public good in A. Because land in A is associated with a lower tax price than is found in B, its price will be bid up and the consumer's surplus gain associated with a lower tax price will be capitalised. Migration will not occur after the point where the joint price is common to both regions. The process of capitalisation chokes off any non-optimal migration.[10]

Thus, there is no reason for Helpman (1978) to be pessimistic about the Tiebout process. Output is maximised in his model, it may be recalled, when the population is divided equally between the two regions. If there are two communities, two lots of public goods are required, and if in *actual* production of public goods constant costs of production prevail, there is a positive disadvantage, because real national income is lower. But any tax advantage arising if one community were to gain population from another would be reflected in its land prices, and thus capitalisation would choke off moves away from the optimum.

The argument, in any case, is appealing more for the theoretical problems it raises than its operational content. What we have here is a situation where the number of clubs is fixed and there is an integer problem – $N/2$ is not an integer, which is the point Pauly (1967) raises. Provided the number of communities can be altered (it is not too costly to do so) and there is no integer problem, decentralisation via the Tiebout process is possible and will achieve efficiency (Helpman (1978)).

Finally, a similar argument was suggested by Wheaton (1975), who considered possibilities for a stable equilibrium under various tax regimes. If individuals differed in income, he concluded that a property tax system would be highly unstable. An individual's tax price in this case is given by $(h/H)p$, where h is his consumption of housing and H is aggregate consumption. This can be rewritten $(h/\bar{h}) p/N$, where $\bar{h}$ is mean consumption of housing. Obviously $\bar{h}$ is higher in rich communities if housing is a normal good. Those with low incomes and consuming small amounts of housing would seek to locate with the rich and thus enjoy a lower tax price for local public goods. This would cause the rich to move on, because an influx of low incomes would lower $\bar{h}$ and raise their tax price; they would form a new community, and so on. There are two problems here. Whether or not one would wish to locate in another jurisdiction in order to enjoy the benefits of a lower tax price depends on the quantity of local public goods one would have to consume in that jurisdiction.[11] This is made clear in Fig. 4.3. Income is measured on the vertical and output of z on the horizontal.

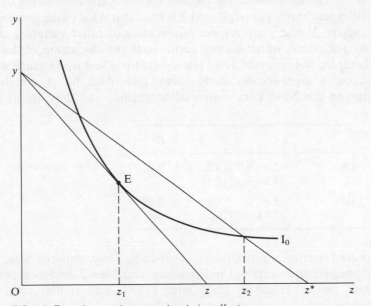

FIG. 4.3 Tax prices and community-choice offsets

Let an individual with income y be located at E on budget line yz. If he moves to another jurisdiction where he can enjoy a tax price reduction, he can locate, say, on budget line yz^*. But the amount of the local public good supplied in his new jurisdiction may not equal z_1 the amount he currently consumes. He will move to the jurisdiction offering him the lower tax price provided the level of z supplied does not exceed z_2; for otherwise he would end up on a lower indifference curve than indicated by I_0, his currently level of utility.

Moreover, Wheaton makes no allowance for the capitalisation process. As we have already indicated and as we shall see below this effectively neutralises the problems Wheaton raises.

CAPITALISATION

If economic agents are rational, a house subject to a high tax rate would, other things equal, sell for less than a lowly-taxed equivalent. Similarly, if for the same tax price, the benefits of public services are higher in one area than another, its property values will reflect that fact. The Tiebout hypothesis maintains that individuals are sensitive to local fiscal variables, and their choice of jurisdiction will be influenced by them. Demand for houses will be high in local 'tax havens', and prices of property there will rise until living in those jurisdictions will be no more advantageous than anywhere else.

Wallace Oates (1969), in an important paper that has since given rise to much discussion, sought to test these propositions in an equation of the following form:

$$V = A + \alpha \ln T + \beta \ln E + \gamma X$$

where V is the capital value of the median house, E the natural log of current educational expenditures per pupil, and T is the natural log of the percentage tax rate; and where X and γ are respectively vectors of other variables and their associated coefficients, which are not germane to the discussion of this section and are therefore not reported here. His results for α and β, on which we focus, are based on a cross-section study using 1960 data for a sample of 53 communities in the New York metropolitan region, and they are as follows:

	α	β	R^2
OLS	−3.6	3.2	0.93
	(4.1)	(2.1)	
TSLS	−3.6	4.9	0.93
	(3.1)	(2.1)	

The bracketed terms are t-statistics. Two-stage least squares was thought necessary because the supposed independent variables T and E depended to some extent on V. Heinberg and Oates (1970) find similar results using Massachusetts data.

Oates concluded two things from this study. First, he calculated that an increase in local tax rates from two to three per cent would on the basis of his results reduce the market value of a $20,000 house by $1500. But using a five per cent discount rate and a 40-year house life, full capitalisation of a *ceteris paribus* tax change of this order would be expected to reduce the house price by $2260. Thus his first conclusion was that tax rate changes appear to be about two-thirds capitalised.

His second point concerns the benefit side. School expenditures account for half the budget of the observations in his sample. Oates's results and additional calculation suggest the downward effect on property values as a result of a tax rise would be virtually wholly offset by the beneficial effects of the expenditure. He concluded: 'If property values do provide a reasonably accurate reflection of benefits from local public services, these results would seem to suggest that these communities have, on the average, expanded public spending to the point where (very roughly) the benefits from an additional unit of output equal marginal cost.' Taken as they stand, these words imply that the property tax acts as a user price. This is a point that should be borne in mind when discussing the incidence of property taxes, and it is one which will be returned to on p.166.

Pollakowski (1973) attempted to replicate these results using California data and was unable to do so. Also he made the legitimate point that in Oates's equations only one local service, schooling, figured whereas the tax revenues supported several. Oates (1973) took this point on board and found in further work that full capitalisation of a tax rate hike was now to be inferred from his point estimates.

At the same time, Oates took the opportunity to make an important point. Despite his original title reference to the Tiebout hypothesis, he emphasised that his results could not be taken to infer that we live in a Tiebout world: merely that some families at least are sensitive to fiscal variables. And to be fair, his original paper only claimed in the text that the results were 'consistent' with the Tiebout hypothesis.

The refinement was timely. Edel and Sclar (1974) drew attention to the absence of any supply responses. If everyone could shop around as in the Tiebout shopping analogue and achieve equilibrium, the situation would be exactly akin to that which obtains in private market places. The property tax would be a perfect user price. With a tax price uniform across communities, individuals shop spatially for the quantity of the public service they want. But if that were the case for everyone, there would be no advantage to owning land in one jurisdiction rather than another. It was not correct for Oates to say his results implied that on average the property tax operated as a user price. As Hamilton (1976b) points out, the 'Oates test rests on the assumption that tax or benefits havens . . . will earn a rent, as reflected in higher housing prices'. Oates's finding must have been due to a disequilibrium in which there is a temporary shortage of fiscal havens, or persistent and systematic differences in production functions either for raising revenue or producing public services. These latter might, for example, include the ratio of middle- to lower-class children, the former being more easily taught; so a high-income community can produce education more efficiently (cheaply) than a poor community. Edel and Sclar emphasise the former reason in accounting for Oates's results. They envisage the replication of communities that are tax havens or are otherwise in short supply. The United States provides real-world opportunities for such replication, although not with the costless ease assumed by economic theorists. Edel and Sclar using Boston data provide results that show a tail-off over time in the importance of regression coefficients associated with fiscal variables. In their view, this is consistent with a supply response. And Hamilton argues that Pollakowski's mixed results, obtained in attempting to replicate Oates's exercise for California, might be explained by a failure of both studies to incorporate important short-run supply variables such as migration rates. The conclusion of Hamilton, Edel and Sclar, and Epple, Zelenitz, and Visscher (1978) is that Oates was testing for the absence rather than the presence of a Tiebout equilibrium; for in equilibrium, there is no reason for house values to be correlated either with benefits from or tax prices for local public goods.

Meadows (1976) criticises Edel and Sclar for concentrating on a single-equation model and failing to consider inter-jurisdictional differences in the housing stock, assessment ratios, and inter-governmental grants. Rosen and Fullerton (1977) look at output measures rather than using data on inputs (expenditure) as a proxy for perceived benefits. The proportion capitalised increases as a consequence. By contrast King (1977) points out that the maintained hypothesis refers to the tax burden (the amount paid) rather than the tax rate. Incorporation of the tax rate involves a spurious correlation and he estimates Oates's results bias the capitalisation upwards by about 40 per cent.

An important criticism of all these results has been made by Linneman (1978). He states that Oates and others estimate equations of the general form:

$$V = V(T', E, X)$$ [9]

where the variables are to be identified as before and with T' representing total tax receipts (actually, Oates has the tax rate in [9]; but that does not diminish the importance of Linneman's point). However, the studies overlook the presence of the local budget constraint:

$$T' = tH = PE - G$$ [10]

where t is the tax rate, H the tax base, P the unit price of z the public good, and G represents any other local finance not raised in taxes. Once [10] is acknowledged, it is not possible to conceptualise $V_T = \partial V/\partial T'$, because if T' alters, so does E. To see the problem Linneman refers to, totally differentiate [9]:

$$dV = V_{T'} \cdot dT' + V_E dE + V_x dX$$

Divide through by dT':

$$\frac{dV}{dT'} = V_{T'} + V_E \frac{dE}{dT'}$$ [11]

In arriving at [11], the author has assumed $dX/dT' = 0$. The problem is clear enough; if tax receipts change then, with the price of the public good and non-tax finance given, E must also change. The regression coefficient does not tell us what we want to know. And the same would be the case if we were to consider dV/dE; β evaluates incorrectly the impact of a change of E on V. And [10] raises yet another problem. There are linear relationships between T' and E and G. If $G = 0$, it is not possible to estimate [9] because of problems arising from the existence of what econometricians call a singular data matrix: increases in E cause linear responses in T'. Among other reasons, the omitted variable G has allowed authors of tax capitalisation studies to derive their results, but as they have not considered G as a determinant of variations in property values, the results and their accompanying interpretations should be received with scepticism.

Epple *et al.* attempt in their paper to lay the foundations for a fresh start. They attempt to distinguish between a world in Tiebout equilibrium and one not so; they ask what would housing demand equations look like derived from the two different sources. They start with utility functions and allow for local and individual budget constraints. The conclusion is that a demand for housing function derived from a system of homogeneous communities would not include the tax rate as an argument, whereas one derived from heterogeneous communities would do so. This result is questioned in Topham (1982b). Moreover, along with Hamilton (1975a), Epple *et al.* state that in Tiebout equilibrium there is no deadweight loss associated with a property tax for homogeneous communities. As Tiebout implies, the choice of public and private goods is identical with that which would obtain in private market places. Topham (1982a) demonstrates that this is incorrect. The problem arises because Epple *et al.* and Hamilton assume, albeit implicitly, that housing stocks are fixed, and there is no mechanism in the model to let housing adjust to a new after-tax price. Although the Tiebout scenario is enormously appealing at an intuitive level, it is theoretically incorrect to assert that his system of spatial selection allows consumers to escape the normal deadweight tax losses associated with any form of commodity tax, including a property tax. But it is easy to agree with the concluding remark of Epple *et al.*: 'to date no meaningful test of the Tiebout hypothesis has been conducted'.

When a tax is imposed on a commodity, individuals will almost invariably curtail their consumption of the taxed product, and the consumers' surplus loss associated with such reduction is known as the deadweight loss of taxation. That is why efficiency demands taxation on commodities with low price elasticities of demand. Deadweight losses occur as economic agents adjust their behaviour to accommodate tax burdens; capitalisation is evident when full adjustment to taxation, especially on the supply side, has not taken place. A failure to appreciate the force of the latter half of this proposition was the cause of further confusion in the literature. Epple *et al.* argued that property values would not be affected by tax-spending decisions in Tiebout equilibrium; for a condition of that equilibrium is that all jurisdictions are homogeneous. The point had been extensively illustrated by Hamilton (1976a). To focus ideas quickly, I am going to use an arithmetic example, which is what Hamilton's notation amounts to. For expositional purposes, I let squires and peasants act as antonomasias. Squires live in mansions, which are assessed for property tax purposes at £30; peasants live in cottages assessed at £15. I assume squires earn more than peasants and their different quantities of consumption of housing services arise because housing is a normal good.

There are three jurisdictions, each with a population of three households. See Table 4.1. Squires live in the homogeneous jurisdiction H, which has a tax base of £90. Jurisdiction L is homogeneous in peasantry and has the lowest tax base; at £45 it is half that of H. Two squires and one peasant live in the heterogeneous jurisdiction M, which has a tax base of £75. Now suppose we are concerned with a private good (say, education) that is being collectively supplied. The 'tax price' faced by an individual is the resource cost of one unit of education multiplied by $h/\bar{h}$, where h is the individual's consumption of housing and $\bar{h}$ is the mean value.

TABLE 4.1

Jurisdiction	Mansions	Cottages	Tax base	Tax prices (£)		Tax rates
				Squires	Peasants	
H	3	0	90	1	n.a	0.5
M	2	1	75	1.2	0.6	0.6
L	0	3	45	n.a	1	1.0

Suppose the jurisdictions each buy 45 units of the collectively-supplied private good whose resource cost is £1 per unit and these are divided equally among the inhabitants. In H, squires pay a tax rate of 0.5 (= 45/90) on their property assessment of £30. A squire's tax bill is £15 and each consumes 15 units of the collectively-supplied private good, valued at £15. Hamilton defines their fiscal residual as the difference between the two amounts: it is zero. Since in his model, fiscal residuals are capitalised, it is clear that no capitalisation occurs in the rich homogeneous jurisdiction. Nor does it in the poor jurisdiction. Peasants in L face the same tax price as squires in H; the tax price is £1 × 1 = 1, and in both fiscal residuals are nil.

The interesting jurisdiction is M, where the tax rate is 45/75 = 0.6. Here the tax price facing each squire is £(1 × 30/25) = £1.2, where £25 is the mean housing value in the mixed jurisdiction. A similar calculation gives a tax price for peasants of £0.6. Squires pay a tax bill of £0.6 (30) in exchange for goods of resource value £15: their fiscal residual is −£3. Peasants pay half this amount to receive the same basket and have a positive fical residual of £6. The stream of tax payments of £3 will be capitalised because other things equal a squire prefers to live in H and pay a lower tax price for the local services than he is required to do in M, and therefore mansions sell for less by the present value of this amount; cottages command a premium equal to the present value of £6.

Note that there are two squires and one peasant: capitalisation is a zero sum game and the aggregate tax base of the jurisdiction is unchanged after capitalisation.

Whilst Hamilton's (1976a) paper is valuable because of its clarificatory qualities, there is much in it that is unsatisfactory. As I shall argue on p. 168, the fiscal residual ought to be defined as the difference between willingness to pay and tax bills, not market value and the latter. The two are the same, given identical utility functions, only in the special case when income and price elasticities are both zero; but a rational indifference map precludes both behavioural parameters simultaneously taking a zero value.

If capital is mobile, units of housing services will in the long run command the same price in all jurisdictions. Therefore, the capitalisation referred to must be attached in some way to the immobile factor land. Hamilton sees this and argues that efficiency requires zoning. Essentially he sees house prices and tax payments as a 'joint' price for housing and local services (see also Barnett and Topham 1980); after capitalisation peasants are treated equally because their joint price is the same in M as it is in L; and for squires the 'joint' price is the same in H as it is in M. To maintain this pattern, land under mansions will sell for less in M than land that is cottaged, and since in the long run an efficiently operated land market would not allow this, Hamilton argues that zoning (planning) regulations necessary to ensure joint prices for mansions (or cottages) are the same in an entire system of communities. As mansions deteriorate through time, they will be replaced by cottages so that landowners can earn a premium. A mixed community, and indeed a homogeneous rich community, can only be preserved if zoning ordinances prevent this.

However, such an enforced equilibrium can hardly be efficient. Efficiency requires a long-run equilibrium where all factors are mobile and earning the same post-tax return across communities. As mansions deteriorate in M they will be replaced by cottages, argue Dyer and Maher (1979); M will convert to a homogeneous community occupied by peasantry; in the long run, they say, all jurisdictions will be homogeneous and capitalisation will be zero. Certainly, it is true that if jurisdictions are homogeneous, capitalisation will be zero, but Dyer and Maher never allow for the fact that jurisdictions like M will always arise whilst ever it is worth the while of a peasant to locate there in order to obtain a lower tax price. The market in housing will eventually equate joint prices, but it remains true that it is movement between jurisdictions that drives up the price of cottages in M. The poor will chase the rich as long as the premium is worthwhile. Thus Dyer and Maher describe a long-run equilibrium that is not easily achieved and they are in turn criticised by those economists who cast doubt on the possibility of attaining a Tiebout equilibrium.

Yinger (1981) points out that full capitalisation will choke off mobility between jurisdictions, since there is no motivation to move once joint prices for housing and local public services are equalised. This raises two points. First, it is not clear whether movement forces up prices or whether rational expectations cause an instant adjustment of joint prices when some disequilibrating event occurs. Some research in this area would be helpful. Second, whether capitalisation chokes off movement in the long run depends on the adjustment possibilities open to agents. As we have seen, capitalisation in mixed jurisdictions is unlikely to endure because eventually mansions will be replaced by cottages. If the source of capitalisation is something that cannot be replicated (for example, a more efficient production of local parks services because of climatic conditions), then the premium on land in that jurisdiction will be secure. Such price adjustments as these, however, merely define the parameters within which the Tiebout mechanism operates. In the long run, capitalisation generates the changes in land use that permit movement for fiscal advantage.

The reader will have noted our change of focus in the capitalisation debate. What started out as a reasonably straightforward investigation of capitalisation of local variations in tax rates and public service levels has evolved into a discussion of whether or not in the long run a system of local governments tends to a Tiebout equilibrium, in which local governments internally are homogeneous in terms of demands for local services. If this is what the debate is about, one can only express surprise at the somewhat oblique way in which propositions are tested. If local governments are in fact adjusting to a Tiebout equilibrium, then voting over the levels of local services will be tending to unanimity in each jurisdiction. A test of that proposition is easily envisaged. There remains, however, a useful role to play in tests of capitalisation itself, for without capitalisation long run adjustment will not take place.

SPILLOVERS

The geographical area over which the benefits from local public goods extend does not always correspond with the jurisdictional boundaries of the providing locality. Some benefits (and costs) spill over into neighbouring communities. There are numerous examples. Educated children from one locality take jobs elsewhere and carry the benefits of their education with them. Clean air in one area is polluted by lack of it elsewhere. In consumer theory, an externality is defined by Meade (1973) in this way: 'An external economy (diseconomy) is an event which confers an appreciable benefit (inflicts an appreciable damage) on some person or persons who were not fully consenting parties in reaching the decision or decisions which led directly or indirectly to the event in question'. A first and obvious way to improve matters in the face of external effects is to rearrange the institutions of society in such a way that the affected persons do become parties to the decision making. And indeed clubs and local governments are themselves the outcomes of strategies to internalise decision making because of external effects. It may be supposed, however, that the external benefits that spill over in the cases to be considered, whilst appreciable, are not sufficient to justify local government consolidations, which would bring in their train welfare losses for many individuals forced to consume non-optimal quantities of local public goods.

In consumer theory, the individual operating in market places equates his marginal evaluation of the private good with the going price. If his consumption of the good creates beneficial effects for another individual (e.g. his painting his house) and if he ignores the externality, then from society's standpoint consumption is too low: Pareto optimality requires him to carry his consumption to the point where

$$MRS^i + \sum_j B^j = p \qquad i \neq j$$

where B^j is the marginal external benefit to the jth individual and p is the market price. Since selfish individuals equate $MRS^i = p$, the standard Pigovian solution is to reduce p by means of a subsidy to induce the level of provision implied by the satisfaction of the equation above.

Weisbrod (1964) and Break (1967) both argued from this standpoint that jurisdictions would ignore any spillins and would under-supply local public goods in aggregate. Williams (1966) in his path-breaking paper responded that it was unrealistic to ignore the spillins that inevitably accrued to jurisdictions when spillovers were pervasive; they would normally regard such transfers 'in kind' as income supplements and 'spend' part on private goods and part on public goods; that is, provided income elasticities of demand for both private goods and public goods were positive, coupling spillins with spillovers would result in an even lower level of provision than Weisbrod and Break envisaged. He went on to demonstrate that Weisbrod's results (i.e. the level of supply implicit in the Weisbrod problem) could conceivably be socially optimal.

To illustrate the issues, consider first of all a situation in which society comprises only two communities. They produce pure public goods that are national in benefit scope. Moreover, public goods production is additive in the sense that if A produces two units and B supplies three units, then each individual in society consumes five units.

When the level of provision in A affects utility in B, residents in B will take account of this fact in determining how much to supply and consume themselves. In this case, Pauly (1970) concludes that under-provision will invariably occur. Figure 4.4 is similar to an Edgeworth box, but only the private good is divisible; both communities consume the same quantity of public good. Private goods are shown on the vertical, public goods on the horizontal. Community B starts out at O_b; it has income O_bC, and its budget constraint is CB'. The line out of the origin – $O_b\beta$ – represents its income-consumption path. The origin for A is O_a; its income is O_aC and its income consumption path is given by $O_a\alpha$. Income consumption paths plot out a locus of tangencies between jurisdictional budget constraints at different levels of income and community indifference curves, as represented by I_a and I_b.

Left to itself, community B would locate at P. However, when B is at P, A is at P', because both must consume the same amount of the public good. Hence residents in A will collectively move to P″ on $O_a\alpha$ when faced with budget constraint CP'P″. If A is at P″, B must be located at P‴. But at P‴, the slope of any community indifference curve will be less than the budget constraint CB'; so B will reduce supply of public goods. So, by 'a series of similar actions and reactions, both communities move along the dotted line in the direction of the arrows to equilibrium at E_a and E_b respectively' (Pauly, 1970:577). Quantity

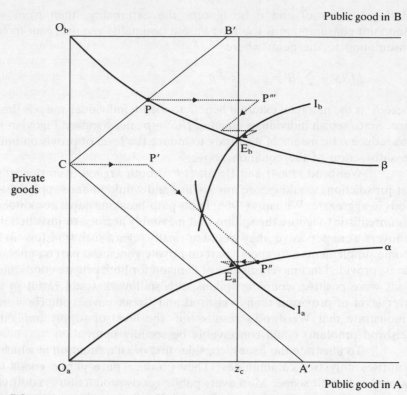

FIG. 4.4 Income expansion paths with spillovers

Oz_c is consumed by all, with production being divided between the two communities.

Now note that each community is located at a point on its income consumption path; and as is well known, at each point along such a path, for a community $\Sigma MRS = MC$. But here we have $\Sigma MRS_a = MC$ and $\Sigma MRS_b = MC$; so that $\Sigma MRS_s > MC$, where the subscripts mean communities A and B and society respectively. Decentralisation leads to underprovision in this case and the Samuelson conditions are not met.

The result is not surprising. As has already been seen on p.132 for pure national public goods optimal jurisdictional size occurs with largest N, and at club sizes less than this, the tax-price (here reflected in the budget constraint in Fig. 4.4) is not minimised. Provided the 'price' elasticity of demand for the public good is not zero, this will imply less public provision in a decentralised than in a centralised situation. One possible remedy is the Williams (1966) solution of, effectively, conferring property rights on spillovers to the supplying jurisdiction. Jurisdictions pay for spillins and are compensated for spillovers.

It has already been indicated that Williams was able to demonstrate that the Weisbrod case, where jurisdictions recognised their own spillover losses as a consequential increase in the opportunity cost of public goods that they faced, might yet produce a level of local public goods provision that was Pareto optimal. However, Williams departed from the pure public goods case in his demonstration. His goods are public within jurisdictions but private between them. The loss of a unit of public good to B deprives A of one full unit. It may be assumed that the public good is attached to persons in some way. Since the number of persons is large, the loss of one person does not appreciably affect size; and so the loss of a unit of the public good is a loss to 'everyone' in the jurisdiction.

There is no space to develop the model, but as Pauly (1970) shows, it is readily translated to Fig. 4.4. However, the flavour of the analysis can easily be appreciated. Suppose of the public goods a jurisdiction supplies, a known fraction will spill over into a neighbouring jurisdiction with a consequential loss to the supplier. Viewed this way, the problem reduces to a standard tax problem. If the fractional loss is 25 per cent of everything produced, this is tantamount to a price increase of about 30 per cent. The jurisdiction will adjust its output of the public good accordingly. If property rights were to be conferred on it for the spillover amount and it was to receive a lump-sum compensation in lieu, this is tantamount to an increase in income and will have a positive income effect. It is possible for these two behavioural parameters to take values that would lead to an excess supply of public goods, as compared with the no-spillover situation. Brainard and Dolbear (1967) point out that Williams's compensation scheme implies a redistribution of income; and Brennan (1969) has drawn attention to the inapplicability of the Williams result to inferior local public goods. Mohring and Maslove (1973) have sought to evaluate the probability of the Williams effect occurring, and claim that there is only a remote chance of the behavioural parameters having the necessary values, but they acknowledge that Williams in private correspondence with them disagreed.

Just as the benefits can spill over from one jurisdiction to another, so can the tax payments, a point that Williams noted in passing. Sandler and Shelton (1972) combined beneficial spillovers with tax exporting, which can occur if the price of goods produced in a community can be hiked in the long run in response to a change in property tax rates. Figure 4.4 is appropriate again, but the analysis must now allow for the fact that tax exporting effectively means that community budget lines will move out and away from their origins. There is an additional income effect. Just as Williams was able to show that paradoxically a generator of spillovers could actually supply more local public good, so with tax exporting, Greene (1975) has shown that a tax exporter could supply less public goods than he would if the jurisdiction was burdened with the full impact of the tax.

If spillovers occur, it is unlikely that a decentralised system of local governments would provide an optimal level of local public goods. Some policy of government intervention, possibly as outlined by Williams, would be necessary to ensure efficiency. In the case of under-provision, grants-in-aid could be designed to ensure that various local governments produced an efficient level of output. The greater the fraction of spillover, the higher the 'price' faced by jurisdictional residents and the greater the grant required fully to compensate the jurisdiction for this welfare loss.

A NON-TIEBOUT WORLD

Individuals operating in market places are typically price takers and quantity choosers. They are commonly both price and quantity takers in the public sector. But as Tiebout reminded us, local governments can play an important allocative role by providing a shopping analogue; households by voting with their feet can become quantity choosers as in the private sector.

Various problems associated with the Tiebout process have already been examined. Some of these implied larger local governments and consequentially, for some individuals at least, a regression to price and quantity taking in the public sector. As Samuelson (1958) pointed out, some people want more of a community than simply a local-public-good supply; they might prefer heterogeneity; they may want to be near the sea or a National Park, close to the arts, or prefer simply to live with 'nice' people (as Tiebout puts it). When this is so, and with central government intervening on the part of the national majority, the Tiebout shopping analogue may be seriously eroded (Topham 1977). A further consideration is that an individual can only shop spatially for one public good; if he shops for a quantity of schooling, for example, he must *take* the associated quantity of police services provided in that geographical area.

The Tiebout process presupposes that local public goods are confined to a small geographical area. In the discussion of optimal club size, however, we reminded ourselves of the obvious: for pure public goods, the optimal size of club is society as a whole. The benefits of any locally-provided service may extend over a wide area and that consideration will be an important factor in determining the spatial size of the club. It will be appropriate to assign some public services to central, some to state and regional, and some to local governments. And of these latter, what is normatively appropriate and what governments actually do may be two different things. Even when local governments have been set up, there is an increasing tendency in the Western world to centralisation. Following receipt of the Redcliffe-Maud Report (1969), in which the input of economic analysis was virtually zero, the British government in 1974 reduced the number of local governments in England and Wales from over 1500 to 522. Similarly, as Hirsch (1970) points out, school districts in the United States have been reduced dramatically since World War II.

In Tiebout's world, individuals are rentiers and are therefore spatially unconstrained; they are free to engage in fiscal shopping untrammelled, as most of us are, by considerations of commuting to and from work. When the analysis is confronted with large local governments or when the focus of analysis is on the outputs of regional or state governments, the Tiebout model is less appropriate.

Salter and Topham (1981) analyse a world with highly-specialised-human capital services. Labour does not receive the same return over all jurisdictions and mobility is necessary if Ricardian (scarcity) rents are to be maximised. But as labour relocates, it commonly finds that on arriving in region J, the constituent jurisdictions j_1 through j_n collectively provide only a limited range of local public goods outputs. In some countries, the number of local governments has been drastically reduced. Choice of jurisdiction is limited. As this limitation approaches unity, as it does with very large local governments in some parts of Britain and as is the case with the outputs of regional and state governments, the individual again reverts to being a price and quantity taker in the public sector.

Now suppose that in period t labour does not know under what jurisdiction it will live in $t + 1$; and further, that all local output decisions are about to be made, implying that incoming migrants to jurisdictions are effectively disenfranchised in the short run. Given some variation in local outputs, the possibility arises that a worker in $t + 1$ will move to an area where the local fiscal basket is less attractive than the one he currently consumes. He will still be a net gainer on relocation, of course; otherwise he would not move; but the reduction in his local fiscal residual will offset to some extent the enhanced Ricardian rent associated with the new job. He would prefer the new job with the old fiscal basket.

A reduction in local fiscal residual is a welfare loss that a utility-maximising individual will seek to avoid. The greater the dispersion in local outputs, the greater the welfare loss that may be expected on moving.[11] Salter and Topham (1981) demonstrate that in these circumstances there is an obligation on central government to offer to moderate every local spending decision by an amount society as a whole approves of. In other words, through the democratic process, central government must seek a more preferred (i.e. reduced) variance of local outputs. What is required is national coercion of local majorities. This argument for central interference in local spending decisions is additional to that associated with spillover effects.

An interesting paper by Rose-Ackerman (1981) points out that voting may be different in a federal structure than in a unitary one. This is because of tactical voting. If a quarter of the country lacks an advantageous facility that the other three quarters have, there may not be a majority vote at a central level for universal provision. Such considerations are ignored in the analysis above.

A PORTFOLIO APPROACH TO THE DISTRIBUTION OF OUTPUTS

In a federal system of government, the individual has two roles to play – as a member of both the national and the local (or regional) community. As a member of the local community, the individual desires maximum freedom in the initiation and pursuance of policies; but as a member of the national community, he does not want members of other local communities to have the same freedoms as he desires for himself. What we have just illustrated is that each individual has a rational, economic interest in what is being done in other jurisdictions. This is so for two reasons. Some of the benefits of what occurs in other jurisdictions will spill over into his own jurisdiction. Second, if each job in society is mapped into a single jurisdiction (i.e. commuting opportunities across jurisdictions are limited) as in Salter and Topham (1981), and if there is a probability that a worker will change his job in a subsequent period, possibly moving to another and as yet unrevealed jurisdiction, then he will be interested in the output of every jurisdiction in society. One day he may live elsewhere.

Thus, the central government, which represents all individuals, has a justifiable interest in all local tax-spending decisions.

Whereas, traditionally, analyses of grants in aid have focused on the response and effects within the recipient locality (see section 5), as early as 1952 Scott asked whether we should not consider the welfare gained by the national government from such donations. As he points out, there must be such a gain in welfare; for if this were not so, why would grants be given at all? By and large, Scott's plea has gone unheeded.

In a recent paper, Barnett and Topham (1977b) have endeavoured to remedy this omission. They consider the distribution of grants-in-aid strictly from the point of view of central government. As we have seen, left to themselves local governments would fail to take account of spillover benefits arising from their provision of local public goods, and therefore the level of provision on *average* would be too low. Further, if local governments are large, the *variance* of outputs may be too great. Central government can be viewed as considering the distribution of local outputs as a portfolio; it can then use its instrument of grants-in-aid to achieve a more desirable distribution of local outputs – move to a preferred mean-variance combination.

Of course, if the Tiebout shopping analogue is operating tolerably well, there is no need for governmental interference to alter local tax-spending decisions. There may still be a spillover problem, of course. But central government, even in a Tiebout world, may be interested in categorical equity, as Feldstein (1975) has termed it; there may be certain categories of goods that the government (i.e. individuals generally) thinks should be equally accessible to all who wish to partake of them. Education is an apposite example here, equal access being a constitutional imperative in the United States.

However, there may be a conflict between spillovers and equity. A frequently quoted example of a spillover in the literature is education. As in Williams's (1966) analysis, it is a spillover that attaches to the person in some way; an individual carries the benefits of an education received in one jurisdiction to work with him in another jurisdiction. But as Barnett and Topham (1977b) point out, if one jurisdiction is educationally conscious, emits a high response to grants-in-aid for schooling, and if its children grow up, achieve fame, and leave it – taking spillover benefits with them; if that is the situation, the spillover literature indicates a grant is required, which leads to more educational inputs, possibly more spillovers, and more grant. Meanwhile, another jurisdiction may have a low collective taste for education and low response rate to any grant-in-aid; but it would attract no grant because its offspring transmit little spillover to neighbouring jurisdictions as they grow up.

This is the nature of the choice analysed by Barnett and Topham (1977b). Society is interested in the outputs of all jurisdictions, and their outputs enter the social welfare function in some way:

$$W = h_1(q_1 \ldots q_J; X)$$

where the q are the outputs of the J jurisdictions and X is a vector of other variables; if the function is separable (i.e. utility from local public goods is not a function of X) we can ignore X. To be interested in every jurisdictional output is tantamount to deriving utility from the distribution of outputs:

$$W = h_2(\mu, \sigma)$$

where μ is the mean of the q and σ is their variance. Society wishes to maximise this function subject to some constraint. Let the output of jurisdiction j be given by

$$q_j = A_1(y_j + g_j)^\alpha$$

where A_1 is a parameter, y_j its average household income, g_j a block grant from central government, and α is the elasticity of demand q with respect to a change in g. Now if the whole of the central-government grant available is divided up between, say, two jurisdictions:

$$G = g_j + g_k$$

The penultimate equation can be solved for g_j (similarly for g_k) and inserted into the above equation; then introducing the statistical definition of μ and σ, it is possible to derive G as:

$$G = f(\mu, \sigma)$$

So the problem is to maximise $W = h_2(\mu, \sigma)$ subject to this consideration. This is the procedure of Barnett and Topham (1977a) and their analysis is illustrated diagrammatically in Fig. 4.5.

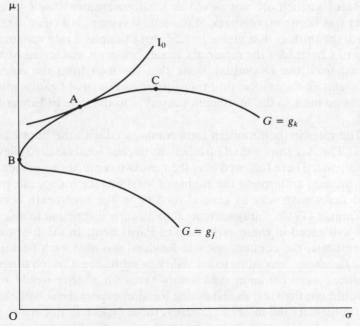

FIG. 4.5 Distribution of local public goods

The mean is shown vertically and the variance of outputs horizontally. Society prefers high μ and low σ here, and that is why the indifference curve (i.e. $\bar{W} = h_2(\mu, \sigma)$) takes the shape it does; a move north-west is a move to a preferable position. The grant can be given all to one jurisdiction or all to the other or something in between; the initial incomes of the jurisdictions and their respective responses to grant aid account for the multivalued, banana shape of the budget constraint facing central government. Society achieves its optimum at A. Note that B (uniformity – zero variance) and C (maximum output in aggregate) will not normally be chosen combinations.

It would have been preferable for Barnett and Topham to have used a matching or an achievement grant, which we refer to on pp.177–81; either grant would allow central government to achieve point A with lower G.

4. Property taxes

HISTORY

The earliest taxes on land predate virtually all structures in Britain, and local taxes of one kind or another have been levied since time out of memory. Danegeld was a Saxon tax on land. Poll taxes as local taxes were levied as early as 1198 and the London riot of that year was a revolt against a tax regime that burdened large families. In the fifteenth century, there are examples of poll taxes in Ipswich, although in this case they varied according to rank and thus incorporated an element of progression.

Rates as such are not as old as local government itself. Much local government was borne on the back of the feudal system. No clear case of rates appears until the thirteenth century. In 1256, for example, a rate was levied from the County of Chester for the repair of Chester bridge; it was levied because the King learned from the Doomsday Book that the men from the county were obliged to maintain the bridge, thus transforming a feudal obligation into a rate. Church rates go back to the fourteenth century – to the time of Edward III and Richard II.

The rates in their modern form commenced with the Poor Law Relief Act of 1601. The Act empowered jurisdictions to raise local taxes to alleviate the plight of the poor. There followed over the next two centuries a number of other Acts of Parliament authorising the raising of local finance for specific purposes. Earmarked taxes gave way to general funding in the nineteenth century.

Cannan (1912)[12] draws attention to an early distinction in assessing tax burdens as evidenced in these early Acts of Parliament. In the fourteenth and fifteenth centuries, the common view in England was that each person should pay in *juxta facultates*, according to his ability or substance. Church tithes (tenths of all produce) were common, and ability taxes for charity would seem but natural. Would not the vicar in first asking for alms expect those with the largest incomes to contribute the most? Eventually, these expectations became require-ments. And as local governments assumed responsibilities for the destitute under the Poor Law and earlier legislation, taxation according to ability for such 'onerous' purposes was adopted without demur.

In the sixteenth century and onwards, however, certain rates were levied according to benefit. An Act of 1532 for destroying crows, and a more comprehensive one of 1566 for the preservation of grain, were both based on this principle. The first was concerned to procure a village net to catch the crows[13] and the latter required the provision of a fund out of which to pay rewards for eggs and heads of birds and vermin, including foxes, which destroyed crops. Under each, proprietors and farmers were taxed in accordance with the portion of lands that they held in the parish. Those with the most lands benefited the most.

The following Act is in the same tradition but is also of relevance to discussions of capitalisation of fiscal residuals. The preamble to an Act of 1545, Cannan informs us, refers to the disrepair of Scarborough Pier, which imperilled the safety of the harbour. Consequently, the inhabitants and dwellers of Scarborough were impoverished, and the rents and farms (i.e. leases) were low. If the pier was repaired, the subsequent trade and prosperity would allow lands and houses to be 'letten for much greater rents or farms'. Masters and keepers of the pier were appointed and a fifth of all rents receivable (that is, a rate of 20p in the £) was to be paid over annually.

The basic principle adopted in these three Acts is taxation according to benefit. In assessing rates according to benefit, the view taken is that all fixed property is raised in value in equal proportion, and so a rate on such property held is levied. Thus we get the notion of *beneficial* local activities, a phrase that has lived on to the present day.[14] Work on sea defences and the like, and, as exampled, the destruction of crows and vermin and the rebuilding of Scarborough pier, all benefited property values.

On the other hand, certain activities a jurisdiction was required to undertake did not raise local property values – at least, differentially they did not – and such taxation was held to be *onerous*. Building jails and conveying prisoners thereto, paying for local Members of Parliament, reimbursing the victims of footpads, and relieving people suffering from the plague, all fall into this class. Onerous taxes were to be borne equably; a person's ability to pay taxes was measured by the land he owned or the house that he occupied. Often the benefit and ability approaches amounted to much the same thing, but it was not invariably so.

The rates as we know them today grew out of the poor rate. At first, the relief of the poor was a matter for charity. People were exhorted to give to the poor each Sunday at church. Gradually such appeals hardened into expectations, and those who did not give were brought before ecclesiastical courts – more feared than civil justice at the time. The principle of *juxta facultates* required people to give as much as they were able: to give according to ability. Such ability must have been measured by property, because in the Middle Ages only a few people had sufficient salaries to live off, and these were usually government employees, such as naval officers, and judges and barristers. Pepys, a high-ranking civil servant even at the time his diary was written, quite clearly had a large salary. On the whole, however, it was property that gave rise to income; poor rates were seen as local income taxes, levied according to ability.

In earlier times, there was much dispute as to what was property. Did it include a watch in a gentleman's pocket, his cattle, his stock-in-trade? Until the nineteenth century, the latter were included, but since 1840 the rates have been strictly a tax on the rental value of immovable property. The rateable value of a propery (the tax base) is the rent at which the property might reasonably be expected to let from year to year if the tenant bore the cost of repairs, insurance, and maintenance generally.

The major exception is agricultural land and buildings, which pays no rates; agriculture has been fully derated since 1929, and prior to that was rated at only 25 per cent of annual value. Likewise, domestic property is partially derated; the domestic element of the central government's rate support grant was the instrument by which the derating of domestic properties was achieved; new legislation in 1980 changed the name only, and the grant by which the government pays a proportion of domestic rate bills is known as the domestic rate relief grant. The amount of aid has increased over the years from 3.6 per cent in 1967/8 to 27.5 per cent in 1975/6, though it has fallen since then. There is a distinction between agricultural and domestic derating; agriculture property is not part of the tax base, but domestic property is and part of its tax bill (18.5p in the £ in 1981/2) is paid by central government.

Less than 40 per cent of local finance comes from the rates. This statistic rises to over 40 per cent if direct charges (e.g. admission charges to facilities, fees, and rents) are ignored. Domestic property accounts for less than half of the total yield from rates. However, in a national context, the rates are an important tax: in terms of yield they rank second only to income tax, and account for over 10 per cent of the revenue received from central and local taxes.

OLD VIEW

The property tax is both a tax on the value of structures and a tax on the value of the land on which they are erected. A distinguishing feature of a system of local property taxes is the lack of uniformity in tax rates levied. Capital is spatially mobile in the long run, whereas land's location is fixed[15], and in the traditional view, recognition of this fact is important in allocating the burden of the tax.

Consider the factor that is perfectly inelastic in supply – land. Its supply schedule is shown in Fig. 4.6 as SS_1. Prior to the introduction of a tax, the price of the factor per unit is p_1. If a tax of x per unit is imposed, the demand curve facing the factor owner falls everywhere by the amount of the tax; because the demand for the factor in use has not changed, willingness to pay remains unchanged, and so the net-of-tax price received by the owner is $p_1 - x$. A tax on a factor in inelastic supply is borne wholly by the owner of that factor.[16]

Figure 4.6 refers to only one time period whereas land is virtually indestructable. If a tax is levied on land and it is thought to be permanent by agents in markets, the price of land will be affected not simply by the tax to be

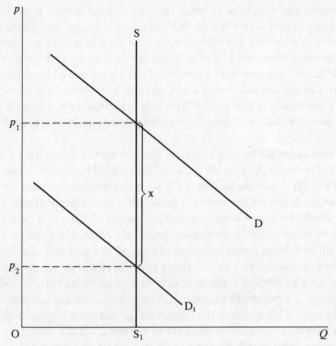

FIG. 4.6 Tax incidence with an immobile factor

paid in the year of introduction of the new tax rate, but by the present value of
the stream of tax payments into the future thought to be associated with that
piece of land. If R is land's resource value prior to the introduction of a tax,
other things equal its after-tax value (V) will be:

$$V = (1 - t)\frac{R}{r}$$ [12]

where t is the tax rate and r is the market rate of interest.[17] Now if in some later
period the tax is raised again, there will be a new after tax value (V') given by:

$$V' = V\left(1 - \frac{dt}{1-t}\right)$$ [13]

where dt is the change in the tax rate. Suppose ownership of the land changed
between [12] and [13] and at a time when t was considered permanent. The new
owner would have paid V per unit for his land. When the tax rate changes from t
to $(t + dt)$, he makes a capital loss of $(dt/r)R$; however, the original owner made
a capital loss of $(t/r)R$, and he was unable to recoup this when he sold his land to
the new owner. In considering how to apportion the burden of a tax on land, it
follows that the burden of the tax rate $t + dt$ falls on the original owner in the
proportion $t/(t + dt)$ and on the new owner by one less this fraction. If it is the
intention to determine the incidence of the property tax *today*, then one has to
take account of the fact that it is the heirs of original owners (or, to be more

precise, those who did not inherit what they otherwise would have inherited) who bear the proportion $t/(t + dt)$ of the existing property tax. Since taxes on land in England have existed for almost 400 years, because various expectations about tax rates have been held, and millions of contracts and bargains struck over the centuries, no one will ever know what the incidence of a property tax on land is. All economists can say is that taxes on land are borne by landowners and assume today's landowners are yesterday's heirs. In this way, taxes on land are held to be progressive because the rich own proportionately more land than the poor.

In sharp contrast to this analysis, the old view concentrated attention on the capital value of propery liable for local taxes, and held that in the long run capital was perfectly variable in supply and by implication perfectly mobile between locations. A tax on the use of a factor that is perfectly elastic in supply will be borne wholly by those who demand the factor.[18] To see why this is so in this context, it is important to recognise that since capital is fixed in the short run, prices of output from structures that are taxed are not initially affected by the tax.[19] Since capital is fixed in the short run, its rewards are in the form of economic rent, and in period 1 the property tax reduces its return. When new decisions are made – whether to replace or relocate – some capital will leave the high-tax jurisdiction. This reduces the supply of the services it provided, and the prices of these services will rise in markets in period 2. If the structure taxed is residential housing, the level of rents will rise until the after-tax return on residential capital is equal to the after-tax return it can expect in another location. Under this view families, as consumers of housing, will bear the consumers' portion of the tax burden in proportion to their housing expenditures,[20] which is roughly proportional to normal income.[21] Land will bear the producers' portion of the tax burden.

To illustrate, Fig. 4.7 describes the market for local housing services. The jurisdiction faces a perfectly elastic supply of capital at a fixed rental rate. As more and more capital is applied to a fixed amount of land, diminishing returns set in, causing the supply curve (S) to slope upwards. Initially, the producer's surplus Ap_1G accrues to landowners as rent. The tax on consumers shifts the demand curve for housing from D to D_t. Price rises from p_1 to p_2 and the quantity demanded falls from q_1 to q_2. Producers receive the after-tax price of p_3. Consumers pay a higher price of p_2 and bear the burden $(p_2 - p_1)q_2$ of the tax yield. Producers lose $(p_1 - p_3)q_2$; and since capital (and labour) is perfectly mobile and land is immobile, landowners bear this part of the burden themselves. The shaded triangle is the welfare-cost of taxation[22]; that is, the producers' and consumers' surplus lost as a consequence of a reduced volume of housing services.

To summarise the old view. Landowners in general are unable to escape the tax on them, although new landowners may bear little of this burden if they are not yesterday's heirs. The tax on structures was passed on to those who demanded their services, because structures were perfectly variable in supply in the long run. Rents rise and fall inversely with property tax changes in the long run. So do the prices of other commodities produced by capital.

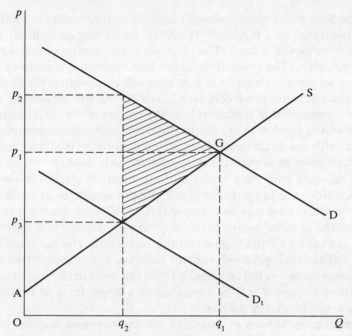

FIG. 4.7 Incidence of a tax on housing

NEW VIEW

Recent work by Harberger (1962) and Mieszkowski (1972) has set property taxes in a general equilibrium framework. The old view was set in a partial equilibrium framework, and it is now seen as suitable only for analysing the distributional effects of a change in its property tax rate by a single jurisdiction; but it is not appropriate in a national setting for analysing the average burdens that property taxes impose on capital.[23]

Short-run incidence

Profit-maximising firms fix prices in the short run on the basis of variable costs; taxes on capital are fixed costs, and do not affect price and output policies. In the short run, property taxes are borne by capital and land, both immobile factors whose rewards are in the nature of economic rents. The value of assets subject to tax fall when the tax is imposed and their owners are unable to escape the tax, since any new contracts of sale would take into consideration future tax payments. Profit-maximising rents are unchanged, and tenants do not pay the tax in the short run.

Long-run incidence

Uniform tax rates. Now consider the long-run effects of a uniform tax on property – in this context, it is assumed that all jurisdictions set tax rates the same.[24] In the long run, capital is fixed in amount neither locally nor nationally, but it is assumed that land is fixed.[25] However, let us suppose initially that the national supply of capital is fixed. The situation is now similar to Fig. 4.6. A tax is levied on occupiers. The price of residence falls by the full amount of the tax, from p_1 to p_2; supply is unchanged at S_1S. Demand by consumers is unchanged, but the after-tax demand producers face is less by the full amount of the tax. Since capital is fixed, so that capitalists bear the burden of the tax, consumers do not bear any of the burden of the tax in this polar case. Both consumer prices and factor rewards are unchanged; there are no distortions in consumer choices and no welfare costs in consumption associated with the tax.

In the long run, even under uniform taxation, capital is *variable* in supply. In addition, the property tax is not comprehensive in its coverage (for example, agricultural land may be exempted). Capital will leave the taxed sector and move into the untaxed sector. In this way, as Mieszkowski pointed out, a tax on property is a tax on capital in general in the economy. The output of housing services will fall and their price will rise; the contrary movement will occur in the untaxed sector, and just as in Harberger's (1962) analysis of the corporation tax, after-tax returns to capital will be equalised at a lower level as capital in the economy as a whole shares the tax.[26]

However, a burden in excess of the tax payment may be borne by capital and land. Housing, for example, is capital intensive and the untaxed sector may not be; so that there will be a decline in the demand for capital relative to that for labour. In such cases, labour would gain and capital would, as it were, be twice burdened. Which way it will go will depend on the initial combination of labour and capital in the two sectors, the substitution elasticities of labour for capital in both sectors, and the elasticities of substitution of one sector's product for the other sector's in consumption. Harberger (1962) felt that these issues did not count for much and capital bore most of the tax.

There are two other effects. As the output price of housing services increases, and that of another sector decreases, there is a change in relative prices. Those for whom the output of the taxed sector bulks large in purchases will suffer a loss of real income. This will add a progressive or regressive effect to the incidence of a uniform property tax as such incomes are high or low. What is significant in such qualifications is that they represent a shift from the polar case of Fig. 4.6 towards the traditional view of incidence set out in Fig. 4.7; the larger the untaxed sector, the more the analysis shifts towards Fig. 4.7 and away from Fig. 4.6.

If the taxed sector is small relative to the untaxed sector, the effects of the tax will be spread widely and its effects imperceptible. Blake (1979) has argued that there are extensive opportunities for firms to avoid the property tax. Investors can move (a) into human capital – education, training, migration, health; or (b) they can transfer into publicly-owned capital and purchase bonds. Neither (a) nor (b) is subject to the property tax. Firms, moreover, 'invest' in more than property – R and D, brand name developments, and management training programmes are forms of untaxed investments for the firm. Multinational firms can invest abroad. If these arguments are accepted, the untaxed sector is indeed extensive, capital is highly elastic in supply, and land as the immobile factor will bear the whole of the tax.

Finally, if capital is untaxed and it is not inelastic in supply, a tax in one sector of the economy that effectively reduces its rate of return overall will lead to a reduction in its supply as savings are reduced. Consequently, because land is fixed in supply, it will bear a disproportionate burden; there is less capital to work with, and land rents will fall. In addition, there will be a reduction in the capital to labour ratio, a lower national income, and a fall in real wages. Whether these effects are large or small is unclear, but Feldstein (1974) has suggested that labour may bear a third of the burden of a tax on capital income.

Differential tax rates. Local tax rates vary. Uniformity in tax rates levied is not a desirable objective because some measure of independence in tax-spending decisions is the essence of local democracy. Thus far the analysis of the new view has been conducted as if rates were uniform, and the time has now come to drop this assumption. However, when the uniform rates assumed represent the average of all jurisdictional tax rates (in the presence of differential tax rates), what has just been discussed is of crucial importance for apportioning tax burdens between various groups in society. Mieszkowski distinguished between the *average* rate of tax for the nation (borne by owners of capital) and local *differentials* around that average, which he called excise effects. These excise effects are now examined. Note that McLure (1977) insists that the new view of the property tax is the analysis of a *national* change in rates, a change *on average* in the property tax rate. Analysis of the excise effects of tax rate differentials is an application of the old view, albeit with more emphasis on the sharing of differential benefits by factors such as land and labour that are tied to local taxing jurisdictions. And it has to be added that increases in the returns to factors in jurisdictions imposing less than average rates was something the old view generally failed to recognise.

The incidence of tax-rate differentials is interesting analytically and important for local decision making; but by and large it is a zero-sum game with, for example, losses to factors in high tax regions of the economy offset by gains associated with low rates elsewhere. As will become clear, it is difficult to unravel the effects of differential tax rates, and the results are heavily dependent on assumptions made about factor mobility.

Suppose now that one small jurisdiction raises its tax rate whilst all others hold theirs at a uniform rate. In the short run, as noted already, price and output policies of profit-making firms are not affected by the tax, and capital in the high-tax jurisdiction bears the tax as a reduction in the economic rent of fixed factors of production. Capital losses are made by existing owners in the way described on p.159 above, and these are never recovered. In the long run, new capital is mobile. In the high-tax jurisdiction, maintenance expenditures on old assets are not pursued and investment in new ventures falls. There is a relocation of capital away from the high-tax jurisdiction. Investment will proceed only up to the point where its after-tax return is the same as elsewhere. In other words, capital is perfectly mobile and therefore *new* owners do not bear any of the incidence of the tax in the long run.

Whom does the tax burden? Consider Fig. 4.7 again. If x is now allowed to denote the local differential, the analysis proceeds as before. The tax is borne locally and shared in some way between producers and consumers.

In this context, suppose labour as well as capital is fully mobile. Labour is both a factor of production and a consumer. Individuals will locate in high-tax jurisdictions only if their real income is not reduced. When the population is mobile, producers are price takers, whether they produce for 'home' consumption or 'export' to other areas. Wages and prices are determined nationally and the whole of the tax burden is borne by land.

There is some argument for this position as Blake (1979) has pointed out. A spatial equilibrium does not imply households can move without costs. Transportation costs affect land prices. But at a given set of transportation prices, products, factors, and households are mobile within the system. This contrasts with the new view that holds labour and land immobile but not capital. Blake's argument amounts to the whole of the differentials incidence being borne by land.

What if all three factors are mobile? If land in a high-tax jurisdiction could be converted back to agriculture and if jurisdictional boundaries are not fixed, then in this special case, over time, the jurisdiction withers away. Land values in urban use could not fall below its agricultural use. An increase in the tax rate reduces the after-tax return to land, causing the factor to revert to agriculture. Factor prices facing jurisdictions are fixed and all local taxes will be set at a uniform rate in this special case. What is interesting about this special case is that it points up two weaknesses in differential tax incidence studies. First, they ignore the benefits associated with tax payments; in this sense, taxes can by viewed as user prices, especially in a local government context. This is dealt with below. Second, and allied to this omission, the demand for housing may be complementary to public-goods provision or it may not. If housing is a substitute for public goods, an increase in the tax rate will cause tax base erosion; but if it is not, then an increase in the tax rate can bring about an expansion in the tax base.

Mieszkowski (1972) devoted his main attention to the scenario where land is fixed, capital fully mobile, and labour imperfectly mobile. The excise effects of differential taxes are shared in some way between consumers, landowners and labourers. Land does not now bear all the tax; part of the burden falls on labour. As the flow of new capital to the jurisdiction raising the tax is reduced, the cost of capital rises, and thus the long-run price of commodities consumed locally also rises. There is a reduction in production. Commodities traded on national markets may face a bigger reduction than home goods if their price is fixed nationally, i.e. if the local producer has no monopolistic power. If, as Mieszkowski assumes, traded goods are location-specific, part of the local tax burden will be passed on, exported, in higher prices.

Two effects influence the after-tax return to the immobile factors land

and labour. Since output is reduced, there is a fall in the demand for their services. However, the prices of land and labour relative to that of capital are reduced, and so entrepreneurs will seek to substitute cheaper land and labour for capital. The output effect depresses and the substitution effect increases the demand for immobile factors. Mieszkowski shows that if the output effect dominates the substitution effect, there is a fall in returns to labour and land relative to those to after-tax capital. Making plausible assumptions about parameter values, Mieszkowski conjectures that when the demand for land is unresponsive to factor price changes, wage rates change little. For low elasticities of substitution between land and labour and land and capital, prices of land fall substantially. He concludes that on the whole one would expect that the burden of tax rate differentials are borne on the producer's side almost wholly by land; land bears up to 40 per cent of the total tax burden, consumers the rest. However, a loss in one jurisdiction is counterbalanced by a gain elsewhere in another jurisdiction; gains and losses will offset each other exactly if production techniques in the two jurisdictions are the same, otherwise there will be a change in the relative rewards to factors nationally with deleterious consequences for national income.

Decisive conclusions are not possible. How the burdens of tax rate differentials are distributed depends on whether industries are jurisdiction specific or not, and if so on whether or not they are relatively capital intensive; on the ease of factor substitutability and mobility; on elasticities of demand; and on the mobility of factors, products, and households. If capital and labour are mobile, the differential burden is borne wholly by land.

INCIDENCE STUDIES

The property tax in Britain is a tax on the rental value of housing, whether it is owner-occupied or rented; it is a tax on the rental income of the capital so employed. The most recently study of its incidence, by the Layfield Committee (1976), concluded that, after rate rebates and supplementary benefits to the poor[27] from central government have been taken into account, rating is broadly progressive in its incidence for low incomes, proportionate over a broad middle band, and regressive at higher income levels.[28] This study, like that undertaken previously for Britain by the Allen Committee (1965) before it, compares actual tax payments with measured income. There is some discussion in an Annexe to the Layfield Report of the distinction between formal and effective incidence of a tax. It recognises that all British studies relate to the formal incidence, or impact, of the tax.[29]

However, even in this Annexe, where some economic theory is being discussed, the effective incidence that is being considered is based on the traditional, the old view of the property tax. The Committee was set up in 1974 and reported in 1976; Mieszkowski had drawn attention to the inadequacies of the old view in 1972.

In the United States in 1974, Pechman and Okner were already researching the incidence of the property tax armed with the new view. They showed that the 'average' reduction in capital income was progressively borne. Their estimates showed a degree of regressiveness in the lower ranges of income, but they use measured income rather than permanent income. And since measured income always contains a number of households who are in any one year experiencing only temporary reductions in purchasing power, and conversely for some upper-bracket incomes, the degree of progression in a tax structure is disguised.[30] Their work is reviewed and updated in an excellent general survey of property tax and its incidence by Aaron (1975) to which the reader is referred.

THE PROPERTY TAX AS A USER PRICE

Consider Samuelson's famous 1954 article. Following Lindahl and Wicksell, Samuelson combines theoretically the two sides of the budget. The theory of public goods envisages *pseudo* tax prices levied as individualised lump-sum taxes; the lump-sum is derived in a theoretically straightforward way – an individual's marginal evaluation times the given quantity of public good supplied. In other words, MRS = 'price' in the public-goods case, just as it does in private-market places. Now in private-market places one does not conduct studies of the *incidence* of market prices, because we know there is no burden there; in private-market places marginal payments are precisely offset by marginal benefits. If we live in a Samuelsonian world, concern with incidence of the property tax is a waste of time. Mieszkowski (1972) and others conduct their analysis, as Blake (1979) aptly puts it, just as if property tax revenues 'were simply redistributed outside the taxing district'. In a word, local benefits from public spending are zero. What is being measured in property-tax incidence studies is the burden of the *fiscal residual*, defined as marginal benefits less marginal tax costs times quantity of public goods; but measured under the special-case assumption of zero benefits.

The incidence literature is not just at odds with public-goods theory: it is at odds with most of the literature of fiscal federalism. The theory of clubs, as we have already seen, treats tax (club) shares per unit as user prices. The economic forces behind the Tiebout shopping analogue (a process of assigning individuals to clubs) are generated by an analysis focusing on user prices. At a more practical level, recent econometric investigations of local government current expenditure using median-voter models naturally have tax-shares or tax-prices as arguments in demand functions for local public goods.[31] Some of the capitalisation literature and papers on the theory of grants also see local taxes as user prices.[32]

Recall the discussion of the historical origins of the property tax. The early statutes distinguished between local activities that were especially beneficial to property values and those that were not. This led Cannan (1912) and Marshall (1920) and lately Foster *et al.* (1980) to distinguish between beneficial and onerous taxes. The incidence literature treats local taxes as onerous; public goods and club theorists, those who see local taxes as user prices, regard local expenditures as largely beneficial. If there is always a perfect correspondence between marginal benefits incurred and incremental tax costs, no further attention need be paid to problems of property tax incidence. The property tax furnishes perfectly a system of user prices. The questions that prompt themselves are: When can the property tax be accepted as a system of user prices? What prior conditions have to be fulfilled to bring about a perfect matching everywhere of benefits and tax costs?

Mieszkowski has significantly moved his position on the property tax. His 1976 essay concerns itself with the property tax as a system of user prices. He follows Hamilton (1975a) in demarcating conditions for this to occur. The underlying model in Hamilton's paper is the theory of clubs; but entry to the club is not determined by existing club membership, as implicitly envisaged in the theory of clubs, but by a zoning regulation on property. As before (p.132), the tax price of a local service is what an individual pays in taxes for one unit of the good. When the local service is truly a local public good, one unit of the good is consumed equally by all. Hence in contrast to the case of a collectively-supplied private good, the tax price to an individual is now $p(h/H)$, where H is the stock of housing in the jurisdiction and where p is the resource cost of public goods. Obviously, given jurisdictions equal in size of population, the tax price you pay is a function of the average size of property in the area.

Suppose, given a system of relative prices, the amount of housing you wish to purchase is h^*. Suppose also that all housing in the jurisdiction is homogeneous, so that the tax-price is p/N, where N is the population of households, and that faced with this tax price the quantity of public goods you wish to purchase is z^*. In Hamilton's zoning system, clubs state the minimum property size acceptable. It is not possible to build a house of size h^* if the zoned minimum is $2h^*$. The house of size h^* must be built in a club where that size is the minimum or one where it is less than that. But if the *effective* minimum is less than h^*, then the average house size is less than h^* and thus the tax price facing a man with house h^* is greater than $(1/N)p$. The optimal strategy is to live up to the minimum, so to speak. Since everyone else in society follows the same strategy, and if a large number of clubs can be formed, all clubs are homogeneous in house size. Provided there are a large number of homogeneous clubs with house size h^*, it is possible to search among them to find the jurisdiction where its z approximates or equals z^*. When this occurs for all individuals, perfect stratification occurs and the property tax is simply a user price.

Marshall pointed out in his famous *Principles* that people would move to escape onerous taxes. In Hamilton's model, we see that the Tiebout process operates and is indeed the driving force, as individuals shop around in an attempt to escape even beneficial taxes; when the system is in equilibrium, individuals have minimised their burden and the property tax is a set of user prices.

Mieszkowski (1976) goes on to point out that given perfect stratification and mobility between jurisdictions the same result would occur with a property tax replaced by a tax on wages or cigarettes. Under a wage tax, high-wage earners congregate together; under a cigarette tax, moderate smokers live with moderate smokers, abstainers with abstainers, and so on. There is one reservation. Hamilton in describing perfect stratification stated that no deadweight loss is incurred with equal-sharing arrangements. This is incorrect.[33] A property tax increases the price of housing, a cigarette tax the price of cigarettes, and similarly with a wage tax. Economic agents, in voting for increments of the local public good or alternatively in deciding whether to move to a jurisdiction with more local public good, will take account of the deadweight loss they incur at the margin because more public good implies a higher level of taxes and thus a higher price for the taxed commodity; some adjustment of spending patterns becomes necessary and a deadweight loss is incurred. Although in homogeneous and perfectly-stratified communities different methods of taxation all yield equal-sharing arrangements, consumers adjust not simply to the tax price but to the full economic costs of taxation at the margin (Atkinson and Stiglitz 1980:492); these costs include the deadweight loss of taxation, and since this is a function (in the case of commodity taxes) of 'price' elasticity of demand for the taxed commodity, it follows that different taxes will give rise to different levels of the local public good – even under equal sharing arrangements. Mieszkowski is not correct in saying that different taxes lead to the same result in these circumstances; not quite, but almost. Likewise, Hamilton makes an error in claiming no deadweight loss for a model with perfect stratification.

The main result that comes out of all this is that in a perfectly stratified and decentralised system, property taxation is tantamount to a system of user prices – ignoring deadweight losses. Mieszkowski (1976) goes on to err again in contrasting this situation with a system where the quantity of public goods is the same in each jurisdiction. In this case, he claims that his 'average' tax result is appropriate. But that result is only appropriate when benefits are zero. Mieszkowski ignores again at this point all consideration of user prices and, to all intents and purposes, assumes zero benefits. But as we know, if an individual's marginal evaluation of the public good equates with his tax bill, the property tax is a benefit tax; whether or not public goods provision is uniform across jurisdictions is irrelevant; if this condition holds the tax is not onerous. To understand the incidence of the tax then, we need to ask: When is the property tax a benefit tax?

EQUITY AND EFFICIENCY

A requirement of the Samuelson conditions for optimality in public goods supply is MRS = tax price for each individual in society, so that ΣMRS = MC. When this condition holds, no individual wants more and none wants less of the public good. In the Samuelson model, the tax system is a set of personalised lump-sum taxes; the personalised lump-sum payment demanded of an individual under this tax regime is $MRS \cdot z$, where z is the level of public goods supply. The pseudo tax price an individual faces is precisely equal to his MRS. Given their various tax prices, all individuals will demand the same level of public goods supply. Such a tax is a benefit tax. The purpose of this section is to outline the circumstances in which a property (commodity) tax would generate a set of pseudo tax prices that would also constitute a benefit tax.

We are concerned with efficiency in the supply of local public goods. The Samuelson tax system is allocatively efficient. When is a property tax efficient? To answer this question, or rather to survey the proposed answers in the literature, the first task is to develop a simple, general theoretical framework. None of the writers surveyed uses this approach, and there are wide differences in stances adopted, but all the main results can be readily evaluated this way. In general, the property tax is efficient if the volume of public goods that is supplied corresponds to the amount consumers would like to see supplied given the tax prices they face. What we seek to emphasise is the clear relationship between equity and efficiency. A tax is usually only efficient in aggregate when individually it is distributionally neutral, when MRS = tax price for everyone in society.

Consider a jurisdiction in which there is no industry. The stock of housing (property) is denoted by H. Let an individual who earns income y own property equal to h. If p is the resource cost of one unit of the public good, y-man is responsible for the fraction (h/H) of p for each unit of the public good supplied by the jurisdiction. His tax price is:

$$p^* = (h/H)p \qquad [15]$$

We suppose that h is small relative to H and that small changes in the former have no perceptible effect on the latter.

Each individual will have a demand function for the public good, and for y-man it is:

$$z = f(y, p^*) \qquad [16]$$

Assume that jurisdictional output equals the median preference of individual voters. Suppose y-man has an income greater than that of the median voter $(y > \hat{y})$, who has demand function:

$$\hat{z} = f(\hat{y}, \hat{p}^*) \qquad [17]$$

Both individuals are assumed to be identical in all but income.

What we seek are the conditions under which $\hat{z} = z$ for a benefit tax; for in that case all want the same level of z supplied; so in this context we need to know when $\hat{z}$ from [16] is the same as z in [17]. Suppose $y - \hat{y} = dy$. That is, y-man is slightly richer than the median voter. Now if the median voter were to receive an increment of income dy, would he still demand $\hat{z}$? For if this is the case, it implies $dz = z - \hat{z} = 0$.

Bearing in mind that $p = f(y)$, we can totally differentiate [16] with respect to z:

$$dz = z_y dy + z_{p^*}\, dp^* = 0$$

Divide through by dy and note that $z_{p^*} = \partial z/\partial p^*$ is negative, but becomes positive as we move it to the RHS:

$$z_y = z_{p^*} \cdot p^{*\prime}(y) \qquad [18]$$

In [18], $p^{*\prime}(y) = dp^*/dy$, reflecting the fact that the tax price facing an individual is related to his property which in turn is linked to his income. We find $p^{*\prime}(y)$ from [15]. The consumer has a demand function $h = h(y, p_h)$, where p_h is the price of housing. Equation [15] can be rewritten:

$$p^* = h(y, p_h) \cdot (p/H)$$

Since p_h, p, and H are all constants:

$$p^{*\prime}(y) = h_y(p/H) \tag{19}$$

where $h_y = \partial h/\partial y$. Before substituting [19] into [18], a little manipulation of [19] is necessary. Multiply the RHS by h/h and by y/y to yield:

$$p^{*\prime}(y) = (h_y \cdot y/h)[(h/H)p](1/y)$$
$$p^{*\prime}(y) = \theta p^*/y \tag{20}$$

where θ is the income elasticity of demand of the taxed commodity. Using [20], [18] becomes:

$$z_y = z_{p^*} \cdot \theta p^*/y \tag{21}$$

Multiply the RHS of [21] by z/z:

$$z_y = \beta \theta (z/y)$$

where $\beta = z_{p^*}p^*/z$ is the absolute value of price elasticity of demand for the local public good. Denote income elasticity of demand for the local public good as $\alpha = z_y \cdot y/z$ and cross-multiply by y/z to obtain:

$$\alpha/\beta = \theta \tag{22}$$

Theta is the income elasticity of demand for the taxed commodity, but additionally it is the elasticity of the tax-price schedule, as becomes clear when both sides of [20] are multiplied by y/p.

Equation [22] states the necessary relationship between three behavioural parameters that must hold for a property tax to be a benefit tax. Buchanan (1964) was the first to state the conditions for tax neutrality in this form. He appeared to derive them intuitively by considering a diagram similar to Fig. 4.8. Y-man and $\hat{y}$-man are identical in all but income and therefore have the same indifference map. Tax-price is a function of income. A person with income y faces budget line B whilst one with $\hat{y}$ faces $\hat{B}$. As defined by Buchanan, full tax neutrality requires MRS = tax price for all y, and this occurs when the respective indifference curves are tangential to their budget lines along the vertical drawn from $\hat{z}$. As income rises, so does an individual's demand if z is a normal good; but at the same time the tax price rises, and this has an offsetting negative effect. On the basis of this demonstration, Buchanan is able to offer the proposition: full tax neutrality occurs when the 'income elasticity of demand for the public good divided by the price elasticity of demand [is] equal to ... the income elasticity of the tax-price schedule' (1964: 229). And that is what we have proved formally.

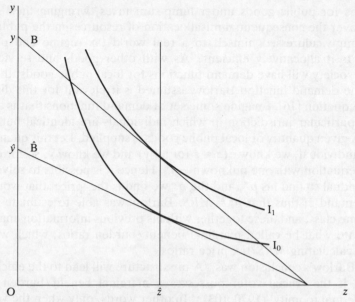

FIG. 4.8 A commodity tax as a benefit tax

We are now in a position to make a number of observations. These concern the incidence of the property tax, its allocative efficiency, and the distributional consequences of levying a tax on property. They are discussed seriatim. The point about incidence need not detain us long, but it is not the less important for that fact. When the tax schedule is fully neutral, the tax price is simply a user price, and once again analysing only the incidence of the tax is a futile exercise. This point is already dealt with in this section; here what are being underlined are the conditions that must hold if a property tax is to be a benefit tax in a heterogeneous jurisdiction. Mieszkowski's (1976) treatment of the property tax as a system of user prices rested on jurisdictions being homogeneous.

The second point concerns a possible relationship between efficiency and neutrality. When a tax schedule is neutral, the associated level of public goods supply ($\hat{z}$) is allocatively efficient. Obviously, if $MRS = p^*$ for all y, then $M\hat{R}S = \hat{p}^*$ and $\Sigma MRS = MC$. Salter and Topham (1981) outline a utility function and income distribution for which $\Sigma MRS = MC$ but $MRS \neq p^*$ for all y not $\hat{y}$; however, Topham (1981) conjectures that the circumstances giving rise to fulfilment of the aggregate Samuelson condition only, with some individuals remaining in disequilibrium, will not normally occur. Be that as it may, it is certainly a *non sequitur* to conclude from $M\hat{R}S \neq \hat{p}^*$ that $\Sigma MRS \neq MC$, and by implication, that if $M\hat{R}S = \hat{p}^*$ then $\Sigma MRS = MC$.

It was an attempt to forge this latter connection that gave rise to a controversy (1973) in the *Journal of Political Economy* following the publication earlier of a fascinating paper by Robin Barlow (1970). Whilst too many economists were devoting time to problems of free riders and non-revelation of preferences for public goods under lump-sum taxes, wringing their hands in agitation over the consequential misallocation of resources in the public sector, Barlow simply addressed himself to a real world tax regime and posed the question: Is it allocatively efficient? As with other goods and services, individuals in society will have demand functions for local public goods; the precise form of the demand function Barlow assumed is irrelevant for this discussion. Consider equation [16]. Imagine some set of demand functions that is appropriate for a particular jurisdiction in which individuals are identical but differ in income. A given quantity of local public goods is supplied. Let this quantity be $\bar{z}$. For each individual, we know $z(z = \bar{z}$ for all $y)$ and we know y; so for everyone [16] is an equation with one unknown $-p^*$. Hence it is possible to solve [16] for each individual to find his p^*, and the p^* we find is the 'price' that would cause him to demand $\bar{z}$; thus that $p^* = MRS$. Barlow was able to estimate taxes for each income class, and these together with his previous information enabled him to formulate what he called marginal benefit/burden ratios, which was tantamount to calculating MRS/tax price ratios.

Barlow's conclusion was: 'A tax structure will lead to the efficient level of output if the crucial voter possesses a marginal benefit/burden ratio-at-efficiency equal to unity' (1970:1031). In other words, only when the voter with the median preference for z is in equilibrium ($M\hat{R}S = \hat{p}^*$) will $\Sigma MRS = p$. As indicated, the paper drew a number of comments, and two of these are of interest. Barzel (1973) pointed out that when private as well as public education is available, Barlow's results represent an excess not a deficiency of public provision. Barzel's result rests on the assumption that education is a purely private good, and therefore families without children at public schools derive no benefit from local provision. Whilst Barzel's analysis is unsatisfactory in a number of ways, his point that the private option should be taken into account is an important one; and the problem was subsequently analysed by Stiglitz (1974).

Bergstrom (1973) dwells on Barlow's *non sequitur*. He points out that even if equation [22] above is not satisfied, it does not follow that the level of public-goods supply is non-optimal. In this paper, he foreshadows Bergstrom and Goodman (1973) who also derive a form of equation [22] for a constant-elasticity demand function for the local public good. Both Bergstrom and Bergstrom and Goodman relate the α/β ratio to elasticity of the tax price schedule.

The tax price confronting the median voter will depend, *inter alia*, on the distribution of incomes; the more leftward skewed this distribution, the lower the tax price facing the median voter, and hence the higher the level of public-goods supply. Bergstrom compares the output that emerges from a median-voter model (that is, an assumption that the voter with the median preference for z determines jurisdictional output and chooses $\hat{z}$) with a Lindahl-Samuelson result. So does Stiglitz (1974).[34] A Lindahl equilibrium is Pareto optimal (Foley 1970), $\Sigma MRS = MC$, but it is not clear that it is the appropriate basis of comparison. The lack of a suitable basis for comparison is also apparent in Topham (1981), who compares public goods supply under various tax regimes. The problem is discussed in Mirrlees (1981).

This brings us finally to the distributional implications of a tax on property. Recall that the neutrality condition of $\alpha/\beta = \theta$ was derived from the supposition $dz = z - \hat{z} = 0$, where z was the amount demanded with income y and $\hat{z}$ with $\hat{y}$. If $y > \hat{y}$ and $z > \hat{z}$, it follows that the MRS/tax price ratio facing y-man is greater than unity; for y-man wishes to purchase $z > \hat{z}$, where his MRS would be equated with his tax price; but he is held back to $\hat{z}$, which is chosen for the jurisdiction as a whole by the crucial, median voter. It is also true in this case that $dz > 0$ and hence equation [22] is replaced by the inequality $\alpha/\beta > \theta$. Whenever this inequality holds, those with income $y > \hat{y}$ enjoy $MRS > p^*$, and conversely for those with $y > \hat{y}$. In these circumstances, the tax regime is redistributive from poor to rich. Although Barlow does not comment on the distributional implications, being concerned only with efficiency, his tabulation shows that the MRS/tax price ratio is an increasing function of income.

An intuitive explanation of tax neutrality is not straightforward when working with α/β. A slightly different perspective allows an insight into what is going on. Imagine two people sitting on a bench looking at a rose garden. Suppose also both derive the same absolute enjoyment from it. If one is rich and the other poor, and assuming diminishing marginal utility of income, the rich man will be prepared to pay more for the pleasure than the poor man. This idea can be linked with previous discussion by using a result from microeconomics first suggested by Pigou. This says that for broad categories of goods (i.e. food, clothing, durables, etc.) the ratio of income elasticity to price elasticity of demand approximates to the elasticity of the marginal utility of income (σ). That is, $\sigma \simeq \alpha/\beta$. The result usually features private goods, but conceptually it is also true for public goods. We can replace equation [22] by the inequality:

$$\sigma > \theta \tag{23}$$

Barlow's estimates of α and β imply a value for σ of 1.89. Pigou's approximation is usually derived from observations on private markets, so it is comforting to find Barlow's estimates falling in the middle of the range of estimates[35] for σ of 1.5 to 2. Estimates[36] for θ approximate to unity.

So far as a property tax is concerned, inequality [23] appears to hold. The intuitive explanation for the non-neutrality of the property tax goes as follows. As income rises, its marginal utility falls; so that at the margin pounds paid in tax are worth less and less. At the same time, expenditure on housing rises for a normal good ($\theta > 0$) and the tax price a consumer faces increases with income. Only if the two offset each other exactly is the tax distributionally neutral; otherwise the sacrifice is not absolutely equal. As Barnett and Topham (1980) and Topham (1981) emphasise, the property tax is not a benefit tax.

5. Grants-in-aid

A TAXONOMY

The various types of grants-in-aid are described in most textbooks on the subject of fiscal federalism as well as those on public finance in general. There is therefore need for only a brief taxonomy here. Wilde (1968, 1971), McGuire (1973), and Waldaver (1973) are useful papers that provide basic outlines and helpful insights; and for a good discussion of the institutional details and the history of British grants see Foster *et al.* (1980).

Grants may be specific or general; they may be subventions in respect of a particular service or allocated to the jurisdiction to spend as it wishes. Local governments usually argue for the latter in the name of freedom and local democracy, but they are always free to refuse grants. The appropriate grant depends on the goals of the donor not the recipient. A second distinction is between matching and non-matching (or block) grants; the first is tantamount to a price reduction and the latter to an income supplement.

In general, matching grants will be more effective than block grants in stimulating local expenditures. Consider Fig. 4.9, where a public good z is measured on the horizontal and private goods are on the vertical. The community can spend all its resources on z or retain them for some other use; it is constrained by its budget line AB and imposes a tax that yields Aa resources to provide z_0 of the local public good. Now suppose central government offers matching aid. It matches local expenditure with a percentage contribution. Such a matching grant is tantamount to a price reduction; so that the local budget line pivots about A to AB'. The locality moves to E on indifference curve I_1. Provided price elasticity of demand is not zero, output will increase; in this case from z_0 to z_m; the resource cost of this latter amount is Ad, of which b'd is

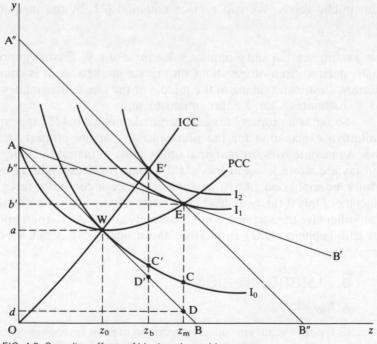

FIG. 4.9 Spending effects of block and matching grants

financed by central government aid and Ab' by local taxes. If the subvention ED had been given as a block grant (that is, as a lump-sum income supplement to the jurisdiction), the local government would have a budget line A"B" and would be able to achieve a more desired position at E', but its output would have been less than at E; z_b is less than z_m because the matching grant is effectively a price reduction which has a substitution as well as an income effect, and this is reflected by the fact that the price consumption curve (PCC) lies to the right of the 'income' consumption curve (ICC) after the initial position.

Note that of the total grant aid ED, the amount EC is received as a form of consumer's surplus by the recipient locality. Had the amount z_m been purchased at the pre-grant price, the jurisdiction would have suffered a welfare loss of amount DC as compared to the starting point W. To induce a jurisdiction to increase consumption from z_b to z_m, that is the minimum amount that would enable such a move to take place. The increase from z_0 to z_b would have required grant aid of only C'D'. McGuire (1973) says that grants in excess of CD when z_m is reached allow a government to redistribute real income to jurisdictions. But on this, see p. 181.

If the price elasticity of demand of the recipient community is greater than unity, a matching grant will induce it to spend more of its own resources on the local public good; if demand is inelastic, a price reduction will cause it to reduce its tax rate on property. This is easily observed by considering the PCC curve in Fig. 4.9. For expositional purposes, Fig. 4.9 was drawn so that the jurisdiction's initial, pre-grant position was the minimum point on its PCC; consequently, any grant would cause a reduction in tax yield – from Aa to Ab' in the case illustrated (Aa to Ab'' for a block grant). Wilde (1968) and other literature refer to this type of reduction as 'leakage'. It occurs whenever price elasticity of demand for the local public good is less than unity. If a grant is given to alleviate taxes, it is necessary that demand be inelastic.

Sometimes grants are close-ended, as opposed to open-ended. If the matching grant in Fig. 4.9 was close-ended after z_m (i.e. if the government was prepared to give matching support up to but not beyond z_m), the budget line would be AEB". But it would make no difference in the case analysed; the jurisdiction would again locate at E, which is just another way of saying that if the donor government is cognizant of price elasticities there is no need to make grants close-ended. Close-ended grants usually reflect a desire to achieve uniformity in supply of z, and almost invariably they are a sign of central government ignorance, a point to which we shall return on p. 177.

Most analyses of grants are conducted as if there was just one local public good. There are usually many. In this situation, Jurion (1979) has shown that complementarity between the aided service and the other services the jurisdiction supplies may result in matching grants being more expensive to the donor government than block grants. Whilst he sets out somewhat unusual circumstances, his results do remind us that we cannot always extrapolate from the specific to the general case.

Circumstances may conspire to give a block grant a price-reducing illusion, as perceived by voters. Oates (1979) considers a society confronted with only two options in a referendum: a larger local budget or the *status quo*. Voters make their decisions on the basis of only two pieces of information – output (z) and their associated short-run marginal tax liability (th), where t is the unit tax from $t = z/\Sigma h$, and h is the housing units consumed by a man with income y. The resource cost of z is taken to be unity. After grant aid G is received, the unit tax changes from t to $t' = (z - G)/\Sigma h$. Since $t > t'$, it follows that tax price $th > t'h$. A block grant effectively reduces the price of the local public good. Note that the after-tax price of property also changes.

OBJECTIVES

Grants-in-aid account for about half the revenue of British local authorities and for about two-thirds of their publicly-financed expenditures. State grants finance about a third of local public expenditure in the United States. As indicated on p.154, the objectives of the donor government have not been much investigated; most activity is centred on the respondent government. By and large, the literature does not analyse the circumstances in which central objectives might be achieved; it contents itself with describing these objectives. (The literature on categorical equity is exceptional in this respect.) The immediate task is to review the aims of a central government in granting aid.

Spillovers. If there is not a correspondence between the area over which benefits emanating from local public service extend and the boundary of the supplying jurisdiction, there may be a case for grants-in-aid. One first has to establish that under-provision is the problem. As discussed on p.154, this objective may conflict with equity considerations. Moreover, a grant system to deal with reciprocal externalities would run up against severe operational difficulties in the real world. So far as the author is aware, no real-world grant has been justified on these grounds.

Horizontal equity. Buchanan (1950) was the first to draw attention to a problem that might arise even though both central and local government might treat equals equally. One jurisdiction might have a lower tax base than another and would have to levy a higher tax rate to be able to provide its citizenry with just the same level of service as the other, richer community. As we shall see in the next subsection, a number of economists have adopted this stance or spoken approvingly of it, including Buchanan (1950), Thurow (1970), Le Grand and Reschovsky (1971), and Le Grand (1975). The usual solution is to base a grant on the basis of benefit/effort ratios, where benefit is utility received from or output of public goods and effort is defined as the tax *rate* – the higher the rate the greater the sacrifice. Unfortunately, these recommendations betray underlying misconceptions of local finance, in particular they ignore the capitalisation process. The point is taken up on p.181.

Needs. This term is ambiguous. To clarify matters, suppose a superior government legislates for, or the constitution of the state or country requires some minimum level of schooling for each child. The expenditure needs of a jurisdiction can then be easily defined as numbers of pupils times the average cost of schooling per child. If one locality has greater needs than another, this may be translated to mean more school children than another. Grants for 'needs' are usually of a block grant kind, with a large number of items listed on which local government can qualify for 'needs' grants – including proportion of elderly, miles of road, and size of population.

A related concept is that of *categorical equity*. The usual example is schooling. The value judgement in this case is that a child's education should not be a function of his parent's (and neighbours') wealth. If education is a normal good, children in rich communities will receive more education than their poorer contemporaries. The discussion below deals with this problem.

Alleviation of local tax burdens. A major consideration in British grant policy has been the possible rise in local tax rates in the absence of supplementary grant orders. That is, central government has been concerned to keep down the *average* level of local tax increases. This is the primary factor in the determination of the amount of grant to be made available in aggregate (Layfield Rèport 1976). A similar policy has existed in Canada (Slack 1980). As already indicated, for such a policy to be successful leakage has to occur, and this will only take place when price (matching grants) or income (block grants) elasticity of demand is low. Slack finds very low income elasticity for her Canadian observations; a $1 increase in block grant would be associated with an increase in local expenditure of only $0.01 to $0.04. Foster *et al.* (1980:284 ff.) also find no response to the income variable in their English study. However, the studies we refer to in section 6, as we shall see, do not find low parameter values for elasticities.

Distribution of local public goods. Central government may decide to use grants to effect a change in the overall distribution of local public goods, as outlined in section 3. It is always possible, however, to suggest a formula for contracting the variance of local outputs and to put it to the vote. Salter and Topham (1981) outline circumstances in which such a majority vote would be affirmative, so that no grant would be required.

CATEGORICAL EQUITY

Societies sometimes display a special interest in the distribution of certain goods and services. As with education in Britain, it may be the case that the legislatively superior government decrees minimum standards of provision, so that education becomes a merit good in jurisdictions that would not otherwise supply to the minimum standard. Often loosely and in public debate recommendations for uniform levels of provision are espoused, but these contradict the spirit of fiscal federalism and will be ignored. What will occupy most of our space in this subsection is the injunction that consumption should not be correlated with income or wealth. Before proceeding with the analysis, it is important to distinguish between categorical and horizontal equity. Categorical equity is associated with the distribution of certain goods and services that are singled out as being of 'fundamental interest'. Health care and education are obvious examples. Horizontal equity merely requires that equals are treated equally and does not distinguish between categories of goods and services; usually all local government goods and services are lumped together for such discussions.[37]

In a landmark judgement in the case of *Serrano v. Priest*, the Californian Supreme Court in 1971 and again in 1974 held unconstitutional those disparities in educational quality between school districts that result from unequal school district property tax bases. It made clear that expenditure per pupil was to be interpreted as a measure of educational quality and the market value of taxable property a measure of local wealth. The Court considered various statistics. The following, which they exampled, crystallises the problem that was before them. Expenditure per pupil is contrasted with tax base per pupil in three Californian school districts.[38] State grants that were operative at the time were insufficient to bring about equality in local tax bases. On the basis of

	Expenditure ($)	Tax base ($)
Baldwin Park	577	3706
Pasadena	840	13706
Beverley Hills	1231	50885

these and other statistics, the Court concluded education was a function of neighbourhood wealth and declared unconstitutional the system of local finance that gave rise to the consequential disparities in expenditure per pupil. However, the Court specifically stated that they did not require local expenditures to be uniform: simply, that a funding scheme that made the quality of a child's education a function of the wealth of his parents and neighbours invidiously discriminates against the poor.[39]

One obvious solution is to give everyone the same tax base. Tax-base equalisation should cause Baldwin Park, the district educating the Serrano children, to increase its per-pupil expenditure. As Feldstein (1975) pointed out, tax base equalisation or DPE (district power equalisation) grants would only fortuitously achieve the Court's objective. Letting E denote education per pupil and W per pupil tax base and A a constant, Feldstein interprets the Court's requirement as a system of grants that neutralise W, one that is tantamount to setting $\alpha = 0$ in:

$$E = AW^\alpha$$

to get:

$$E = A$$

where A is a portmanteau containing variables not germane to the argument.

As yet there is no price term; for the price of expenditure is unity. However, by a system of matching grants, it is possible to reduce the prices of expenditure faced by the various school districts. Post-grant the relevant equation for a particular school district would be:

$$E = AW^{\alpha} P^{-\beta}$$

where P is 'price' post-grant and $-\beta$ is 'price' elasticity of demand. What should this price be to achieve the previous equation? By inspection, it is clear that we must have $P = W^{\alpha/\beta}$ to get:

$$E = AW^{\alpha}[W^{\alpha/\beta}]^{-\beta} = A$$

As matters stand, all local expenditures will be less than they otherwise would be because W (wealth) no longer features as a positive determinant. What has been suggested thus far is not a grant system but a vector of local taxes positively correlated with wealth. Recognising this, Feldstein set $P = kW^{\alpha/\beta}$, where all local expenditures would be stimulated by a constant factor $k^{-\beta}$, with k set to achieve any level of expenditure thought desirable.

In his paper, Feldstein interpreted the Serrano judgement as a 'more precise rule that the elasticity of local educational spending per pupil with respect to the value of local taxable property per pupil be zero' (p.77). That is true, but the Court expressed views about the level of educational provision, as is clear from their comment: '. . . only a district with a large tax base will truly be able to decide how much it really cares about education. The poor district cannot freely choose to tax itself into an excellence which its tax rolls cannot provide.'[40]

The problem the Court posed was: How much would a district spend on education if it were rich? Design a grant system to enable it to achieve that amount. This is the direction Barnett and Topham (1977a) take.[41] In order to conduct the exposition with indifference curves, let the tax base be income y, measured on the vertical in Fig. 4.10, with the local public good measured on the horizontal. The poor jurisdiction confronts constraint yz, locates at a, and supplies z_0 to its citizens. A target jurisdiction with tax base y_t would supply z_1. The amount z_1 is found by using the formula for income elasticity of demand for z:

$$\alpha = \frac{dz}{dy} \cdot \frac{y}{z}$$

Hence:

$$\frac{dz}{z} = \alpha \frac{dy}{y}$$

where the elasticity value α is assumed constant over the range. The proportionate change in z should equal α times the proportionate change in income that would occur if the poor authority's tax base were to be increased to equal that of the rich jurisdiction. In that case it moves to b and increases its provision of z from z_0 to z_1.

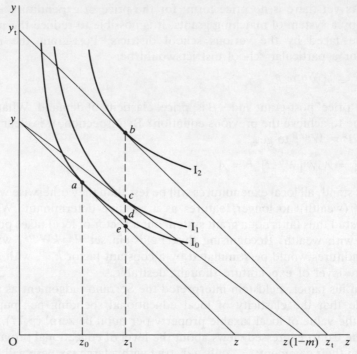

FIG. 4.10 Designing grants for wealth neutrality

For the state, the most economical way to provide grant aid is a matching grant rather than an income supplement of $y_t - y$. The price of expenditure is to be reduced from P to $P(1 - m)$ where $m < 1$ is the matching rate. The change in price is $dP = -mP$. So the question is, What price reduction would cause it to consume z_1? This is found by using the formula for price elasticity of demand (β) for z:

$$\frac{dP}{P} = \frac{1}{\beta} \frac{dz}{z}$$

The proportionate change in price should equal the proportional change in z required times the reciprocal of price elasticity. Hence by substitution:

$$\frac{dP}{P} = m = \frac{\alpha}{\beta} \frac{dy}{y}$$

Only if $\alpha = \beta$ would be it be appropriate to equalise tax bases, letting the new budget constraint facing the poor authority run from y to z_t. Unusually, Feldstein's estimates give $\beta < \alpha$, and so the matching rate does not have to be as generous as implied by base-equalisation schemes to achieve z_1.

It is a simple matter to revert from indifference curves and income to wealth (w) neutrality. The formula for wealth elasticity $[\alpha' = (dz/dw) \cdot w/z]$ is used in these equations and z_1 found in that way.

To revert to Fig. 4.10. A block grant of *eb* would achieve z_1, as would a matching grant of *ec*. However, of this amount *ec*, only *ed* is necessary to achieve z_1. Provided a jurisdiction could move costlessly from *a* to *d*, it would be indifferent where it was located. A matching grant of *ec* on the other hand allows it to improve its welfare; it moves from I_0 to I_1 on its indifference map. Barnett and Topham argue that the Court judgement did not require any increase in real income; its concern with equity was singular and categorical. Thus the compensating surplus for the price fall (*cd*) should not be paid. A block grant of *de* should be offered, together with a small inducement premium, to be paid when the jurisdiction achieves z_1. In other words, Barnett and Topham simply compensate a jurisdiction for any welfare loss incurred in compliance with the wishes of a superior government.

Of course, it is always possible to kill two birds with one stone and use the pretext of educational neutrality to bring about a change in the distribution of income. McGuire (1973) suggested this use of such grants; but there are difficulties (see p.186) when grants are paid to jurisdictions rather than people. But McGuire does at least recognise the consumers' surplus his block grant would entail; whereas when matching grants are given it is never calculated. Using Feldstein's regression estimates, Barnett and Topham are able to find an expression for the community indifference curve I_0 and thus calculate their proposed grant *ed*. They find[42] that *ec* exceeds *ed* by a factor of five. Moreover, base equalisation, because it would bring about an expansion of educational provision beyond z_1, could result in inordinate grant aid payments.

Thurow (1970) pointed out that base equalisation would achieve z_1 only if $\alpha = \beta$; if $\beta > \alpha$, jurisdictions would go beyond z_1. He appeared to approve of such expansion. Two points are relevant. First, as Feldstein points out, if $\alpha \neq \beta$, base equalisation does not achieve wealth neutrality; for example, if $\beta > \alpha$, the poor would spend more than the rich, because the response by the poor locality to the price reduction the grant allows is greater than the enhanced provision the wealthy jurisdiction provides. There may be arguments for that, but it is not what the Court required.[43] Second, grant payments can quickly become astronomical with open-ended matching grants. Base equalisation would result in grant payments 57 times in excess of *ed* in Feldstein's case.[44]

Finally, it is not true, as Hamilton (1976a) asserts, that capitalisation undercuts the *Serrano* judgement. The Court found a relationship between tax base and expenditure and declared it unconstitutional. Capitalisation, as Hamilton himself makes clear (see p.147), is a zero-sum process within jurisdictions, and therefore does not affect the issues discussed in this section.

EQUALISING GRANTS

Whilst categorical equity is concerned with the distribution of local outputs, equalising grants are a response to the application of the principle of 'equal treatment of equals' to local finance. Equals should be treated equally unless they are dissimilar in some relevant respect. People living in property assessed uniformly for tax purposes should be treated equally unless benefits derived from public goods (a relevant respect) differ. If benefits are the same, tax rates should be the same. Many economists subscribe to this view, including Buchanan (1950), Thurow (1970), Le Grand and Reschovsky (1971), Le Grand (1975, 1977), the Layfield Report (1976), Kay and King (1980), and Foster *et al.* (1980), although the latter are much more cautious than earlier writers. To his great credit, Cannan (1899) was an early demurrer, but his work was ignored. Foster *et al.* show the way in which the principle of equal treatment of equals has affected grant design. They mention other British supporters of DPE. They include the British government. Unfortunately, as we shall see, base equalisation does not treat equals equally.

Individuals may face differences in 'tax price' for either or both of two reasons. Needs may differ. Expenditure per pupil may be the same in two authorities, but if they are identical except for the fact that one has twice the number of children as the other, the tax prices for units of output *per capita* facing individuals in the fecund jurisdiction will be higher. For simplicity in what follows, we shall assume needs are the same, which does not affect the analysis in any material way. The second reason for differences in tax prices arises from unequal tax bases, and this is the reason we concentrate on.

In this context, consider Fig. 4.11. Imagine two jurisdictions, one with tax base B_t and one with B. We may regard the base of the tax as income, or we may assume that income is a suitable proxy. Tax base is on the vertical in Fig. 4.11 and expenditure on the local public good (z) is on the horizontal. Since both axes are in terms of money, initial budget lines have a slope of minus one. The richer jurisdiction faces constraint B_t B_t' and we suppose it elects to give up

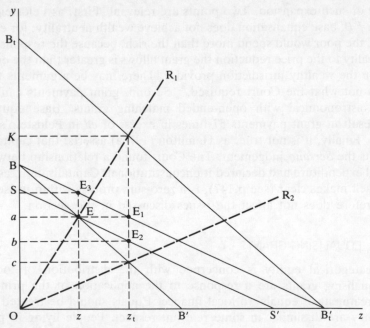

FIG. 4.11 Equalising grants

B_tK income to secure z_t of the local public good. The ray from the origin (R_1) is the reciprocal of the tax rate: the steeper the ray the lower the rate of tax. If the poorer jurisdiction levied the same rate of tax, it would sacrifice B_a income to secure only z of the local public good. And to obtain z_t it would have to move out along R_2 – levying tax rate Bc/OB.

Base equalisation schemes envisage the superior government stepping in as residual tax payer. This pivots the lower jurisdiction's tax base from BB' to BB'_t. It levies the original tax of Ba/OB to secure z whilst a government grant of ac finances the increment of output zz_t. Such a grant is tantamount to a price reduction in all the items of expenditure on which citizens of the poorer jurisdiction collectively spend their money.

In this critical discussion of equalisation grants, it is important to point out that the level of public goods is not an issue. Issues of merit goods and categorical equity are handled separately. Indeed, if all that is required is that the poorer jurisdiction provide z_t for its residents, all that is necessary is that the Slutsky line SS' is drawn in Fig. 4.11. Hypothetically, BS is withdrawn from the poor jurisdiction and with a matching grant it is offered local public goods at the cheaper, base-equalising 'price'. The old basket E is still open to choice. However, the superior government offers cb if z_t is attained at the real resource cost given by BB'. The locality goes from E to E_2 rather than E_1. It increases its tax rate, now sacrificing bc income to obtain z_t. The Slutsky compensation surplus for the price fall is not given as grant aid. This avoids many of the pitfalls of equalising grants.

It must be assumed that income and property are closely correlated for grants-in-aid to stand any chance of achieving income-based equity between individuals (Boyle 1966). Assume that to be the case. The principle of equal treatment of equals implies unequal treatment for unequals, and presumably the objective is egalitarian. Suppose that a grant is given to a locality, and 'price' elasticity of demand for the local public good is zero; the grant simply alleviates the property tax. In Fig. 4.11, the jurisdiction moves from E to E_3 receiving aS in grant aid; the whole of the grant 'leaks' away. But this is not egalitarian. Within the jurisdiction, the tax bill an individual faces falls from $(h/H)z$, where z denotes expenditure, h the individual's consumption of the taxed commodity, and H is aggregate consumption in the jurisdiction. After the grant the tax bill falls to $(h/H)[z-Sa]$, where Sa comes from Fig. 4.11. Now consider an individual with lower y consuming $\hat{h}$: his tax bill after the grant is $(\hat{h}/H)[z-Sa] < (h/H)[z-Sa]$. The rich gain most within jurisdictions. Taking benefits as well as taxes into account, Barnett and Topham (1980) outline the circumstances under which the rich gain most within a jurisdiction and conversely.

Base equalisation is applicable to two internally homogeneous jurisdictions that differ in average income. As we saw on p.146 and illustrated in Table 4.1, the individuals in the two jurisdictions pay the same price whether they are in the richer or the poorer locality, just as they would in market places. A system of grants implying that each locality, rather than levying different tax rates finance identical levels of provision is tantamount to pricing local services on a percentage basis: the price of education is, say, 3 per cent of income for each individual in the two jurisdictions. In employing tax rate as a measure of effort, advocates of base-equalising grants make the implicit assumption, as Feldstein (1975) points out, that all marginal utility of income schedules are identical and of the Bernoullian type. That is, the schedule of the marginal utility of income takes the form of a rectangular hyperbola with an x per cent decrease in income (a tax rate of x per cent) leading to an x per cent increase in marginal utility irrespective of the level of income.

Le Grand's support for base equalisation rests on the assumption that a jurisdiction's tax base is beyond its control. In one sense, because capitalisation is a zero-sum process, it is; but in another and more important sense it is not. The amount of housing a person consumes depends on his demand function. Let $h = h(y, q, z)$ express this demand function, where q is the after-tax price of housing, and equal to $p_h + t$, with t the unit tax on h and p_h its resource cost. If a jurisdiction is profligate and spends money wastefully on services from which its citizens derive little benefit, the amount of h consumed will shrink with a rise in q not offset by any perceptible change in z. Inman (1975) takes into account second-round effects of this nature in his discussion of grants-in-aid. Obviously, if a donor government offsets each base reduction with larger grants it provides insurance for the recipient authority against inefficient behaviour.

The most telling criticism is that these grants ignore the Tiebout mechanism and the associated capitalisation process. If residents in two identical houses derive the same benefits from local public goods but pay different prices for the privilege, that fact will be reflected in market prices for housing. Hence it is not what an individual pays in local taxes that is important; what matters is the amount paid for the joint basket comprising housing and local public services. Mobility between jurisdictions will ensure that joint prices are equalised across jurisdictions. Mieszkowski (1976) conducts his analysis of the property tax in just this way, and as Cannan (1899) pointed out using the same analytical framework: 'Occupiers are clearly just as well off in places where rates for unproductive purposes have long been high as in places where they have long been low' (p.191). Horizontal equity is not a problem once full capitalisation has taken place (Hamilton 1976a), and we know from Oates (1969) and the subsequent discussion that some capitalisation occurs because people are sensitive to fiscal variables.

A grant changes the tax price of residents in the recipient community. How they respond collectively depends on the operative price elasticity of demand in the jurisdiction. A system of equilibrium prices would have prevailed prior to receipt of grant by a jurisdiction; the equilibrium will be disturbed. House prices in the jurisdiction in receipt of grant almost invariably will rise. Individuals will be willing to pay more for such houses if they feel better off in them. The new circumstance is a fall in tax price accompanied by an expansion (perhaps) in local public goods provision in the recipient jurisdiction.

Consider an individual in another jurisdiction. In Fig. 4.12 he is located at A where he is, say, the decisive voter – or at any rate, where the level

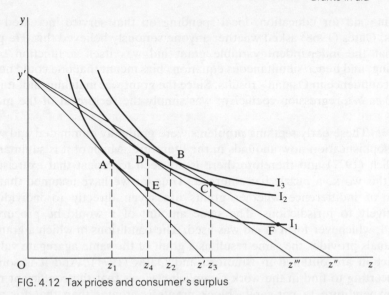

FIG. 4.12 Tax prices and consumer's surplus

of public goods is the one he would have chosen freely. He consumes z_1. After the neighbouring jurisdiction receives grant aid, he could on moving there consume at a lower tax price. Ideally, he would like to take up position B; but since he is not the median voter in the new jurisdiction, suppose he is obliged to locate at C on a lower indifference curve (I_2). How much better off is he? Construct budget line $y'z'''$. Faced with this constraint and free choice he would select point D. At D he is indifferent to C. Hence, the consumer surplus for the hypothetical price fall as measured by DE represents the income equivalent of the gain in welfare. This is similar to Barnett's (1981) measure. Note that if a level of z to the right of F were chosen, the consumer would not move – a point overlooked by Wheaton (1975). The main point (Barnett and Topham 1980) is that what is capitalised is the consumers' surplus for the price change, not the fiscal residual at the old quantity, as proposed by Hamilton (1976a). However, both analyses basically completely undercut the case for equalising grants.

Finally, Dyer and Maher (1979) point out that Hamilton (1976a) was not considering the long run. In the long run, more and more poor houses would be supplied in mixed jurisdictions and segregation would occur in equilibrium. However, it is always in the interest of the poor as well as the rich to insist on zoning for new property at above the existing average property size; otherwise tax prices will rise. After equalising grants are introduced, this is no longer necessary. Segregation is more likely in their presence than their absence.

IMPACTS OF GRANTS ON SPENDING

Depending on the behavioural parameters evinced by the local governments, grants in aid may alleviate local taxes or encourage local expenditure. Exploration has built up a large literature. Some early studies showed remarkable responses to grant aid. For example, Osman (1966) found that for each dollar of matching aid for education, local spending on that service increased by 5.1 dollars. Oates (1968) asked whether anyone seriously believed this. He pointed out that the independent variable grant aid was itself a function of local spending, and hence simultaneous equations bias meant that one could not place much confidence in Osman's results. Since the grant was matching aid, it is likely that Osman's regression coefficient was simply the reciprocal of the matching rate.

These early teething problems were gradually eliminated and work of some sophistication now abounds in the literature. Much of it is summarised in Gramlich (1977) and therefore there is no need to repeat that exercise here. From this work, a puzzle has emerged. Thus far we have assumed that it is a matter of indifference whether grants are given directly to individuals or collectively to jurisdictions. The same amount of z would be procured, we implied, whichever form of aid was used. The conditions in which a grant to all individuals provides the same result as a grant of the same aggregate value to a jurisdiction are outlined in Bradford and Oates (1971). And it is somewhat disconcerting to find in the work Gramlich reviews that the coefficient relating local expenditure to per-capita block grants is greater than that for average jurisdictional income. Okun is reportedly said to have called this the flypaper effect: money sticks where it hits. Oates (1979) has provided a possible theoretical answer in suggesting lump-sum grants have a price effect because of misperceptions of voters: hence block grants would have a substitution as well as an income effect.

Another possibility is that block grants can be converted into a matching grant by bureaus when funds are fungible. This consideration has been examined in a sophisticated model by McGuire (1975) who has been able to disentangle price from income effects. Most consumer models maximise a utility function subject to a constraint in order to derive estimating equations to check against the results. McGuire's approach is based on the supposition that the constraint is unknown to the researcher. Additional restrictions on the utility function enable him to let the observed data tell us what the constraint is as well as grant recipient's response to it.

Foster *et al.* (1980) appear to find that the Bradford-Oates equivalence theorem is unsupported by evidence. In some of their models, the coefficient on income is actually negative. However, Slack (1980) found virtually no response from a variable that combined income and block grants, suggesting that grants achieved Canadian objectives of alleviating property taxes. And Feldstein (1975) consistently found the coefficient on income to exceed that on block grants.

The flypaper effect is compatible with the economics of bureaucracy, but estimation is not straightforward and the evidence is still too conflicting to form a balanced judgement. If we accept Oates (1979), then we expect the coefficient on block grants to be higher than that on income, because of price effects. This argument runs counter to the equivalence theorem and has the advantage of providing a theoretical explanation for the empirical results Gramlich reviews.

6. Median voter models

Fiscal federalists have long been interested in the likely explanation of observed variations in local expenditures. They serve as a manifestation of the case for local governments outlined in section 2. Some variations will be determined by differences in tastes and incomes. Bearing in mind the discussion of the previous section, we may expect differences in grant support to account for some of the variation. And if there are scale economies, population might enter as an argument. If we were to proceed in this *ad hoc* way, other possibilities would soon suggest themselves. We would ask ourselves: What precisely are the determinants of observed differences in local tax spending decisions? A number of the most important positive responses to this question are reviewed by Hirsch (1970). By and large, what these studies lack is a theoretical structure.

Henderson (1968) was one of the first economists to suggest a theoretical structure, and he adopted an approach based on the concept of the social welfare function. He postulated that the local social welfare function took the form:

$$w = f(y, g, N) \cdot \ln z + x$$

where y is per capita income, g is grant-aid, N is population, z and x represent public and private expenditure levels respectively. The budget constraint is obviously $y + g = z + x$, and maximising w with respect to z and x, gives the estimating equation:

$$z = f(y, g, N)$$

Henderson estimated a stochastic form of this function. His results were both plausible and interesting. Unfortunately, his treatment of grant aid was unsatisfactory; he drew no distinctions between block and matching grants, and did not consider the possible interrelationship between g and all the other variables in the estimating equation.

However, we saw in section 2 that the quantity of local services depends on the tax price confronting voters. Are local governments mindful of what voters actually want? And if this is so, of the N members of the electorate, whose preference will dominate? Consider again Fig. 4.2 on p.137. Focus on the left-hand panel. Suppose preferences for the local public good z (measured on the horizontal) are normally distributed. The mean and median preference is $z = \mu$. Now if the electorate are continuously consulted about issues as in a direct democracy, or occasionally as with a referendum, any suggested level of z greater than μ will not secure a majority vote when it is paired with $z = \mu$; for all those who prefer μ and all those who want less than μ will vote for μ rather than $z' < \mu$. Likewise all suggestions involving levels of z less than μ will be defeated. In this way the preferences of the median voter dominate, and this remains true even if the distribution of preferences is skewed. Mueller (1979) discusses voting in the context of public choice.

Before proceeding with this consideration, it is as well to clarify another aspect of the matter. The Tiebout model envisages consumers in a system of local governments shopping spatially and costlessly for levels of z. His model can be seen as one where city managers exogeneously determine levels of z, and voters shop once they have the necessary information for the various jurisdictions. Hamilton (1975a, 1976a) adopts this stance. But it is a misconception; for Tiebout (1956) distinctly says that in determining levels of z, the city manager 'follows the preference of the older residents of the community' (p.419). As in the theory of clubs, output levels are based on individual preferences, and the city manager is not constrained by voting with feet. Mobility occurs, of course; but those who vote with their feet are the minorities who, if they stayed in their existing jurisdiction, would suffer a welfare loss from consuming what is for them a non-optimal level of the local public good.[45]

Thus, it is reasonable to suppose that expenditures are related to individual preferences as expressed in a democracy. A pioneer paper was that of Barr and Davis (1966) who adopted 'the basic postulate ... that in a democratic society individual voters are the underlying determinants of political decisions'. Following Downs (1957) and Buchanan and Tullock (1962), Barr and Davis assume politicians make tax-spending decisions in order to win elections; they choose the fiscal basket around which can be formed a dominant coalition, and since voters attempt to maximise over utility, the level of z approximates the median choice. The constraint on local politicians is generated by fear of losing elections rather than voting with feet exercising a discipline on local fiscal choices. They then go on to assume a utility function for individuals that has private goods and public goods as arguments and a budget constraint containing a tax price for the public good. There were one or two omissions such as a failure to specify that the taxed commodity would be affected by changes in z; indeed for private goods they drew no distinction between post-tax and pre-tax conditions. Nevertheless, the approach set the tone for future exercises.

Two studies, by Borcherding and Deacon (1972) and Bergstrom and Goodman (1973), postulate demand functions for public goods of the general form:

$$q = Ay^{\alpha}(ap)^{\beta}$$

where a is a parameter associated with tax share. Both studies use a more detailed function, but their main features are captured in this way. One problem that they pursue (omitted here) is estimation of a crowding parameter, and both find that the services the local governments in their studies provide are approximately private goods.

The parameter a is given by $h/\bar{h}$ where h is the housing units consumed by an individual with income y and $\bar{h}$ is the mean consumption. If $h = By^{\theta}$ where B is a parameter and θ is income elasticity of demand for housing, and if $\bar{h}$ is the consumption of a man with $\bar{y}$, then $a = (y/\bar{y})^{\theta}$. Thus we have:

$$q = ky^{\alpha + \theta\beta}$$

where $k = A(p/\bar{y}^{\theta})^{\beta}$, which is common to all individuals. As Bergstrom and Goodman point out, the quantity of local public goods demanded is monotonic and increasing in y provided $\alpha > \theta\beta$; that is, if $\alpha/\beta > \theta$, which is the formulation discussed in our discussion of property taxes. Where this condition holds, those with $y > \hat{y}$ demand $q > \hat{q}$.

Bergstrom and Goodman compare the level of provision chosen by the median voter with the amount he would choose under Bowen (1943) and Lindahl (1919) pricing regimes. However, both Bowen and Lindahl assume lump-sum tax regimes, whereas property taxes are operative in the real world. Borcherding and Deacon assume head taxes but Bergstrom and Goodman model property taxes. However, they neglect the deadweight losses property taxes impose and therefore their discussion of efficient levels of output is deficient (Topham 1981). Because the various tax regimes have differing distributional effects, it is necessary to invoke a social welfare function to choose between them.

Denzau and MacKay (1976) have pointed out that benefit shares as well as tax shares will affect the quantity of local public goods the median voter will demand. An increase in benefit share is equivalent to a reduction in price per unit of local public service enjoyed, and consequently a lower local 'budget' will be required by the median voter if his demand for the service is price inelastic. However, unless it can be shown that benefit shares are functions of y in some way, this point does not seem to take us very far.

A number of studies have questioned whether the median voter hypothesis is tested in such exercises. Whilst the median voter is the maintained hypothesis, the alternative is not put. The issue is discussed in Atkinson and Stiglitz (1980). Pommerehne (1978) points out median voter models work better where the local institutions are consistent with their adoption; evidence from Swiss municipalities suggests demand-orientated median voter models are superior for democracies with referenda than without. Some interesting observations on these issues are made by Romer and Rosenthal (1979). They ask how we can be sure that the levels of local expenditure observed are those that median voters actually want. They go on to point out that all local expenditures may be above or below optimum levels. It might have been better, they say, if regressions had been run on those at the top and bottom of the distributions as well as for the median; in that way, the equation with the best fit would indicate the dominant preference. However, the author is a trifle sceptical of uncovering much by this procedure, since he would expect some jurisdictional bureaucracies to be 'pushers', others to be 'sleepers'; so that whether and the amount to which a particular government's local expenditure is in excess of what its median voter requires will most likely vary from observation to observation. However, voting with feet does allow consumers some room for manoeuvre, and to that extent one would anticipate local outputs according more closely with median preferences than would central outputs. Incidentally, it will be recalled in this context that Barlow's (1970) evidence suggested that the MRS/tax price ratio for the median voter was less than unity, implying an output in excess of what he required.

Barkume (1977) approaches matters directly from the ballot box. He asks what the proportion of Yes votes in a local referenda might tell us. All who vote for a marginal rise in property tax rates must have their MRS/tax price ratio in excess of unity. Voting behaviour rather than public expenditure variations is also a guide to efficiency in school finance. After some manipulations in statistical theory, Barkume derives an equation in which the proportion voting Yes is the dependent variable with income, price, and other variables as regressands. The paper is interesting in suggesting a fruitful new approach; however, his finding that voters would approve a property tax increase in circumstances in which $\alpha/\beta < \theta$ might be regarded with some scepticism for the moment.

As will be apparent by now, median voter models concern themselves with local government data simply because cross-sectional data is readily available and does not raise many of the problem of violation of *ceteris paribus* conditions associated with times series data. Clearly, however, the debate has moved from explaining variations in local behaviour to the more general topic of public sector efficiency.

7. Concluding remarks

Fiscal federalism spans virtually the whole field of public economics. Research activity is high and likely to remain so as economists grapple with emerging theoretical problems. For example, the stability conditions of a Tiebout equilibrium have yet to be satisfactorily specified, even on a simple basis. As with the theory of clubs, allowing for differing tax regimes will give rise to new analytical problems. And although capitalisation is much discussed, its incorporation into the more esoteric theoretical models has yet to occur.

The next decade is likely to see much attention devoted to the distributional implications of grants-in-aid to local governments. Nobody, for example, has yet analysed the distributional implications of the whole system; we do not know whether equalising grants to local governments have an egalitarian effect on the distribution of income as a whole when central government taxes to finance the grant are incorporated into the analysis. And when such judgements are made, there remains the question of what the policy implications are once the grant exists and capitalisation has occurred; most writers operate on the implied assumption that they have a *tabula rasa* on which they can write any story they wish.

Both the old view and the new view of the property tax, whilst helpful, divert attention from the real issues. To what extent is a property tax a user price and how does the system of finance affect the efficiency of local public goods supply? A closely related problem concerns the relevance of median voter models for the real world. Perhaps there is a role for the economics of bureaucracy here if coupled with a careful specification of how a system of local governments acts as a constraint on local bureaucrats.

But research activity is not simply a function of theoretical deficiencies. Economists are creatures of their time. They respond to the issues of the day, and to predict future activity we would have to know, as we do not, what these issues might be, what new policy will be introduced. Politics, they say, is the art of the possible, research the art of the soluble. Solutions exist for all real world problems; the only difficulty is how to find them.

Notes

1. This is not always the case. Some analyses of clubs are concerned with discrimination – see De Serpa (1977). This is not part of our concern. Jurisdictions do not have the power to discriminate between individuals: free mobility of labour is taken for granted. Thus the population (N) does not figure here as an argument in the utility function.
2. There is not much evidence to suggest local government service could be supplied more cheaply at a centralised level. Flat-bottomed curves seem to be in evidence. See Hirsch (1973) for United States evidence.
3. The seminal paper is Buchanan (1965). A useful introduction is supplied in Boadway (1979). Note that the focus in this survery is on maximising per-capita benefits. Ng (1973) has suggested total benefits should be maximised, which implies that the benefits to newcomers as well as existing members of the club should be taken into account. A recent survey by Brennan and Flowers (1980) is apposite. Stiglitz (1977) adopts a singular approach by assuming that new members to the club increase real income but at a diminishing rate of return. The constraint on membership is derived from this line of reasoning rather than crowding of facilities. He is concerned with pure rather than impure public goods.
4. The Samuelson condition is based on the supposition that lump-sum taxes will be levied, as here, albeit without crowding.
5. Derive as follows. Since $p^* = \alpha p / N$

$$\frac{\mathrm{d}p^*}{\mathrm{d}N} = \frac{\alpha'(N)pN - \alpha p}{N^2}$$

$$= \frac{\alpha p}{N} \left(\frac{\alpha'(N)}{\alpha} - \frac{1}{N} \right)$$

Multiply by N/N:

$$= \frac{\alpha p}{N^2} (r - 1)$$

6. For example, if an indifference map can be specified by $y = ax^2 - bx + c$, then $MRS = p = b - 2ax$, which is independent of y if the parameter 'a' and 'b' are not functions of y.
7. See Topham (1977).
8. There is a problem here. Both MRS and $\overline{\Sigma}MRS$ are functions of the level of public-goods supply. Calculations of the full economic costs individuals face should take into account the way in which the fraction $MRS/\overline{\Sigma}MRS$ (and thus the tax price) changes at the margin for each individual. Only if the elasticity of both numerator and denominator for a change in public-goods supply are equal to one another for all individuals is it permissible to ignore this consideration.
9. Cebula and Curran (1978) produce evidence to suggest that climate is an important factor in migration decisions. This is the type of attribute one has in mind here, but it

is not altogether appropriate since the Tiebout shopping analogue is normally taken to be sub-regional. Nevertheless, some individuals are not tied by specific skills to one locality or region, and clearly do locate in warmer climates, other things equal. A full analysis would have to take account of the effects of climate on production and consumption. This Cebula and Curran fail to do, but it is not for nothing that Alaska and Greenland are sparsely populated.

10. Some writers, e.g. Izraeli (1977), argue that different tax prices will reflect themselves in different wage rates. But, as is outlined on p.163 when the incidence of the property tax is discussed, the burden of a tax and thus any associated benefits manifest themselves in the prices of immobile factors.

11. This is obviously true if we consider only homogeneous jurisdictions. A move away from one's own jurisdiction implies a welfare loss. The argument goes through for heterogeneous jurisdictions.

12. The next few paragraphs are all drawn from this excellent book, which is highly recommended.

13. Can this enter *The Guinness Book of Records* as the first local public good – crow-free skies!

14. Marshall (1920) uses it in Appendix G to his *Principles*, and Foster *et al.* (1980) make much of the distinction between beneficial and onerous taxes.

15. Jurisdictional boundaries are assumed fixed here. The assumption is relaxed later.

16. By contrast, if the factor is perfectly elastic in supply, it bears none of the tax. Aside from these two special cases, the division of the impact of a tax between consumers and producers is given by ratio of the elasticities of demand and supply.

17. If a stream of payments (tR) is thought to be *permanent*, its present value is given by tR/r.

18. See note 16.

19. Profit-maximising prices are a function of variable costs, not fixed costs.

20. Housing expenditure includes the imputed values of rents in the case of owner occupiers.

21. See Aaron (1975) for supporting evidence.

22. The welfare costs of taxation are ignored in this outline. They are, however, not unimportant. See Browning (1976).

23. And these are the important burdens because differential tax rates cancel out.

24. Which is tantamount to focussing on the average of all rates prevailing in jurisdictions.

25. If land has a backstop agricultural use and boundaries are not fixed, so that land can move in and out of the city, this assumption is not appropriate. The implications of its relaxation are examined below.

26. An elementary outline of the Harberger model can be found in Musgrave and Musgrave (1980: 293–300). See also chapter 2 by Sumner in this volume.

27. Rates rebates and supplementary benefits relieve $2\frac{1}{2}$ million people of rates payments altogether. See Layfield (1976: 267).

28. Layfield, p.159.

29. Layfield, p.422.

30. Aaron (1975: 45–49). The incidence of the property tax is discussed in two *AEA* conference papers by Aaron (1974) and Musgrave (1974).

31. See, for example, Bergstrom and Goodman (1973) and Borcherding and Deacon (1972).

32. For example, Bradford and Oates (1971), Feldstein (1975), Barnett and Topham (1980), and Hamilton (1976b).

33. Whilst it is true that under such a property tax equal sharing arrangements occur, as under a poll tax, the level of public goods supply is not the same and deadweight losses occur. This is true even for a club of one person. See Topham (1982).
34. Stiglitz (1974) shows over-provision occurs if $\sigma > 1$ (i.e. $\alpha/\beta > 1$). He analyses a tax that is proportional to income. The elasticity of such a tax-price schedule is 1. School finance is, however, derived from taxes on property, and only by coincidence is the income elasticity of demand for property equal to that value.
35. Brown & Deaton (1972) and Stern (1977) summarising the evidence suggest a value for σ of 2.
36. Income elasticity of demand approximates to unity in most studies. See Aaron (1975).
37. Le Grand (1977) appears to find even this too categorical and would ideally extend the principle of equal treatment of equals more extensively.
38. See *Serrano v. Priest* in *96 California Reporter* 608: 1971.
39. Ibid., p.604
40. Ibid., p.620.
41. They failed to distinguish their own approach from Feldstein's and assumed he intended their solution; but k is left open in his analysis.
42. Similar, though slightly reduced, estimates are found when the Slutsky compensation for the price fall is calculated.
43. Thurow (1970) was not in fact commenting on the Serrano case.
44. Barnett and Topham (1977:340).
45. It is assumed here that joint price for housing and local public goods have been equalised.

References

Aaron, H. J. (1974) A new view of property tax incidence, *American Economic Review*, **64**, 212–21.
Aaron, H. J. (1975) *Who Pays the Property Tax?* Brookings Institute: Washington DC.
Committee of Inquiry into the Impact of Rates on Households (1965) *Report*, R. G. D. Allen, Cmnd. 2582.
Atkinson, A. B. and Stiglitz, J. E. (1980) *Lectures in Public Economics*, McGraw Hill: London.
Barkume, A. J. (1977) Tax-prices and voting behaviour: the case of local educational financing, *Economic Enquiry*, **15**, 574–86.
Barlow, R. (1970) Efficiency aspects of local school finance, *Journal of Political Economy*, **78**, 1028–40.
Barnett, R. R. (1981) A True Measure of Capitalisation, *mimeo*.
Barnett, R. R. and Topham, N. (1977a) Achievement grants and fiscal neutrality in school finance, *Applied Economics*, **9**, 331–42.
Barnett, R. R. and Topham, N. (1977b) Evaluating the distribution of local outputs in a decentralised structure of government, *Policy and Politics*, **6**, 51–70.
Barnett, R. R. and Topham, N. (1980) A critique of equalising grants to local governments, *Scottish Journal of Political Economy*, **27**, 235–49.
Barr, J. L. and Davis, O. A. (1966) An elementary political and economic theory of the expenditures of local government, *Southern Economic Journal*, **33**, 149–65.
Barzel, Y. (1969) Two propositions on the optimum level of producing collective goods, *Public Choice*, **6**, 31–37.

Barzel, Y. (1973) Private schools and public school finance, *Journal of Political Economy*, 174–86.

Bergstrom, T. C. (1973) A note on efficient taxation, *Journal of Political Economy*, 187–91.

Bergstrom, T. C. and Goodman, R. P. (1973) Private demands for public goods, *American Economic Review*, **63**, 280–96.

Boyle, L. (1966) *Equalisation and the Future of Local Government Finance*, Oliver & Boyd: Edinburgh.

Blake, D. R. (1979) Property tax incidence: an alternative view, *Land Economics*, **55**, 521–31.

Boadway, R. W. (1979) *Public Sector Economics*, Winthrop.

Borcherding, T. E. and Deacon, R. T. (1972) The demand for services of non-federal governments, *American Economic Review*, **62**, 891–901.

Bowen, H. R. (1943) The interpretation of voting in the allocation of economic resources, *Quarterly Journal of Economics*, **58**, 27–48.

Bradford, D. and Oates, W. E. (1971) The analysis of revenue sharing in a new approach to collective fiscal decisions, *Quarterly Journal of Economics*, **85**, 416–39.

Brainard, W. C. and Dolbear, F. T. (1967) The possibility of over-supply of local 'public' goods: a critical note, *Journal of Political Economy*, **75**, 86–90.

Break, G. F. (1967) *Intergovernment Fiscal Relations*, Brookings Institution: Washington, DC.

Brennan, G. (1969) Optimal provision of public goods, *Journal of Political Economy*, **77**, 237–41.

Brennan, G. and Flowers, M. (1980) All 'Ng' up on clubs?: some notes on the current status of club theory, *Public Finance Quarterly*, **8**, 153–69.

Brown, A. and Deaton, A. (1972) Models of consumer behaviour, *Economic Journal*, **82**, 1145–1236.

Browning, E. K. (1976) The marginal cost of public funds, *Journal of Political Economy*, **84**, 283–98.

Buchanan, J. M. (1950) Federalism and fiscal equity, *American Economic Review*, **40**, 583–99.

Buchanan, J. M. (1964) Fiscal institutions and efficiency in collective outlay, *American Economic Review*, **54**, 227–35.

Buchanan, J. M. (1965) An economic theory of clubs, *Economica*, **32**, 1–14.

Buchanan, J. M. and Goetz, C. J. (1972) Efficiency limits of fiscal mobility: an assessment of the Tiebout model, *Journal of Public Economics*, **1**, 25–43.

Buchanan, J. M. and Tullock, G. (1962) *The Calculus of Consent*, Ann Arbor: University of Michigan Press.

Buchanan, J. M. and Wagner, R. (1970) An efficiency basis for federal fiscal equalisation, in Julius Margolis (ed.): *The Analysis of Public Output*, Columbia UP: New York.

Cannan, E. (1959) Evidence to Royal Commission on local taxation (1899) reprinted in Musgrave, R. A. and Shoup, C. S. (eds): *Readings in Economics of Taxation*, George Allen and Unwin: London.

Cannan, E. (1912) *A History of Local Rates in England and Wales*, P. S. King: London.

Cebula, R. J. and Curran, C. (1978) Property taxation and human migration, *American Journal of Economics and Sociology*, **37**, 43–49.

Deaton, A. (1974) Reconsideration of the empirical implications of additive preferences, *Economic Journal*, **84**, 338–48.

Denzau, A. and MacKay, R. (1976) Benefit shares and majority voting, *American Economic Review*, **66**, 69–76.

De Serpa, Alan C. (1977) A theory of discriminatory clubs, *Scottish Journal of Political Economy*, **21**, 33–41.

Downs, A. (1957) *An Economic Theory of Democracy*, Harper: New York.

Dyer, J. C. and Maher, M. D. (1979) Capitalisation of intrajurisdictional differences in local tax prices: comment, *American Economic Review*, **69**, 481–84.

Edel, M. and Sclar, E. (1974) Taxes, spending and property values: supply adjustment in a Tiebout-Oates model, *Journal of Political Economy*, **82**, 941–54.

Epple, D., Zelenitz, A. and Visscher, M. (1978) A search for testable implications of the Tiebout hypothesis, *Journal of Political Economy*, **86**, 405–26.

Feldstein, M. S. (1974) Incidence of a capital income tax in a growing economy with variable savings rates, *Review of Economic Studies*, **4**, 505–13.

Feldstein, M. S. (1975) Wealth neutrality and local choice in public education, *American Economic Review*, **65**, 75–89.

Flatters, F. R., Henderson, V. and Mieszkowski, P. (1974) Public goods, efficiency, and regional fiscal equalisation, *Journal of Public Economics*, **3**, 99–112.

Foley, D. (1970) Lindahl's solution and the core of an economy with collective goods, *Econometrica*, **38**, 66–72.

Foster, C. D., Jackman, R. and Perlman, M. (1980) *Local Government Finance in a Unitary System*, George Allen & Unwin: London.

Giertz, R. (1976) Decentralisation at the state and local level, *National Tax Journal*, **29**, 201–9.

Gramlich, E. M. (1977) Intergovernment grants: a review of the empirical literature, in Oates, W. E. (ed.) *The Political Economy of Fiscal Federalism*, Lexington Books: Lexington, Mass.

Greene, K. V. (1975) Fiscal federalism, spillovers, and the export of taxes: a comment, *Kyklos*, **28**, 412–8.

Hamilton, B. W. (1975a) Zoning and property taxation in a system of local government, *Urban Studies*, **12**, 205–11.

Hamilton, B. W. (1975b) Property taxes and the Tiebout hypothesis: some empirical evidence, in Mills, E. S. and Oates, W. E. (eds) *Fiscal Zoning and Land Use Controls*, Lexington Books: Lexington, Mass.

Hamilton, B. W. (1976a) Capitalisation of inter-jurisdictional differences in local tax prices, *American Economic Review*, **66**, 743–53.

Hamilton, B. W. (1976b) The effects of property taxes and local public spending on property values: a theoretical comment, *Journal of Political Economy*, **84**, 647–50.

Harberger, A. C. (1962) The incidence of the corporation income tax, *Journal of Political Economy*, **70**, 215–40.

Heinberg, J. D. and Oates, W. E. (1970) The incidence of differential property taxes on urban housing, *National Tax Journal*, **23**, 92–98.

Helpman, E. (1978) On optimal community formations, *Economic Letters*, **1**, 289–93.

Henderson, J. M. (1968) Local government expenditure: a social welfare analysis, *Review of Economics and Statistics*, **50**, 156–63.

Hirsch, W. Z. (1970) *The Economics of State and Local Government*, McGraw-Hill: New York.

Hirsch, Werner (1973) *Urban Economic Analysis*, McGraw-Hill: New York.

Inman, R. P. (1975) Grants in a metropolitan economy: a framework for policy, in Oates, W. E. (ed) *Financing the New Federalism*, Johns Hopkins Univ. Press: Baltimore.

Izraeli, O. (1977) Differentials in nominal wages and prices between cities, *Urban Studies*, **14**, 275–90.

Jurion, B. J. (1979) Matching grants and unconditional grants: the case with *n* goods, *Public Finance*, **34**, 234–44.

Kay, J. A. and King, M. A. (1980) *The British Tax System*, 2nd edition, OUP: Oxford.

King, A. T. (1977) Estimating property tax capitalisation, *Journal of Political Economy*, **85**, 425–31.

Layfield Report, Report of Committee of Inquiry (1976) *Local Government Finance*, May, Cmnd. 6453, HMSO: London.

Le Grand, J. (1975) Fiscal equity and central government grants to local authorities, *Economic Journal*, **85**, 531–47.

Le Grand, J. (1977) Fiscal equity and grants to local authorities: reply, *Economic Journal*, **87**, 780–2.

Le Grand, J. and Reschovsky, A. (1971) Concerning the appropriate formulae for achieving horizontal equity through federal revenue sharing, *National Tax Journal*, **24**, 475–86.

Lindahl, E. (1958) Just taxation – a positive solution (1919), in Musgrave, R. A. and Peacock, A. T. (eds) *Classics in the Theory of Public Finance*, Macmillan: London.

Linneman, P. (1978) The capitalisation of local taxes: a note on specification, *Journal of Political Economy*, **86**, 535–38.

Litvak, J. M. and Oates, W. E. (1970) Group size and the output of public goods: theory and an application to state local finance in the United States, *Public Finance*, **25**, 42–58.

McGuire, M. (1972) Private-good clubs and public-good clubs: economic models of group formation, *Swedish Journal of Economics*, **74**, 84–99.

McGuire, M. (1973) Notes on grants-in-aid and economic interactions among governments, *Canadian Journal of Economics*, **6**, 207–21.

McGuire, M. (1974) Group segregation and optimal jurisdictions, *Journal of Political Economy*, **82**, 112–32.

McGuire, M. (1975) An econometric model of federal grants and local fiscal response, in Oates, W. E. (ed.) *Financing the New Federalism*, Johns Hopkins Univ. Press: Baltimore.

McLure, C. E. (1977) The 'new view' of the property tax: a caveat, *National Tax Journal*, **30**, 69–75.

Marshall, A. (1920) *Principles of Economics*, Macmillan.

Meade, J. E. (1973) *The Theory of Economic Externalities*, Sijthoff-Leiden: Geneva.

Meadows, G. R. (1976) Taxes, spending and property values, *Journal of Political Economy*, **84**, 869–80.

Mieszkowski, P. (1972) The property tax: an excise tax or a profits tax, *Journal of Public Economics*, **1**, 73–96.

Mieszkowski, P. (1976) The distributive effects of local taxes: some extensions, in Grieson, R. E. (ed.) *Public and Urban Economics*, Lexington Books: Lexington, Mass.

Mieszkowski, P. and Oakland, W. H. (eds) (1979) *Fiscal Federalism and Grants-in-Aid*, The Urban Institute: Washington, DC.

Mirrlees, J. A. (1981) Discussant's comments: property taxes and commodity taxes and public sector efficiency, in Curry, D., Peters, W. and Peel, D. A. (eds) *Essays in Contemporary Economics*, Croom Helm: London.

Mohring, H. and Maslove, A. (1973) The optimal provision of public goods, yet another comment, *Journal of Political Economy*, **81**, 778–85.

Mueller, D. C. (1979) *Public Choice*, CUP: Cambridge.

Mullen, J. K. (1980) Role of income in explaining state-local fiscal decentralisation, *Public Finance*, **35**, 300–08.

Musgrave, R. A. (1974) Is a property tax on housing regressive? *American Economic Review*, **64**, 222–29.

Musgrave, R. A. and Musgrave, P. B. (1980) *Public Finance in Theory and Practice*, 3rd edn, McGraw-Hill: New York.

Ng, Y. K. (1973) The economic theory of clubs: Pareto optimal conditions, *Economica*, **40**, 291–98.

Oates, W. E. (1968) The dual impact of federal aid on state and local government expenditure: a comment, *National Tax Journal*, **21**, 220–23.

Oates, W. E. (1969) The effects of property taxes and local public spending on property values: an empirical study of tax capitalisation and the Tiebout hypothesis, *Journal of Political Economy*, **77**, 957–71.

Oates, W. E. (1972) *Fiscal Federalism*, Harcourt Brace: New York.

Oates, W. E. (1973) The effects of property taxes and local public spending on property values: a reply and yet further results, *Journal of Political Economy*, **81**, 1004–8.

Oates, W. E. (1979) Lump-sum intergovernmental grants have price effects in Mieszkowski, P. and Oakland, W. H. (1979).

Osman, J. W. (1966) The dual impact of federal aid on state and local government expenditure, *National Tax Journal*, **19**, 362–72.

Pauly, M. V. (1967) Clubs, commodity, and the core: an integration of game theory and the theory of clubs, *Econometrica*, 314–24.

Pauly, M. V. (1970) Optimality, 'public' goods, and local governments: a general theoretical analysis, *Journal of Political Economy*, **78**, 572–85.

Pechman, J. A. and Okner, B. A. (1974) *Who Bears the Tax Burden?* Brookings Institution: Washington, DC.

Pollakowski, H. O. (1973) The effects of property taxes and local public spending on property values: a comment and further results, *Journal of Political Economy*, **81**, 994–1004.

Pommerehne, W. W. (1978) Institutional approaches to public expenditure: empirical evidence from Swiss municipalities, *Journal of Public Economics*, **9**, 255–80.

Redcliffe-Maud Report, (1969) *Report of Royal Commission on Local Government in England*, Cmnd. 4040, HMSO: London.

Romer, T. and Rosenthal, T. (1979) The elusive median voter, *Journal of Public Economics*, **12**, 143–70.

Rose-Ackerman, S. (1981) Does federalism matter? Political choice in a federal republic, *Journal of Political Economy*, **89**, 152–65.

Rosen, H. S. and Fullerton, D. J. (1977) A note on local tax rates, public benefit levels, and property values, *Journal of Political Economy*, **85**, 433–40.

Salter, S. J. and Topham, N. (1981) The distribution of local public goods in a non-Tiebout world, *The Manchester School*, **49**, 51–69.

Samuelson, P. A. (1954) The pure theory of public expenditure, *Review of Economics and Statistics*, **36**, 387–9.

Samuelson, P. A. (1958) Aspects of public expenditure theories, *Review of Economics and Statistics*, **38**, 332–8.

Sandler, T. M. and Shelton, R. B. (1972) Fiscal federalism, spillovers, and the export of taxes, *Kyklos*, **25**, 736–53.

Scott, A. D. (1952) The evaluation of federal grants, *Economica*, **19**, 377–94.

Slack, E. (1980) Local fiscal response to inter-governmental grants, *Review of Economics and Statistics*, **62**, 364–70.

Stiglitz, J. E. (1974) The demand for education in public and private school systems, *Journal of Public Economics*, **3**, 349–86.

Stiglitz, J. E. (1977) The theory of local public goods, in Feldstein, M. S. and Inman, R. P. (eds) *The Economics of Public Services*, Macmillan: London.

Stern, N. (1977) The marginal valuation of income, in Artis, M. J. and Nobay, A. R., *Studies in Modern Economic Analysis*, Blackwell: London.

Thurow, L. Aid to state and local governments, *National Tax Journal*, **23**, 23–25.

Tiebout, C. M. (1956) A pure theory of local expenditures, *Journal of Political Economy*, **66**, 416–24.

Topham, N. (1977) Consumer mobility and the distribution of local public goods, *Public Finance*, **32**, 254–64.

Topham, N. (1981) Property and commodity taxes and public sector efficiency, in Curry, D., Peters, W. and Peel, D. A. (eds) *Microeconomic Analysis*, Croom-Helm: London.

Topham, N. (1982a) A note on zoning and property taxation in a system of local governments, *Urban Studies*, **19**, 197–9.

Topham, N. (1982b) A note on testable implications of the Tiebout hypothesis, *Public Finance*, **37**, 120–9.

Waldaver, C. (1973) Grant structures and their effects on aided government expenditures: an indifference curve analysis, *Public Finance*, **28**, 212–25.

Weisbrod, B. (1964) Collective consumption services of individual consumption goods, *Quarterly Journal of Economics*, **78**, 471–7.

Wheaton, W. C. (1975) Consumer mobility and consumer tax bases: the financing of local public goods, *Journal of Public Economics*, **4**, 377–84.

Wilde, J. A. (1968) The expenditure effects of grants-in-aid programmes, *National Tax Journal*, **21**, 340–8.

Wilde, J. A. (1971) Grants-in-aid: the analytics of design and response, *National Tax Journal*, **24**, 143–56.

Williams, A. (1966) Optimal provision of public goods in a system of local governments, *Journal of Political Economy*, **74**, 18–33.

Yinger, J. (1981) Capitalization and the median voter, *American Economic Review*, **71**, 99–103.

CHAPTER FIVE

Public and private enterprise: comparative behaviour and relative efficiency

Robert Millward and David M. Parker*

1. Introduction

In recent years there appears to have been some shift in the literature on the economics of public enterprises from prescriptive welfare economics to an examination of the actual behaviour and performance of publicly owned firms. Notably there has been growing interest in the relative behaviour and efficiency of public and private enterprises to see whether there is any difference and to identify the cause of observed differences.

The economics literature in the 1960s contained numerous studies which prescribed for public enterprises the adoption of 'optimal' pricing and investment policies to achieve economic efficiency.[1] The literature emphasised the case for prices to be set according to marginal economic costs, the need for social cost-benefit studies where 'spillover' effects existed and investment to be determined by discounted cash flow techniques using an optimal rate of discount. Both prices and investment were to be determined so as not to distort the allocation of resources between the public sector and private sectors of the economy. This prescriptive welfare literature, stressing allocative efficiency, arguably reached a high point of respectability in the UK with the publication of the Government's 1967 White Paper on the Nationalised Industries which endorsed marginal cost pricing and introduced a Test Rate of Discount for public enterprise investments, supposedly equivalent to the opportunity cost rate in the private sector.

It would be wrong to say that interest in allocative efficiency declined in the public enterprise literature in the 1970s, but it was qualified and complemented by a growing interest in the behaviour and performance of public ownership. In the UK one cause of this was the apparent failure to implement the 1967 guidelines. There was some indifference to the guidelines within the industries and in addition government intervention in pricing and investment policy in the 1970s as part of anti-inflation policy became the dominant characteristic of government dealings with the industries.[2] Largely independent of these issues however there has been a growing neo-institutionalist literature, especially in the USA, concerning the economic theory of organisational forms

*Thanks are due to the editors and other participants in this volume for comments and suggestions.

which, as a by-product, has considered whether differences in the performance of public and private enterprises can be traced to differences in forms of ownership. To a degree the theoretical literature has links with studies in the field of business economics which consider the goals of firms where ownership and control are divorced.[3] Also, by considering motivation and incentives, the literature strongly complements earlier work on the internal efficiency of organisations.

As in many areas of applied economics there is a chasm between analytical work and empirical tests. The problem is compounded here because for some types of comparison like the relative costs of producing certain outputs, it is important that public and private firms are assessed on a like-with-like basis. In particular it is usually an advantage for the two types of firm to be producing the same type of good or service. This is rarely found in the UK where public firms often have national monopolies. Hence much of the empirical work under review relates to North America where public and private firms coexist in electricity, water supply, transport, refuse collection, though studies for industries in Australia, Indonesia and Switzerland have also been published.

An interest in the relative behaviour of public and private enterprise need not imply any judgements about what is good or bad and part of this survey is concerned with such 'positive' theories of public firms. Since in addition judgements *are* made, usually in the context of 'efficiency' we need to understand measures of efficiency. One type is 'economic efficiency' which is treated extensively in many books on microeconomics and public finance. Our interest in this concept stems partly from its use as a normative criterion of performance and, since policy guidelines for public enterprises have been derived from considerations of economic efficiency, partly from its possible implications for the behaviour of public firms relative to private. In the next section we therefore provide a brief introduction to this topic. The main sections of the survey are therefore:

- Economic efficiency
- Economic organisation, contractual forms and ownership
- The behaviour of the public firm
- The measurement of efficiency
  (this section may be omitted by readers acquainted with problems involved in the estimation of cost functions and with the recent literature on measures of productivity).
- Empirical comparisons of public and private firms
  (productivity in transport – the cost of electric power in USA – cost studies in water supply, refuse collection, and others – market structure and ownership – pricing, politics and profitability).

2. Economic efficiency

The classic concern of public finance has been with methods of raising taxation which do least harm to the allocation of resources. Little attention initially was

devoted to the analysis of the public services for which finance was being raised –
law and order and defence being seen not only as inescapable commitments of
governments but also as delimiting the scope of public services. During this
century both the range of public services and the economic analysis of them have
expanded considerably. Little of this work was however initially directed to
analysing *the behaviour of public enterprises* for two reasons. Firstly, the major
objective – which is also characteristic of the study of taxation – has been that
of devising optimal solutions, that is, as we shall show shortly, of developing
prescriptions for policy; if industries are publicly owned, what should be their
pricing and investment policy?

  Secondly, though the *theory of public goods* can be viewed in part as
an explanation of why some goods are financed through government, its
relevance for public enterprise is limited. The focus of this theory is on goods
which are necessarily supplied simultaneously to large groups of consumers. The
technology of schemes for flood protection, noise abatement, clean air, pest
control, national defence, etc. are such that if one person in a defined group is
supplied so also necessarily are other members of the group. An individual in
such a population will not fully reveal his preferences for these goods; the
provision of the service will not be contingent on the amount he is willing to pay
and if the service is supplied he cannot be excluded from enjoying the benefits.
Hence the amounts which consumers are prepared to pay for such schemes
cannot be revealed through market prices and the revenue would have instead to
come from central or local taxation – even though the actual construction or
running of such schemes could, so far as the analysis above is concerned, be
undertaken by private firms, on contract from government agencies. Thus at
the heart of the theory of public goods is the systematic underrevelation of
preferences by users. That part of this survey which is concerned with public
production is however devoted to goods and services where full preference
revelation is assumed – coal, railways, electricity and gas supply, airlines, water
supply being typical examples of areas inhabited by public enterprise.

  The rest of this section therefore briefly[4] considers the policy prescriptions for the operation of public enterprises or the control of private enterprise
which emanate from the precepts of economic efficiency. Tangential to this we
also consider whether these theoretical issues have any implications for the
relative behaviour of public and private enterprises; that is, if public enterprises
did follow the policy prescribed would that imply a different behaviour from
private enterprises? Models of economic efficiency usually consider an economy
with a number of different 'firms'. The latter are often defined by the location
and/or technology of production rather than by their organisational features.
Production efficiency is deemed to exist when (a) it is not possible by shifting
inputs or outputs from one firm to another, to raise the quantity of any product
without lowering the quantity of another product, (b) it is not possible to lower
the use of any one input, given a certain pattern of outputs, without increasing
the use of other inputs. Clearly this would require that the marginal product of
any input should be the same in each firm producing the same kind of good. This
would further imply that the ratio of the marginal products of two inputs should

be the same in firms producing the same goods. The ratio of the marginal products of two inputs is often referred to as the marginal rate of technical substitution and this has to be the same in all firms even when they produce different products, for otherwise a reallocation of inputs could raise the output of one firm without decreasing that of another. Clearly one way of attaining production efficiency would be to try and ensure that each firm is faced with a common set of prices for inputs. In such circumstances standard microeconomic analysis implies that each firm will choose its input combination so that the marginal technical rate of substitution is equal to the (common) relative prices of the inputs.

A second major issue of economic efficiency and one which has tended to dominate the policy prescriptions for public enterprises relates to the scale and patterns of outputs. To analyse this it is useful to work with a hypothetical example. Consider a product, say coal, which can be produced under conditions of constant returns to scale – doubling all constant quality units of management, labour, capital equipment and coal deposits is assumed to double coal output. Whether or not wage-rates, the price of equipment and the availability of good managers changes with the volume of production is not of central significance for the moment and hence, for simplicity we assume they do not vary. The geological conditions of mines vary considerably so that it is usually not possible to continue to open new mines with the same technical working conditions. Thus although constant returns to scale prevail, average production costs (including a 'normal' return to capital) in the 'marginal' mine, as shown by LL' in Fig. 5.1, would rise as the industry expanded and so coal is produced at rising long-run marginal costs (LL'). In the short run, variations in production can take place only by changes in the intensity of use of a given stock of equipment and mines. The associated changes in the amount of the variable factor, say labour, could

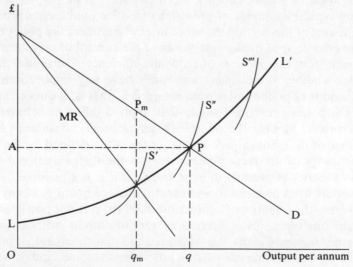

FIG. 5.1 The optimal quantity of coal

therefore be expected to be subject to diminishing returns. Thus with given stocks of equipment and mines short-run marginal costs associated with such capacity levels would be indicated by lines like S', S'' and S''' in the diagram. The standard precepts of economic efficiency suggest that output should be expanded to the point where marginal cost equals the valuation of extra output by consumers. The latter is indicated by the ordinates of the curve D in Fig. 5.1, so that the optimal amount in this case is where price equals marginal cost.

If this rule is followed in every sector of the economy then the associated allocation of resources is optimal in the following sense. Increases in output beyond q would involve the use of resources whose valuation to consumers is less than their marginal costs, that is, less then their value in other parts of the economy. A contraction of output below q would involve releasing resources whose value to consumers in other parts of the economy is less than their value in coal mining. The precise positions of the demand curves for each commodity will reflect the pattern of relative valuation of different goods and services. This pattern will be determined – and space precludes a rigorous demonstration of this – by the distribution of income in the economy which itself will reflect, amongst other things, the initial ownership of resources. There is no unique economically efficient allocation of resources but rather a limited range of allocations, all efficient but varying with the distribution of income.

One implication is that if governments have views about the desirability of a certain distribution of income this should be attained by lump-sum redistributions of income, that is by taxes and transfers unrelated to the volume or value of production, input supplies and sales. They should not, that is, break the link between marginal costs and the marginal valuations of output. Indeed since government production in other areas like education and defence are financed by taxation then such taxes would, ideally, also have to be lump-sum. However, transfers of income unrelated to occupation, sales, etc. are virtually impossible to devise; in practice therefore some taxes will be related to the rewards of inputs and the prices of outputs. Moreover the rule of pricing at marginal cost only works if it is applied in each and every sector. If there are 'uncontrolled' sectors where price is not equal to marginal costs – such as private sector monopolies – the 'first best' marginal cost rule may no longer be appropriate for the 'controlled' public sector. For both these reasons a literature[5] has developed on 'second-best rules' which are designed to promote efficiency in resource usage subject to such constraints. Essentially this involves analysing what the appropriate relationship between price and marginal cost should be in the 'controlled' public sector given that there are distortions in other parts of the economy. This is a complex literature which at present provides no simple policy guidelines. It is not explored further, the not unreasonable justification for this omission being that where considerations of economic efficiency have entered the public/private debate at the empirical level, it is the 'first-best rules' which have dominated so far.

Returning then to our main theme, if the production of coal in the above diagram is under public ownership, we may think of the public enterprise as controlling production in all the mines and facing a demand curve D. The long-run marginal cost to the enterprise of expanding production by opening up new mines is to be taken as LL'. Associated with various volumes of capacity are short-run marginal cost functions such as those shown by the S lines. In essence then the efficiency rule would require the public firm to expand the usage of any *given* capacity to the point where price equals short-run marginal cost and to expand capacity as long as long-run marginal cost is less than price. If the public enterprise did behave in this way then its optimal output is at q where price, P, is equal to both short- and long-run marginal cost. In the case of private ownership, *if* the industry is competitive then the same result would emerge. Consider a situation where each of the myriad of mines is worked by separate companies who pay royalties to the owners of land for permission to exploit the coal deposits. Each of the mining companies is unable to influence the price of coal and therefore produces where price equals the *firm's* short-run marginal production costs. The latter are not shown in Fig. 5.1 but the horizontal sum of the short-run marginal production cost curves of each of a given number of firms would constitute the industry's short-run supply function such as S' in Fig. 5.1. Long-run expansion involves the entry of new mining companies working more and more geologically difficult deposits. Thus the *industry* marginal cost is approximately equal to the average production cost of the marginal mining company. The marginal company will just earn normal profits, so that it will operate where its own average production costs are at a minimum – and therefore equal to its marginal costs and the market price. Thus the long-run supply curve of the industry is LL'. In long-run equilibrium, the perfectly competitive industry produces at q where price is equal to the average production costs of the marginal mining company. Any differences between production costs in the marginal company and production costs in other companies will be competed away in the form of royalties from the mining companies to accrue as differential rent to the owners of the inelastic factor of production, coal deposits.[6] Hence each mining company's average costs (covering both production and royalties) all equal qP. Moreover, since landlords reap where they do not sow, the taxation of the royalty rents by the state would not affect the quantity of such natural resources available to the country.

Of course, if for some reason private ownership involves monopoly, then the demand curve facing the one mining company would be D in the diagram and the marginal revenue of the firm is no longer equal to price, but to the MR line. The private monopolist[7] produces at q_m. Put otherwise, if a public and a private firm faced the same cost and demand conditions, prices in the public firm will be less than in the private firm and the difference will be greater the smaller is the elasticity of demand over the relevant range (cf. Funkhouser and MacAvoy 1979, who compare public and private enterprise prices largely on this basis). However, this is not a strong theoretical reason for expecting differences in the behaviour of public and private enterprise unless the propensity of private ownership to lead to monopoly is stipulated. In particular the constant returns to scale technology is quite consistent with expansion occurring through a growth in the number of firms in a highly competitive setting. Moreover, even if private ownership did lead to monopoly, public provision is not the only alternative for attaining efficient output levels. Fixing of the price at P and monitoring of rates of return by a regulatory body could force the private firm to sell quantity q in the diagram. To say the least, this is not an easy exercise and the question of price regulation is considered later in the survey in the context of the empirical studies.

At this point it is useful to mention one other argument which, as we shall see later, is sometimes used for public ownership – even though it is not directly connected with questions of economic efficiency as conventionally defined. This is the problem of *declining industries*. Consider for example the impact of a substantial fall in the demand for coal on the employment of labour in the competitive coal industry. Previously we assumed mining labour was available at a fixed wage independent of the scale of mining output; of more interest is the case where mining labour is not in perfectly elastic supply to the mining industry; thus the industry marginal cost line LL' can now be interpreted to slope upwards for a further reason – expansion of the industry raises wage rates for each mining company. Thus, starting from the equilibrium position at P, a large leftwards shift in the demand function would initially involve a decline in employment and wage rates as the industry moves down its short-run supply curve S". The long-run adjustment would involve bankruptcies of mining companies, closure of mines and further declines in prices, employment and wages as the industry moves down the long-run supply curve LL'.

Now governments of the twentieth century have not been able to ignore such developments, especially where large and rapid employment changes are involved and the effects are concentrated in specific regions – compare the coal, railway and steel industries in Britain. If a government objective is to slow down the rate of contraction and spread the adjustments over a longer period, it might do this by taking the industry into public ownership and ignore considerations of economic efficiency. Initially, for example the level of output and employment might be maintained despite the decline in price, with the government accepting the financial implications and also accepting that large amounts of resources are not being released to other parts of the economy where, in the long run, their value to consumers exceeds their value in coal mining.

On the face of it then, publicly owned declining industries would have lower prices, more capacity, larger outputs and more employment than in comparable privately owned declining industries. However, public ownership is not the only policy instrument available. If the industry remained in private ownership, its rate of contraction could be reduced by government subsidies to the mining companies per unit of coal sales. This would shift the supply curves to the right with the same potential impact on output and employment. The subsidies would be financed by tax payers, including, of course, any tax receipts from owners of coal deposits. Hence the underlying hypothesis about the differential behaviour of public and private enterprise is analytically weak (cf. Pashigian 1976) unless it can be argued, on other grounds, that the propensity to subsidise is likely to be bigger when industries are publicly owned than when they are privately owned.

Finally we consider the strongest case where considerations of economic efficiency suggest different behaviour between public and private enterprise, i.e. *economies of scale and natural monopoly*. When increasing returns to scale operate for a product, a given percentage increase in constant quality units of equipment, labour, management, etc. leads to a more than proportionate increase in output. Thus even when the prices of inputs do not vary with the scale of operations – as we shall assume for simplicity – the long-run average costs of the product decline as output expands (in contrast to the previous case of constant returns to scale where with given input prices long-run average cost would be constant). An expansion of the size of generating plants, transmission lines and distribution networks in electricity for example, can lead to more than proportionate increases in output per unit of time simply because of the engineering characteristics of such assets. Thus the industry long-run marginal cost (MC) lies below average cost (AC) in Fig. 5.2 and the economically efficient scale of operations is at q (or zero output, a vital qualification which we will consider later).

Following the marginal cost rule, a public enterprise setting a uniform price per unit of output of P would have sales receipts less than its total costs. Hence resort would have to be made to levying on consumers an additional charge unrelated to the size of purchases (such as an annual rental charge for connection to the electricity system) or to carrying a deficit financed ultimately from taxation. In the case of private ownership the first firm into the field is likely to be able to undercut potential competitors since its costs (in real terms) would fall as it expanded sales. No such possibility arises with constant returns to scale. The present case is therefore often termed a natural monopoly. The private profit maximising monopolist with marginal revenue, MR, will sell q_m at

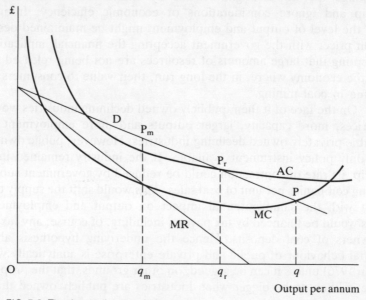

FIG. 5.2 The decreasing cost industry

a price P_m – and this is true whether or not connection charges are levied since such lump-sum charges affect only whether a customer is connected, not how much he buys.

On the face of it then private ownership involves a problem which is solved by public ownership which is predicted to involve a larger output and lower price. However we must, as before, ask whether the solution to the problem intrinsically requires public ownership and in this case there are two rather different issues involved. Whilst economies of scale with private ownership might involve monopoly *in* the field it is quite consistent with competition for the field (Demsetz 1968). In particular, government could invite bids for the contractual right to supply, exclusively, electricity to some defined area over some defined period (as local governments sometimes do for contracts for refuse collection). Provided there is active competition in the bidding process, the entry or franchise fee would be bid up to the level of monopoly profits; the successful bidder would finish up with average costs, including the franchise fee, equal to P_m in the diagram, or even higher if lump-sum connection charges are possible. At the time the contract is due for renewal, potential entrants would again bid, with of course the first entrant's assets open for sale if necessary.

Now there are lots of problems with contracting – the size of transactions costs, the information advantages of the first entrant (cf. Williamson 1971) – but even if there were not it is clear from the diagram that competition for monopoly of the field will only, at best, eliminate monopoly profits; it will not yield the efficient scale of operations, q. As an alternative to contract bidding, consider the case where the government allows a private monopolist to emerge but regulates its prices. (We shall postpone to a later section of this survey the possibility that price regulation, in so far as it affects the rate of return on capital and hence the degree of capital intensity, affects costs.) By specifying that prices have to be lowered when monitored rates of return are seen to be above normal, the regulator would drive down prices and profit rates from the unconstrained monopoly position and therefore induce an expansion of output beyond q_m. The limit of this, however, is q_r in Fig. 5.2, since any further reductions of the exogeneously given uniform price below P_r would lower the monopolist's rate of return below what could be earned elsewhere in the economy. An important qualification is necessary if lump-sum consumer charges are possible and here we find ourselves finally in a situation exactly analogous to the public enterprise. If such charges were sufficient to allow a public enterprise to break even, i.e., earn a normal rate of return, with a per unit price of P then so also would they allow the private monopolist, faced with a regulated price of P, to earn a normal rate of return. If the lump-sum charges are insufficient then the public enterprise would have to carry a deficit if it sold q at price P and the deficit would be financed from taxation. Exactly the same result would emerge however by government capital subsidies to a private monopolist facing a regulated price of P. Products which it is difficult for consumers to resell, like electricity, are of course ripe for discriminating charges both as between different units of output (like the two-part tariff we have been suggesting) and across consumers. However, the major problem, at least analytically, is that if such limited[8] discriminatory charges are inadequate for normal rates of return, there is no obvious way of knowing whether the subsidies are warranted – that is, whether *any* production at all is warranted. The basic problem of increasing returns to scale is that one is faced with an indivisibility (the extreme example being an uncongested bridge with zero running costs) and the *marginal* cost rule is really inappropriate for an *indivisible* change. Imagine the case, for example, where the demand curve is everywhere to the left of the AC curve. There is no price which yields enough revenue to cover total costs and yet production might still be warranted to the extent that consumers' total valuation, as indicated by the area under the demand curve, exceeds total costs at some output levels. To ascertain empirically the area under the demand curve is however a formidable exercise when discriminatory charges are not possible. The only consolation in the present context is that the same issue arises whether the industry is in private or public ownership.

In summary, economic efficiency considerations predict that public enterprise will build more capacity, employ more labour and sell more output at lower prices than private enterprises if, and only if, two conditions are met:

(a) public enterprise operations are based solely on considerations of economic efficiency;
(b) either
   (i) any tendency for private ownership to lead to monopoly is unconstrained by price regulation
   or
   (ii) subsidies to public enterprise are more likely than subsidies to private enterprise even when both face the same economic problems.

These hypotheses about the *actual* behaviour of public enterprise will, at a later point in the survey, be compared with other hypotheses.

3. Economic organisation, contractual forms and ownership

The traditional analysis of economic efficiency was primarily concerned with the broad objectives of firms in the area of pricing, input choice and scale of operations. It paid little attention to factors internal to the firm affecting the success with which given objectives were achieved. The very terms 'public' and 'private' relate however to different organisational forms. An important question therefore is whether the two organisational types involve any systematic differences in the success with which objectives are achieved, irrespective of what are the objectives. Hypotheses on this issue have emerged as a by-product of a growing literature on the theory of economic organisation. The focus here will be on three issues: (a) the factors theoretically affecting the success of *management* in achieving the owners' objectives, i.e. factors affecting what is sometimes called 'organisational slack' (Williamson 1963a) or 'X inefficiency' (Leibenstein 1966); (b) the minimisation of the costs of a given output, a common corporate objective which will be used here for illustration – the whole issue of efficiency of different kinds is considered in section 5; (c) the degree to which the ownership features of public and private firms imply different performances from management.

FIRMS VERSUS MARKETS

Recent developments in the theory of economic organisation suggest that the 'firm' can be thought of as a nexus of contracts between varying parties, notably labour, management, financiers, raw material suppliers. Since all exchanges of resources involve contracts, formal or informal, then each organisational form and each transaction in the economy will be characterised by particular types of contractual arrangements. It is often helpful to focus on broad groupings of contract types. In so far as we are interested in public and private *firms*, then it would seem useful first of all to draw a distinction between the direction of resources within firms as opposed to their direction across markets.

A producer can make a market contract with resource owners for goods and factor services. Alternatively, he can 'employ' such resource owners, i.e. enter into a contract which essentially gives the producer more flexible control over the resource owners. A car producer could buy pressed body parts from other producers; accounts work could be undertaken by an independent accountancy firm for a fee; office and factory cleaning could be 'contracted out'; haulage work could be undertaken by an independent haulier. A classic explanation of such 'vertical disintegration' would be the economies of scale that accrue from specialisation at each stage of production (Stigler 1951). The alternative is to manufacture own body parts, employ own accountancy staff, cleaners and hauliers. The broad distinguishing feature of this alternative is the greater flexibility given to the producer in his direction of the resource owners. For example, accountancy staff may always be on hand and maintain confidentiality; own haulage capacity will always be available for a firm's use at short notice. Other contractual forms are possible beside the simple ones of employment or market contracting with autonomous suppliers – for example franchising agreements, between say producers and retailers or the establishment of subsidiary companies to specialise in certain work or services. Whilst space precludes further exploration of these other forms, they do carry the implication that the economic boundaries of the 'firm' are blurred (Rubin 1978). The important point in the present context is that differing contractual forms will have differing benefits and costs and one might expect that the chosen form is that which yields the largest net benefits. Difficulties in contracting in markets with autonomous suppliers is now understood to be an important reason for the existence and expansion of firms. Market contracting costs seem to result from information problems. Coase (1937) identified a number of costs of transacting in markets which essentially arise from information imperfections, notably the difficulties market contracting faces where uncertainty about future events exists, where long-term decisions regarding resource use are involved, or where difficulties exist in discovering mutually beneficial prices.

This 'transaction costs' approach to explaining the existence of resource allocation within firms rather than in markets has been developed and refined in recent years and a considerable literature now exists (Stigler 1961, Demsetz 1969, Alchian 1969, Alchian and Demsetz 1972, Hirshleifer 1973, Arrow 1975, Spence 1975).[9] Outstanding in this literature, however, is the contribution of Oliver Williamson (1973, 1975, 1976a, 1976b, 1979), who has identified a number of possible costs of market transacting to explain why resources are sometimes organised in 'firms', or what he prefers to refer to as 'hierarchies'. In particular:

(a) costs resulting from what he calls 'bounded rationality'. He argues that individuals have a limited ability to absorb and process the complex issues necessary to reach a position of completely objective and rational behaviour. Therefore, people are sometimes unable to identify easily, and hence cheaply, future contingencies and write these, and adaptations thereto, into market contracts. Successive short-term contracts may overcome this but at the price of larger transactions costs.

(b) costs resulting from 'opportunism', i.e. where one or other of the parties to a contract withholds information pertinent to a mutually beneficial contract, or has special skills, information or position which allow that party to bid up the recontracting price, thereby imposing costs on the other party. Such 'opportunist' behaviour will be especially prevalent where the number of potential bidders for a contract is smaller, i.e. where competition for a contract is limited, giving market power to one of the parties to the contract.

(c) costs results from 'information impactedness', i.e. a producer may have varying information about potential contractors, some of whom, though genuine, are unable to convince the producer that they have the ability, as well as the will, to fulfil a contract. This problem is exacerbated by 'opportunism' in market contracts and suggests that where there are asymmetries in the levels of information available to the parties to a contract, the party with the least information may suffer costs, and contracts unfavourable to that party may be negotiated.

In other words, Williamson is essentially saying that contracting parties in markets sometimes require considerable information about current and future circumstances, which may be unavailable. Firms or hierarchies, however, may have more sophisticated information bases. To illustrate, Williamson, along with Wachter and Harris (1975), has suggested that the recruitment of labour within firms may have advantages over market contracting with autonomous suppliers of labour in markets, where: (a) complex contingent claims contracts would be required in a market contract to offset a lack of information about future conditions; (b) there are information asymmetries favouring workers, which would reduce the benefits of purchasing labour in markets; (c) firms need to create an environment in which labour will have incentives to train other labour in skills important to the long-term success of the firm. Hence we would expect employment contracts to be preferred in circumstances where labour has to be moved between tasks or geographically to meet changing requirements which are difficult to predict accurately; where workers once trained would be able to exert considerable pressure upon management to obtain exceedingly favourable contracts unconstrained by potential suppliers of alternative labour services in the labour market; and where workers would be unwilling to train if they saw them as potential competitors in future recontracting.

Williamson also rejects the idea of a frictionless capital market in which shareholders have perfect knowledge. Instead he argues that shareholders suffer from bounded rationality and the capital market in general suffers from information impactedness. Therefore he suggested that capital markets involve significant transaction costs and conglomerate firms acting as mini, internalised, capital markets may avoid such costs and be superior allocators of capital, since they can benefit from superior information relating to the allocation of capital. Thus in the case of two important inputs, labour and capital, there may be circumstances in which employing resources is more efficient than contracting for resources with autonomous suppliers in markets.[10]

INCENTIVES WITHIN FIRMS

Organising resources within firms also involves costs which parallel the 'transaction costs' found in markets. By considering the costs in hierarchies we gain a further understanding of why different organisational forms are adopted for allocating resources and, importantly, we can identify the role of management within firms. This leads to a consideration of the way incentives to management may differ in public and private firms.

The basic unit of analysis in an organisation is taken to be the individual, whether a member of the labour force or management, for it is the individual who owns, supplies or hires factor services. It is assumed individuals have utility functions which include both pecuniary and non-pecuniary variables and which they attempt to maximise or at least pursue.[11] Pecuniary items are financial receipts, notably wages, bonuses and salaries and non-pecuniary items are other 'rewards' such as a pleasant working environment, a pretty secretary, a quiet life ('low stress') and ability to avoid work or effort ('shirking'). Given that there are these two broad forms of income we may conjecture that where individuals are unable to alter their pecuniary income directly, by say working harder, they will attempt to raise their income and hence utility by raising non-pecuniary income. In particular, individuals will raise their non-pecuniary income by pursuing an 'easier life' at work as long as this has no effect on their pecuniary income. Since 'shirking' and related activity raises a firm's costs of production in the form of reduced labour productivity or directly increasing other costs, a major function of management is checking the pursuit of non-pecuniary income by the labour force. The same point, and we return to this later, applies to management. Managers will also pursue non-pecuniary variables, unless they are prevented from doing so by, say, external factors, such as pressure from shareholders, or by the existence of pecuniary incentives such as profit sharing agreements or plain entitlement to profits. In contrast, where resources are allocated in markets competition and exchange in the market place, at least where competition does exist, will produce rewards to factors of production which reflect their productivity, producing incentives to be efficient. In such circumstance an increase in 'shirking' would reduce an individual's productivity, leading to a fall in the supply of services and hence a decline in his pecuniary income. In firms the marginal products of individual workers have to be directly identified by management and at the same time the productivity of management also needs to be metered, if pecuniary payments are to be related to their productivity.

Incentives for labour inputs to perform efficiently and contribute to the success of the firm are determined by management and can take two broad forms: (a) incentives can be related to 'prices'; for example, payments to factors can be related to output through the adoption of piecework modes of payment, productivity bonuses, profit sharing schemes and at least for some grades of the labour force the 'carrot' of promotion with associated higher earnings is an apparent spur to greater effort; (b) directives and control procedures can be implemented; these procedures include the introduction of set working hours and meal breaks, job specifications, direct supervision of work, standards relating to the quantity and quality of work, managerial directives, disciplining procedures, and the use of work study and similar techniques.

The form and success of such 'incentives' is not the subject of this review, per se;[12] we are more concerned with the motivation of management, in the private and public sectors of the economy, to identify and introduce the optimal 'incentives' structure in their firms to ensure minimum production costs at any given output level. Firms are in a sense hierarchies in which incentives to be efficient are necessary at all levels. The costs of introducing, operating and enforcing incentives related to 'prices' or of making directives and control procedures, will rise where internal signals or information flows between different levels of the firm hierarchy become blurred or incomplete. Therefore an important function of management in firms is to develop efficient information flows, which will involve introducing organisational forms and employment contracts which economise on the costs of monitoring.

In addition, the terms of the employment contract between labour and management may economise on monitoring costs by creating incentives to limit 'shirking'. However complex, detailed contracts are costly to write and enforce; therefore actual employment contracts usually contain relatively few provisions, each of which serve several purposes. The reasons for this relate to the market 'transaction cost' arguments and particularly the problems of writing long-term detailed contracts emphasised above.[13] More specifically, writing detailed employment contracts is difficult where the future use of inputs cannot be fully foreseen or specified easily, where future work requirements are unclear, or where the nature of the work concerned is non-routine. In such cases, to allow flexible use of labour, employment contracts tend to outline only general duties or areas of responsibility. A contract for piecework introduces direct incentives to be efficient but can only be adopted where the work is routine, easy to detail and agree at the time of employment and where the quantity and quality of the product can be cheaply identified and monitored.

In other cases, management has to monitor labour inputs and outputs directly (McNeil 1974, Goldberg 1974a, Leibenstein 1979). Furthermore, even where inputs and/or outputs can be more clearly detailed in the employment contract, monitoring activity is not redundant. Inputs and/or outputs will need to be monitored if the employment contract is to be enforced; that is there will be 'enforcement costs' (McManus 1976). Where the details of a job can be clearly specified and agreed at the time of employment the *quality* of performance will still need to be monitored.

There are likely to be particular difficulties in establishing detailed employment contracts with inputs and in monitoring inputs and outputs, including enforcing contracts where there are problems in identifying the productivity of individuals within a firm and hence in relating pecuniary rewards to productivity. In particular, in such cases the self-policing 'price' incentives referred to above cannot be relied upon to stimulate effort. Identifying each individual's productivity becomes especially difficult where 'team production' occurs, that is where each input contributes simultaneously to a given task. For example, where four men are jointly involved in lifting items on to lorries the contribution or effort of each individual cannot be easily identified. Each individual has no separable output; only the team has an output and the assessment of each person's contribution involves monitoring costs.[14]

Where such joint production occurs the opportunity for individuals to increase their non-pecuniary income by 'shirking' increases. Some or all individuals in a 'team' could gain extra pecuniary income if 'shirking' was curbed, as rewards available to the team would rise as output rose, but there is no automatic incentive for any particular individual to reduce his 'shirking' unless he can be certain that other individuals in the 'team' will do likewise. In other words, 'non-shirking' in a 'team' is a public good in the sense that the benefits of 'non-shirking' will be shared out indiscriminately amongst all the 'team'. Individuals in a team who do not 'shirk' will share the benefits of 'non-shirking' with those who do. In such circumstances which are characteristic of many production activities, we can expect that close monitoring of factor inputs and/or outputs will be needed and this will require, especially when large numbers are involved, management time, effort and resources.

AGENTS, PRINCIPALS AND INCENTIVES FOR MANAGEMENT

Since management monitoring of factor inputs requires time and effort, management itself needs incentives. In the small firm, where the owner of the firm is the manager, incentives exist for the owner-manager to minimise 'shirking' and other activities which raise costs of production. Any such inefficiencies will reduce the residual income left to the entrepreneur after payments to contracted factor inputs, thereby reducing his pecuniary income. Hence his freedom to take 'income' in non-pecuniary forms, e.g. an afternoon on the golfcourse, involves a direct cost in terms of a lower pecuniary income.

Turning to large firms in the private sector, which are often the nearest equivalents to publicly owned enterprises, control of the firm's resources lies with a management whose pecuniary income takes the form largely of salaries – though links with profits are not uncommon. Ownership rights in such firms are held by shareholders (stockholders), including small shareholders taking no direct active part in management policy and large institutional investors, such as banks, insurance companies and pension funds, which also, at least in the UK, refrain from interference, at least openly, in the management of the firms in which they invest. In some cases shares may be held by directors of the firm or other senior management, although in the UK the shareholdings of directors are a very small percentage of total shareholdings.

A number of studies relating to managerial and behavioural theories of the firm suggest that there is a significant divorce of ownership and control in the private sector and that this may lead to an alteration in the objectives of firms away from the pursuit of profit to some other goal, such as sales, growth or utility maximisation or 'expense preference', where profit is a constraint rather than a goal.[15] By implication there will be differences across firms in the degree of success in achieving the owners' objectives – there will, that is, be variations in 'organisational slack' and 'X inefficiency'.

Such behaviour will presumably only be possible where a firm's 'owners' are unable or unwilling to invest time, effort and resources to limit managerial behaviour to the pursuit of high efficiency and profits. Hence, the pressure placed by 'owners' on management to monitor factor inputs or outputs efficiently becomes an important determinant of efficiency differences between firms. A useful way of analysing this, and one which is particularly helpful in the context of comparison of public and private firms, is from the perspective of 'agency relationships' and property rights.

In agency relationships 'principals' appoint 'agents' to undertake stipulated duties. If both principals and agents are maximisers of their respective utilities then there is no good reason for assuming that agents will act in the best interests of principals, unless some limit to the discretionary behaviour of agents is introduced. Such a limit will normally be imposed and hence generate monitoring costs for the principals.[16] In firms where ownership and control are divorced, the owners of the firm are the principals who appoint directors ('agents') to manage the firm on their behalf. This agency relationship involves an attenuation (restriction) of the property rights of owners over their firms' assets.[17] Such property rights consist of the right to receive the reward from the employment of resources, the right to direct the use of resources and the right to transfer these ownership entitlements to others, which may be summarised as the rights to benefit from, control and dispose of resources.

In a business with the traditional single 'entrepreneur', the owner's property rights are unattenuated, except in so far as they may be constrained by general legislation relating say to the environment, employment or taxation. The entrepreneur can direct the use of resources, sell his property rights and, importantly, fully benefit from the use of his property through having complete entitlement to any residual income remaining in the firm after payments to all contracted inputs. It is this entitlement to the residual income which leads to the presumption that there are incentives to minimise production costs in owner-controlled firms (cf. Cho 1977). Where ownership and control are divorced the property right to control resources is transferred to management, while the right to benefit from ownership (to benefit from the residual income) remains with the 'owners' of the firm. Management are given powers to hire, fire and organise inputs; the ultimate right to dispose of the ownership rights in the firm remains with the 'owners'.

In such cases, we might infer that where principals are unable to limit managerial freedom significantly and where management pursue their own rather than owners' utility, incentives to minimise costs are lower than where ownership and control are not divorced. To limit managerial behaviour which diminishes owners' utility, 'owners' will need to monitor management activities. Such monitoring activity will be costly in time, effort and resources and hence there are 'agency costs' where ownership and control are divorced. Contracts between shareholders and directors and other similar agreements may limit these costs as would the linking of management salaries to profits. So will company law, which defends shareholders against managerial fraud and lays down minimum information requirements relating to companies' affairs. However, the costs will not disappear and, in particular, detailed contracts will again be difficult to write, monitor and enforce.

THE OWNERSHIP FUNCTION IN LARGE PRIVATE SECTOR COMPANIES

The argument that privately owned joint stock companies are likely to be more efficient than public enterprises, frequently derives from study of the different attributes of ownership in publicly and privately owned companies, that is the differing property rights or, alternatively, agency relationship involved (Alchian 1965, Alchian and Demsetz 1972, Demsetz 1964, 1966, 1967, de Alessi 1969, 1974a, 1974b, 1975, 1977, Furubotn and Pejovich 1972, 1974). We have noted that management requires incentives to monitor inputs efficiently and that if management has no direct interest in the residual income of the firm then these incentives could be imposed by pressures from 'principals'. In the case of private sector companies a great deal depends upon the ability of shareholders to limit managerial behaviour to the pursuit of maximum efficiency and profits. It has been suggested that shareholders are able to do this at firms' annual general meetings when they can elect and fire directors, act in consort with other shareholders to establish block votes to impose policy changes and generally badger management. On the other hand, it appears that AGMs are rarely occasions where shareholders and management clash.

Three other factors are perhaps of more significance. Firstly there is the market for shares enabling shareholders to signal their confidence in management policy through day-to-day buying and selling of shares. This involves some expense and effort but will usually be less costly than organising direct action at AGMs. By selling, shareholders can signal disapproval of management policy, which may in itself change management attitudes as share prices fall, and in the extreme could encourage 'take-over' of the firm, possibly by more effective management. In addition, the ability to buy and sell shares in companies permits specialisation in shareholding. Thus individuals with a special interest or expertise in shipbuilding will be able to specialise in owning shares in shipbuilding concerns. Poor managerial decisions are more likely to be spotted by owners who specialise. Secondly, it has been suggested that competition in the market for top management, from lower levels of management within the firm or from potential management outside, may be a further constraint on managerial behaviour in the private sector. Furthermore, 'principals' will be able to reflect their confidence in the quality of the management they are hiring, in the salaries they pay their managers, and so transfer the costs of any *anticipated* higher production costs (Alchian 1977a, Alchian and Demsetz 1972, Furubotn and Pejovich 1972, Fama 1980). Thirdly, company law in so far as it requires regular independent audits and financial statements, would appear to be a further restriction upon managerial freedom of action.

In other words, in private companies where ownership and control are divorced, the existence of markets for ownership rights and management, along with legislation regulating the publication of information relating to the company, limit the costs to owners of monitoring management behaviour. Of course, the extent to which these constraints actually do limit managerial behaviour is an empirical matter and unfortunately studies to date provide no firm conclusions. Some undertaken in the UK and USA suggest that in manager controlled firms a lower profit is earned than in firms where a clear divorce between ownership and control does not exist (see for example, Monsen, Chiu and Cooley 1968, Radice 1971, Palmer 1973, Round 1976, McEachern 1978).[18] Some research into the relationship between the pay and tenure of top management and the goals of large firms has suggested that profit maximisation is not so important as growth and sales maximisation, a result which is consistent with the proposition that management can adopt discretionary behaviour to increase their own rather than owners' utility.[19] Not all empirical studies, however, support such a view and there is a similar lack of consensus about the actual operation of capital markets in modern industrial economies. On the one hand, there are those who endorse an 'efficient markets hypothesis' and who support the view that owners do limit the behaviour of management by buying and selling shares. On the other hand, a number of studies have pointed to inefficiencies in capital markets. In particular, some studies have stressed that the costs of buying and selling shares or uncertainty about the current and future performance of firms, or shareholder inertia in the face of costs of obtaining information about firms and shares, permit management to deviate from policies which maximise shareholders' utility.[20]

Therefore, although shareholders in the private sector do appear to have powers to limit managerial behaviour, there is some suggestion that the agency relationships, which exist where ownership and control are divorced, are important and permit at least some degree of discretionary behaviour by management which reduces owners' utility. On the other hand, it seems reasonable to presume that there will be a minimum level which a firm's profits cannot fall without provoking a response from shareholders at an AGM or in the stock market.

THE OWNERSHIP FEATURES OF PUBLIC ENTERPRISE

Agency relationships also exist for public enterprise. For example, in the UK the public in effect delegate powers to ministers and government departments, who themselves delegate powers to the boards of the public corporations. Hence the boards act as agents of government and more indirectly the public. Where such agency relationships exist property rights and in particular rights to the residual income of enterprises are affected. The boards, their chairmen and other senior management in public enterprises will normally have no direct interest in the residual since they do not benefit directly from a high residual, although status, career prospects and survival in office could be linked to the performance of their enterprise.

In addition, government departments and ministers are usually pre-' vented from directly benefitting from the residual. In the UK it would be judged improper for civil servants or politicians to receive financial benefits from public enterprises. Therefore, while civil servants may have an incentive to promote the size and scope of public ownership, as this may mean more and better paid civil service posts, and politicians may promote low prices and high employment in public industries to win votes, there may be no direct incentive for government to pressure public boards (or similar agencies) to minimise production costs and maximise the residual.

The public, of course, have a direct interest in the performance of public enterprises, as they consume the products or services supplied by these enterprises and act as ultimate financiers of the industries losses through the tax system. Just as shareholders in joint stock companies need to monitor management in these companies, so the public need to monitor the activities of the public enterprise. In both instances a divorce of ownership and control occurs. However, there is a difference between joint stock companies and public enterprises from an agency and property rights perspective. Whereas in joint stock companies the residual may act as a direct incentive for shareholders to monitor management and in the extreme shareholders may terminate their property rights by selling shares, in the case of public ownership, the public, the 'principals', find the monitoring of their 'agents' more costly. Each owner, that is each member of the public, will normally find that the cost of influencing the policy of the enterprise or government policy will considerably outweigh any benefits that he or she will gain from a change in policy. Unlike shareholders in joint stock companies who can sell their shares, their property rights, the cost of terminating ownership rights in public industries is much greater since these ownership rights are compulsory by virtue of residence. Migration from one jurisdiction to another will terminate these rights and would be a costly action if undertaken just for that reason. Alternatively, the public may actively support political changes which will terminate public ownership, for instance by supporting a political party which will 'denationalise'. This also is a high cost strategy, involving time, effort and perhaps money, and which may have uncertain results. In both cases, whether moving residence or political action, the cost to an individual is likely to be far greater than any resultant benefit the individual might receive. We may therefore conclude that, on a priori grounds at least, the lack of a capital market where ownership rights can be exchanged makes the cost of monitoring agents by principals far greater in the case of public ownership than in the case of private ownership where capital markets exist (Alchian 1965b). Similarly, whereas in the case of private ownership specialisation in ownership reduces monitoring costs by permitting ownership by those who have special knowledge of an industry's affairs, in the case of public ownership specialisation is impossible. All members of the public hold an equal and very small share in the ownership of the enterprise and are unable to sell or trade this ownership.

We may conclude from this fundamental difference between private and public ownership that, since that cost of terminating property rights in publicly owned industries is high in relation to resultant benefits, the public may be expected to acquiesce in their continued ownership of the respective industries and to playing a very passive role as 'owners', conceding all control over the industries to government and management. Supportive of this view is the oft-cited lack of interest or even outright opposition to public industries discovered in public opinion polls.

Finally, it should be re-emphasised that problems of agency relationships can, on a priori grounds, be expected to exist in the private sector. Whilst the analytical literature points to these problems being greater in the public sector, in the end the question is an empirical matter. The empirical studies considered in the last section of the survey are therefore of prime importance.

4. The behaviour of the public firm

The previous section has two broad implications for the analysis of public firms. Firstly it focuses attention on economic organisation, i.e. on the contractual arrangements distinctive to 'public' ownership and in particular the form of constraints on the behaviour of individuals working in public enterprise. Secondly in portraying the citizen of a political jurisdiction as the ultimate owner of the enterprise and in contrasting his powers as owner with those of the shareholder of the private firm, it makes explicit the potential importance of civil servants and politicians in any explanation of the behaviour of public firms, even though these issues cannot be handled solely within the framework of the property rights theory of the firm.

The latter set of issues thrusts us into a very wide-ranging and complex areas. For example, to understand the behaviour of a public enterprise, it is not irrelevant to ask why it was bought into public ownership. One approach might be to analyse which particular income groups or occupational categories benefit from specific acts of nationalisation. One could then contrast the behaviour of the enterprise with that which would have occurred under private ownership. Useful though this approach may be, it has to be recognised that if the coal mines and railways had not been nationalised in for example the UK in the 1945–50 period, the whole political climate could well have been different (if not explosive) and hence 'what otherwise would have occurred' with private ownership requires treatment of a barely discernible scenario. Secondly, in so far as the motivation of politicians is relevant to the behaviour of public firms, an analysis of vote-getting and related electoral issues is necessary. This is an area where economists have started to make a contribution – under the heading of public choice theory (see Mueller 1976). Nevertheless, the area is in an embryonic state, much is still highly theoretical and studies of public enterprise behaviour which draw explicitly on public choice theory are few in number.

The empirical work on public firms has not therefore been able to draw on a well articulated set of theoretical concepts. There are several broad approaches which individually or in combination have provided a starting point for empirical work. One approach has already been mentioned in section 2, i.e. the comparison of public and private under the rather restrictive assumption that public enterprise operations are based on the precepts of economic efficiency. We now consider three further approaches.

THE ORIGINS AND STATED ECONOMIC OBJECTIVES OF PUBLIC OWNERSHIP

Economists, by nature, are prone to attach little weight to the public statements of political leaders usually because the statements on economic matters are vague by the standards of logic required in economic theory or a vested interest is suspected to lie in the background. No doubt these strictures are in part applicable to what we know of the stated reasons for public ownership and the stated objectives of public enterprises. Nevertheless, economists do not yet have tested models to explain acts of nationalisation and it would therefore be foolish to ignore the extensive public debate on these subjects. Some of the electoral aspects of public ownership are considered later in this survey. Students should also read some of the economic history of nationalisation movements (see Eldon Barry (1965), Chester HMSO 1975, Trebing (1976)). Here we propose to illustrate some of the issues by several features of note in the origins and stated economic objectives of public ownership in Britain.

Firstly the public ownership of key industries in Britain in the 1945–50 period can be viewed in part as an expression of a political philosophy with a long history which would embrace Spencean socialists, Chartism, Marxism, 'gas and water' socialism, Syndicalism and Guild socialism – though the role of this philosophy in explaining public ownership has perhaps been overstated. A major theme was the redistribution of economic power and hence the political power that goes with it. Whilst this cannot easily be translatable into conventional economic terminology, it did above all imply a downgrading of the role of profit and the use of public industries to promote the general economic welfare of the poor. Private profit was to be 'confiscated' and used to improve the welfare of the workers in the industry and the public at large. The Nationalisation Acts did not include profit as an objective. The industries were required to break even and any profits earned were to remain in the industries to improve services and working conditions. To many in the labour movement profits came from the surplus value created by the workforce and therefore belonged to the workers. The introduction of public ownership was intended to change the pattern of production and income distribution and for the Labour Party public ownership had its roots in Clause IV of the Party's constitution which aimed to secure for workers 'the full fruits of their industry and the most equitable distribution thereof'. Moreover, Herbert Morrison, who inspired the establishment of an early public corporation to run London Transport and who was perhaps the key architect of the public corporation in Britain, expected (1933) that one benefit of nationalisation would be the provision of 'socially necessary' services and all the Nationalisation Acts contained a 'public purpose' clause requiring that the new enterprises provide cheap and abundant coal and gas, electricity supply to rural areas, an 'adequate' railway system, etc.

Secondly, the nationalised industries were also to be a tool in national economic planning. Here the background of the inter-war period is vital. To many in the labour movement private ownership had failed the nation and permitted mass unemployment and social deprivations. Economic planning would overcome this and amongst other things this required public ownership of the commanding heights of the economy. In fact up to the mid 1970s unemployment was not a major problem in the British economy though the investment programmes of the nationalised industries have been adjusted on occasions, as with other items of public expenditure, to meet the requirements of macroeconomic management. Perhaps the best illustration of the general phenomenon is the way in which the industries' prices were controlled in the 1970s as an arm of counter-inflation policy, the choice of this instrument being motivated in part by the belief that this would especially benefit people with low incomes (cf. Millward 1976).

Thirdly, it can be argued that the promotion of economic efficiency and of management efficiency *did* play a very important part in arguments for public ownership. How this was to be reconciled with the first two points was never and has never subsequently been satisfactorily resolved. Notwithstanding what we have argued in the previous section on economic efficiency, it was felt that economies of large-scale production could lead to monopoly abuse if the industries were left in private ownership. After the slump of the 1920s and 1930s the labour movement felt there was a need to reorganise and rationalise a number of key industries and pressure groups allied to the labour movement, such as the Railway Nationalisation Society, declared the need for efficient management of publicly owned industries, (Eldon Barry 1965: 237). Herbert Morrison (1933) expected that one benefit of public ownership would be that the industries would be efficiently and economically conducted. This was a view which had found some sympathy in the case of electricity supply in the unlikely quarter of the employers' pressure group the Federation of British Industries (now the Confederation of British Industries) in the mid-1920s. Though some Conservative back-benchers opposed the establishment of a publicly owned Central Electricity Board to rationalise and develop the nation's electricity supplies, the FBI supported the move on the grounds that it would mean cheaper electricity. Thus the argument that public ownership was necessary for the exploitation of economies of scale and rationalisation seems to have found some favour even outside the labour movement.

Moreover the view that management efficiency was important for the proponents of nationalisation can be defended in the structure and form which public ownership eventually was to take. The acceptance by 1945 of *public corporations* as the vehicle for public ownership resulted from a belief that such corporations would be the best method to ensure efficient operation of publicly owned industries. Direct government control through government departments was rejected on the grounds that government ministers did not stay long enough in one department to gain expertise in an industry's affairs and the civil service had no experience and received no training in the running of industries. It was hoped that the boards of public corporations could play a role somewhat like the boards of joint stock companies, an argument put forward by the Liberal Party in its 'Yellow Book' in 1928 and which Morrison acknowledged as a source of his faith in public ownership through public corporations, cf. HMSO Chester 1975:385–6. Since joint-stock companies separated ownership and control in industry, why should public corporations which did the same be any less efficient? Thus the final legislation was designed with the intention that the Corporations would be independent of government in a significant way, thereby promoting initiative, enterprise and a basically commercial ambience. The assets were vested in new bodies which were given a corporate status free from Treasury supervision of personnel and from day to day supervision by the Minister or Parliament. The fixed terms of the Board's members were seen to provide some immunity from the changes in the political party in office. These features were buttressed by the clauses which required the industries to break even and which have been described (HMSO Chester 1975:1046) as the sheet anchor of the thinking of the Ministers who introduced the nationalisation legislation. It was hoped, that is – and how subsequent experience has proved this a vain hope! – that any threats of wage claims leading to deficits would be converted to a trade-off between wages and prices. Moreover the break-even clause was intended to reinforce independence from government by divorcing the accounts from the national budget – though not entirely since for some corporations specific privision was made for deficit grants and capital finance was also linked to the Treasury.

BUREAUCRACY

A further feature of public firms stems from the analysis in section 3 of the survey. This is the line of argument which links the property rights analysis of the public firm to the behaviour of *management* without necessarily giving an explicit role for politicians and civil servants. Managers of public firms are seen, in this approach, to have more scope than in private firms for promoting their own welfare at the expense of the owners' welfare. The specific manifestations of this will depend on the specific control framework in each firm but some general points can be made. In the simplest type of production theory the employment of a factor of production is extended until its pecuniary income is equal to its marginal value product and the marginal physical product of a factor is larger, the bigger is the volume of co-operating factors of production. Where a factor has several uses, its time will be allocated among activities such that each activity yields the same marginal value product. Where the factor is management, it has to be recognised that such an allocation of time will rarely coincide with the management's preferred allocation of time. For owners supervising management, there are costs (in terms of time and effort) in devising the monitoring reward systems such that the total input of management and its allocation of time between activities corresponds more closely to profit-maximising patterns. As a result of the ownership characteristics of public firms, the incentive to devise and monitor such reward systems is less.

The first implication of this is that since the physical productivity of management is always difficult to discern and the span of control is often used as a rough proxy, then management will itself attempt to raise the volume of co-operating resources beyond profit-maximising levels in order that management's own pecuniary income is raised. Capital equipment is an obvious example and the predication is (de Alessi 1969, 1974b) that public enterprises will use lower interest rates than private firms in evaluating the time-stream of revenue and costs of an investment project. Consider two projects which yield the same stream of revenue net of operating costs but where A involves a capital outlay now whereas B involves capital expenditures spread out through time. *Ceteris paribus*, the lower is the interest rate used for discounting the larger will be the present value of B's future capital expenditures and the more favourable becomes A, that is, the more favourable becomes the project which activates large volumes of co-operating resources *now*.

The second implication is that management will have more scope for promoting its non-pecuniary income – of attaining an allocation of its time nearer to its preferred allocation and of obtaining types and volumes of co-operating resources which more fully promote management welfare rather than that of the owners. Moreover and paradoxically, public enterprises, and especially those closely integrated with government, sometimes lay down strict operating guidelines for pecuniary income when the productivity of management is less easy to judge in terms of profitability. If pecuniary income is so constrained and yet detailed monitoring of management is limited, the 'cost' to management of extending non-pecuniary income is reduced. Job perks of comfortable surroundings are commonly quoted but some authors have extended this to more strategic aspects of the firm's behaviour. Since the design of complicated price structures to reflect complex cost characteristics, hard bargaining with buyers and sellers, customer complaints about the product and industrial relations problems all make life difficult to management, then for example de Alessi (Fall 1974) predicts that, as compared to private firms there will in public firms *ceteris paribus*, be less product differentiation, higher prices paid for inputs and lower prices received for outputs, higher quality products (to minimise customer complaints) and better conditions for a larger work force.

BALLOT BOX MODELS

The main prediction of the bureaucracy approach is that public enterprises will expand their output and capital equipment beyond profit-maximising levels. By its focus on the attenuated rights of citizen-owners its theoretical force depends on a muted role for government. Explicit models of the effect of government on public enterprises are small in number though growing. Their main focus has been politicians motivated by the desire for re-election[21] and their ability to influence the operations of public enterprises to enhance voter support. This is seen to take the form of directly conferring economic benefits on voters or in some cases to use public enterprise operations to raise the volume of campaign resources in cash or in kind.

Considering first the direct appeal to voters, attention has concentrated on two key blocs of votes, consumers and owners, and a contrast drawn with the behaviour of a firm maximising profits. Two simple ideas are involved. The significance of an individual consumer to a profit maximising firm is as a source of profit whilst to the public firm it arises from the possibility of his having one vote; similarly the significance of an owner arises from his having one vote whereas for the profit maximising firm it arises from the size of the owner's entitlement to profit. Secondly any departure from the profit-maximising price structure involves a net gain to an individual if the rise in his tax bill as citizen owner is less than the saving he makes as a consumer (ignoring the consumer surplus elements of any increase in consumption). The aggregate of all such net gains over all individuals cannot be positive but this still leaves the possibility that some change in the price structure may involve a larger *number* of gainers than losers (cf. Peltzman 1971).

If we assume that taxes are related to income, then there will be no possibility of raising votes if each individual has the same preference for goods and services and the same income level and each qualifies for one vote. Consider however the case where preferences are different, implying that the demand for the product of the enterprise varies across individuals. A price reduction will yield greater benefits to those with heavy demands for the product whilst enterprise losses associated with this will be spread evenly over the taxpaying population. If the heavy demanders of the product are numerous their net economic gains will mean larger gains in votes than are lost from the minority group paying the uniform tax but consuming only small amounts of the product. A good illustration of this possibility is the case of urban bus transit systems in the USA. The smaller is the proportion of car-owning non-users of buses in the voting population of any metropolitan area the bigger, *ceteris paribus*, would we expect to be the financial losses on publicly owned transit systems; evidence collected by Pashigian (1976) for 40 transit systems in the years 1960 and 1970 is consistent with this hypothesis. When tax liabilities differ, more complex possibilities are involved.

This approach has several implications. Firstly, we would expect a downward price bias since prices *above* the profit-maximising level injure both consumers and taxpayers. Secondly, non-voting users – such as those users located outside the jurisdiction of citizens who own the enterprise – can be expected to pay higher prices than owners. (On this whole general area see the N. Topham survey in this volume.) Thirdly, Peltzman (1971) has argued that in public firms differences in the costs of supplying different customer groups are not likely to be reflected in the price structure as closely in public firms as in private firms. Thus two customers with similar demand functions for the product but who occasion, perhaps because of location, different costs to the enterprise will not face the same set of prices if they are supplied by a profit-maximising firm but, *ceteris paribus*, might be treated equally by the public firm since each consumer has at most only one vote. Finally in this context we may note the case were the size of the subsidy to the enterprise is fixed and the key decision involves the rate of price subsidy across the customer population. Sometimes it may be possible to focus on one dimension of the good or service being supplied – for example whether the subsidy to travellers on a commuter rail service (cf. Cooter and Topakian 1980) should vary with trip length or be generalised across all users. A hypothesis consistent with this general approach would be that the fare would be set to maximise the subsidy to that group of voters whose trip length was the median of all voters. The median trip length is such that 50 per cent of voters have smaller trip lengths than the median and the remaining 50 per cent of voters have trip lengths greater than the median. Hence with fares set to maximise the subsidy to the group of voters whose trip length is the median, the number of voters desirous of a bigger subsidy per mile and a smaller lump-sum generalised element would be less than 50 per cent and hence 'outvoted'. Similarly those wanting a bigger lump-sum element and a smaller subsidy per mile would be 'outvoted'.

Finally we may note that, on the face of it, an important class of voters would be the employees of the public enterprise. In fact little systematic work has been performed on this area. In the British context the problem of being unable to compare public and private firms in the same industry undermines what otherwise would have been a good data base, namely the coincidence in some cases of parliamentary constituency boundaries with groups of employees working in divisions or plants of nationalised industries. In the American context it is the municipal firm which dominates numerically in many of the empirical studies, such that the proportion of the voting population who are consumers of the municipal utility is likely greatly to exceed the proportion who are workers in the firm. Crain and Zardkoohi (1978), however, have argued that public firms will extend employment beyond profit-maximising levels with the aim, in the USA context, of increasing the army of campaign workers. The further implication that the labour-capital ratio[22] is higher in public firms than private is of some interest since in contrast the bureaucracy approach puts much stress on the advantages to management of size, and specially, large volumes of capital equipment, i.e. is pointing to higher capital-labour ratios in public firms.

5. The measurement of efficiency in firms

(This section may be omitted by readers acquainted with problems involved in the estimation of cost functions and with the recent literature on ideal measures of productivity.)

In the previous section various hypotheses about the *behaviour* of public firms have been explored. In some cases these have carried direct implications about pricing, output levels, capacity size and employment in public firms relative to private firms. An expectation that, for example, prices in public firms will be less than in private firms faced with the same cost and demand conditions can be deduced from several of the approaches discussed. The empirical studies considered later in this survey will be examined in part in relation to these hypotheses about behaviour. In this section we introduce a further general consideration, namely that of efficiency. Whether or not a lower price level is a good or a bad thing involves a *normative judgement*. One needs a standard by which things are to be classified as good and bad. When the term 'efficient' is used in relation to pricing levels or output or resource usage, the writer is characterising behaviour according to some such standard even though this is sometimes not stated explicitly. We suggest that 'the efficiency of an enterprise' is a phrase which has a normative significance only in relation to the objectives of the enterprise. If the objective is to raise the real income level of the poor, then an efficiency measure would have to reflect that – the size of costs per unit of output or the level of the achieved rate of profit on capital may be completely inappropriate.

The efficiency measures that have been used by economists are much less sophisticated in scope. Even so the problems of measurement and interpretation remain complex. Three commonly found measures are: (a) productivity, (b) costs, (c) profits. In this section we consider precise formulations of these measures for firms and assess the extent to which they successfully measure the achievement of the following objectives:

(i) maximising the income of owners,
(ii) economic efficiency in the allocation of resources in the economy as a whole.

Clearly enterprises which are ruled by other objectives will, rightly or wrongly, often be seen to be inefficient by such measures. At the least, however, a clear understanding of the measures will indicate what has not been measured.

PRODUCTIVITY

The fundamental idea behind productivity comparisons of firms is to measure the *volume* of resources used to produce a *given* pattern of outputs. For firms producing several products and/or using several inputs, the aim of obtaining a volume measure is complicated, as we shall see, by the necessity of aggregating outputs and inputs with weighting systems which usually involve the use of prices. Consider therefore to start with enterprises which are known to produce only one product with one input. Firms A and B in the next diagram are observed to produce the same output but B uses larger amounts of labour. Provided that all labour working in the firms involves a cost to the enterprise, the difference in the volume of labour employed is a measure of the relative efficiency with which the enterprise owners' income is being enhanced. Similarly, provided that all labour employed involves a cost to the economy, the differing amounts of employment are a measure of the relative economic inefficiency of firm B. The qualification is important since in an economy with large-scale unemployment the alternative use value of the 'surplus' labour may be insignificant.

    With this as background we now consider some of the general problems of measuring productivity. Firm C in Fig. 5.3 is producing a different output level to Firm A and in such circumstances it is tempting to compare the two firms by examining output per unit of input, Y/X. The fact that the firms are producing different output levels may be due to several factors including the different ownership characteristics of A and C. If at the same time technology is such that different output levels involve different output/input ratios then a simple comparison of Y/X would be confusing the two issues. Suppose however that it is known with certainty that the production technology involves constant returns to scale. Within each firm a given percentage increase in labour yields on equal percentage increase in output – though the labour/output ratio differs across firms. We would then be sure that measured differences in Y/X between

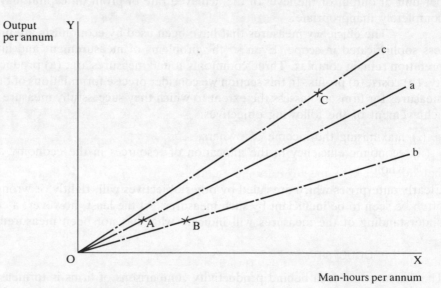

FIG. 5.3 Productivity with one input

A and C would be mirrored in different volumes of X were each firm to produce the same output level.

One obvious point may also be noted at this stage. Measures of value of output per man and costs per unit of output are not substitutes for the Y/X measure since they may be picking up factors other than productivity. If P is the price of the product then PY/X may be measuring, in part, differences in prices between firms. Such price differences may be due to factors unconnected with ownership (such as the particular markets served) and in some cases they may be due to ownership characteristics (such as government imposed price constraints on public firms). Similarly the price of labour, W, might be higher in public firms because management are under less financial pressure to bargain with unions or the difference may be due to differing work locations; a measure of unit costs, WX/Y, would pick up these factors. The productivity measure Y/X is, in other words, designed to be independent of these problems and figures of value of output per man or costs per man are not necessarily reflecting differences in productivity.

Productivity comparisons are usually *presented* in the form of growth rates or indexes. The assumption of constant returns to scale would imply that the production function for firm A takes the form shown by the broken line 'a' in Fig. 5.3, whilst for B it is line 'b' and for firm C it is 'c'. Each enterprise exhibits varying skills in the deployment of labour in production. We could in fact think of there being a general production technology for this product involving certain returns to scale between Y and X but with a shift factor, T, representing different institutional arrangements. Thus

$$Y = f(X, T) \tag{1}$$

A common presentation of the productivity differences would then be the *growth rate of productivity as T changes*, that is as we move from one ownership structure to the next. To prepare the way for the more complex cases of several inputs we may note that for infinitely small changes the growth rate of output associated with a change in T is

$$\frac{d \log Y}{dT} = \frac{d \log f(X, T)}{dT} = \frac{\partial \log f}{\partial T} + \frac{\partial \log f}{\partial \log X} \frac{\partial \log X}{\partial T} \tag{2}$$

The growth of output thus arises in part from a growth in input associated with the change $(\partial \log X/\partial T)$ multiplied by the elasticity of output with respect to input $(\partial \log f/\partial \log X)$. The remaining element in the growth rate of output is that due purely to the institutional change $(\partial \log f/\partial T)$; this is therefore the growth rate of productivity which we see from rearranging [2] is

$$\frac{\partial \log f}{\partial T} = \frac{d \log Y}{dT} - a \frac{\partial \log X}{\partial T} \tag{3}$$

The elasticity of output, denoted by a in the above, will be equal to 1 if there are constant returns to scale so that the productivity measure for an infinitesimally small change would be the growth rate of output minus the growth rate of input.

For a discrete change from ownership structure t to ownership structure t' the productivity measure[23] emerges simply as

$$r_y - r_x \qquad [4]$$

where $r_{y'}$ the growth rate of output, would be measured as the log of $Y_{t'}/Y_t$ and r_x, the growth rate of input, measured as the log of $X_{t'}/X_t$. We cannot always assume constant returns to scale especially for products like electricity and transport. In fact empirical studies often have to start with no prior information. Production functions like [1] would then have to be estimated and if they cannot be estimated because of insufficient data the use of simple productivity measures would be misleading indicators of productivity unless there are compelling reasons to assume constant returns to scale.

Turning to the situation where firms use several inputs, the same basic issues apply. Instead of [1] we have

$$Y = f(X_1, X_2, \ldots, X_i, \ldots, X_n; T) \qquad [5]$$

which again is deemed to depict a general production technology for the product but now with n inputs. Instead of [3] we therefore have

$$\frac{\partial \log f}{\partial T} = \frac{d \log Y}{dT} - \sum_i a_i \frac{\partial \log X_i}{\partial T} \qquad [6]$$

where $a_i = \partial \log f / \partial \log X_i$.

This 'total factor' growth rate of productivity comprises the growth rate of output minus the sum of the growth rates of inputs each weighted by the elasticity of output with respect to changes in that input. For a discrete change from t to t' we have, instead of [4]

$$r_y - \sum_i a_i r_i \qquad [7]$$

where r_i is the growth rate of input X_i and where a_i would have to be treated as an elasticity averaged over the old and new output levels. In fact, unless there have been prior studies, the estimation of the elasticities would be close to estimating the whole production function. A short cut is available involving the use of factor shares of total cost as weights, instead of the elasticities. As we shall show shortly, apart from bringing in new efficiency considerations, the short cut requires an assumption of constant returns to scale for which no compelling *a priori* reason may exist.

There is a related reason for not presuming too much about the production function. So far we have assumed the firms produce just one product. In practice railways, for example, produce freight-ton miles as well as passenger-miles. Moreover the *dimensions* of output can be complex. Electricity can be supplied at different voltages and in geographical areas with varying terrain for laying power lines. Refuse collection can be once weekly, twice weekly, collected from flat or house or only at the curbside. If these factors are not made explicit in the output measure, then the comparison would be reflecting issues other than productivity. Whilst electricity supply by a public firm to a remote part of mid Wales may be unprofitable or indeed inefficient in the economy's use of resources, this does not necessarily imply that the firm has a low productivity or cost effectiveness. What we wish to show in the present context is whether *given the same job*, public firms are less cost effective than private firms. Whether or not the range of outputs is efficient is an important, though separate issue.

In these circumstances with different products or output dimensions denoted by Y_1, Y_2, etc. the production function in [5] has to be replaced by

$$g(Y_1, Y_2, \ldots, Y_i, \ldots, Y_m) = f(X_1, X_2, \ldots, X_n; T) \qquad [8]$$

In the productivity measure [6], the symbol Y essentially has to be replaced by $g(Y_i, \ldots Y_m)$. Now

$$\frac{\mathrm{d} \log g}{\mathrm{d} T} = \sum_j \frac{\partial \log g}{\partial \log Y_j} \frac{\partial \log Y_j}{\partial T}$$

where $\partial \log g / \partial \log Y_j$ is the elasticity of inputs with respect to a change in Y_j in the initial situation. For the discrete change, the productivity measure in [7] becomes

$$\sum_j v_j r_j - \sum_i a_i r_i \qquad [9]$$

where r_j is the growth rate of output Y_j and where v_j is the elasticity of input with respect to output Y_j averaged over the old and new output levels. The growth rate of productivity now consists of the sum of the growth rates of the various outputs minus the sum of the growth rates of inputs weighted by their respective input and output elasticities. Thus now we require further information about the production function. A short cut is again available by using revenue shares instead of v_j but, as we shall see later, apart from bringing in new efficiency considerations, this also requires an assumption of constant returns to scale. There is now even less basis for assuming this on *a priori* grounds since it requires that a given percentage increase in all inputs increases the volume of each product by the same percentage.

COSTS

The productivity measures discussed so far are essentially measuring the degree to which different firms would use different volumes of resources if they produced the same set of outputs. From the point of view of economic efficiency or the income of owners, they can be interpreted as reflecting the varying facility with which the enterprises combine and use inputs to produce outputs. To illustrate (cf. Farrell 1957, Rowley 1977), Fig. 5.4 shows the input combinations of six firms all assumed to be producing the *same* output. Firm E uses less inputs than firm E', firm F uses less than F' and firm G uses less than G'. Provided the technology is sufficiently adaptable to allow small changes in the factor combination then firms exemplified by E, F and G could be shown as being on one production line K whilst the other group are on another line, K', which, be it

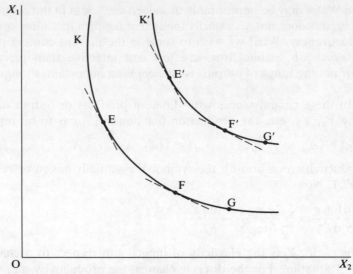

FIG. 5.4 Productivity and input price inefficiencies

noted involves the *same* level of output. On the previous measures then, a positive growth of productivity would be recorded in moving from E′ to E or from G′ to E but none in the move from G to E, which is what is required.

In particular the productivity measures are independent of factor prices. Suppose now that firms E and E′ faced an exogenously given factor price ratio equal to the slopes of the (parallel) dotted tangents at E and E′. Both firms would have chosen the least cost factor combination to produce the given level of output, notwithstanding that the institutional structure of E′ involves a lower productivity level. The input price ratio is equal to the slope of the production lines which reflects the relative marginal products of the two inputs in the respective firms. Firm G is assumed to face the same price ratio so its chosen input combination is not the least cost combination open to it. It is less 'price efficient' than E in its choice of inputs even though, in terms of productivity, there is no difference between the two. This is then a source of inefficiency with respect to the objective of maximising owners' income additional to that involved in the productivity measure [7]. The same point applies for economic efficiency provided factor prices are reflecting economic costs. Now the essential difference between firm E and firm G (and between E′ and G′) lies in the extent to which the relative marginal products of the two inputs correspond to the input price ratio. It can be shown[24] that this difference is, with constant returns to scale, precisely equal to the difference between the output elasticities of inputs and their respective share of total costs. If then constant returns to scale prevail, we can replace a_i, in the productivity measures of equations [6], [7] and [9] by the share of outlays on input X_i in total cost and this will have achieved three things. Firstly it means that the estimation of output elasticities in the production function is circumvented; all we need is data on expenditure on inputs. Secondly it means that the measure will not only reflect the productivity differences such as those between E and E' but it will also pick up the price inefficiencies of G relative to E. Thirdly it will pick up the two sources of difference between E and G', assuming both face the same input prices; that is, the G' firm has a lower productivity and is less price efficient than firm E. Although the two effects cannot be unscrambled, the simplicity of the factor share weighted productivity measure explains its pervasive use.

However, the assumption of constant returns to scale is crucial. We have already given reasons why we cannot *a priori* be sure of this property and why therefore several writers adopt the approach of estimating the whole production function. In practice it is usually the *cost function* which is estimated. In part this is because data on the volume of input supplies is not always readily available; in other cases data on input prices are limited so that all one has are figures of costs in different firms, some indications of output dimensions and little information on differences in input prices between firms.

Thus for the simple one product/one input case instead of estimating [1], total costs are estimated as

$$C = f(Y, P_x, T) \tag{10}$$

where P_x is the price of X, which we are assuming for the time being is the same in all firms. Two of the approaches used for estimation are as follows. Firstly one collects data from each of the population of firms for the years in question on total costs, output and input prices and then examines how in general costs vary with output and prices and whether, with the latter two held constant, costs are sensitive to the institutional structure, that is whether they are higher in public firms than private. Whichever way the cost-function is initially specified,[25] it would obviously be desirable to allow that the results could yield various possible scale economies. A typical form of the function would be, with total costs expressed in log form and now allowing several inputs and outputs,

$$\log C = A + a_1 \log Y_1 + a_2 \log Y_2 + a_3 \log P_l + a_4 \log P_k + a_5 D \tag{11}$$

where P_l is the wage rate, P_k the price of capital and where A, a_1, a_2 etc. are assumed constant and their values derived from the estimation. Here the cost function has been constrained to have constant elasticities with respect to output ($a_1 = \partial \log C / \partial \log Y_1$ etc.), their size reflecting the types of return to scale. The major point about [11] however is that the institutional structure is included in the form of a dummy variable D which takes a value of 1 under one ownership structure (say public) and 0 under private. Hence the coefficient $a_5 = \partial \log C / \partial D$ shows the percentage change in costs when one shifts from the set of private firms to the set of public firms, holding outputs and input prices constant. An alternative method of presentation might be to estimate two cost functions, one public and one for private and then examine whether the coefficients are significantly different.

If firms face different input prices it is important to examine the reasons for the difference. There is some evidence for example that wages and salaries in the public sector grew faster than in private sector in the UK in the late 1960s and the early 1970s (Dean 1975, 1977, Hawkesworth 1976). However, a public firm's wage bill may differ from that of a private firm simply because, though wage rates of given skill grades are the same, a different mix of skilled and unskilled workers is employed. In principle this means that different categories of labour input should be reflected in the production function and a range of associated wage rates in cost functions like [11]. The question then reverts again to whether the public firm has chosen a less cost-effective factor combination than the private firm and this will be picked up in the productivity measures and in the a_5 coefficient. Similarly if wage rates of a given grade of labour tend to be higher in the public firm because of the work location this again, in principle, will be picked up in these measures.

It may be the case however that public firms, *ceteris paribus* do pay higher wages or face lower interest charges than private firms. It is a frequent supposition (cf. Pryke 1971, Wallace and Junk 1970, Neuberg 1977) that public firms get their capital cheaper, i.e. at lower interest rates, than do private firms, notwithstanding that governments sometime require public firms to use a discount rate (cf. in the UK, the Test Discount Rate) in evaluating investment projects, different from the rate of interest actually charged. Such differences would not show up in the productivity or cost function measures for these treat input prices as exogenous to the firm. Although public firms, in the above circumstances, would have relatively more expensive labour and less expensive capital than the majority of private firms, it could still be the case that the factor combination chosen is just as cost effective as the combination that private firms would choose *when faced with the same input prices* – and indeed there could be some private firms in the sample in precisely such circumstances. To illustrate, firm F in the previous diagram has no different productivity than firm E and if F faces an input price ratio indicated by the dotted tangent at F then it is also price efficient. In productivity measures like [7], the two firms would be revealed to have the same efficiency. If, in the absence of data on production elasticities, input shares are used as weights, the measure would record no change as long as there are constant returns to scale and as long as each firm chooses that input combination which minimises costs for the given input prices.[24] Similarly in the estimated cost function [11] and assuming good data on input prices are available, the dummy coefficient would only pick up an ownership effect if the public firm's input choice differed from what private firms would choose at such input prices.

If then the difference in prices is intrinsic to the ownership characteristics *other measures are necessary*. When it is felt, on grounds of economic efficiency in resource allocation, that the cost to the nation of capital supplied to public firms is larger than the nominal cost, then the total costs of the public firms in the sample are sometimes revalued at a higher shadow cost. Thus in calculating total factor productivity in British public enterprise, Pryke (1971) revalues the weight attached to capital by using the rate of return then earnable in private manufacturing industry. In Neuberg's electricity cost functions (1977) the total costs of public firms are revalued upward to account for a higher shadow cost of capital. Such revised productivity measures or the a_5 coefficient in a revised cost function would then pick up the fact that at the same standardised interest rate, public firms will use relatively more capital and hence, to this extent, would be recorded as economically less efficient than private firms. These then would be measures geared to economic efficiency. They are not geared necessarily to the objective of maximising the income of owners, since for the owners the true cost of a factor may be its nominal price. On the other hand, when the input price differences are attributable to management – for example when a weak management bargains ineffectively with trade unions – one needs a measure which includes the input price differences. Thus, for cost functions, the input prices would have to be excluded as independant variables. When constant returns to scale prevail the simplest replacement for the factor-share weighted productivity measure would be costs per unit of output. In summary the way in which input prices are treated significantly affects the conclusions that can be made from the efficiency measures.

PROFITS

Variations in profitability across firms are commonly used by the media and laymen as indicators of efficiency. Figure 5.5 on p.234 shows that the profitability of publicly-owned industry in the UK has, in the post-war period, been consistently less than in private industry. There are three elements which contribute to the variability of profits across firms. Firstly there is the productivity of each firm as defined earlier. Secondly there is the degree to which firms are 'input price efficient' – i.e. choose input combinations which minimise costs. Thirdly, there is the volume and range of products chosen and the level of prices set for each product. It is clearly possible then for a public firm to have a lower rate of profit than a private firm even though its productivity performance is superior. It is also possible for a public firm to be more cost efficient than a private firm and yet still have a lower rate of profit because of factors connected with the volume and range of its products and the structure and level of its product prices. Some of these issues will be discussed in the next section of the survey. Here we conclude the basic theme of this section by examining firstly how the productivity measure can be estimated when there are several products and secondly the extent to which the choice of products and product prices is itself a question of efficiency.

When firms have the same productivity performance and are equally efficient with respect to exogenously given input prices, any differences in their promotion of owners' income essentially lies in the range of outputs produced, their quality dimensions, the rate of production and the level of prices. When public and private firms face the same set of exogenously given product prices then the more 'price-efficient' firm from the point of view of the owners is that where rates of production or range of outputs more nearly corresponds to the point where marginal costs equal price since this is the profit-maximising position. This would also be an economically efficient outcome if marginal costs reflected the economic costs to the country.

Putting matters this way allows us to return again to the productivity measure which, as we saw, becomes difficult to estimate if there are many

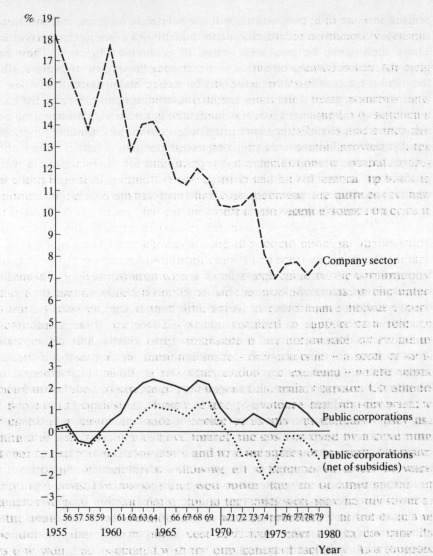

FIG. 5.5 Rate of profit in public and private industry in the UK 1955–79 (Gross trading profits including stock appreciation but net of capital consumption as a percentage of net capital stock)

Source: *National Income and Expenditure Blue Books*, Central Statistical Office, HMSO.

products since knowledge of the input elasticity of each product is required. Now with constant returns to scale it can be shown[24] that the difference between relative product prices and relative marginal costs is precisely reflected in the difference between the elasticities of products and their respective shares of revenues. Hence we can circumvent the estimation of elasticity by replacing v_j in equation [9] by product Y_j's share of total revenue and any difference in 'price efficiency' will be picked up by a productivity measure where inputs are weighted by factor shares and products by revenue shares. Of course again the constant returns to scale assumption is crucial. If this cannot reasonably be assumed and if it is desired to include a price efficiency effect one could estimate a profit function taking output, unit costs and product prices as independent variables and include an institutional dummy as in the cost function discussed before.

When, of course, the firms are not price takers it is not in the owners' interest for prices to be equal to marginal costs. If the objective is profit then the measure should be profit even though that measure will be reflecting pure productivity considerations, input price efficiency and differences in product prices intrinsic to ownership. The last mentioned will reflect monopolistic elements in earned profits in the same way that any monopsonistic elements in factor prices would be reflected in a measure of costs per unit of output.

In conclusion let us summarise how owners' income and economic efficiency are reflected in each of the measures we have considered:

(a) The proportionate difference in costs between public and private firms, as revealed by cost functions which treat output and input prices as independent variables, reflect 'pure' productivity differences plus differences in input price efficiency, provided such prices are truly exogenous to the enterprise.
(b) With the same proviso but also a further one of constant returns to scale, factor-share weighted productivity measures will reflect the same thing.
(c) If input prices are in part endogenous, reflecting the bargaining context and market structure, the level of unit costs would be a better indication of efficiency with respect to a profit objective but for economic efficiency such a measure would reflect both monopsonistic power and the performance of management.
(d) If input prices facing the firms are not, on economic efficiency grounds, deemed to reflect economic costs, shadow prices could be used but the measure would also be reflecting input price efficiency.
(e) Difference in profits, usually measured as a rate of profit on capital, will reflect all the forces mentioned already plus 'product price efficiency' and any monopolistic market power.

6. Empirical comparisons of public and private firms

If the sole focus of interest in the performance of enterprises was the income accruing to owners, there would be considerably more public/private studies than exist at present. The relevant indicator would be profitability, usually expressed as the rate of profit on capital advanced by owners. Since the owners' interest so measured does not vary with the location or type of products or inputs, cross industry and cross country comparisons could be made, with allowances perhaps for the way in which the cycles of booms and depressions have affected the observations. There are basically three reasons why economists have not been satisfied with studies which restrict themselves to profit measures. Firstly there has been an interest in the behaviour of public and private enterprises independently of any question of efficiency. Secondly where efficiency considerations have been introduced these have often embraced the objective of economic efficiency rather than simply the objective of enhancing owners' income. Thirdly the previous section has shown that little can be deduced about the *sources* of inefficiency from summary measures like profitability; a firm might be minimising the costs of its chosen output levels even though the volume of production in different areas is not adjusted to the point where relative prices equal relative marginal costs; the latter may be due to price restraints imposed by government or it may indeed reflect poor management decisions.

As a result empirical comparisons of public/private have been restricted to areas where the two types of institutions have been doing a broadly similar job – especially producing a similar type of output but more generally where differences and the types of differences can be isolated and attributed to ownership rather than other factors. This has meant a rather patchy collection of studies, scattered across different countries and even then involving results subject to varying interpretations. Since the coverage of particular product areas like transport or water supply have not been systematic nor has that of particular countries (with the USA perhaps an important exception) we propose to discuss the studies in terms of the themes of (a) productivity, (b) costs, (c) market structure versus ownership, (d) pricing, politics and profitability.

PRODUCTIVITY IN TRANSPORT

Few public/private comparisons have been able to approach the essence of the 'ideal' productivity measure discussed earlier in this survey, i.e. to measure the degree to which different volumes of resources are used to produce a given pattern of outputs. Two recent studies of Canadian railways and Australian airlines have however got closer than any others. Moreover they were both designed as attempts to test the proposition that the structure of property rights is such that pressure on management from owners is less in public firms than private firms and that this will manifest itself in lower productivity and/or higher unit costs. Discussion of these studies reveals problems which, we shall show, are at the heart of attempts to compare the public and private sectors of industry in the UK.

Railways throughout the world have in this century had radically to reduce their capacity in the face of competition from new long-distance modes of transport. The Canadian railways were no exception but by the mid-1950s the system had settled down to two main companies – the publicly owned Canadian National and the private Canadian Pacific, in competition with each other over many routes and subject less and less to rate regulations. For each of the years from 1956 to 1975, Caves and Christensen (1980) calculated the growth rate in productivity in moving from one rail company to the other using a presentation with some similarities to equation [9] which we reproduce here

$$\sum_j v_j r_j - \sum_i a_i r_i \qquad [9]$$

where r_j is the growth rate of output j in moving from one institutional structure to another and measured as the log of $Y_{jt'}$ output in institutional structure t' minus the log of $Y_{jt'}$ output in the other institutional structure. The growth rate, r_i, of input i is measured in an analogous way. The input elasticity of product j is denoted by v_j and the output elasticity of input i by a_i. Such elasticities are averaged over the old and new output levels and essentially act as weights for aggregating the growth rates. The authors identified four grades of labour input which, together with fuel, equipment, materials and structures formed the main input categories. Data on passenger miles and freight-ton miles were available as two indicators of output. The growth rate in productivity in any year as one shifts from CP to CN, is measured as the sum of the growth rates of the two outputs (aggregated by weights to be discussed shortly) minus the (weighted) sum of the growth rates of inputs. Taking 1967 as an example, the growth rate of productivity so calculated was 0.041 which implied that productivity in the public firm was some 4.1 per cent higher than in the private firm (see Table 5.1). Analogous figures for the other years are reproduced in Table 5.1 from which Caves and Christensen concluded there was little difference in productivity and hence no support for the proposition that the property rights structure of public firms leads to lower 'production efficiency' than in private firms.

TABLE 5.1   Productivity in Canadian railways (Percentage growth rate in productivity in moving from CP to CN)

1956	1957	1958	1959	1960	1961	1962
(−)5.5	(−)8.1	(−)7.6	(−)7.1	(−)8.1	(−)8.6	(−)7.6
1963	1964	1965	1966	1967	1968	1969
(−)4.1	(−)5.1	(−)3.2	2.5	4.1	6.4	4.9
1970	1971	1972	1973	1974	1975	—
4.5	2.5	2.9	2.1	0.8	2.9	—

Source: Calculated as the logarithms of the entries in the last column of Table 2, Caves and Christensen 1980, showing CN total factor productivity relative to CP.

This is, of course, only one aspect of economic efficiency. Canadian railways have for a long time been subject to control with respect to the hauling of grain and flour and the transport of such crops for export has been subject to rate regulation. In addition the abandonment of track in the prairies, where regulation has held grain rates below variable costs, has also been controlled by government. Railways rates then do not reflect marginal costs in some areas and Caves and Christensen suggest this phenomenon affects Canadian National more than the privately owned Canadian Pacific. Indeed, in order to exclude this factor, Caves and Christensen did not weight outputs by revenue shares since, as was argued earlier, this would have picked up such 'inefficiencies' in product pricing. Instead data on the cost elasticity of each product were obtained from some separate work on US railroads and used as product weights. As note 24 demonstrates, such weights will be reflecting any differences in input price efficiencies as well as the underlying input elasticities of each product.

A similar point applies to the way inputs were each weighted not by their output elasticities, a_i, but by their shares of total cost. If there are differences in the facility with which each firm adjusts its input combination to the input prices it faces, these will be reflected in the measure which, given the aim of reflecting productivity and/or unit costs, is no bad thing as long as input prices are truly exogenous to the enterprise. It could be however that any differences in input prices such as cost of capital are intrinsic to the ownership differences. Caves and Christensen do not discuss this, apparently relying on the observation that railroads purchase inputs in unregulated factor markets. Finally their measure could be a distortion of productivity differences if constant returns to scale do not apply since the use of cost shares as a proxy for the theoretically ideal weights of the output elasticity of each input would then obscure the differences in productivity due simply to scale of operation. Fortunately Caves and Christensen were able to claim that the information on returns to scale from US studies was such that the hypothesis of constant returns to scale could not be rejected for the broad range of output over which the Canadian railways were operating.

The case of Australian airlines has some similarities to the above in being another instance where a public firm (Trans Australian Airlines) coexists with a private firm (Ansett Transport Industries) in the same product area in the same country. Indeed the very possibility of this comparison stems from a peculiar institutional structure. Where the two airlines operate on inter-state routes, government policy has been to equalise practically every aspect of their operations, that is, routes, ports of call, frequency of stops, aircraft capacity and types, import licences for aircraft, take-off times, engineering and airport facilities, seating arrangements, fares, freight rates. Since available aircraft are the same in each airline as, apparently, are the prices of all inputs, then productivity measures can focus on output per man provided the use of materials and fuel is not too dissimilar.

In Davies' oft-quoted studies (1971, 1977, 1980) for the period 1958–74, the most striking statistics are those which indicate freight tonnage per employee vastly higher in the private firm. The first column of Table 5.2 shows figures for three years which are representative of the results for the whole period. Two immediate questions are whether freight tonnage is the only dimension to output and whether constant returns to scale operate. Forsyth and Hocking (1980) point out that the private airline operates on local short routes as well as the inter-state routes and hence ton kilometres is a better measure of output. The second column of Table 2 shows, for the same three years, their adjusted figures which also exclude operations in Papua New Guinea where, it is claimed the airlines operate in very different circumstances. The differences in labour productivity so calculated are now less marked. Moreover the private airline carries a much larger volume of freight than the public firm so there is a danger of attributing productivity differences arising from scale of operation to ownership factors unless constant returns to scale prevail.

In any case freight is not the only output – it accounts for less than 20 per cent of each airline's revenue and the employment figures relate to all

TABLE 5.2 Labour productivity in Australian airlines

	Freight tonnage per employee (Davies)	Freight-ton km per 1000 employees (Forsyth-Hocking)	Passengers per employee (Davies)	Passenger-km in 1000s per employee (Forsyth-Hocking)	Revenue in $1000 per employee (Davies)
1964/5	5.0 (12.1)	29 (32)	287 (352)	245 (251)	8.5 (9.7)
1969/70	5.8 (9.3)	40 (42)	390 (414)	341 (336)	13.1 (14.1)
1973/4	6.0 (10.0)	48 (50)	496 (532)	433 (431)	19.1 (21.4)

Sources: Davies 1980, Table 1; Forsyth and Hocking 1980, Table 1
Note: Figures shown are for the public airline, TAA, with figures for the private airline, ATI, in brackets

activities. From Davies' point of view this difficulty disappears with the fact that output per man in the other product category, passengers, is also, he argues, higher in the private firm, as the third column of Table 5.2 shows. When the Forsyth-Hocking adjustments are made to the passenger figures, however, we see from the fourth column of Table 5.2 that the public firm is, if anything, showing a better performance, again subject to the returns to scale qualification. It is therefore necessary to use some form of weighting system to aggregate outputs in the manner of the productivity measure of expression [9]. All that is available is the data shown in the last column of Table 5.2. In the words of Forsyth and Hocking 'the significance of revenue per man is obscure' as a productivity measure. The observed proportionate differences between the two firms (of the order of 5 per cent) are at best a very crude approximation to a measure of the sum of the rates of growth (in moving from TAA to ATI) of freight ton kilometres and passenger kilometres (disaggregated by routes and each weighted by revenue shares) minus the growth rate of labour. Such a measure would be consistent with expression [9] if constant returns to scale prevail. It would in any case be picking up efficiency factors additional to productivity – namely the degree to which passenger and freight volumes on both the inter-state and local routes were expanded to the point where marginal costs equal the price per kilometre. Having said all this, the major conclusion that can be drawn from the case of Australian airlines is similar to that for Canadian railways – there is no significant evidence that productivity is lower in public firms than private firms. It may be noted here that in both countries the public firm does not have a monopoly of its service and we return in a later section of this survey to explore the relationship between market structure and ownership.

PRODUCTIVITY IN PUBLIC AND PRIVATE INDUSTRY IN THE UK

The reservations about figures of revenue per man apply with equal force to the sort of comparisons that have sometimes been made between the private manufacturing sector and the public enterprise sector in the UK. In fact the figures of the value of net output per man for one particular year, 1971, shown in the first row of Table 5.3 are of even less significance than the Australian figures since there is no basis for presuming that non-labour inputs are the same in each sector. G. and P. Polanyi (1972, 1974) felt in particular that the nationalised industries had excessive capital and thus expressed net output as a ratio of expenditure on labour and capital, and obtained the figures shown in the second row of Table 5.3 which they called 'productivity indicators'. Such ratios are meaningless as productivity measures for two reasons. Firstly the use of a value measure of output would not be unreasonable if prices are equal to marginal costs in each sector and for each product within each sector and if constant returns to scale prevailed since in such circumstances revenue shares are an exact proxy for each product's cost elasticity as required in expression [9]. It is well known however that UK governments have in some periods held prices down in the public sector in the interests of counter-inflation policy and generally intervened in the relationship between prices and costs of different products (Millward 1976). Whilst the Polanyis' measure could reasonably be interpreted as in part reflecting one aspect of economic inefficiency it is not a measure of productivity. Indeed the figures in row B are primarily reflecting differences in the profitability of the two sectors. The Polanyis view the annual costs of capital as consisting of two components; one part is the return that could have been earned by the use of capital elsewhere in the economy (estimated at 10 per cent); the other part is the depreciation in the capital stock. Since 10 per cent was the sort of return being earned in the private sector it is not surprising that their 'productivity' indicator for manufacturing comes out near to 1.0. As Fig. 5.5 on p.234 shows, the rate of return on capital in the nationalised industries has been consistently lower than the private sector so that the results shown in row B of Table 5.3 are not at all surprising.

The second major problem is that the two sectors are producing completely different products. This means that, in the present state of the art, it is impossible to use the kind of productivity model discussed in the previous section and in particular to use expression [9]. Moreover the concept of returns to scale embracing the two sectors is now meaningless, as also would be comparisons of costs per unit of output. Of course one could calculate productivity changes over time in each sector. This is precisely what Pryke (1971) has done in his extensive work on UK public enterprise. Roughly speaking[26] Pryke calculated for the manufacturing sector a growth rate of productivity with some similarities to expression [9], treating labour and capital as the main inputs and with the change in question being that from one year to another (rather than from one ownership form to another). His results showed productivity, so conceived, growing at an average of 2 per cent per annum in manufacturing in the period 1948–68, as can be seen in section C of Table 5.3. Similar calculations were performed for various nationalised industries and Pryke felt able to conclude that the performance of the nationalised industries was probably slightly better than private manufacturing. However, since Pryke's method implicitly involved the use of revenue shares as weights for products and

TABLE 5.3   Some 'productivity' measures for public and private industry in the UK

	Nationalised industries	Manufacturing
A. Value of net output (£) (1971) ÷ number of employees	2529	2040
B. Value of net output (1971) ÷ (wages bill + capital consumption + 10% capital stock)	0.67	0.99
C. Annual average % growth rates of output per unit of composite input		

	Nationalised industries					
	Electricity	Coal	Railways	Gas	Airways	Manufacturing
1948–58	3.6	0.4	0	0.7	7.8	1.5
1958–68	3.1	3.0	2.4	3.7	9.1	2.4
1948–68	3.4	1.7	1.1	2.2	8.4	2.0

Sources: Section A and B from G. and P. Polanyi 1974, Table 6; Section C from Pryke 1971, Table 9

cost shares as weights for inputs, his measures are picking up 'price inefficiencies' as well as pure productivity factors. More significantly, Pryke's approach at most allows one to compare the two sectors in terms of their *respective* growth rates of productivity *over time*. It is not possible to compare productivity *levels* in the two sectors nor therefore to calculate, for any year, the change in productivity in moving from the private sector to the public sector.

THE COST OF ELECTRIC POWER IN THE USA

The American electricity supply industry has probably been studied, with respect to public/private comparisons, more intensively than any other industry in the world. Essentially this is due to the very large number of both private and public firms. The objectives of the studies of costs have not always been made explicit though they can be viewed as being relevant to the hypothesis tested for the transport productivity studies – that the ownership structure of public firms implies less pressure on management to raise productivity and lower unit costs.

Now whilst the aim has usually been to measure the degree to which different volumes of resources are used in producing and distributing given patterns of electricity supply, data limitations forced the studies to be directed to differences in *costs* between firms, allowing for any differences in output levels and in input prices. That is, one attempts to estimate whether costs would be different in public and private electricity firms if they faced the same input prices and produced the same output levels, as we have illustrated in the context of equation [11] in an earlier part of the survey. One implication of this is that usually returns to scale are estimated rather than presumed. In addition the studies, for the large part, treat input prices as exogeneous to the firms. Most importantly of all however at this point is to note that by treating costs as the main indicator of efficiency, one is including a measure of the 'input price inefficiencies' of different firms as well as their production inefficiencies.

Whilst the US electric utility industry is possibly '... as close to perfection in public/private comparability as any other imaginable real world case' (Yunker 1975:66) it does contain problems arising from the size distribution of firms. Most of the research studies of the industry discussed in this survey were completed during the last five years and refer to cross sections of data drawn from within the period 1964–72 and sampled from a basic population which included all but the smallest firms. Many of the latter, in the case of municipally owned firms, as Wallace and Junk (1970) have noted, continue to generate their own power thriving on a subsidised cost of capital. In this period there were 67 Federal projects, involving largely hydroelectricity, producing 12 per cent of the nation's power, wholesaling about half of this to other utilities. Of the 536 municipal firms in the basic population many were small and the 210 private firms in the basic population produced 77 per cent of the nation's power.

Yunker's study (1975) was explicitly motivated by a desire to test the property-rights proposition that the ownership structure put less pressure on management in public firms which are thereby 'economically inefficient', the best indication of which he felt was a measure of unit costs. He estimated costs as a function of output and the number of customers for 1969. Concerned at the different size distribution in the public and private industries, he restricted attention to private and municipal firms producing 0.5 to 4 million megawatt hours per annum and further restricted to firms with at least 1,000 customers since some firms sell to only a very small number of business or government users. Looking at the remaining 24 public and 49 private firms his equation suggested costs were lower in public firms but the results were not statistically significant. He concluded therefore that there was no evidence that private firm costs were lower than public firm costs. Yunker had however no data on input prices and therefore any production inefficiencies in public firms might be obscured if public firms had lower input prices. Put otherwise, he had not estimated what costs would be in the two sets of firms if both had faced the same input prices. Moreover the firms, in a sense, differed in their output composition in that some were just distributing whilst others were generating, transmitting and distributing.

Meyer (1975) felt that cost studies could reveal the degree to which new technologies or organisational methods were being adopted. He also lacked data on input prices which he felt might vary regionally and therefore attempted a partial offset by grouping the basic population geographically, excluded firms which were not engaged in all three functions and then drew a quota sample, 30 public and 30 private; a review of size of firms by volume of generation indicated that the composition of the public and private samples was quite similar. He found that from observations for each of the three years 1967, 1968, 1969 the cost structures of the two types of firm were significantly different in all the different functions. Generating costs per megawatt hour declined with the number of megawatt hours and were generally lower for public firms. Total transmission costs were primarily determined by the number of customers, with the results pointing to lower costs for public firms. The percentage of sales to resale customers was not found to affect either transmission or distribution costs. Neither were distribution costs per megawatt hour affected by the split of sales between residential and non-residential consumers but they were affected in a complex way by both output and the number of customers, but Meyer did not identify the pattern of the differences between public and private. In each of the above estimates he excluded maintenance costs which were found, separately, to be primarily determined by plant size, and maintenance costs per megawatt of capacity were significantly lower in public firms. Similar separate estimates of (a) sales and account expenses and (b) general and administration expenses, again pointed to lower costs in public firms.

The work of Yunker and Meyer was important in being the first attempts to allow systematically for output levels in assessing relative cost efficiency in electricity but the estimates related simply to *operating costs* embracing, therefore, only labour, fuel and raw materials. Data deficiencies were the main problem but it does mean that, in addition to the problem of input prices, the results have significance only if the similar size composition of firms in the two samples control precisely for differences in capacity and technology, that is for capital costs and Meyer's public sample included the Federal projects which involve much larger production units than in many other firms. Neuberg (1977) overcame some of these problems in his detailed study of distribution where he also argued that some of the complex features of customer characteristics and location could be picked up by allowing for miles of overhead distribution line (S_2) and the square mileage of the territory (S_3). From the basic population of firms he excluded the Federal projects and some 25 private firms not involved in distribution. Then a questionnaire survey was made of the remaining private firms and a sample of the municipal firms, finishing up with data from 90 private firms and 75 municipal firms for the year 1972. Costs embraced distribution proper, sales, customer accounts and a proportion of general and administrative expenses. Neuberg was concerned to allow for the suggestion that public firms had a lower cost of capital than private firms. He therefore credited all firms with the same cost of capital using a 10 per cent interest rate and adjusted each firm's costs accordingly. Neuberg's main results are illustrated in the following cost function. It expresses costs per final customer as a function of output, wages rates and ownership. In log form we have

$$\log C_n = 6.1 - 0.40 \log Y + 0.01 \log Y^2 + 0.25 \log (S_1/Y)$$
$$- 0.92 \log (S_2/Y) + 0.97 \log (S_3/Y) + 0.30 P_L - 0.09 D \quad [12]$$

where Y is the number of ultimate customers, S_1 is megawatt hours of electricity, P_L is the wage rate and D takes a value of 1 for public and 0 for private firms.[27] Thus in moving from the set of private firms to the set of public firms, holding output and wage-rates constant, costs fall by about 10 per cent.

If the incentive to minimise costs is weak in publicly owned electric distributing firms, this might manifest itself in the prices paid for bought-in power, clearly here a major input. De Alessi (1975) indeed argued that municipal buyers have less incentive to bargain and more incentive to conclude convenient agreements. There was however no evidence in support of this proposition in the prices paid by public and private firms to his sample of firms for the year 1969. There were 209 firms in the sample and all were generating electricity and then transmitting it (as wholesale sellers) to the public and private retail distributors. Allowing for the size of the wholesaling firm, input prices, the number of customers, the degree to which customers had multiple sources, regional effects, de Alessi found that electric power sold to municipally owned retail distributors did not involve any higher prices than that sold to private retail distributors.

Neuberg did not of course cover the actual production of electricity. We therefore finally consider the study by Pescatrice and Trapani (1980) who considered generation data for the years 1965 and 1970. They were able to estimate a cost of capital for each firm and in addition explored differences in generating technology. They argued that capacity could be similar in age and in the general method of production but differ in technology and this would be reflected in unit costs. From the basic population they therefore excluded firms for which adequate data were not available and which were not generating by a common production method, that is by coal, gas or oil. For each of the remaining 33 private firms and 23 municipal firms, they calculated a weighted average age of equipment. An equation was then estimated for costs per megawatt hour as a function of output (the number of megawatt hours generated), the prices of labour, capital and fuel, the age of equipment and finally the ownership form. The results indicated that a shift from private firms to public firms lowered average costs by the order of 25 per cent, a significant contribution to which was the considerably higher level of technology embodied in the plant of public firms.[28]

Thus none of the cost studies support the proposition that public electricity firms have a lower productivity or higher unit costs than private firms, allowing for differences in output and in factor prices though one qualification may be mentioned at this point. The possibility that public firms have a lower cost of capital is dealt with explicitly in Neuberg's work. In Pescatrice and Trapani's study, figures on cost of capital for each firm were available and whilst their cost function would not pick up any 'economic inefficiencies' arising from an unduly low cost of capital, at least, by treating the cost of capital as an explicit variable, public firms are not credited with lower costs simply because their cost of capital is less. Such data, however, all related to one year; if *in the past* cost of capital in public firms, *relative* to that in private firms, was lower than at present then the new technology which that might have induced will in part be reflected in current operating cost data and any relative cost superiority attributed to the ownership factor would be overstated. Such problems can be overcome only by a vastly superior data base than exists at present.

STUDIES OF UNIT COSTS IN WATER SUPPLY, REFUSE COLLECTION AND OTHER AREAS

Estimating cost *functions* has the decided advantage of offering possibilities for separating ownership issues from effects due to scale of operation and quality dimensions of output. The remaining cost studies that we now consider do have one common feature, also found in electricity but not so markedly, namely problems arising from public firms producing at a different scale or different dimensions of output to private firms.

Funkhouser and MacAvoy (1979) have examined the large number of private and public firms coexisting in many industries in Java, Sumatra and Bali. The nationalisation of Dutch companies in Indonesia in the 1950s and 1960s was such that during the 1960s and 1970s public and private firms coexisted in shipping, rubber, palm oil, cement, fertilisers, trading, banking, insurance and construction (embracing contractors, engineers and architects). Data was collected for one year, 1971, from balance sheets, banks and tax records supplemented in the case of public firms by reports to the Ministry of Finance and, in the case of private firms for which data was generally inaccessible, by extensive interviews. Whilst Funkhouser and MacAvoy felt able to claim that, for each firm in the same industry, production conditions, demand conditions and public policies on import licenses and local taxes were roughly the same, no data was available on input prices nor on capital employed and the two types of firm did not always sell the same product or market in the same area. The basic cost information then was production costs (excluding interest and depreciation – cf. Yunker and Meyer for electricity) plus a single dimension measure of output yielding figures of direct costs per ton in cement, fertilisers and shipping and per kilogram in rubber and palm oil; in finance and construction the output measures were in value terms. Such data were available from 54 public and 40 private firms and the authors suggested that unit variable costs were significantly higher in public firms. Whilst higher costs (and lower profit margins) were most noticeable in finance and construction, averaging over all industries unit costs in private firms were some 12 per cent lower than the industry averages. A restricted sample was constructed by pairing public and private firms in the same industry on the basis of comparable level of sales. For the resulting 31 paired observations, the cost difference disappears, both types of firms showing unit costs some 11 per cent below the full industry average. The significant public firms excluded from these samples are large public companies in fertilisers and cement and some very small companies in rubber and trading. As Funkhouser and MacAvoy comment, '. . . the public companies "out of scale" with respect to their industries appear to have had higher costs as well as lower profit margins' (1979: 365). Thus there is no evidence that public firms are less cost efficient than private firms of the same size. However, the problem is complicated by another of their findings, namely that unit production costs did not, generally, tend to vary with scale. Since the majority of firms at the top end of the scale spectrum are public, the basic sample of private firms is not sufficiently spread to allow one convincingly to conclude that their costs would have been lower than public firms if they had operated at such output levels.[29]

Scale effects are also important in the work by Crain and Zardkoohi (1978, 1980) on *water supply* in USA, which they found was an industry subject to increasing returns to scale. They examined data from the American Water Works Association on 1970 cost figures embracing operation, maintenance, administration and depreciation. Utilitics with inadequate data were excluded and in addition any public firm larger than the biggest private firm was excluded. This left 24 private and 88 public. Pooling all firms they estimated unit costs (C = costs per million gallons of water) as a function of the wage rate (P_L), the price of capital (P_k), output (Y = million gallons of water supplied) and with a dummy variable for ownership effects. The approach was therefore similar to that exhibited in equation [12] above for Neuberg's study of electricity. The results suggested that shifting from private to public raised unit costs by an order of 25 per cent. Of particular interest are the cost functions for the separate samples.[30] Thus in log form for the public firms we have

$$\log C_n = 0.93 - 0.24 \log Y + 0.67 \log P_L + 0.33 P_k \qquad [13]$$

and for the private firms

$$\log C_p = 1.97 - 0.14 \log Y + 0.84 \log P_L + 0.16 \log P_k \qquad [14]$$

The coefficient on the output variable shows the elasticity of average cost with respect to output. Thus for the sample of private firms we see that the fall in average costs for a 100 per cent rise in output is 14 per cent ($= \partial \log C_p / \partial \log Y$). Such economies of scale are even larger for public firms where the elasticity is ($-$) 0.24. Large public firms who would presumably benefit most from such economies are however excluded from the sample. On the other hand, there are no comparably large private firms and where firms of the same size are taken the private firms show lower unit costs for any given set of input prices. Both this case and the Indonesian case shows the danger of sampling from a basic population where public and private do not coexist over the whole spectrum of scales of operation. Nevertheless for American water utilities the evidence is consistent with the proposition that public firms have higher costs than private firms.

There have, finally, been studies of unit costs in areas which are often not embraced in the public 'enterprise' sector in so far as that term is commonly used to encompass public agencies levying prices, i.e. direct user charges. Thus both public and private provision of refuse collection services, health and fire services can be found though only refuse collection has been studied in any depth in terms of cost efficiency. Since taxation rather than user charges is the more common source of finance, they are rather different animals to electricity, railways, etc. The broad results of the studies are that public provision involves higher unit costs than private provision. A fruitful line of inquiry for future research may well be that of examining the extent to which the source of finance and associated budgeting procedures affects cost efficiency. In this survey however we merely provide a brief outline of the findings.

Apart from the fact that an impressive volume of work has now been done on *refuse collection*, one source of interest is the complex characteristics of output reinforcing the general problem in cost studies of ensuring that the public and private firms are compared under similar circumstances. Since public and private refuse collectors rarely work the same geographic area then costs should ideally be expressed as a function of the various dimensions of output, viz.

frequency of service, customer density, location of pick-up points, weight and type of garbage, climatic factors, topographic variations, distance from disposal site. Unless such variations are covered, cost measures would be picking up efficiency considerations related to the choice of the quality and quantity of output.

A second source of interest lies in the fact that, whilst in the UK refuse is generally collected by departments of local authorities, in several other countries a variety of patterns is found. A Columbia University survey of 1975 (see Savas, Policy Analysis 1977) involved data on mixed residential waste collection in 2052 cities embracing one third of the US population. In nearly 20 per cent of cities citizens self-hauled their garbage to disposal sites. In 40 per cent of the cities self-hauling was allowed to coexist with arrangements where householders could alternatively pay user charges (in some cities regulated) to private firms. In some cities private firms had to have hauling licences and in some cities area franchise agreements had been reached with municipal authorities. After allowing for other variables which might affect costs, such as location and frequency of service, Edwards and Stevens (1978) found that in 77 cities sampled the price charged per household showed no significant variations as between these various arrangements.

This study and one by Bennett and Johnson (1979), who considered residential refuse collection in Fairfax, Virginia, contrast with several studies which have found private firm/household arrangements to be more expensive than municipal provision (Hirsch 1965, Pier, Vernon and Wicks 1974, Savas, Policy Analysis 1977, Pommerehne and Frey 1977). It is not surprising to find municipal provision cheaper than private firm/household agreements since municipal provision invariably involves an area monopoly for a specific type of garbage, which means that it can reap economies from the contiguity of customers quite apart from any economies of scale which may be open to both types of firm. A more valid comparison would therefore be between municipal firms and those private firms operating in cities where self-hauling is prohibited and where the firms have area franchises or exclusive contracts under which the householder has no choice of service level, does not pay user charges and where the municipal authority pays the private contractor. The Edwards and Steven study found prices (as contract fees or user charges on households) in such cases to be lower than where 'free market' private firm/household agreements existed. The difference was attributed to economics of contiguity and scale.

Most studies have found that franchise and contract arrangements also involve lower costs than municipal provision, though it has not always been possible to control properly for differences in input prices. Sampling from the Columbian University survey B. J. Stevens (reported in Savas, Policy Analysis 1977) found municipal provision involved significantly higher costs after standardising for the total volume and weight of refuse, household density, wage rates, temperature, frequency and location of service.[31] Savas (Policy Analysis 1977) considered the case of Minneapolis, where in 1971 a new system of residential waste collection was introduced, with one area served by the local

Sanitation Division and another by a consortium of private firms. It emerged that the cost per ton for the Sanitation Division, excluding overheads, was some 10 per cent higher in 1971 than the consortium's contract income per ton and costs expressed per household were 15 per cent higher (Savas, Policy Analysis 1977). However, this cost difference disappeared by 1975!

General evidence pointing to lower costs for private franchise and contract arrangments has been found in countries other than the USA. Kitchen's cost data (1976) for 48 Canadian municipal areas for 1971 suggested that the costs of public provision were higher than private sector provision after standardising for wage rates and many of the dimensions of output. Pommerehne and Frey from a sample of 103 Swiss cities in 1970, embracing half the Swiss population, confirmed that user charge arrangements are more costly than other forms of provision and that private contract provision is some 20 per cent cheaper than public residential refuse collection.

Turning to *hospital* services we are dependent upon one major study by Clarkson (1972) who compared proprietary (for profit) with non-proprietary short-term stay general hospitals with a 50 to 99 bed capacity. Non-proprietary included government owned hospitals as well as non-profit making charitable institutions. Clarkson argued that differences in performance between non-proprietary and proprietary hospitals would exist partly because certain rights or claims to benefits in non-proprietary organisations are not for sale as they are in proprietary organisations; in addition managers or workers in non-profit organisations do not have exclusive claims on the residual income remaining after costs have been met. From his sample of hospitals in California, Clarkson felt able to make two broad conclusions. Firstly, there is evidence that non-proprietary hospitals have different and more explicit rules than proprietary hospitals, including a greater tendency to have formal budgets approved by a governing board, written staff regulations and standing committees of the staff. Clarkson suggested that non-proprietary hospitals were less likely to use price and wage information provided by markets and were more likely to use other sources of information such as opinion polls; this latter conclusion may be questioned, since the majority of non-proprietary as well as proprietary hospitals in the sample did not use opinion polls. Secondly, from payroll data covering 26 separate worker classifications for short-term general hospitals in Los Angeles and San Francisco, supported by other *ad hoc* indicators of inputs, Clarkson concluded that variability in the choice of factor input combinations was higher in non-proprietary than proprietary hospitals, a result which is attributed to the lower concern with market prices. However, sample sizes are not made explicit and the input variability observed may result from factor price differences and technology. Wage rates differ across hospitals, as Clarkson acknowledges, so that efficient input usage would require differing factor combinations. Moreover, technology in this industry may allow a fair amount of factor substitutability and various input combinations may be therefore equally efficient. Finally, the problem of output dimensions is side-stepped. In the field of health care output and, therefore, input requirements will vary not only according to quantity but also quality.

In the case of *fire services* Ahlbrandt (1973) calculated costs of public provision from data collected relating to cities and fire districts in the Seattle-King County area and from some additional cities within the state of Washington. The estimated costs were contrasted with the actual cost for a competitive firm supplying Scottsdale, Arizona, as well as other communities in that state. The private firm's rate of profit was regulated and Ahlbrandt considered that costs would be held in check by potential competition from alternative municipal provision or other producers. His results showed costs to be significantly lower for the private firms. However, Ahlbrandt conceded that much of the cost difference arose from differences in the employment of fire fighters and equipment, resulting in differences in the quality and quantity of services supplied, notwithstanding that this may be reflecting superior knowledge of demand characteristics under private contracting.

MARKET STRUCTURE VERSUS OWNERSHIP

A characteristic of the cost studies discussed so far is the attempt to isolate those features of the behaviour and efficiency of public and private firms which are not intrinsic to ownership differences. One further feature is however rather difficult to unscramble from the institutional setting. In Western mixed economies the coexistence of public and private firms is often found where large economies of scale and contiguity are believed to exist. Geographic areas then often finish up with one firm, either a regulated private utility or a public enterprise. There are important exceptions. Of the studies already cited, Indonesian public firms and the Canadian National railway faced competition. In US electricity many private utilities are unregulated. When we observe the relative behaviour and efficiency of public and private firms, it is clearly important to distinguish the effects of the presence of competition and regulation from the role of the ownership factor. To date only a small number of studies have considered this problem.

Meyer (1975), it may be recalled, had found electricity operating costs to be significantly lower in public firms than private. Each of the firms in the sample was presumed to have a monopoly of its area of supply and in order to examine whether the cost differences were reflected in prices he calculated for one year, 1969, the average revenue per kilowatt hour for various customer groups. For the groups 'residential', 'small commercial' and 'other' he found that the public firms' prices were lower than for private firms and suggested that the margin was consistent with the cost differences, given that purchased kilowatt hours per customer were found to be similar in both types of firm. For the 'resale' group, consumption per customer was much bigger in public firms and, given block tariffs, he felt this accounted for the considerably lower price charged by public firms. Whilst consumption per 'large commercial' user was sufficiently lower in the sample of public firms, to expect higher prices in public firms than private firms, Meyer found that the two sets of prices were very similar and indeed average revenue was noticeably lower than in any other customer group (except resale). 'Large commercial accounts ...' suggests Meyer (p.398) '... have a competitive threat open to them, which is not available to other customers, since they may be large enough to make setting up generating capacity for themselves an economically and financially feasible alternative.'

Indirect though this example may be, one can search in vain for clear examples where competition affects the relative prices of public and private firms. Other evidence on the effects of competition relates, perhaps surprisingly, to cost efficiency. Caves and Christensen (1980) had found no significant difference in productivity between the two Canadian railroads and concluded that the performance of the publicly owned Canadian National showed '. . . the impact of competition in offsetting the negative aspects of public ownership. Our results indicate that the impact of competition can be substantial' (p.974). In presuming that publicly owned firms are cost inefficient the authors (cf. also Spann 1977) do not appear to have been aware of the recent evidence on costs in electricity but have rather relied on Davies' work on airlines (see pp.238–9 for a criticism of this), studies of the inefficiencies of *price* structures in US electricity and on studies of fire services (Ahlbrandt 1973) and hospital services (Clarkson 1972, Lindsay 1976) which are rather different animals to public corporations. There is at present, no general support for the proposition that public enterprises are less cost efficient than private firms. The Canadian railroads experience confirms that – it cannot, *per se*, be adduced in support of a role for competition. Of rather more direct relevance is the exploitation by Primeaux (1977, 1978) of the fact that there are some American cities – a total of 49 in 1966 if those with populations less than 25,000 are excluded – where public electricity firms faced competition from other firms, mainly private. Consumers can in some of the cities switch from one firm to another whenever they want; in other cities, new customers have a choice of supply but thereafter they are committed to that firm. Primeaux compared the costs of these municipal firms with other municipals of the same size and with the same power source but which had a monopoly of their area. Allowing for differences in levels of sales, capacity, fuel costs, the cost of purchased power, the rate of consumption per consumer, and geographical area he found that costs were significantly lower in the municipals facing competition. He concluded therefore that the effects of competition in making firms more cost conscious offset any excess capacity effects that would be associated with the duplication of facilities. As a footnote to this we may note that for refuse collection in Minneapolis Savas suggested that the mere coexistence of the two types of firms in the city (doing the same job but in different areas) seemed to reduced cost differences. In summary there is some evidence pointing to competition improving the cost efficiency of public firms but the relative magnitude of this effect on public and private firms has not yet been explored.

Given their access to government subsidies, it is not clear even on theoretical grounds why competition should affect public firms though it may be that the performance of managers in different firms is more readily comparable. Turning now to the effects of *regulation*, the theoretical issues have received much more attention but little agreement between writers, (cf. Stigler 1971, de Alessi, Fall 1974). Space precludes any extended discussion of the regulation literature. On the one hand regulated firms are well placed to collude and have an incentive to influence regulators who in any case have little vested economic interest of their own in acquiring the full information needed for effect. Thus in the Australian airline case discussed earlier, Forsyth and Hocking argue that while '. . . it might appear that the industry is regulated by the Department of Transport, in fact it is to a large degree self-regulating. The airlines agree issues between themselves and submit their proposals to the Department of Transport. The Department has imperfect information about the operations of the airlines and this gives some freedom of operation' (1980:182–3). On the other hand, regulators might well be under pressure from vested interests – consumers, potential contractors – a force making for active regulation.

Precise evidence on the effects of regulation *vis-à-vis* the effects of ownership is inconclusive as yet. Regulation usually involves control of tariffs or fares and the prescription of a maximum average rate of return on capital. Suppose that the latter is less than what an unconstrained firm would earn. Theory suggests (Averch and Johnson 1962, Baumol and Klevorick 1970) that the imposition of such a required rate of return would reduce actual profits but that some of these profits can be restored if the firm raises its output and capital/labour ratio, ensuring all the time that the *average* rate of return is not exceeded. Thus the regulatory constrained profit maximising position involves 'over-capitalisation'. Of particular relevance to the public/private issue is a finding of Crain and Zardkoohi (1980) that changes in the capital/labour ratio in private water utilities were not responsive to changes in the relative prices of capital and labour – which one would expect for an unconstrained private firm. Since the public water firms in the sample were found to have higher costs than the private utilities, the authors concluded that the overcapitalisation effects of regulation of the private firms were offset by ownership factors. Davies (1971, 1977, 1980) comes to similar conclusions about Australian airlines but there is some doubt attached to his claim that the public airline is less cost efficient. Evidence of regulation effects on private electricity utilities in the USA have been found (Courville 1974, Spann 1974) but in the one study to date which examined such effects in conjunction with ownership factors, the costs of public electric firms were significantly lower than the private utilities. Pescatrice and Trapani (1980) found very little evidence of the standard 'static' overcapitalisation effects of regulation. Since however they attributed the cost superiority of public firms to more technically advanced production methods, they speculated that the input distortion arising from regulation was manifesting itself in the excessive acquisition by private utilities of equipment with old fashioned technology.[32]

In summary, whilst the results are rather mixed, there is some evidence that competition does reduce the costs of public firms and regulation raises the costs of private firms. Neither finding is inconsistent with the findings about the effects of 'ownership' on costs – namely that, balancing the results of electricity and railroads against water, airlines and refuse collection, there is no general indication that private firms are more cost efficient than public firms.

PRICING, POLITICS AND PROFITABILITY

The unprofitability of the UK nationalised industries has been a favourite debating theme for some time. Figure 5.5 shows rates of profit in the UK public and private enterprise sectors. Whether or not allowance is made for subsidies and for the pervasive problems of measuring profits and capital, the rate of return has been consistently and considerably lower in the public sector. For reasons already discussed it is not possible, at a sectoral level, to compare the productivity or even cost efficiency of these two institutional types in the UK. Some of the cyclical movements in the prices and profitability of the public sector, relative to the private sector, can sometimes be traced to the machinations of macroeconomic policy (Millward 1976). For deeper insight in this context we turn to the USA where the coexistence of public and private in the same product areas is more common.

Very broadly the main findings have been that, standardising for other factors, (a) prices are lower and output higher in public firms than in private firms, (b) for different types of product and consumers, relative prices are not as closely geared to relative marginal costs in public firms as they are in private firms, (c) one or both of the above two factors have contributed to the lower profit rates sometimes found in public firms.

These findings emerged from the earliest comparisons of public and private firms and led some to the conclusion that public enterprises were generally inefficient (Peltzman 1971, de Alessi, Fall 1974). Subsequent work on productivity and costs in electricity and transport in the USA suggests that such a conclusion cannot be drawn. In any case, one of the major problems in assessing the findings on 'price inefficiencies' and output levels is to what extent they can be uniquely attributed to a particular hypothesis about the behaviour of public firms relative to private. In what follows we shall try to link these results to three different explanations, discussed earlier in this survey: (a) public firms as a vehicle for harnessing the political support of voters, (b) the straight property rights prediction that public firms are more bureaucratic than private firms, (c) public firms as an instrument of government economic and social policy especially in the area of income redistribution and macroeconomic policy.

Considering first the average level of prices, in US electricity some of the earliest interpretations have to be revised in the light of the subsequent work on costs. Peltzman (1971) assumed that managers of public firms were interested in the continued existence of the enterprise and their jobs, the vehicle for which was political support. In particular he expected that prices would tend to lie below the profit maximising level and examined the 1966 electricity bills, in various customer classes, of a sample of firms each serving at least 10,000 customers and embracing both municipal firms and private firms, the latter tending to operate in cities with larger populations. A straight comparison of the bills revealed the customers of public firms had consistently lower bills and Peltzman attributed this to the preferential tax treatment of public firms. He had not however properly standardised for production costs[33] and, as we have already seen, Meyer's detailed study of electricity operating costs had concluded that, in conjunction with block tariffs, they were consistent with the differences in prices between public and private firms. An indirect implication of all this is that electricity profit rates in the public sector will not be too far out of line with profits in the private sector. In Table 5.4 we reproduce some data from Mann (1970) which broadly bears this out. The rate of return on capital varies much more across the sample of public firms than it does for private but the average return is quite similar. Many US electricity firms have a monopoly of their geographic areas and hence different prices reflecting different costs is plausible. In contrast many Indonesian public firms face some sort of competition in which case, with broadly similar prices, differences in costs could well be reflected in differences in profit margins. Funkhouser and MacAvoy's study of Indonesian firms (1979) had started with a working hypothesis that public firms were a vehicle of government economic and social policy with the specific objective of so setting prices as to maximise consumer benefits subject to profits not falling below prescribed levels. As already hinted, whilst profit margins were found to be generally lower in public firms than in competing private firms, especially in finance and construction and in large firms, the authors attributed this to differences in costs or to public firms being 'out of scale'.

In the monopoly context it would be surprising not to find some association between prices and costs. Different tests from the above are needed to see if there is anything over and above cost differences which is influencing the general level of prices. Pashigian (1976) found differences in prices and profits between public and private firms remained, after allowing for costs, in his study of urban bus transit systems, each of which had semi-monopolistic positions in their respective cities and were generally subject to fare regulations. Of the systems in the 117 largest US cities several were excluded because of data limitations, leaving Pashigian with a sample of 58 transit systems with 1970 data of which 40 had adequate data for a 1960–70 comparison. Pashigian estimated an equation for prices (revenue per vehicle) as a function of operating costs and of regulatory and ownership factors. Since costs had been allowed for and did prove to be an important factor, then the remaining differences in prices

TABLE 5.4   Rates of profit in public and private electric utilities in USA, 1966 (percentages)

Rate of return	Proportion of public firms	Proportion of private firms
Less than 5	18	5
5–7	23	25
7–8	6	36
8–10	12	30
More than 10	41	4
Average rate of return	7.1	6.7

Note: Rate of return equals electric utility operating income as a percentage of net electric fixed assets. There were 494 (non-Federal) public firms in the sample and 185 private firms (but the average figure for the latter of 6.7 is based on 213 observations). Source: Mann (1970)

between transit systems which were not attributable to costs but rather to regulatory and ownership factors were mirrored in differences in gross profit margins (revenue net of operating costs, expressed as a proportion of revenue).

Now Pashigian did find evidence that publicly owned transit systems had lower prices, after allowing for costs, and therefore lower profit margins, than private firms.[34] He observed however that this could be consistent with several explanations. Thus in so far as these systems represent declining industries or are subject to economies of scale both with respect to the transporter's costs and the users' waiting time they are, so one argument goes, either naturally unprofitable or become unprofitable from heavy regulation of fares; particularly unprofitable systems are therefore abandoned by private utilities and operated by publicly owned systems. To add substance to these arguments one would have to add the presumption that governments are more willing to subsidise publicly owned firms than private ones. On this basis the occurrence of government ownership would be greater in those cities where, allowing for the growth of population, car ownership had grown most and thereby undermined the profitability of bus transit systems. In fact, Pashigian finds precisely the opposite to be the case; urban bus transit systems have tended to become publicly owned in cities where the level of car ownership is low. Now the lower for any city is the level of car ownership the larger tends to be the proportion of low income families and the larger is the proportion of the city population travelling to work by transit. Thus it could be that urban authorities are consciously holding down fares and taking firms into public ownership as part of more general policies to redistribute income to the poor. An alternative explanation, for which Pashigian finds supportive evidence, rests on electoral issues. Transit systems, whether publicly or privately owned, are sometimes regulated by a district based metropolitan authority, sometimes by a city council, sometimes by a state commission. As one rises from district to city to state the more non-bus users there are in the voting population to which the regulatory body is answerable and the larger therefore is the number of non-users who would have to finance subsidies. Thus Pashigian finds that private utilities have lower prices, allowing for cost differences and therefore lower profit margins, when they are regulated by city or district bodies than by state agencies,[35] a phenomenon he attributes to voter opposition to subsidies from rural and semi-rural areas. Similarly the proportion of firms which are publicly owned is bigger the lower is the level of the regulatory body. Thus the earlier observation that a shift to government ownership has occurred less where car ownership has grown more, is consistent also with an electoral hypothesis that car-owning non-users constitute a voting opposition to strong regulation and heavy subsidies.

One final question in the context of the general level of prices is that, if political factors are present, under what circumstances are they stronger than others? Pashigian's findings suggest that private firms are not immune from political factors, a tendency which was revealed in Mann's study (1974) of electricity where he did standardise for cost differences between firms. For 196 publicly owned electric firms, he calculated whether monthly residential bills during 1967, allowing for size of plant and various cost categories, were a function of the apparent degree of political activism in the firm's county (measured by the proportion of the county population who cast votes in the last Presidential election) and/or of the strength of the majority party. He found no role for political activism but prices did tend to be significantly less the larger was the percentage vote difference between the majority and minority parties. A similar exercise for 46 private utilities found however the same variable to be important so that publicly owned firms were not as distinctive as first thought.

Turning now to the structure of prices of different products and different consuming groups Peltzman did in this case find some evidence consistent with his stress on political factors. He argued that though the cost of supplying Group A might be greater than the cost of supplying Group B, price differences would not completely reflect this since a lower price for Group B might gain less votes than were being lost from Group A. The prediction is therefore that the tariff structure of public electricity firms is less differentiated with respect to customer groups and less reflective of differences in costs as between groups. The only cost data which Peltzman had related to the whole system of each firm. He argued however that the cost per kilowatt hour for a firm supplying a group of consumers with particular cost characteristics would be equal to the system-wide unit costs less amounts that get bigger the larger is the ratio of that group to the total customer population. Prices were then regressed on system-wide unit operating and capital costs and variables to reflect the varying proportions of residential/non-residential customers and, within each, high and low consumption. For private firms he found that the prices of high consumption residential customers were significantly related to these variables whereas the public firm prices were not; a similar result emerged for non-residential customers. In confirmation of this de Alessi found that the 1966 selling prices of municipal wholesaling firms were less significantly related to regional variables than were the prices of private firms. Indeed by putting the price of one group as an independent variable in the price equation for the other group, Peltzman found that his residential and non-residential prices were highly and significantly intercorrelated for public firms but not for private firms. Thus costs of particular groups are reflecting themselves in public firms in the overall tariff structure rather than the prices of particular groups. Suggestive evidence on the same lines can be found in Peltzman's other work[36] on liquor prices in state-owned and private stores.

Independently of cost differences, one might expect that, since electricity is non-storeable and consumers can change monopoly area suppliers only inconveniently by shifting residence, firms will operate price discrimination. On the grounds that private firms are more geared to maximising their owners' wealth and less geared to the ballot box than public firms, more price discrimination might be expected in private firms. Peltzman hypothesised that, given the same average price, standardising for differences in the number of customers, their income levels and any regional effects, a more enthusiastic execution of price discrimination would raise the volume of kW sales per customer. The results indicated significantly higher volumes for private firms. He also found that private utilities tended to have a larger number of rate schedules but this result was not standardised for other variables. De Alessi's careful examination (1977) of rate schedules in 1970 involved allowing for regional differences in income and state regulation, differences in city sizes, the residential/non-residential mix and sources of power, by the selection of matching pairs of municipal and private firms. He finished up with 20 pairs and found that public firms had significantly lower numbers of peak schedules and of total schedules.

Private utility electricity tariff structures seem therefore to be more profit orientated than those of public firms. A key problem again however is whether this is consistent with more than one explanation. In some countries, railroad rates have been equal across customer groups, independently of any cost differences, partly as a heritage from the days of the rail monopoly of long distance transport and associated rate regulation. In the UK the Nationalisation Acts often required the provision of gas, electricity, railway services throughout the country, which was meaningless if for example the prices levied in remote areas were to reflect costs. Such uniformity in rates, fares and tariffs is therefore consistent with the use of industries to further wider goals of economic and social policy (Millward 1978). As a further alternative to the electoral explanation, it may be noted that the drawing up and monitoring of price schedules related to complex cost structures would be economically attractive for a management with a strong economic incentive to raise profits; de Alessi (Fall 1974, 1977) contrasts therefore with Peltzman in attributing the 'price inefficiencies' of public firms to the reduced pressure on management arising from the attentuated property rights of the owner of public firms. To distinguish between bureaucratic and electoral hypotheses requires more stringent tests.

One attempt to date, though not conclusive, warrants mention. Rail transport for travellers in the San Francisco Bay area is managed by the Bay Area Rapid Transit District (BART) a publicly owned body managed by a board of directors directly elected by voters in the counties and cities it serves. Cooter and Topakian (1980) attempted to explain the fares charged in one year (1975/6) to passengers commuting from 33 stations grouped on four arms radiating from the central business district. Their focus was on short-run allocation decisions (since capital investment in an expansion of BART was not likely) and on the structure of fare subsidies rather than the total subsidy from the Metropolitan Transport Commission which was treated as given. At any one station the subsidy conferred on the average passenger, i.e. with average trip length for passengers embarking from that station, would be the cost to BART of that journey less the relevant fare. Rail costs in the short-run would be restricted to fuel, engine wear and tear, track maintenance. How these should be allocated across different segments of track is itself a complicated exercise. The dotted line in Fig. 5.6 shows Cooter and Topakian's estimate of the various possible subsidy structures open to BART given the total subsidy available, the cost assumptions and other assumptions relating to demand elasticities.[37] The mileage of the passenger estimated to receive the largest daily subsidy was estimated as 13.5 miles and was equivalent to a per mile subsidy of 19 cents plus an amount unrelated to mileage and working out at (−) 127 cents. This may be

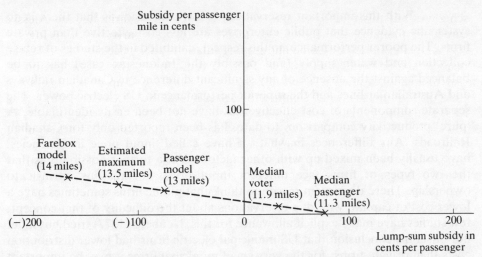

FIG. 5.6 Subsidy structures on the San Francisco Bay Area Rapid Transit District Railway 1975/6
Source: Adapted from Fig. 1 of Cooter and Topakian 1980

compared with the predictions from models of BART's behaviour. Thus Cooter and Topakian calculated the subsidy structure that would emerge from a bureaucracy model; two variants were covered, one where BART is deemed to maximise total revenue (the farebox model) and another where passenger mileage is maximised. Finally, by examining the distribution of the voting population, they considered an electoral hypothesis by estimating what subsidy structure would maximise the subsidy accruing to the passenger whose trip length was median and what subsidy structure would maximise the subsidy accruing to the voter (whether or not he used the railway) whose distance from the central business district was median. In the latter case it was presumed the voting non-user would have a preference similar to his rail travelling neighbour on the grounds that road congestion costs would vary symmetrically with the subsidy structure. As can be seen from Fig. 5.6 the bureaucratic models predicted best, yielding a subsidy structure favouring journeys between 13–14 miles. Unfortunately these results were extremely sensitive to the cost and demand assumptions – so much so that Cooter and Topakian had to allow that no hypothesis could be rejected under a reasonable range of assumptions.

7. Conclusions

It seems likely that in the future the data basis for comparing public and private firms will improve. At present observations are often available only for selected years with long time series conspicuous by their absence. This is not a problem unique to this area of applied economics but the requirement of comparing the two institutional forms on a similar product basis certainly makes life more difficult.

With this important reservation, a first conclusion is that there is no systematic evidence that public enterprises are less cost effective than private firms. The poorer performance, in this respect, exhibited in the studies of refuse collection and water supply (and possibly the Indonesian case) has to be balanced against the absence of any significant difference in Canadian railways and Australian airlines and the superior performance in US electric power. The separate components of cost effectiveness have not been easily identifiable. A 'pure' productivity comparison, to date, has been reported only for Canadian Railroads. Any differences in what we have called 'input price inefficiencies' have usually been mixed up with other factors. Yet a further possibility is that the two types of firms face different input prices for reasons intrinsic to ownership. There does seem reason to think that public firms sometimes have a lower cost of capital, with due reservations about the difficulty of that concept; few studies have made explicit allowance for this; Neuberg (1977) tried but it did not offset his conclusion that US municipal electric firms had lower distribution costs than private firms; for the very small municipal firms it may be important (see Wallace and Junk 1970). The possibility that wages are higher in public firms has not been widely explored though Hamermesh (1975) did not find that unionised US bus drivers and construction workers received higher compensation in government than in private industry.

Some proponents of the property rights theory of the firm have certainly predicted that unit costs would be higher in public firms, after allowing for any differences in input prices and scale of operation.[38] This line of analysis is particularly attractive in its attempt to understand organisational forms by looking at the contractual underpinnings and to base the analysis firmly on individuals within the organisation. In contrast to the property rights approach to individuals in firms, the role of management labour markets remains relatively unexplored. Is it possible, for instance, that competition amongst managers helps to equalise performance levels in the public and private sectors? Do managers' salaries reflect their likely contribution to raising profits (cf. Fama 1980)? In other words, does the management labour market operate so as to transfer the costs of any management inefficiency from shareholders to managers' own salaries, thereby creating incentives for management to pursue efficiency? In a perfect labour market, with perfect information, we would predict this outcome; in practice, information is imperfect and the extent to which managerial salaries do reflect managerial efficiency is a grey area. A further problem is that public and private firms often coexist where markets are in any case regulated. Perhaps both public enterprises and regulated private firms attract a similar kind of management in that dealings with para-statal bodies are part of the job. It is likely also that further studies will give a better picture of the respective roles of ownership, competition and regulation.

Clear differences between public and private firms do appear when we turn to pricing and profitability. In particular the broad picture emerging from North American electricity supply and transport is that where firms have monopoly coverage of a geographic area, the prices of private firms are more closely geared to the marginal costs of different products and services and, *ceteris paribus*, public firms have lower prices and bigger output levels. This is consistent with what can be gleaned in the UK by looking at the nationalised industries on their own. Since British economists have for long been preaching that prices should be related to marginal costs, they are well aware that practice differs. Whether however the behaviour of public firms here is attributable to political influence or to the empire building of bureaucratic management and civil servants or to explicit execution of social objectives with respect to the poorer regions and groups is still largely an open matter. That voting pressure plays at least some part in the USA is convincingly suggested by Pashigian's work (1976) on urban bus transit systems. One other potential influence merits final mention. 'Labour' was instrumental in furthering public ownership, yet paradoxically they finished up in Britain with no explicit representation on the boards of the nationalised industries and no preferential rights apart from due recognition of centralised bargaining; moreover with the exception of Hamermesh's US study the role of trade unions has been largely unexplored.

Notes

1. See for instance R. Turvey (1968) and J. R. Nelson (1964).
2. 'The criteria for control of nationalised industries, which have been established by government in the past, have not only been invalidated by subsequent government price restraint policies but have in any case taken insufficient account of the circumstances of individual nationalised industries. As a result it is doubtful whether they have made a material contribution to improving the allocation and effective use of resources.' (HMSO 1976).
3. Baumol (1958, 1959), Marris (1963, 1964), Williamson (1963, 1964, 1970).
4. For an extensive discussion see Rees (1976).
5. See Baumol and Bradford (1970), Rees (1976) and more generally Atkinson and Stiglitz (1980).
6. Equal to the area APL on Fig. 5.1. Very similar issues are involved if mine managers are not equally efficient; a rental return accrues to the more efficient mining companies since management is not in perfectly elastic supply to the industry.
7. We ignore the complication that the one company would be a monopsonistic leaser of coal deposits.
8. If perfect price discrimination is possible, then the demand curve also indicates marginal revenue. Total revenue would then equal the area under the demand curve, i.e. the total valuation by consumers. If in such circumstances the enterprise cannot break even, no production is warranted on grounds of economic efficiency.
9. For a review of the argument that the firm is an economy in miniature and that information problems are central to the literature on the internal organisation of resources see Spence (1975). For a further view on issues raised in this section see Marris and Mueller (1980).
10. For a review of some other reasons for the growth of firms and especially the role of monopoly policy see Kessler and Stern (1959) especially pp.1–20.
11. Whether maximisation of a generalised utility function is a meaningful or useful approach is a debate which we will not enter into here; for a sceptical view see Leibenstein (1979) especially p.495. Pursuit rather than maximisation of utility

would presumably satisfy Leibenstein and does not appear to alter the essential argument.

12. On the problems of control and information in organisations and hence the need for enforcement and operating rules for members of organisations, see for example, Alchian and Kessel (1962) and Arrow (1964). On the design of incentives within firms see for example, Hurwicz (1973), Mirrlees (1976), Harris and Raviv (1978), Kleindorfer and Sertel (1979), and references therein and Cohen (1980).

13. If employment contracts completely specified all duties, leaving no room for discretionary behaviour without recontracting or writing contingent claims contracts, then allocating resources within firms would presumably suffer from the same information and contracting costs as allocating in markets.

14. On the general background to the concept of 'teams' see Marschak and Radner (1972) and Radner (1972); on the problems of 'shirking' in teams, Alchian and Demsetz (1972), and Furubotn and Pejovich (1972). For a complementary approach see Radner and Rothschild (1975). In Alchian and Demsetz's approach factor complementarity is the root cause of 'team production'. McGuire in his study of 'clubs' (1972) has argued: 'Increasing applications of one factor, in combination with others enhance the marginal products of the other factors (and *vice versa*). This reciprocal conferral of marginal benefits leads to multifactor operation; economies are internalised in production clubs called "firms".' McManus (1976), especially pp.348–9 argues, however, that the problem in identifying marginal products lies in the technical characteristics of the inputs and outputs rather than 'team production' as such. Auster (1978) emphasises the importance of simultaneity in time of factor contribution in making the identification of marginal products difficult.

15. Baumol (1962), Marris (1964), Rees (1974). The argument that, where ownership and control are divorced, management may pursue goals other than maximum profit, has been explored in some detail since the late 1950s, but does predate this period. For instance, in 1935 Sir John Hicks discussed management pursuit of 'the quiet life', in 1947 Rothschild emphasised 'long-run survival' as a goal of management, and in 1952 Papandreou anticipated the later work of Simons, Cyert and March and suggested that the goals of firms arose out of interactions within firms. For a review of theories relating to the goals of firms see, for instance, Cyert and Cedrick (1972). On utility maximisation see Williamson (1963, 1964, 1970) and Alchian, November (1965).

16. In some circumstances agents may incur costs to guarantee behaviour conducive to the interests of principals, referred to as 'bonding costs'. The difference between the value of a firm without 'monitoring' and 'bonding' costs and with these costs defines the 'total gross agency costs', that is the costs of the agency relationship. See Jensen and Meckling (1976) and more generally on the theory of agency Ross (1973) and Mitnick (1975).

17. The agency and property rights literature have in the main developed independently, even though the issues they deal with are clearly complementary. For an early study which does discuss the two approaches together see Alchian (1965b). For a general study of the concept of property rights see Becker (1977).

18. For a recent review of these and other studies, see the various contributions to *Managerial Finance* 4, 1978.

19. McGuire, Chiu and Elbing (1962), Marris (1964), Meeks and Whittington (1975), McEachern (1978), Boyes and Schlagenhauf (1979). Some studies of pricing policy have also suggested that management may not pursue profit maximisation policies (e.g. Lanzillotti 1958). Other studies, however, question the view that the divorce of

ownership and control is as widespread as some suggest or that it is especially important in determining firms' objectives (for example, Kania and McKean (1976), Cooper (1977) and Nyman and Silberston (1978)). Differences in the results of empirical studies may arise from differing definitions of owner and management control and from differences in the samples of firms studied. For recent support for this view see Glassman and Rhoades (1980).

20. Kaysen (1965), Grabowski and Mueller (1975), Kuehn (1975), Singh (1975), McEachern (1976), Smiley (1976) and Owen (1979), Brown (1978) suggest stock market prices do adjust to information but not instantaneously. Some other studies also support, sometimes with some reservations, an 'efficient markets' approach and hence the view that shareholders do react in the stock market to managerial policy; for example, see Sullivan (1977) and Koutsoyiannis (1978). The power of shareholders and the efficiency of the capital market is clearly still something of a grey area.

21. In the USA there is often a close link between management and politicians, especially at the municipal level.

22. Crain and Zardkoohi invoke a further argument for expecting a less capital-intensive technique. The owner of a private investment can pass on his accumulated wealth to heirs but for a public investment the expected benefits after death cannot, suggest Crain and Zardkoohi, be capitalised and bequeathed to heirs. Hence citizens would want managers of public firms to use techniques of production with short gestation periods; a similar argument is seen to apply for citizens who may be switching their jurisdiction. This argument however loses some weight to the extent that heirs reside in the same constituency and thereby reap some of the benefits of the public investment and to the extent that other jurisdictions are making similar public investments.

23. An *index* measure of productivity change would be the growth rate of output divided by the growth rate of input which for a discrete change would be measured as r_y/r_x. For the many input/many product case discussed later the index measure is

$$\sum_j v_j r_j \Big/ \sum_i a_i r_i$$

where a_i is the elasticity of output with respect to input x_i and v_j is the elasticity of input with respect to output Y_j, both elasticities being averaged over the old and new output levels. For further discussion of these 'Divisia' measures of growth see Crew, Kleindorfer and Sudit (1979) and Caves and Christensen (1980).

24. Consider for simplicity the case of two inputs (X_1, X_2) yielding one output, Y. The output elasticity of X_1 is

$$a_1 = \frac{\partial Y}{\partial X_1} \frac{X_1}{Y} = \frac{X_1}{Y/\partial Y/\partial X_1}$$

Now the crucial property of constant returns to scale is that the sum of the output elasticities is equal to 1. Intuitively the explanation is that, since the output elasticity of an input is the proportionate response of output to an increase in the input then when all inputs are increased, the proportionate responses of output must add up to unity if constant returns to scale prevail. This property is usually written in the following form:

$$Y = X_1 \frac{\partial Y}{\partial X_1} + X_2 \frac{\partial Y}{\partial X_2}$$

Substituting in the expression for a_1 and denoting input prices by P_{x1} and P_{x2} yields

$$a_1 = \frac{X_1}{X_1 + X_2\left(\dfrac{\partial Y/\partial X_2}{\partial Y/\partial X_1}\right)} = \frac{X_1 P_{x1}}{X_1 P_{x1} + X_2 P_{x2}\left(\dfrac{\partial Y/\partial X_2}{\partial Y/\partial X_2}\dfrac{P_{x1}}{P_{x2}}\right)}$$

Clearly then the output elasticity a_1 is equal to the share of expenditure on X_1 in total costs if the expression in the last brackets is equal to 1, that is if

$$\frac{\partial Y/\partial X_2}{\partial Y/\partial X_1} = \frac{P_{x2}}{P_{x1}}$$

which is the standard requirement for the least cost input combination, namely that relative input prices equal relative marginal products. Moreover for a firm which is technologically efficient and operating under constant returns to scale, the degree to which it is 'price efficient' with respect to its input choices, is reflected in the degree to which the input's share of total costs corresponds to the output elasticity of that input.

When a firm produces several products (say Y_1 and Y_2), the relevant weight for each product in the productivity growth measures is that product's input elasticity, that is the proportionate increase in the bundle of inputs divided by the proportionate increase in the volume of that product. Under certain circumstances a proxy to that elasticity is the cost elasticity of the product. To show this, it should be recognised that we now have a production function of the following form

$$Y(Y_1, Y_2) = X(X_1, X_2)$$

The input elasticity of product Y_1 is

$$V_1 = \frac{\partial X}{\partial Y_1}\frac{Y_1}{X} = \frac{\partial Y}{\partial Y_1}\frac{Y_1}{Y}$$

If the production function is linearly homogeneous of degree D then

$$Y = \left(X_1\frac{\partial Y}{\partial X_1} + X_2\frac{\partial Y}{\partial X_2}\right)\frac{1}{D}$$

where D is a constant and would be equal to unity for constant returns to scale. Hence

$$Y = \left(X_1 + X_2\frac{\partial Y/\partial X_2}{\partial Y/\partial X_1}\right)\frac{\partial Y/\partial X_1}{D}$$

If the firm is price efficient in its choice of inputs then

$$Y = (X_1 P_{x1} + X_2 P_{x2})\frac{\partial Y/\partial X_1}{D P_{x1}}$$

For small changes in the usage of inputs $\partial Y/X_1$, D and P_{x1} will not change. Hence

$$\frac{\partial Y}{\partial Y_1} = \frac{\partial Y/\partial X_1}{D P_{x1}}\frac{\partial (X_1 P_{x1} + X_2 P_{x2})}{\partial Y_1}$$

Substituting back into the expression for V_1 yields

$$V_1 = \frac{\partial (X_1 P_{x1} + X_2 P_{x2})}{\partial Y_1}\frac{Y_1}{X_1 P_{x1} + X_2 P_{x2}}$$

which is the cost elasticity of product Y_1, that is the proportionate change in total costs divided by the proportionate change in Y_1. When not even cost elasticity data is available the revenue shares of each product can be used as proxies for input elasticities under certain circumstances. The expression for the input elasticity of product Y_1 can be presented as

$$V_1 = \frac{Y_1}{X / \partial X / \partial Y_1}$$

If constant returns to scale prevail, the input elasticities of all the products add up to unity, that is

$$X = Y_1 \frac{\partial X}{\partial Y_1} + Y_2 . \frac{\partial X}{\partial Y_2}$$

Substituting into the previous equation yields

$$V_1 = \frac{Y_1}{Y_1 + Y_2 \left(\frac{\partial X / \partial Y_2}{\partial X / \partial Y_1} \right)}$$

Denoting the product prices by P_{y1} and P_{y2}, we have

$$V_1 = \frac{Y_1 P_{y1}}{Y_1 P_{y1} + Y_2 P_{y2} \left(\frac{\partial X / \partial Y_2}{\partial X / \partial Y_1} \frac{P_{y1}}{P_{y2}} \right)}$$

Thus the input elasticity of product Y_1 is equal to that product's share of total revenue if relative product prices equal relative marginal product costs, i.e.

$$\frac{\partial X / \partial Y_2}{\partial X / \partial Y_1} = \frac{P_{y2}}{P_{y1}}$$

25. This survey does not presume any prior knowledge of econometric methods. For a good discussion of dummy variables see Stewart (1976) ch. 3–10.
26. The precise calculation that Pryke makes is not entirely clear from chapters 2 and 6 of his book (1971) but a statistical appendix has been available from D Pryke at Liverpool University. It appears that for each sector, such as manufacturing, an *index* of productivity for year t' with year t as base is calculated by

$$\sum_j R_j Y_{jt} \bigg/ Y_{jt} \div \sum S_i X_{it'} \bigg/ X_{it}$$

where R_j is the share of value added in manufacturing taken by product j and S_i is the share of total costs taken by input i. These weights appear to be averages from two years, 1954 and 1958 and applied irrespective of the values for t' and t. Apart from that, the index is similar to the ideal index given in footnote 23 with the difference that $r_j = \log (Y_{jt'} / Y_{jt})$ and $r_i = \log (X_{it'} / X_{it})$. The costs of one of the inputs, capital, was estimated by Pryke in a manner analogous to that used by the Polanyis and described in the text of this survey; 10 per cent was the assumed rate of return. The average annual rate of growth of productivity between year t and t' is then calculated as the log of the above index, divided by the number of years between t' and t.
27. For those interested in significance tests, the F and t tests were significant at the 0.01 level for all coefficients except S_3 and D; the latter was significant at the 0.09 level.

Both Neuberg and Meyer estimated, in addition, separate cost equations for public and private and found they were significantly different, using Chow tests.

28. For further discussion of the Pescatrice and Trapani study see Millward (1981).

29. Bearing this in mind, as well as the absence of data on input prices and capital employed, one feels Funkhouser and MacAvoy may have overstated the case in the following observations: 'For the public enterprises in question, higher costs ... cannot be traced either to their operating with different factor input ratios or their desire to provide more output. Indeed it seems that all cost elements in the public firms are higher and it is this phenomenon which requires explanation' (p.366).

30. In the pooled sample all coefficients were significant with t and F tests at the 0.05 level. The cost structures of the two separate samples were found to be significantly different. For further discussion of the Crain and Zardkoohi results see Millward (1981).

31. The cost of contract collection was not significantly different from municipal provision in cities with populations less than 50,000 (quoted in Savas, Policy Analysis 1977). The Pier, Vernon and Wicks study (1974) found public provision to be cheaper but the only variable in their cost function was number of pick-ups.

32. Recall however our earlier observations about changes over time in the relative cost of capital. For further discussion of regulation in the public/private context see Millward (1981).

33. Similarly in his 1975 study, de Alessi had hypothesised that management in public firms would not bargain hard in obtaining selling prices. His results suggested that such public firm prices were some 30 per cent lower than in private firms but he had no explicit cost variable in the equation for selling prices.

34. For the group of public and private firms regulated by state bodies. Where regulation was by city or district there was no significant difference.

35. Whether private utilities were regulated by city rather than district had no significant effect on the profit margin. At the same time, the profit margin of public firms tends to be bigger the lower is the level of the regulatory body, a phenomenon which Pashigian does not discuss and which does need reconciling with the experience of private firms.

36. See the last part of his 1971 article.

37. In what follows their 'best' cost assumption and constant demand elasticities are taken for illustration.

38. See in particular the expectation that management will be inferior in public firms in Alchian (1965:827), Rowley (1977:13), Davies (1971:150), Crain and Zardkoohi (1978:398), Pommerehne and Frey (1977:223), Peltzman (1971:111), de Alessi (May 1974:646, Fall 1974:7, 1977:9).

References and further reading

Ahlbrandt, R. (1973) Efficiency in the provision of fire services, *Public Choice*, **16**, 1–15.

Alchian, A. A. (1959) Private property and the relative cost of tenure, in Bradley, P. D. (ed.), *The Public State in Union Power*, University of Virginia Press: Charlottesville.

Alchian, A. A. and Kessel, R. A. (1962) Competition Monopoly and the Pursuit of Pecuniary Gain, in *Aspects of Labour Economics*, Bureau of Economic Research, Princeton.

Alchian, A. A. (1965a) The basis of some recent advances in the theory of management of the firm, *Journal of Industrial Economics*, **November**, 30–41.

Alchian, A. A. (1965b) Some economics of property rights, *Il Politico*, **30**, 816–29, reprinted in Alchian, A. A., *Economic Forces at Work*.

Alchian, A. A. (1969) Information cost, pricing and resource unemployment, *Western Economic Journal*, **7**, 109–28, reprinted in Alchian, A. A., *Economic Forces at Work*.

Alchian, A. A. (1977a) Corporate management and property rights, in Mann, H. (ed.), *Economic Policy and the Regulation of Corporate Securities*, 227–57, American Enterprise Institute: Washington, reprinted in Alchian, A. A., *Economic Forces at Work*.

Alchian, A. A. (1977b) *Economic Forces at Work*, introduction by Coase, R. H., Liberty Press: Indianapolis.

Alchian, A. A. and Demsetz, H. (1972) Production, information costs and economic organisation, *American Economic Review*, **62**, reproduced in Furubotn, E. G. and Pejovich, S. (1974) and Alchian, A. A., *Economic Forces at Work*.

Alchian, A. A., Klein, B. and Crawford, R. G. (1978) Vertical integration, appropriable rents and the competitive contracting process, *Journal of Law and Economics*.

Amacher, R. C. and Tollison, R. D. (1976) Property rights within government and devices to increase government efficiency, *Public Finance Quarterly*, **4**, 151–8.

Arrow, K. J. (1975) Vertical integration and communication, *Bell Journal of Economics*, **6**, 173–83.

Arrow, K. J. (1964) Control in large organisations, *Management Science*, **10**, 397–408.

Atkinson, A. B. and Stiglitz, J. E. (1980) *Lectures on Public Economics*, McGraw Hill: New York.

Auster, R. (1975) Some economic determinants of the characteristics of public workers, in Leiter, R. D. and Sirkin, G. (eds), *Economics of Public Choice*, **2**, 185–98.

Auster, R. (1978) Shirking in the theory of the firm, *Southern Economic Journal*, **45**, 867–73.

Auster, R. and Morris Silver (1976) Comparative statics of the utility maximising firm, *Southern Economic Journal*, **42**, 626–32.

Averch, H. and Johnson, L. L. (1962) Behaviour of the firm under regulatory constraint, *American Economic Review*, **52**, 1052–69.

Barry, E. E. (1965) *Nationalisation in British Politics: The Historical Background*, Cape.

Baumol, W. J. (1958) On the theory of Oligopoly, *Economica*, **25**, 187–98.

Baumol, W. J. (1959) *Business Behaviour Value and Growth*, Macmillan: London.

Baumol, W. J. (1962) The theory of the expansion of the firm, *American Economic Review*, **52**, 1078–87.

Baumol, W. J. and Bradford, D. (1970) Optimal departures from marginal cost pricing, *American Economic Review*, **60**, 265–83.

Baumol, W. J. and Klevorick, A. K. (1970) Input choices and rate of return regulation: an overview of the discussion, *Bell Journal of Economics*, **1**, 162–90.

Becker, L. C. (1977) *Property Rights: Philosophic Foundations*, Routledge and Kegan: London.

Beesley, M. and Evans, T. (1978) *Corporate Social Responsibility: A Reassessment*, Croom Helm: London.

Bennett, J. T. and Johnson, M. H. (1979) Public versus private provision of collective goods and services: garbage collection revisited, *Public Choice*, **34**, 55–63.

Berle, A. and Means, G. (1933) *The Modern Corporation and Private Property*, Macmillan: London.

Blair, R. D. and Kaserman, D. L. (1980) Vertical control with variable proportions: ownership integration and contractual equivalents, *Southern Economic Journal*, **46**, 1118–28.

Boyes, W. J. and Schlagenhauf (1979) Managerial incentives and the specification of functional forms, *Southern Economic Journal*, **45**, 1225–32.

Brown, S. L. (1978) Earnings, changes, stock prices and market efficiency, *Journal of Finance*, **33**, 17–28.

Buchanan, J. M. et al. (1978) The economics of politics, in *Institute of Economic Affairs Readings*, **18**: London.

Carrol, T. M., Ciscil, D. H. and Chisholm, R. K. (1979) The market as a commons: an unconventional view of property rights, *Journal of Economic Issues*, **13**, 605–27.

Caves, D. W. and Christensen, L. R. (1980) The relative efficiency of public and private firms in a competitive environment: the case of Canadian railroads, *Journal of Political Economy*, **88**, 958–76.

Chester, D. N. (1952) Management and accountability in the nationalised industries, *Public Administration*, **Spring**, 27–47.

Chester, T. E. (1976) The public sector – its dimensions and dynamics, *National Westminster Bank Quarterly Review*, **February**, 31–44.

Cho, J. H. (1977) Moral implications of acquisitive instinct under the separation of ownership and control, *Review of Social Economy*, **35**, 143–8.

Clarkson, K. W. (1972) Some implications of property rights in hospital management, *Journal of Law and Economics*, **15**, 363–84.

Coase, R. H. (1937) The nature of the firm, *Economica*, **November**, 386–405, reproduced in Boulding and Stigler (eds) (1953) *Readings in Price Theory*, and Neel, R. E. (ed.) (1973) *Readings in Price Theory*.

Coelho, P. R. P. (1976) Rules, authorities and the design of not-for-profit firms, *Journal of Economic Issues*, **10**, 416–28.

Cohen, S. I. (1980) Incentives, iterative communications and organisational control, *Journal of Economic Theory*, **22**, 37–55.

Comanor, W. S. and Leibenstein, H. (1969) Allocative efficiency, x-efficiency and the measurement of welfare losses, *Economica*, **36**, 304–9.

Coombes, D. (1971) *State Enterprise: Business or Politics*, Allen and Unwin: London.

Cooper, D. (1977) Some limitations of tests of the effect of control on firm performance, *Revista Internazionale di Scienze Economiche e Commerciali*, **24**, 167–74.

Cooter, R. and Topakian, G. (1980) Political economy of a public corporation: pricing objectives of BART, *Journal of Public Economics*, **13**, 299–318.

Copeland, T. E. and Smith, K. V. (1978) An overview of non-profit organisations, *Journal of Economics and Business*, **30**, 147–54.

Courville, L. (1974) Regulation and efficiency in the electric utility industry, *Bell Journal of Economics*, **5**, 53–74.

Crain, W. M. and Zardkoohi, A. (1978) A test of the property rights theory of the firm: water utilities in the United States, *Journal of Law and Economics*, **40**, 395–408.

Crain, W. M. and Zardkoohi, A. (1980) Public sector expansion: stagnant technology or property rights, *Southern Economic Journal*, **46**, 1069–82.

Crew, M. A. and Kleindorfer, P. R. and Sudit, E. F. (1979) Managerial discretion and public utility regulation, *Southern Economic Journal*, **45**, 696–709.

Crew, M. A. and Sudit, E. F. (1979) Incentives for efficiency in the nationalised industries: beyond the 1978 White Paper, *Journal of Industrial Affairs*, **7**, 11–15.

Crew, M. A. and Rowley, C. K. (1970) Anti-trust policy: economics versus management science, *Moorgate and Wall St. Review*, 19–34.

Cyert, R. M. and Cedrick, C. L. (1972) Theory of the firm, past, present and future: an interpretation, *Journal of Economic Literature*, **10**, 398–412.

Davies, D. G. (1971) The efficiency of public versus private firms: the case of Australia's two airlines, *Journal of Law and Economics*, **14**, 149–65.

Davies, D. G. (1977) Property rights and economic efficiency – the Australian airlines revisited, *Journal of Law and Economics*, **20**, 223–6.

Davies, D. G. (1980) Property rights in a regulated environment: a reply, *Economic Record*, **June**, 186–9.

de Alessi, L. (1969) Implications of property rights for government investment choices, *American Economic Review*, **59**, 13–24.

de Alessi, L. (1974a) Managerial tenure under private and government ownership in the electric power industry, *Journal of Political Economy*, **82**, 645–53.

de Alessi, L. (1974b) An economic analysis of government ownership and regulation: theory and the evidence from the electric power industry, *Public Choice*, **Fall**, 1–42.

de Alessi, L. (1975) Some effects of ownership on the wholesale prices of electric power, *Economic Inquiry*, **13**, 526–38.

de Alessi, L. (1977) Ownership and peak-load pricing in the electric power industry, *The Quarterly Review of Economics and Business*, **17**, 7–26.

Dean, A. J. H. (1975) Earnings in the public and private sectors, *National Institute Economic Review*, **74**, 60–70.

Dean, A. J. H. (1977) Public and private sector manual workers pay 1970–77, *National Institute Economic Review*, **82**, 62–66.

Demsetz, H. (1964) The exchange and enforcement of property rights, *Journal of Law and Economics*, **7**, 11–26.

Demsetz, H. (1966) Some aspects of property rights, *Journal of Law and Economics*, **9**, 61–70.

Demsetz, H. (1967) Toward a theory of property rights, *American Economic Review*, **57**, 347–59.

Demsetz, H. (1968) Why regulate utilities?, *Journal of Law and Economics*, **11**, 55–65, in Rowley, C. K. (ed.) (1972), *Readings in Industrial Economics*, **2**, 173–86.

Demsetz, H. (1969) Information and efficiency: another viewpoint, *Journal of Law and Economics*, **12**, 1–22.

Downs, A. (1967) *Inside Bureaucracy*, Little Brown: Boston.

Edwards, F. R. and Stevens, B. J. (1978) The provision of municipal sanitation services by private firms: an empirical analysis of the efficiency of alternative market structures and regulatory arrangements, *The Journal of Industrial Economics*, **27**, 133–47.

Elliott, R. F. (1977) Public sector wage movements, *Scottish Journal of Political Economy*, **24**, 133–51.

Fama, E. F. (1980) Agency problems and the theory of the firm, *Journal of Political Economy*, **88**, 288–307.

Farrell, M. J. (1957) The measurement of production efficiency, *Journal of the Royal Statistical Society*, series A, **120**, 253–81.

Florestano, P. S. and Gordon, S. B. (1980) Public versus private: small government contracting with the private sector, *Public Administration Review*, Jan/Feb., 29–34.

Forsyth, P. J. and Hocking, R. D. (1980) Property rights and efficiency in a regulated environment: the case of Australian airlines, *Economic Record*, June, 182–5.

Fosler, R. S. (1978) State and local government productivity and the private sector, *Public Administration Review*, **38**, 22–27.

Foster, C. D. (1971) *Politics, Finance and the Role of Economics*, Allen and Unwin: London.

Funkhouser, R. and MacAvoy, P. W. (1979) A sample of observations on comparative prices in public and private enterprise, *Journal of Public Economics*, **11**, 353–68.

Furniss, N. (1978) Property rights and democratic socialism, *Political Studies*, **26**, 450–61.

Furubotn, E. G. and Pejovich, S. (1972) Property rights and economic theory: a survey of recent literature, *Journal of Economic Literature*, **December**, 1137–62 and in Fels, R. and Siegfried, J. S. (eds), *Recent Advances in Economics: A Book of Readings*, Irwin: London.

Furubotn, E. G. and Pejovich, S. (1974) *Economics of Property Rights*, Ballinger Pub. Company: Cambridge, Mass.

Gay, D. E. R. (1978) Property rights and the theory of the firm under Hungary's new economic mechanism, 1968–73, *Rivista Internazionale de Scienze Economiche e Commerciali*, **25**, 1021–8.

Glassman, C. A. and Rhoades, S. A. (1980) Owners versus manager control effects on bank performance, *Review of Economics and Statistics*, **62**, 263–70.

Goldberg, V. P. (1974a) Public choice – property rights, *Journal of Economic Issues*, **8**, 555–79.

Goldberg, V. P. (1974b) Protecting the right to be served by public utilities, *Research in Law and Economics*, **1**.

Gordon, R. A. (1961) *Business Leadership in the Large Corporation*, CUP: London.

Grabowski, H. G. and Mueller, D. C. (1975) Life-cycle effects of corporate returns on retention. *Review of Economics and Statistics*, **57**, 400–9.

Gravelle, H. S. (1976) Public enterprises under rate of return financial targets, *The Manchester School of Economic and Social Studies*, **44**, 1–16.

Gravelle, H. S. E. and Katz, E. (1976) Financial targets and x-efficiency in public enterprise, *Public Finance*, **31**, 218–34.

Gunderson, M. (1979) Earnings differentials between public and private sectors, *Canadian Journal of Economics*, **12**, 228–42.

Hamermesh, D. S. (1975) The effect of government ownership on union wages, in Hamermesh, D. S. (ed). *Labour in the Public and Non-Public Sectors*, Princeton University Press: Princeton.

Harris, M. and Raviv, A. (1978) Some results on incentive contracts with application to education, employment, health, insurance and law enforcement, *American Economic Review*, **68**, 20–30.

Hawkesworth. R. I. (1976) Public and private sector pay, *British Journal of Industrial Relations*, **14**, 206–13.

HMSO (1961) *The Financial and Economic Obligations of the Nationalised Industries*, Cmnd. **1337**.

HMSO (1968) *Ministerial Control of the Nationalised Industries*, HC **371**.

HMSO (1967) *Nationalised Industries: A Review of Economic and Financial Objectives*, Cmnd. **3437**.

HMSO (1975) *The Nationalisation of British Industry 1945–1951*, Sir Norman Chester.

HMSO (1976) *A Study of UK Nationalised Industries: A Report to the Government by the National Economic Development Office*.

HMSO (1978) *The Nationalised Industries*, Cmnd. **7131**.

Hirsch, W. Z. (1965) Cost functions of the urban government service: refuse collection, *Review of Economics and Statistics*, **47**, 87–92.

Hirshleifer, J. (1973) Where are we in the theory of information?, *American Economic Review*, **63**, 31–9.

Hirshleifer, J. and Milliman, J. W. (1967) Urban water supply: a second look, *American Economic Review*, **58**, 169–78.

Hurwicz, L. (1973) The design of mechanisms for resource allocation, *American Economic Review*, **63**, 1–30.

Jacob, N. L. and Page, A. N. (1980) Production, information costs and economic organisation, *American Economic Review*, **70**, 476–78.

Jensen, M. C. and Meckling, W. H. (1976) Theory of the firm: managerial behaviour, agency costs and ownership structure, *Journal of Financial Economics*, **3**, 305–57.

Kania, J. J. and McKean, R. N. (1976) Ownership, control and the contemporary corporation: a general behaviour analysis, *Kyklos*, **29**, 272–91.

Kaysen, C. (1965) Another view of corporate capitalism, *Quarterly Journal of Economics*, **79**, 51–51.

Keating, B. (1979) Prescriptions for efficiency in non-profit firms, *Applied Economics*, **2**, 321–32.

Keating, B. and Keating M. A. (1975) A non-profit firm model, *Atlantic Economic Journal*, **3**, 36.

Kessler, F. and Stern, R. N. (1959) Competition contract and vertical integration, *Yale Law Journal*, **69**, 1–129.

Kitchen, H. M. (1976) A statistical estimation of an operating cost function for municipal refuse collection, *Public Finance Quarterly*, **4**, 56–76.

Klein, B., Crawford, R. G. and Alchian, A. A. (1978) Vertical integration, appropriable rents and the competitive contracting process, *Journal of Law and Economics*, **21**, 297–326.

Kleindorfer, P. R. and Sertel, M. R. (1979) Profit maximising design of enterprises through incentives, *Journal of Economic Theory*, **21**, 318–39.

Koutsoyiannis, A. (1978) Managerial job security and the capital structure of the firm, *Manchester School*, **46**, 51–75.

Kuehn, D. (1975) *Takeovers and the Theory of the Firm: An Empirical Analysis for the United Kingdom 1957–1969*, Macmillan: London.

Lanzillotti, R. F. (1958) Pricing objectives in large companies, *American Economic Review*, **48**, 921–40.

Leavitt, H. J. (1978) *Managerial Psychology: An Introduction to Individuals, Pairs and Groups*, 4th edn, University of Chicago Press.

Lecraw, D. S. (1977) Empirical tests for x-efficiency: a note, *Kyklos*, **30**, 116–20.

Leibenstein, H. (1975) Aspects of the x-efficiency theory of the firm, *Bell Journal of Economics and Management Science*, **6**, 580–606.

Leibenstein, H. (1966) Allocative efficiency versus x-efficiency, *American Economic Review*, **June**, 392–415.

Leibenstein, H. (1972) Comment on the nature of x-efficiency, *Quarterly Journal of Economics*, **86**, 327–31.

Leibenstein, H. (1976) *Beyond Economic Man: A New Foundation for Microeconomics*, Harvard University Press: Cambridge, Massachusetts and London.

Leibenstein, H. (1978) X-inefficiency xists – a reply to an xorcist, *American Economic Review*, **68**, 203–11.

Leibenstein, H. (1978) On the basic proposition of x-efficiency theory, *American Economic Review, Papers and Proceedings*, **68**, 238–32.

Leibenstein, H. (1979) A branch of economics is mission: micro-macro theory, *Journal of Economic Literature*, **17**, 477–502.

Lindsay, C. M. (1976) A theory of government enterprise, *Journal of Political Economy*, **84**, 1061–77.

McCain, R. A. (1975) Competition, information, redundancy: x-efficiency and the cybernetics of the firm, *Kyklos*, **28**, 286–308.

McEachern, W. A. (1976) The managerial revolution and corporate performance, *Challenge*, **19**, 36–40.

McEachern, W. A. (1978) Ownership, control and the contemporary corporation: a comment, *Kyklos*, **31**, 491–6.

McGuire, M. (1972) Private good clubs and public good clubs: economic models of group formation, *Swedish Journal of Economics*, 85–9.

McGuire, M., Chiu, J. S. Y. and Elbing, A. O. (1962) Executive income, sales and profits, *American Economic Review*, **52**, 753–61.

McKean, R. N. (1965) The unseen hand in government, *American Economic Review*, **55**, 496–505.

McKean, R. N. (1972) Property rights within government and devices to increase government efficiency, *Southern Economic Journal*, **39**, 177–86.

McManus, J. C. (1976) The costs of alternative organisations, *Canadian Journal of Economics*, **9**, 334–50.

McNeil, I. R. (1974) The many futures of contracts, *Southern California Law Review*, **47**, 691–816.

Mann, P. C. (1970) Publicly owned electric utility profits and resource allocation, *Land Economics*, **46**, 478–83.

Mann, P. C. (1974) User power and electricity rates, *Journal of Law and Economics*, **17**, 433–43.

Mann, P. C. and Seifried, E. J. (1972) Pricing in the case of publicly owned electric utilities, *Quarterly Review of Economics and Business*, **12**, 77–89.

Marks, M. (1980) State and private enterprise, *The Business Economist*, **11**, 3–16.

Marris, R. (1963) A model of the 'managerial' enterprise, *Quarterly Journal of Economics*, **77**, 185–209.

Marris, R. (1964) *The Economic Theory of Managerial Capitalism*, Macmillan: London.

Marris, R. and Mueller, D. C. (1980) The corporation, competition and the invisible hand, *Journal of Economic Literature*, **18**, 32–63.

Marschak, J. and Radner, R. (1972) *The Economic Theory of Teams*, Yale.

Martin, J. E. (1976) Applications of a model from the private sector to federal sector labour relations, *Quarterly Review of Economics and Business*, **16**, 69–78.

Meeks, G. and Whittington, G. (1975) Directors pay, growth and profitability, *Journal of Industrial Economics*, **24**, 1–14.

Meyer, R. A. (1975) Publicly owned versus privately owned utilities: a policy choice, *Review of Economics and Statistics*, **57**, 391–99.

Millward, R. (1976) Prices and incomes policy and the UK nationalised industries, in Laidler, D. E. W. (ed.), *Study on the Possible Part Played by Certain Primary Non-Employment Incomes in the Inflationary Process in the UK*, Commission of the European Communities, Medium Term Economic Policy Series, **6**, 124–81.

Millward, R. (1976) Price restraint, anti-inflation policy and public and private industry in the UK, *Economic Journal*, **86**, 226–42.

Millward, R. (1978) Public ownership, the theory property rights and the public corporation in the UK, *Salford Papers in Economics 78–1*.

Millward, R. (1982) The comparative performance of public and private ownership, in Lord Eric Roll (ed.), *The Mixed Economy*, Macmillan: London.

Mirrlees, J. (1976) The optimal structure of incentives and authority within an organisation, *Bell Journal of Economics*, **7**, 105–31.

Mitnick, B. M. (1975) The theory of agency: the policing paradox and regulatory behaviour, *Public Choice*, **24**, 27–42.

Monsen, R. J. Jr. and Downs, A. (1965) A theory of large managerial firms, *Journal of Political Economy*, **73**, 221–36.

Monsen, R. J. Jr., Chiu, J. A. and Cooley, D. E. (1968) The effect of separation of ownership and control on the performance of the large firm, *Quarterly Journal of Economics*, **82**, 435–51.

Moore, T. G. (1970) The effectiveness of regulation of electric utility prices, *Southern Economic Journal*, **36**, 365–75.

Morrison, H. (1933) *Socialisation and Transport*, Constable & Co.: London.

Mueller, D. C. (1976) Public choice: a survey, *Journal of Economic Literature*, **14**, 395–433.

Munkirs, J. R., Ayers, M. and Grandys, A. (1976) Rape of the ratepayer: monopoly overcharges in the 'regulated' electric utility industry, *Anti-trust Law and Economics Review*, 57–68.

Nelson, J. R. (ed.) (1964) *Marginal Cost Pricing in Practise*, Prentice-Hall: London.

Neuberg, L. G. (1977) Two issues in the municipal ownership of electric power distribution systems, *Bell Journal of Economics*, **8**, 303–23.

Niskanen, W. A. (1971) *Bureaucracy and Representative Government*, Aldine–Atherton: New York.

Nyman, S. and Silberston, A. (1978) The ownership and control of industry, *Oxford Economic Papers*, **30**, 74–101.

Ostergaard, G. N. (1954) Labour and the development of the public corporation, *The Manchester School*, **22**, 192–226.

Owen, G. (1979) Stopping the rot in companies, *Financial Times*, **27 Sept.**, 22.

Palmer, J. (1973) The profit performance effects of the separation of ownership from control in large US industrial corporations, *Bell Journal of Economics*, **4**, 293–303.

Park, Y. J. (1979) On x-efficiency and output differences, *Rivista Internazionale di Scienze Economiche e Commerciali*, **26**, 73–83.

Pashigian, B. P. (1976) Consequences and causes of public ownership of urban transit, *Journal of Political Economy*, **84**, 1239–59.

Peel, D. A. (1973) Some implications of utility maximising firms: a note, *Bulletin of Economic Research*, **25**, 148–51.

Peltzman, S. (1971) Pricing in public and private enterprises and electric utilities in the United States, *Journal of Law and Economics*, **14**, 109–47.

Pescatrice, D. R. and Trapani, J. M. III (1980) The performance and objectives of public and private utilities operating in the US, *Journal of Public Economics*, **13**, 259–75.

Pier, W. J., Vernon, R. B. and Wicks, J. H. (1974) An empirical comparison of government and private production efficiency, *National Tax Journal*, **27**, 653–6.

Polanyi, G. and Polanyi, P. (1972) The efficiency of nationalised industries, *Moorgate and Wall Street Review*, **Spring**, 27–49.

Polanyi, G. and Polanyi, P. (1974) *Failing the Nation: The Record of the Nationalised Industries*, Fraser Ansbacher Limited: London.

Pommerehne, W. M. and Frey, B. S. (1977) Public versus private production efficiency in Switzerland: a theoretical and empirical comparison, *Urban Affairs Annual Review*, **12**, 221–41.

Prescott, E. C. and Visscher, M. (1980) Organisation capital, *Journal of Political Economy*, **88**, 446–61.

Primeaux, W. J. (1977) An assessment of x-efficiency gained through competition, *Review of Economics and Statistics*, **59**, 105–8.

Primeaux, W. J. (1978) The effect of competition on capacity utilisation in the electric utility industry, *Economic Inquiry*, **April**.

Pryke, R. (1971) *Public Enterprise in Practice*, MacGibbon and Kee: London.

Pryke, R. (1981) *The Nationalised Industries: Policies and Performance since 1968*, Martin Robertson.

Radice, H. K. (1971) Control type, profitability and growth in large firms: an empirical study, *Economic Journal*, **81**, 547–62.

Radner, R. (1972) Teams, in McGuire, C. B. and Radner, R. (eds), *Decision and Organisation: A Volume in Honour of Jacob Marschak*, ch.10, North-Holland: Amsterdam.

Radner, R. and Rothschild, M. (1975) on the allocation of effect, *Journal of Economic Theory*, **10**, 358–76.

Rees, R. (1974) A reconsideration of the expense preference theory of the firm, *Economica*, **41**, 295–307.

Rees, R. (1976) *Public Enterprise Economics*, Weidenfeld and Nicholson, London.

Richardson, H. (1973) On public ownership, *New Society*, **28 June**, 748–9.

Robson, W. A. (1962) *Nationalised Industry and Public Ownership*, 2nd Edition, Allen and Unwin: London.

Ross, S. A. (1973) The economic theory of agency: the principal's problem, *American Economic Review*, **62**, 134–9.

Round, D. K. (1976) The effect of the separation of ownership and control on large firm profit rates in Australia: an exploratory investigation, *Revista Internazionale di Scienze Economiche e Commerciali*, **23**, 426–35.

Rowley, C. K. (1980) Industrial policy in the mixed economy, British Association for the Advancement of Science, Salford, in Lord Eric Roll, (ed.), *The Mixed Economy*, Macmillan: London.

Rowley, C. K. (1971) *Steel and Public Policy*, McGraw-Hill, London.

Rowley, C. K. (1976) The x-efficiency factor, *New Society*, **15 January**, 97–8.

Rowley, C. K. (1977) Efficiency in the public sector, paper 2 in Bowe, C. (ed.), *Industrial Efficiency and the Role of Government*, Department of Industry, HMSO: London.

Rubin, P. H. (1973) The expansion of firms, *Journal of Political Economy*, **81**, 936–49.

Rubin, P. H. (1978) The theory of the firm and the structure of the franchise contract, *Journal of Law and Economics*, **21**, 223–33.

Samuels, W. J. (ed.) (1976) *The Chicago School of Political Economy*, Michigan State University: Michigan.

Samuels, W. J. and Mercuro, N. (1976) Property rights, equity and public utility pricing, in Trebing, H. M. (ed.), *New Dimensions in Public Utility Pricing*, MUS Public Utility Studies, Michigan State University: Michigan.

Sandler, T. (1975) The challenge of property rights, the human prospect discussion, *Futures*, **7**, 523–25.

Sandler, T. and Cawley, T. (1980) A hierarchical theory of the firm, *Scottish Journal of Political Economy*, **27**, 17–29.

Savas, E. S. (1974) Municipal monopolies versus competition in delivery of urban services, in Hawley, W. D. and Rogers, D. (eds), *Improving the Quality of Urban Management*, Saga Publications: Beverly Hills, California, 473–500.

Savas, E. S. (1977) An empirical study of competition in municipal service delivery, *Public Administration Review*, Nov/Dec, 717–24.

Savas, E. S. (1977) Policy analysis for local government: public versus private refuse collection, *Policy Analysis*, **3**, 49–74.

Schmid, A. A. (1976) The economics of property rights: a review article, *Journal of Economic Issues*, **10**, 159–68.

Shapiro, D. L. (1973) Can public investment have a positive rate of return?, *Journal of Political Economy*, **81**, 401–13.

Silver, M. and Auster, R. (1969) Entrepreneurship, profit and limits on firm size, *Journal of Business*, **42**.

Simon, J. L. (1968) State Liquor Monopolies, in Turvey, R. (ed.), *Public Enterprise: Selected Readings*, Penguin: Harmondsworth, 365–77.

Singh, A. (1975) Take-overs, national selection and the theory of the firm: evidence from the post-war UK experience, *Economic Journal*, **85**, 497–515.

Smiley, R. (1976) Tender offers, transactions costs and the theory of the firm, *Review of Economics and Statistics*, **58**, 22–32.

Smith, S. (1975/6) Pay differentials between federal government and private sector workers, *Industrial and Labour Relations Review*, **29**, 179–97.

Spann, R. M. (1974) Rate of return regulation and efficiency in production: an empirical test of the Averch-Johnson thesis, *Bell Journal of Economics*, **5**, 38–52.

Spann, R. M. (1977) Public versus private provision of government services, in Borcherding, T. (ed.), *Budgets and Bureaucrats: The Sources of Government Growth*, Duke University Press: Durham NC.

Spence, A. M. (1975) The economics of internal organisation, *Bell Journal of Economics*, **6**, 163–72.

Stein, B. A. (1976) Collective ownership, property rights, and control of the corporation, *Journal of Economic Issues*, **10**, 298–313.

Stewart, J. (1976) *Understanding Econometrics*, Hutchinson: London.

Stigler, G. J. (1951) The division of labour is limited by the extent of the market, *Journal of Political Economy*, **59**, 185–93.

Stigler, G. J. (1961) The economics of information, *Journal of Political Economy*, **69**, 213–25.

Stigler, G. J. (1971) The theory of economic regulation, *Bell Journal of Economics*, **2**, 3–21.

Stigler, G. J. (1976) The xistence of x-efficiency, *American Economic Review*, **66**, 213–6.

Stigler, G. J. and Friedland, C. (1962) What can regulators regulate? The case of electricity, *Journal of Law and Economics*, **5**, 1–16.

Stiglitz, J. E. (1975) Incentives risk and information: notes towards a theory of hierarchy, *Bell Journal of Economics*, **6**, 552–79.

Sullivan, T. G. (1977) A note on market power and returns to stockholders, *Review of Economics and Statistics*, **59**, 108–13.

Tawney, R. H. (1921) *The Acquisitive Society*, G. Bell & Sons: London.

Tivey, L. (1978) *The Politics of the Firm*, Martin Robertson: London.

Trebing, H. M. (1976) The Chicago school versus public utility regulation, *Journal of Economic Issues*, **10**, 97–126.

Tulkens, H. (1976) The Publicness of public enterprise, in Shepherd, W. G. (ed.), *Public Enterprise: Economic Analysis of Theory and Practice*, Lexington Books: Lexington.

Tullock, G. (1965) *The Politics of Bureaucracy*, Public Affairs Press: Washington DC.

Tullock, G. (1971) Public decisions on public goods, *Journal of Political Economy*, **79**, 913–28.

Turvey, R. (ed.) (1968) *Public Enterprise Economics*, Penguin: Harmondsworth.

Turvey, R. (1968) *Optimal Pricing and Investment in Electricity Supply*, Allen and Unwin: London.

Wallace, R. L. and Junk, P. E. (1970) Economic inefficiency of small municipal electricity generating systems, *Land Economics*, **46**, 98–104.

Weisbrod, B. A. (1978) The forgotten economic sector: private but non-profit, *Challenge*, **21**, 32–6.

Williamson, O. E. (1963a) Managerial discretion and business behaviour, *American Economic Review*, **53**, 1032–57, reprinted in Furubotn and Pejovich (1974).

Williamson, O. E. (1963b) A model of rational managerial behaviour, in Cyert, R. M. and March, J. G. (eds), *A Behavioural Theory of the Firm*, Prentice-Hall: Englewood Cliffs, NJ.

Williamson, O. E. (1964) *The Economics of Discretionary Behaviour, Managerial Objectives in a Theory of the Firm*, Prentice-Hall: Englewood Cliffs, NJ.

Williamson, O. E. (1970) *Corporate Control and Business Behaviour*, Prentice-Hall: Englewood Cliffs, NJ.

Williamson, O. E. (1971) The vertical integration of production: market failure considerations, *American Economic Review Papers and Proceedings*, **61**, 112–23.

Williamson, O. E. (1973) Organisational forms and internal efficiency. Markets and hierarchies: some elementary considerations, *American Economic Review, Papers and Proceedings*, **May**, 316–25.

Williamson, O. E. (1975) *Markets and Hierarchies: Analysis and Antitrust Implications: A Study in the Economics of Internal Organisation*, Free Press: London.

Williamson, O. E. (1976a) The modern corporation as an efficiency instrument, in Pejovich, S. (ed.), *Government Controls and the Free Market: The US Economy in the 1970s*, Texas Press, 163–94.

Williamson, O. E. (1976b) The economics of internal organisation: exit and voice in relation to markets and hierarchies, *American Economic Review*, **66**, 369–77.

Williamson, O. E. (1977) Firms and markets, in Weintraub, S. (ed.), *Modern Economic Thought*, University of Pennsylvania Press, Blackwell, ch.10, 185–202.

Williamson, O. E. (1979) Transaction cost economics: the governance of contractual relations, *Journal of Law and Economics*, **22**, 233–61.

Williamson, O. E., Wachter, M. L. and Harris, J. E. (1975) Understanding the employment relation: the analysis of idiosyncratic exchange, *Bell Journal of Economics*, **6**, 250–78.

Young, D. R. (1974) The economic organisation of refuse collection, *Public Finance Quarterly*, **2**, 43–72.

Yunker, J. A. (1975) Economic performance of public and private enterprise: the case of US electric utilities, *Journal of Economics and Business*, **28**, 60–67.

Author index

Subject index